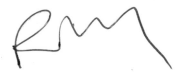

TUC:
The Growth of a Pressure Group
1868–1976

TUC:
The Growth of a
Pressure Group
1868–1976

Ross M. Martin

Professor of Politics
La Trobe University
Melbourne

CLARENDON PRESS · OXFORD
1980

Oxford University Press, Walton Street, Oxford OX2 6DP

OXFORD LONDON GLASGOW
NEW YORK TORONTO MELBOURNE WELLINGTON
KUALA LUMPUR SINGAPORE HONG KONG TOKYO
DELHI BOMBAY CALCUTTA MADRAS KARACHI
NAIROBI DAR ES SALAAM CAPE TOWN

*Published in the United States by
Oxford University Press, New York*

British Library Cataloguing in Publication Data

Martin, Ross M
   TUC, the growth of a pressure group,
   1868–1976.
   1. Trades Union Congress – History
   2. Trade-unions – Great Britain – Political activity
   I. Title
   331.88′06′241   HD8383.T74   79-41040
   ISBN 0-19-822475-3

*Printed in Great Britain
at the University Press, Oxford
by Eric Buckley
Printer to the University*

To
Anne, Leitha, Lois, Vivienne and,
as always, Nadia

PREFACE

THE 100th Congress of the world's oldest national trade union confederation was held in September 1968. Over one thousand delegates, representing almost nine million unionists, packed into the Blackpool opera house. Their deliberations, minutely reported by press, radio, and television, were also watched by official observers from 20 government departments and agencies, 12 embassies, and the trade union movements of 38 countries. Their executive body's 300-page report listed eight specialized departments staffed with some 70 full-time personnel, and recounted numerous discussions on major political issues of the day with the Prime Minister, his colleagues, and officials. Their chairman was a member of the House of Lords, their secretary a Privy Councillor; and they elected to their executive two other lords, two knights, another Privy Councillor, and eight recipients of lesser royal honours.

The first Congress had met in June 1868. Its 34 delegates, representing something over 100,000 unionists, required only a small room of the Mechanics' Institute in David Street, Manchester. Their proceedings, while of some interest to the local press, attracted no observers from government departments, embassies or from such foreign unions as there were. They had no executive body and no full-time staff. They did not even contemplate discussing policy issues of interest to them with public servants, let alone with ministers. They were men who would have been dazzled by the thought of being appointed a Justice of the Peace: a knighthood or a peerage for one of their number could only have seemed a tale told by an idiot.

It is the contrast between the circumstances of these two Congresses which epitomizes, in one way, what this book is about: the changing role of the Trades Union Congress.

There has been one consistent thread in this role. The TUC has always been concerned with influencing, at some remove, the decisions of national government. That is, it has always functioned as a political pressure group. This book, then, is a study of a pressure group. But it differs from almost all other

similar studies owing to its historical emphasis. And that
emphasis, in a work by one who does not profess to be a
historian, springs from two beliefs. First, that organizations are
largely prisoners of their history; and, second, that their contemporary character and situation are more perceptively
weighed against the comparative dimension which history
provides. The book thus attempts, if on a much more modest
scale, what Samuel Beer brilliantly achieved on the broader
canvas of his *Modern British Politics*.

Central to this attempt is an assessment of the nature and
process of institutional change. For this reason, my main concern is with what may be described as the developmental
period of the TUC's career. That period extends from 1868 to
1940, when the TUC attained a level of political recognition
which it has essentially retained ever since.[1] Nevertheless, if
relatively sketchily, the book also deals with the years from 1940
to 1976.[2] It does not, however, pretend to be a definitive history,
or to supplant B. C. Roberts's *The Trades Union Congress, 1868–
1921*. Much that would find a place in such a history is either
omitted or dealt with only so far as it is relevant to the TUC's
specifically political role. This selective approach requires a
statement of the criteria of relevance; and that is provided in
chapter 1.

A study of an organization, like a biography, invites justification—if only because both are too often the work of hagio-
graphers. As a case-study, the TUC is of interest for two reasons
in particular. In the first place, it occupies a singular position
in the hierarchy of contemporary British pressure groups. It is
marked out as an organization of distinctive character and
apparent influence by its wide-ranging policy concerns, its
myriad formal and informal links with government, its close
association with the Labour party, its sheer bulk in numerical
terms and its capacity for attracting public attention.

In the second place, the TUC's unusually long history of
continuous political involvement provides a unique test, over
time, of a hypothesis first concisely expounded by Harry

[1] This point is confirmed, though they differ from each other in their approach
to the matter, by both Samuel Beer (*Modern British Politics*, p. 215) and Alan
Bullock (*The Life and Times of Ernest Bevin*, vol. II, p. 137).
[2] Specifically, to 5 April 1976 when the last Wilson government ended.

Eckstein.[3] This predicates that the nature and outcome of pressure group activities are determined primarily by four factors: the structure of government; the scope of public policy; the political culture or politically-relevant attitudes prevalent in a society; and the attributes or resources of specific pressure groups. The point is that the TUC's lifetime spans a period during which all these factors were transformed. In the case of governmental structure, there was a decisive shift in the balance of power between cabinet and parliament, and also in the political weight of the public bureaucracy. In the case of public policy, there was the massive expansion in the scope of government concerns which distinguishes the welfare state and managed economy of the mid-twentieth century from the virtual *laissez-faire* state of the 1860s. In the case of political culture, there was the transition, first, from an age when organized groups operated on the periphery of political respectability to a time when their legitimacy, in principle, is scarcely doubted; and, second, from a society that firmly equated political capacity with social class to one in which that equation is, at least, widely questioned. Finally, in the case of group attributes, there was the enormous change both in the electoral importance of trade unionists and in the political significance of their peculiar weapon, the strike.

A word about the first and the last chapters, and specifically the fact that they are replete with footnotes of a substantive character. In general, I prefer, as far as possible, to avoid using footnotes for other than the citation of sources—a principle that has been strictly applied throughout the intervening chapters, apart from one case in chapter 7 (concerning the definition of 'general strike'). I have made an exception of chapters 1 and 11 in this respect because they are concerned with the theorizing aspects of the study and it seemed helpful, to the reader, to state the propositions and arguments involved as sparingly as possible, consigning to footnotes those further elaborations, qualifications and illustrations that I would otherwise have felt compelled to include in the text.

---

[3] *Pressure Group Politics*, chap. 1. See also his Introduction to Part VI of Eckstein and Apter (eds.), *Comparative Politics: A Reader*, for an admirably succinct account and a penetrating critique of 'group theory'—of which, as he explains, pressure group analysis and his hypothesis are, in a sense, the illegitimate offspring.

I have accumulated a wealth of debts in the course of writing this book. The greatest is to Hugh Clegg, of the University of Warwick, who has been familiar with the project from its uncertain beginnings many years ago. His critical encouragement has survived both the passage of time and, in the case of several chapters, the reading of more than one draft. His scholarship has rescued me from numerous errors. I am also grateful for valuable comments from Richard Spann, of the University of Sydney, who read the whole book in draft; and from David Winchester, of the University of Warwick, who read chapters 1, 10, and 11.

Marilu Espacio, with great skill and monumental patience, bore the main burden of typing my drafts. Annemarie Flanders, Anne Peterson, Margaret Prebble and Jean Brierley cheerfully and efficiently shouldered the same task at different times. Nadia Martin fashioned the index with meticulous care. The institutional debts, involving the provision of facilities, finance, or both, are to the Rockefeller Foundation; the Warden and Fellows of Nuffield College, Oxford; Monash University; La Trobe University; the Industrial Relations Research Unit of the Social Science Research Council at the University of Warwick; and to the staff of the TUC itself who gave me access to early TUC reports and to the minutes of the Parliamentary Committee and the General Council before these became available on microfilm. The book also profited from early interviews with Len Murray, in 1959, and Lord Citrine, in 1966.

R. M. M.

October 1979

CONTENTS

I

Lines of Approach

LARGE organizations, as a rule, lead complicated lives. The
Trades Union Congress is no exception. Penetrating that
complexity, in order to assess the evolution of the TUC's
political role, involves two tasks. One is to describe the ways in
which relevant activities of the TUC have changed over time.
The other is to explain why such changes occurred when they
did. This chapter is concerned with the chief considerations
that have guided the present attempt to grapple with these
tasks.[1]

THE EXPLANATORY TASK

Three 'determinants' of the general character of pressure group
politics (structure, policy, attitudes), and one determinant of
the activities of specific groups (attributes), have been delineated by Harry Eckstein.[2]

1. Structure: the structure of government in particular, but
also of pressure groups, with reference to the organizational
locus of effective decision-making.

2. Policy: the scope and character of government policy
concerns.

3. Attitudes: above all, broad social attitudes concerning the
propriety of pressure-group activity in general, and the standing
of particular groups; but also the attitudes of pressure-group
constituents towards involvement with government.

4. Group Attributes: the politically-relevant resources of
specific pressure groups, such as wealth, electoral influence,
expertise, prestige.

---

[1] Methodologically, of course, the descriptive task is prior to the explanatory
task. But, on what amount to aesthetic grounds, I have chosen to deal here with
the latter first because the approach adopted to it can be set out very much more
briefly than is possible in the case of the descriptive task.
[2] *Pressure Group Politics*, chap. 1.

The history of the TUC's political role has been examined with these four factors particularly in mind. This is one reason why, in each of the main empirical chapters of this study (chaps. 3–9), the discussion concerned specifically with the TUC's activities is prefaced by sections on 'Government' and 'Trade Unions'. Such an arrangement facilitates consideration of Eckstein's four causal variables.[3] Thus the 'Government' section is concerned largely with issues relating, during the period in question, to the structure of government, the scope of public policy, and attitudes (especially of government leaders) towards trade unions and their officials. In the 'Trade Unions' section, correspondingly, attention is paid mainly to the structure of trade union organization, the policy concerns of union leaders, their attitudes to government and to forms of political action, and, finally, the nature of the unions' political resources.

The principal concerns of the third section, 'Trades Union Congress', are the subject of the remainder of this chapter.

THE DESCRIPTIVE TASK

Description is intrinsically less difficult than explanation, since the nature of an event is usually more readily established than its cause. But even description, if it is to be more than a chronological mish-mash, requires assumptions, categories and criteria which enable events to be ordered, related and interpreted.

The Aspects of a Role

There are seven aspects of the TUC's political activities which enclose the main elements in its relations with government.[4] They are points of access, methods of communication, forms of pressure, scope of relations, intensity of concern, quality of relations, and, finally, effectiveness.

[3] The arrangement, in any case, is justified on the ground that the role of a political intermediary, like the TUC, cannot be adequately appreciated without an understanding of the character and concerns of the institutions it stands between.

[4] These categories owe much to those formulated by Eckstein, *Pressure Group Politics*, chap. 1.

1. Points of access: the particular institutions of government (e.g., parliament, a department) and the level within them (e.g., ministerial, civil servant) towards which the TUC has directed its efforts to influence the course of public policy and administration.

2. Methods of communication: the ways in which the TUC's claims have been made known to government office-holders.[5] The primary distinction is between direct methods (e.g., lobbying backbench MPs, ministerial deputations, consultative bodies) and indirect methods (e.g., correspondence, demonstrations, sponsoring parliamentary candidates).Direct methods are distinguished from indirect methods both by their face-to-face element and by the fact that they alone require a measure of positive cooperation from government office-holders.[6]

3. Forms of pressure: techniques the TUC has used, threatened to use or appeared capable of using to support its claims. The major examples are reasoned argument, electoral opposition, strike action and withholding administrative co-operation.

4. Scope of relations: the range and variety of policy issues involved in claims which the TUC and government have made on each other.

[5] 'Government office-holders', for present purposes, include *all* parliamentarians.
[6] In other pressure group studies (as pointed out by Grant and Marsh, *The Confederation of British Industry*, pp. 122–3) it has been usual to emphasize the categories of formal and informal methods, the distinction here customarily being seen as between *ad hoc* discussions (including telephone conversations) and more or less regular meetings within the framework of an officially constituted consultative body. This is a useful distinction, and I have taken advantage of it at a number of points below. At the same time, its utility is limited in the case of a work which is concerned, above all, with the historical dimension. For one thing, both of the formal/informal categories are concerned with direct or face-to-face (or phone-to-phone) contact. This concentration on direct methods of communication is adequate enough for studies concerned with major groups in the mid-twentieth century and later; but it ceases to be so when the perspective is longer because, historically, the great shift in methods of communication has been from the *indirect* to the direct—at least in the case of the TUC. This is why the direct/indirect distinction must be given pride of place in the present work. In addition, however, the formal/informal typology, as normally interpreted, tends to obscure or ignore some changes which have to do with the formality of group-government dealings. The ministerial deputation is perhaps the key example in the TUC's case. For many years meetings between TUC deputations and ministers were conducted on highly formalistic lines which precluded anything like genuine discussion. But eventually, especially after the first world war, such meetings came more and more to involve serious discussion between ministers and TUC spokesmen. The standard formal/informal distinction cannot accommodate this change because it is locked into the *form* of the meeting on the assumption (often, of course, justified) that this tells you as much as you need to know about the character of the proceedings.

5. Intensity of concern: the importance which the TUC's constituent trade unions and government office-holders, respectively, have attached to the TUC's political function, in comparison both to its other functions and to the political activities of other union-associated bodies.

6. Quality of relations: the character of dealings between TUC spokesmen and government office-holders, in terms of two continua. The intimate-antagonistic continuum concerns the ease or congeniality of dealings, ranging from 'old boy' confidences to open hostility. The soft-hard continuum relates to the element of bargaining involved, ranging from *pro forma* consultation to stern negotiation.

7. Effectiveness: the extent to which the TUC has succeeded in winning acceptance of its claims on government. In assessing effectiveness, commentators almost invariably confine their attention to claims concerning substantive policy and administrative issues. But, as argued below, procedural claims for access to government office-holders arc also highly significant in this connection.

The Focus: Authority

The political activities of a pressure group like the TUC are directed primarily towards achieving goals specified in the claims it makes on government. Implicit in each and every such claim, moreover, is a claim to acceptance of the group's right to act in this way. So far as government is concerned, this implicit claim is for acknowledgement that the group has a legitimate role in the process of government decision-making. The group, in other words, is asking for recognition of its authority in this respect. The goal of authority, underlying as it does all the TUC's political activities, provides the focus of the present inquiry.

The authority of the TUC, however, has two faces. The TUC does not so much confront the institutions of government as stand between them and its own constituents, the affiliated trade unions. Its role as a political pressure group is essentially that of an intermediary. When it presents claims to government it is, as it were, facing two ways simultaneously. It is not only claiming government recognition of its authority to be heard; it is also asserting, in relation to its constituents, the authority to speak on their behalf.[7]

There is thus both an external and an internal face to the TUC's authority as a political intermediary. Its external authority, or lack of it, is reflected in the reactions of government office-holders to its claims. Its internal authority is reflected in the corresponding reactions of affiliated union leaders. Moreover, the reactions on each side affect those on the other. Given the basic requirement that each side sees some value in dealing with the other, their respective reactions to the TUC's claim to act as their intermediary depend heavily on their perception of the other's reaction to that claim. Thus, if government office-holders believe that the TUC's ability to speak for the unions is questionable, they are less likely to take notice of it; and, similarly, if union leaders perceive the TUC as lacking weight in government eyes, they are less likely to rely on it as an intermediary. In other words, the external authority and the internal authority of the TUC are, to a degree, interdependent. Each can be adequately understood only in the light of the other.

Measuring Authority

For more than a century the TUC, with varying frequency and in varying ways, has acted as an intermediary between trade unions and government. That is to say, it has plainly had *some* political authority throughout this period. What is less clear is (to put it crudely) *how much* authority it has had.

Authority, in the present context at least, is a complex and essentially non-quantifiable attribute. The attempt to measure it, therefore, must be largely a matter of rough judgement and can be expected to yield only imprecisely defined estimates. Even so, the roughness of the judgement may be mitigated by specifying two things as precisely as possible: first, a standard

[7] As this passage implies, the term 'TUC' here refers to the organization's official leadership enclosed in its executive organ (originally known as the Parliamentary Committee, latterly as the General Council), with its associated full-time administrative staff and committees drawn exclusively or predominantly from its own membership. This is the sense in which 'TUC' is generally to be interpreted when used in this book. It will be evident from the context when the term is employed in a more comprehensive sense to include, as well, affiliated unions and the annual Congress at which they are individually represented, together with committees on which Parliamentary Committee/General Council members are not in the majority.

of comparison; and, second, relevant and observable indicators susceptible to comparative assessment.

The first question, then, is: what is the authority of the TUC to be measured against? The short answer is that it is to be measured against itself. This is not the only feasible standard of comparison.[8] But it is appropriate, as well as practicable, because the present study is concerned less with the TUC's authority at any particular time than with *changes* in it over time. Thus the immediate standard of comparison, in the case of the TUC's authority in a specific period, is its authority in the preceding period; and the ultimate standard is its authority during its earliest years.

The question of indicators is more complicated. Of the factors involved in the various aspects of the TUC's political activities (outlined above), there are some which are more readily observable than others and which, also, seem to be more directly relevant than most to the issue of authority. The TUC's claimed function, of acting as an intermediary between unions and government, has three dimensions bearing on the authority derived from discharging it. These are the dimensions of exclusiveness, control and importance.

1. Exclusiveness: the extent to which the TUC's intermediary role pre-empts the field, in the sense of excluding direct dealings between government and the trade unions or other union-associated organizations.

2. Control: the extent to which the TUC (specifically, its executive body and officials) effectively determines three things—the content of the claims it carries forward as an intermediary, the manner in which it discharges its intermediary function and the channels through which it does so.

3. Importance: the significance attached to the TUC's

---

[8] One possible alternative is a model or ideal-type construct: this is the sort of standard, typically of the One Big Union type, which seems to inspire (usually implicitly) most complaints about lack of internal authority in the case of peak union bodies. Another alternative is the assumed authority of another or other pressure groups operating in the same political system during the same period. A third is the authority of similar or corresponding organizations operating in different political systems: for attempts to employ this standard to assess internal authority, see R. M. Martin, 'The Authority of Trade Union Centres', *Journal of Industrial Relations*, Vol. 4, 1962, pp. 1–17 (reprinted in J. E. Isaac and G. W. Ford (eds.), *Australian Labour Relations Readings*, 1966); John P. Windmuller, 'The Authority of National Trade Union Confederations', in D. B. Lipsky (ed.), *Union Power and Public Policy*, pp. 91–107.

intermediary role by trade union leaders, on the one hand, and by government office-holders on the other.[9]

In the case of each of these dimensions, there are observable indicators. Because the two faces of a pressure group's authority are not necessarily symmetrical[10] (although interdependent to a degree, as we have seen), the relevant indicators are best outlined separately in relation, first, to the TUC's internal authority and, second, to its external authority.

Internal authority. *Exclusiveness* is indicated by the extent to which claims on government affecting the interests of specific unions are channelled through the TUC, rather than being handled by concerned unions themselves or by other union-associated bodies.[11] *Control* is indicated by the extent to which the TUC leadership selects (and rejects) union claims for submission to government, and determines the form in which they are presented and the procedure by which they are communicated. A subsidiary indicator in this connection is the proportion of TUC executive members, or nominees, on TUC deputations and on the union side of government advisory and administrative bodies. *Importance* is indicated by the nature of the policy issues which the TUC leadership handles and, in particular, by the extent to which those issues relate to the central concerns of the trade unions, especially their legal status or their sectional industrial interests.[12]

[9] This dimension, while involving indicators which are less readily observable than in the case of the other two, is crucial. In terms of exclusiveness and control, the TUC's authority would be maximized if the TUC's executive body totally monopolized union-government dealings and had absolute power to determine the manner and content of such dealings. But the *quality* of the authority involved, even in these circumstances, obviously depends on whether the issues handled by the TUC are of small or great importance to trade union officials and government office-holders.

[10] For example, so far as the dimension of importance is concerned, a pressure group's internal authority can be expected usually to be greater on this score than its external authority because the policy concerns of its constituents are invariably more concentrated than those of government leaders.

[11] Both the exclusiveness and the control indicators, of course, imply the possibility of competition in relation to the TUC's intermediary function. This may come from individual trade unions (affiliated or not), from its constituent unions acting collectively in opposition to the TUC executive through the annual Congress, or from other union-associated bodies ranging from industry federations of unions to the Labour party. The competitive threat posed by the Labour party in particular is, in fact, a major theme in the TUC's history.

[12] The assumption involved here is that the primary concern of British trade unionists and their leaders is with wages and working conditions, and with the legal freedom of their unions to act in customary ways to protect and promote their interests in these matters.

External authority. *Exclusiveness* is indicated by the extent to which government office-holders show themselves willing to confine their dealings with the trade unions to TUC representatives. *Control* is indicated by the extent to which office-holders either initiate such dealings or enter into them in the form requested by the TUC. *Importance* is indicated by four distinct factors: (a) the extent to which the emphasis in government concerns falls on matters close to the central concerns of the TUC and its constituents; (b) the extent to which government office-holders are prepared to discuss policy issues remote from the industrial and organizational matters of traditional union concern; (c) the frequency of face-to-face dealings between TUC representatives and ministers, particularly senior ministers; and (d) the extent to which TUC-government dealings involve a bargaining element.

It will be noted that the indicators of external authority all involve factors figuring in the aspects of the TUC's political activities outlined earlier. Most of these aspects thus have some relevance to the assessment of external authority. The only one that does not is forms of pressure; its relevance is to the explanation rather than the description of external authority. But there is also another aspect (effectiveness) which is excluded from the indicators in one important respect, and this omission is less obviously appropriate.

The Question of Effectiveness

Effectiveness, the extent to which the TUC has won acceptance of its claims from government, was defined earlier in terms of two kinds of claims: those concerning access to government office-holders, and those concerning substantive policy matters. The indicators of external authority, set out above, include effectiveness in relation to access claims, but not in relation to policy claims. The omission may seem odd. For there can be no question that a pressure group's ability to translate its claims into government policy is the ultimate and decisive indicator of its external authority. The difficulty is that, however conclusive this indicator may be in conception, its utility as a tool of empirical investigation is very limited indeed.[13]

[13] Most pressure group studies briefly acknowledge that there are problems about assessing effectiveness in policy terms—but then proceed, with few explicit qualms,

The problem of 'secrecy'[14] is one obvious obstacle to assessing a pressure group's policy effectiveness, especially with the modern shift in group-government dealings away from the relatively public arena of parliament to the secluded rooms of administrative departments. But the problem of causation is much the more fundamental.[15]

The inclusion in government policy of a claim made by a pressure group does not in itself resolve the question of whether the group's action was a determining, reinforcing, minor or irrelevant consideration in the minds of government decision-makers. *Post hoc, ergo propter hoc*, is a tempting refuge, especially for pressure group leaders,[16] but its accuracy is always questionable. More often than not, too, the issue is further complicated by a considerable time-lag, sometimes of decades, between the initial submission of a claim and its embodiment in public policy. Nor are these the only difficulties. How, for example, are a pressure group's serious or 'real' claims to be distinguished from those advanced either primarily to appease internal political pressures or as an initial bargaining gambit? Then there is the associated problem of where the line is to be drawn between effectiveness and ineffectiveness when, as so often,

---

to affirm the substantial effectiveness of their chosen group or groups. The most notable exceptions, although not canvassing all the possible complications, are Graham Wootton's *The Politics of Influence* (see chap. XXVI), Martha Derthick's *The National Guard* (see chap. 1) and G. L. Kristianson's *The Politics of Patriotism* (see chap. 10), which follows Wootton, if in less guarded vein.

[14] Which provided S. E. Finer with a provocative theme, an eye-catching title (*The Anonymous Empire*) and a resounding concluding plea ('Light! More Light!').

[15] This problem is examined in a limited context in R. M. Martin, 'Trade Unions and Labour Governments in Australia', *Journal of Commonwealth Political Studies*, Vol. 2, 1963, pp. 59–78; reprinted in Colin A. Hughes (ed.), *Readings in Australian Government*. But the partial solution proposed and applied there is less appropriate in the British case because of government's smaller statutory involvement, as compared with the Australian case, in industrial relations.

[16] Thus the flamboyant attribution by George Howell, first secretary of the TUC, of credit for 122 highly diverse legislative measures between 1868 and 1901 to 'the influence of labour leaders': Howell, *Labour Legislation, Labour Leaders and Labour Movements*, 2nd ed., Vol. II, pp. 469–72. Thus, also, the more limited attribution of a later TUC secretary, reporting on TUC representations for pensions increases in relation to certain former public employees. On the last occasion the claim was raised, by a TUC deputation, the Chancellor of the Exchequer had explicitly rejected it. A year later a different Chancellor, 'without any warning to the TUC', introduced legislation granting pensions increases to a variety of former public employees, including the category with which the TUC had been concerned. The TUC secretary interpreted this sequence of events as meaning that 'the case put by the deputation must have made an impression'— even though a different Chancellor was involved. W. M. Citrine, *The TUC in War-time*, June 1944, p. 22.

government policy incorporates a more or less heavily modified version of a claim,[17] or deals with a related issue in a way that is open to interpretation as an off-setting concession. Again, how is the effectiveness of a particular pressure group to be assessed in the case of a claim actively backed by other groups— especially when the origin of the claim lies elsewhere?[18] Then there is the difficulty of weighing 'successes' (total or partial) against 'failures' (total or partial): a calculation which is further complicated not merely by variations in the importance of the claims involved but also by the likelihood of differing assumptions about the significance of such variations.[19]

Moreover, the difficulty of assessing policy effectiveness is heightened in the case of the present study by two other considerations. In the first place, the study is concerned with a long time-period during which the nature and the range of the TUC's policy claims, along with much else, changed radically. One problem this poses is that there is no stable and comprehensive set of policy concerns common to the whole period. Even in the case of the single persistent policy issue (the legal right to strike) it is uncertain how properly to evaluate the TUC's fluctuating fortunes, which include legislative failure in 1871, success in 1875 and 1906, failure in 1927, success in 1946, failure in 1971, and success in 1974.[20] Then there is the problem

[17] A small example: the TUC in 1935 pressed for the limit entitling widows' pensions, from superannuation funds, to exemption from Estates Duty to be increased from £25 to £100. The limit was raised in the Budget of that year to £52. The TUC reported this 'small concession,' and described it as 'not satisfactory': *TUC Report*, 1935, pp. 189, 191. A large example: 'the TUC's advocacy', the General Council claimed, 'has brought about a perceptible change of emphasis in Government [economic] policy': *TUC Report*, 1972, p. 249.

[18] A major case in point is the issue of old-age pensions which the TUC advocated from 1899, along with other politically active groups, but did not initiate.

[19] Thus Eckstein (chap. IV), while making no bones about the monumental failures of the British Medical Association in relation to government medical policy since the turn of the century, can still conclude on the basis of lesser successes that it has had 'great political influence'. Others might as readily and, perhaps, as reasonably conclude that it is the great failures which really count.

[20] As the history of this issue also suggests, the time factor further complicates the problem of assessing policy effectiveness because the success of one year may crumble into the failure of another. For example, the TUC scored a great success in 1911 when the unions were given a major role in the administration of unemployment insurance. But then, as the government's need for such cooperation faded, they were gradually eased out after the first world war. There is a similar problem in assessing the weight that ought to be given to a small success which breeds greater. Perhaps the classic case, as far as the TUC is concerned, is provided by the Beveridge report of 1942, immensely influential and with a farreaching impact on British social policy. On Beveridge's own testimony, the 'commissioning

of the weight to be given this particular issue within the pro-
gessively expanding range of other large issues with which the
TUC has been concerned between the first and the last of these
dates.

The second special consideration is the expanse of the TUC's
policy concerns. Eckstein points out, in connection with dealings between the British Medical Association and the Ministry
of Health (the BMA's relations with other departments involving only 'relatively minor' matters), that it 'is an under-
statement to say that the range of subjects . . . is very broad'.[21]
But that range is set within the boundaries of the Ministry of
Health's fairly well defined jurisdiction. In contrast, it is impossible, without hopeless distortion, to define the TUC's
principal concerns in terms of the jurisdiction of one, or even
two, ministries. Least of all is it feasible to reduce the TUC-
government relationship to a single distinctive issue of continuing and dominating importance, as in the case of the
National Farmers' Union (annual farm price review) and the
British Legion (war pensions).[22] Even designating broad policy
areas of consistent TUC concern in recent years (such as
industrial relations, employment and social welfare) scarcely
simplifies matters. Not only is the variety of major issues involved in these areas very great, but they omit much else of
acknowledged importance to the TUC. For the TUC's policy
concerns for most of its lifetime have been remarkably wide—
much wider, indeed, than those of any other recognized British
pressure group outside the labour movement. This further
complicates the already formidable problem of assessing its
policy effectiveness.

These difficulties, however, do not mean that all judgements
of policy effectiveness are invariably pointless or necessarily
deceptive. They do not totally rule out informed guesses and
considered approximations. They do warn against straining for
resounding but intrinsically flabby conclusions. Above all, in

of the inquiry' which produced the report 'was due to the driving force of the
Trades Union Congress': Beveridge, *Power and Influence*, p. 317. In these circumstances, it might well be argued that the TUC's little-noticed achievement, in
relation to the formation of the Beveridge committee, is actually one of its most
momentous successes—perhaps, even its greatest.

[21] *Pressure Group Politics*, pp. 49n., 78.

[22] See Peter Self and H. J. Storing, *The State and the Farmer*, chap. III; Wootton,
The Politics of Influence, chaps. XI, XX.

the particular case, they establish the uncertain precision of
policy effectiveness as an indicator of changes, especially long-
term changes, in the TUC's external authority.

The contrast is with the indicators outlined earlier in relation to external authority, and specifically in relation to the
control dimension. The key indicator of control concerns
effectiveness, but it is effectiveness in terms of claims for access
to government office-holders, not of policy claims. The advantage of the reception given access claims, as a criterion of
effectiveness, is that greater precision is possible because the
problems of secrecy, causation and standards of success or
failure are reduced in complexity. As to secrecy, it is usually
immeasurably simpler, for example, to ascertain if and between
whom a meeting has been held, and what issues were raised at
it, than it is to discover the terms of the discussion—let alone
the extent to which the subsequent actions of the participants
were influenced by it. As to causation, groups almost invariably
press access claims on their own initiative and without external
support; there is little or no room for bargaining gambits in the
case of such claims; the time-lag problem is largely obviated
except, possibly, in the case of some claims for representation
on existing consultative bodies or for the creation of new
bodies. As to standards of success or failure, there are strict
limits to the ways in which an access claim may be modified by
the recipient (for example, by redirecting a proposed ministerial deputation to a civil servant or suggesting, instead, contact
by correspondence); and, in any case, flat rejection or total
acceptance, if the TUC's experience is any guide, is more usual
in the case of access claims than policy claims. In addition, the
range of claims is not only more limited in comparison with
policy claims, but is capable of a very much smaller and less
diversified expansion over time: thus the range of the TUC's
access claims extends no further than from claims for deputations to ministers in the nineteenth century to claims for representation on administrative bodies in the twentieth century.
For all these reasons, the fate of access claims provides a
comparatively precise indicator of effectiveness.

There is thus a strong practical reason for preferring an
indicator which relates to effectiveness in the narrow sense of
access to government, rather than in the broader sense of policy

achievements. But the preference can be justified on more substantial grounds as well; and, indeed, it must be if it is to meet the obvious criticism that the preferred indicator, while easier to apply, is not worth the effort.

Primary and Secondary Effectiveness

Access has customarily been ignored as a measure of effectiveness in pressure group studies. There appear to be two reasons for this. In the first place, access has been relegated to subsidiary status on the (usually implicit) assumption that it is merely 'the facilitating intermediate objective' of a pressure group.[23] In the second place, the studies have been almost exclusively concerned with major Western pressure groups during the recent twentieth century, a period in which such groups have had, on the whole, few serious problems of access. In those studies with a more than sketchy historical dimension, in which varying patterns of access emerge, the tendency has been to treat access as an indicator of effectiveness but *only* on the assumption (again, usually implicit) that it relates to or reflects policy outcomes.[24]

The present argument, on the contrary, is that the fate of access claims, whether viewed in historical or contemporary terms, provides an indicator of effectiveness which is both independent of policy outcomes and substantial. It qualifies on both counts because access claims happen to be of singular importance to group leaders.

Truman, while coining the phrase 'facilitating intermediate objective', has also described access, more accurately, as 'the basic objective' of pressure groups.[25] Without access, in some form, a group's policy claims cannot reach government office-holders. Access of a sort may be gained from a distance, as it were, by such means as public demonstrations, newspaper advertisements and letter-writing. But *direct* access, involving closer contact of the face-to-face or phone-to-phone kind,

[23] The phrase is David B. Truman's (*The Governmental Process*, p. 264), who has given greater attention than most to the question of access: see ibid., esp. pp. 264 ff., 450 ff., 506–7.
[24] Thus when Samuel Beer, in his *Modern British Politics*, writes of 'a system of consultation' which, from 1940, 'gave the unions a position of power' (p. 211), he is plainly (and the indications are not restricted to this page of his book) tying access to policy outcomes.
[25] *The Governmental Process*, p. 264.

requires the consent of office-holders. In other words, it is a
precondition of the direct communication of a group's policy
claims that government is presented with, *and accepts*, a claim
to the group's right to be heard.

The leaders of British pressure groups representing economic
interests have consistently tended to treat indirect methods of
communicating their policy claims either as a last resort or as a
means of adding emphasis.[26] Their consistent preference, and
there is no reason to doubt that it echoes their constituents',
has been face-to-face dealings with government office-holders.
This is reflected in the pains taken, even by those heading
securely established groups like the modern TUC, to reassure
their constituents that they have direct access to the ear of
government.

One reason for this preference is the assumption that there is
a likely correlation between close dealings and policy outcomes—which is not to say that group leaders assume a precise
correlation but rather that they expect, as Eckstein remarks in
a particular case, that 'whatever promotes intimate relations
between the [British Medical] Association and the Ministry
[of Health] also helps the Association to influence the Ministry's
decisions'.[27] But they also have a second reason for their preference; and it is a reason which is not associated with policy
achievements.

A pressure group's internal authority as an intermediary
obviously depends on the group being perceived by its constituents as actually discharging an intermediary role. The
minimal function which that role entails is the effective communication of policy claims. Effective communication, in other
words, is a source of authority, irrespective of policy outcomes.
And since effective communication tends to be seen by group
leaders and constituents as involving direct dealings with
government, a group's success in securing direct access affects
conceptions of its authority. The sensitivity of group leaders on
this point is suggested not only by continual references in their

[26] There are, of course, other politically-involved groups of whom this is not
true. In some cases, as with groups which confine themselves to organizing public
demonstrations on political issues and satisfy their constituents by doing so, there
is no serious attempt to act as an intermediary (in any relevant sense of the term)
between constituents and government.
[27] *Pressure Group Politics*, pp. 109–10.

reports to the directness and closeness of their dealings with government, but also by their efforts to monopolize such access by excluding other groups claiming to speak for similar or related interests. Beer appears to have had external authority in mind when he pointed out, in relation to group representation on government advisory bodies, that 'the symbolism of formal status enhanced the position of the consulted groups';[28] but the point applies with at least equal force to internal authority.

As a source of internal authority, direct access to government has a bearing on the stability of a pressure group—at least in terms of relationships within it, and ultimately in terms of its survival.[29] Without access, aspiring pressure groups have died,[30] or have been severely constrained.[31] Government recognition in this form, therefore, is of extreme value to a pressure group, and specifically to its leaders. It is virtually *sine qua non*. As such, it takes priority over policy achievements—not merely in the sense that communication of a policy claim is logically prior to a governmental decision on that claim, but also in the sense of the *importance* attached to communication as distinct from decision.

Underlying this conclusion are two considerations which have been commonplaces of organizational theory since Robert Michels' classic work. One is that survival in itself becomes a dominant group goal;[32] the other is that the interests of group leaders and constituents are not identical.[33] Thus while the constituents of a pressure group tend to regard access claims

---

[28] *Modern British Politics*, p. 339.

[29] The survival point fully applies only in the case of an organization claiming little or nothing apart from a pressure-group function. In fact, of course, organizations claiming this function often not only discharge other functions but frequently display great powers of adaptation, developing new functions in place of, or alongside, old ones. In any case it is conceivable that a failed pressure group's constituents may be retained, if only for a time, by other factors (lack of alternatives, habit, loyalty, hope, ignorance). But cohesion in these circumstances is likely to be least certain in the case of a group like the TUC whose constituents are not individuals but organizations with distinct functions, substantial resources, and often with conflicting interests and a capability as autonomous political actors.

[30] For example, see Wootton, *Politics of Influence*, p. 110.

[31] See Self and Storing, *The State and the Farmer*, p. 219.

[32] 'Thus, from a means, organization becomes an end. To the institutions and qualities which at the outset were destined simply to ensure the good working of the party machine . . . a greater importance comes ultimately to be attached than to the productivity of the machine': Michels, *Political Parties*, p. 390.

[33] 'Every organ of the collectivity . . . creates for itself, as soon as it becomes consolidated, interests peculiar to itself. The existence of these special interests involves a necessary conflict with the interests of the collectivity': ibid., p. 406.

as no more than a means to the end of policy effectiveness,[34] leaders are more likely to regard access as an end in itself. The failure of specific policy claims may well damage the internal authority of leaders. But an inability even to communicate those claims, by preferred means, is likely to pose a sterner and more pressing threat to their position. For such a failure places the group's *raison d'être* more firmly in question because, unlike policy failures, it deprives constituents of hope in relation to future policy claims on other issues.

Of course, this divergence of viewpoint between leaders and constituents might conceivably be reduced or even eliminated in an organization like the TUC whose executive body resembles, in Truman's phrase, 'a collection of ambassadors' from its member-unions.[35] There are, indeed, notable cases of TUC executive members acting out an ambassadorial role. But they are far from typical. Generally speaking, part-time executive members appear to have placed a high value on the prestige and prominence conferred by their office. Their actions, other than on issues of singular significance to their own union, suggest that they have tended to identify their personal interests with those of the TUC as an organization. There is no doubt that this has been the identification of the TUC's full-time officials.[36]

For TUC leaders in general, then, it would seem that the *primary* criterion of effectiveness is the TUC's success in securing, maintaining and extending its direct access to government office-holders. From this standpoint, policy successes provide a *secondary* criterion of effectiveness, in that they confirm rather than establish the TUC's ability to fill an intermediary role.

This conclusion echoes, in one respect, the assumption of most other pressure group studies: that access claims are of a different order from policy claims. But the conventional

[34] There are politically-involved groups of which this may not be true. For example, as a participant in the student movements of the 1960s has explained, 'the means the students used *were* the ends of the movement': Gerald Rosenfield in Paul Jacobs and Saul Landau (eds.), *The New Radicals*, p. 217. But groups of this character fall outside the concerns of the present study.

[35] Truman, *The Governmental Process*, p. 178.

[36] 'The staff of the TUC', their most senior member once commented, 'have a keen sense of the authority, the dignity and the prestige of the TUC': George Woodcock, *TUC Report*, 1965, p. 561.

attribution of subsidiary status to access claims[37] is here denied, on the ground that for group leaderships access possesses a value of its own quite independent of policy outcomes.[38] It follows that an indicator based on access claims not only provides, as argued earlier, a more accessible and precise measure of effectiveness over time than one based on policy claims; it also provides a measure of effectiveness involving issues of crucial concern to key actors in the political process.

[37] The major exception is Wootton's *The Politics of Influence*, which places unusual emphasis on access claims (see chap. XI), but at the same time redresses their down-grading in other studies only to the extent of equating certain of them with policy claims by attributing to them an ideological content (in relation to ex-servicemen's associations). Thus claims to membership of government advisory bodies are characterized as claims for 'democratic representation', and of administrative bodies as claims for 'democratic control'. My point is that the interest of group leaders in such claims involves much more than a belief (though it may involve that also) in principles of democratic representation and control.

[38] Quite independent, that is, except in the conceivable but unlikely case of a group which has adequate access to government office-holders but, over a substantial period, persistently fails to secure anything at all that its leaders can present to their members as a policy gain.

2

The Environment by 1868

THE society in which the TUC emerged was, for its time, kinder than most to trade unionism. Outright repression was a thing of the past, although the unions' legal position remained uncomfortably exposed to the attentions of a judiciary from which they could expect little sympathy. Trade union officials were no longer quite the pariahs they had been. William Gladstone suddenly modified his opposition to extending the franchise after seeing some union spokesmen on another matter in 1864: their demeanour, he informed a startled House of Commons, had convinced him that some sections of the working class possessed qualities (including 'regard for superiors') making them worthy of the vote.[1] Some time later the Conservative Lord St. Leonards treated two union leaders to 'an excellent luncheon, affably showed us his pictures and library, especially the books he had himself written or edited, and otherwise entertained us' at his home.[2]

At the same time, union officials were still unable to secure recognition from most employers; and in cases where they did, they usually 'received scant courtesy when they were admitted into the employers' presence'.[3] In 1866 Robert Lowe, echoing Palmerston, could garner support for the Liberal revolt against Gladstone's Reform Bill by raising the spectre of 'the extensive and powerful tyranny which would be exercised through the bill by trade unions'.[4] His opponents in the middle-class National Reform Union found it prudent to rebuff a proposal from the trade union-sponsored National Reform League for a combined campaign in support of the bill. And towards the

---

[1] Philip Magnus, *Gladstone: A Biography*, pp. 160–1.
[2] George Howell, *Labour Legislation, Labour Movements and Labour Leaders*, vol. II, p. 438.
[3] ibid., p. 439.
[4] Quoted in S. Maccoby, *English Radicalism, 1853–1886*, p. 83.

18

end of the same year the 'Sheffield outrages' revived middle-class fears of union violence, and prompted claims that the 'unions must be stamped out as a public nuisance'.[5]

Nevertheless, the climate of opinion was favourable enough in 1867 to permit the passage not only of Disraeli's Reform Bill but of a Master and Servant Bill removing some handicaps on union activity, together with other industrial measures which some Conservatives viewed as a means of 'putting us right with the Working Classes'.[6] In that year, too, union leaders were given unprecedented access to the royal commission on the Sheffield outrages. Formerly, they had appeared as witnesses before similar bodies, 'but never once had a workmen's representative a chance of examining an employer'; they had also felt 'placed at a disadvantage by the secrecy or semi-secrecy of the inquiries'.[7] This time, they secured the appointment to the commission of two middle-class sympathisers, Thomas Hughes and Frederic Harrison, and they were allowed to send representatives to attend its hearings.

THE TRADE UNIONS

The total union membership in 1867 is unknown, but there are clear indications that it had expanded significantly since the mid-point of the century. Trade unionism in the 1860s was largely the preserve of skilled workers. Union organization was strongly local in character. However, the trend towards a broader geographic base was already well-established in the 'new model' amalgamations which laid the foundations of national craft unions.

Viable inter-union organization was confined to the local level up to the mid-sixties. It took the shape of trades councils formed in major urban centres, from the forties, culminating in the formation of the London Trades Council in 1860. Attempts to set up *national* inter-union bodies had either died quickly, like Robert Owen's Grand National Consolidated Trades Union of the 1830s, or failed to gain general acceptance, like the Sheffield-based National Association of United

---

[5] Quoted in Howell, *Labour Legislation*, vol. I, p. 162.
[6] Quoted in Paul Smith, *Disraelian Conservatism and Social Reform*, pp. 44, 86.
[7] Howell, *Labour Legislation*, vol. I, p. 163.

Trades. The mid-sixties, however, witnessed a burst of crea-
tivity at this level which culminated in the foundation of the
Trades Union Congress.

A campaign for reform of the law relating to contracts of
employment, initiated earlier by the Glasgow Trades Council,
led to the formation of a widely-representative lobbying committee in 1864 and, eventually, to the Master and Servant Act
of 1867. Another single issue, electoral reform, produced the
predominantly trade-unionist National Reform League in
1865, and the slightly more radical London Working Men's
Association the following year. 1866 also saw the emergence
of the more broadly-based United Kingdom Alliance of
Organized Trades intended to promote industrial coordination,
though its financial resources soon proved inadequate. The
court decision of *Hornby* v. *Close*, signifying that unions had
no legal protection against embezzlement, prompted leading
affiliates of the London Trades Council to set up the Conference
of Amalgamated Trades in 1867. This 'Junta', as named by
the Webbs, subsequently handled the trade union case before
the royal commission on the Sheffield outrages. For a time, the
role was shared with the less select Conference of Trades,
initiated by the London Working Men's Association but including union bodies outside London. The eventual exclusion
of the latter's observer from hearings of the commission, leaving
the field to the Junta, angered provincial union leaders. One
outcome was the decision of the Manchester and Salford Trades
Council to propose an annual trade union 'Congress', and to
convene the first meeting in June 1868.

These developments in inter-union organization involved a
trade unionism dominated by skilled workers who shared in the
prosperity of the golden years of British industrialism by virtue
of their ability both to restrict entry to their trade and to
secure wage rates far higher than those of manual workers in
general. They formed in their own eyes, as in the eyes of observers, an 'aristocracy of labour'. Their manners and life-style
were closer to those of the small employer than to those of the
unskilled labourer; and their unions were designed to protect
them as much against competition from the unskilled as against
oppression by employers. Accordingly, they saw themselves as
possessing a distinctive social status, conferred on them by skill,

organization and a disposition towards sobriety and self-improvement. They tended to be fiercely critical of traditional socio-political distinctions, but their temper was far from revolutionary. Like the middle-class Radicals, they attacked 'Old Corruption' not for supporting class distinctions, but for supporting distinctions based on 'privilege' rather than 'merit'. And they were inclined, before they won it, to regard 'the franchise as a symbol of social recognition, rather than as an instrument to . . . rearrange society'.[8] Typically, too, they accepted the principal tenets of the *laissez-faire* orthodoxy in economics, but with a crucial qualification favouring collective (i.e., trade union) action on their own part.

Trade union methods of action reflected these preconceptions. The emphasis was on collective self-help. Unions normally provided insurance facilities covering one or more contingencies such as unemployment, sickness, accident, superannuation and funeral costs. These provisions underpinned the unions' industrial aims of controlling the supply (by way of apprenticeship requirements), the use and the payment of skilled labour—matters which were usually determined unilaterally by a union, on the basis of 'customary' conditions, and enforced by the threat that its members would not accept employment on lesser terms. Unemployment benefit made it easier for unionists to refuse or leave work not complying with union rules. The other types of benefit helped dissuade them from accepting such employment because the penalty, expulsion from their union, meant forfeiting past investment as well as future benefit. Strikes were typically highly selective and very limited, the preferred form being the 'strike-in-detail', entailing the withdrawal of small groups or of individual employees supported by unemployment benefit rather than strike pay. Large-scale strikes were comparatively rare.

The product, particularly after the emergence of the 'new model' amalgamations aiming at national coverage, was unions with large and well-husbanded funds, whose leaders were intensely proud of their independence. Their attitudes to political activity followed suit.

The embryonic union organizations of the eighteenth and early nineteenth centuries had financed court actions to

[8] F. B. Smith, *The Making of the Second Reform Bill*, p. 235.

enforce old statutes regulating wages and apprenticeship; they
had also promoted and opposed new legislation by employing
counsel to appear before parliamentary bodies, by lobbying
parliamentarians, by organizing petitions and demonstrations,
and sometimes by trying to influence elections in particular
constituencies. The repeal of the old regulatory legislation and
the growing prevalence of *laissez-faire* sentiments (not least
among unionists themselves) reduced the point of political
activity for industrial purposes. In the middle years of the
century, union leaders in general tended to steer clear of
official political involvement—although the coal and textile
unions continued to agitate for regulatory legislation in their
own industry, and individual unionists were active in support
of electoral reform and other political causes.

The 1861 constitution of the London Trades Council pre-
saged a change in the wind with its reference to 'the general
interests of labour . . . both in and out of Parliament'.[9] Momen-
tarily, however, caution was still the keynote. In the same year,
a council majority was prepared to take political action for the
purpose of preventing a War Office contractor from employing
army labour, but they backed away from official involvement
in campaigns for electoral reform and reform of the law of
master and servant. Nevertheless, the council was officially
active on both issues by the mid-sixties.

When the first Trades Union Congress met in 1868 the
burning trade union issues of the day were political in character
—the pending report of the Royal Commission on Trade
Unions, with its likely legislative sequel; and the *Hornby* v.
Close decision, which only legislation could remedy. In addition,
political action had been marvellously vindicated the previous
year by the passage of the second Reform Act and, above all,
the Master and Servant Act, 'the first positive success of the
Trade Unions in the legislative field'.[10]

THE STRUCTURE OF PRESSURE GROUP ACTIVITY

Pressure group activity along recognizably modern lines was
already a feature of British politics by the 1860s. The groups
that have tended to take the eye of historians of the period are

[9] Quoted in B. C. Roberts, *The Trades Union Congress, 1868–1921*, p. 18.
[10] S. and B. Webb, *The History of Trade Unionism*, p. 253.

of the 'single-cause' type—like the Anti-Corn Law League of the 1840s and the National Reform Union of the 1860s—with limited goals, no significant non-political functions and, usually, a short life. But mingled with them, increasingly, were other politically-involved associations based on specific and permanent interests. They often possessed non-political functions as well. They clustered, in particular, around issues of trade and religion.

The relative modernity of these pressure groups was signalled most clearly by the way they communicated their claims to government. In the eighteenth century, government office-holders had tended to regard as legitimate only those organized group pressures which were channelled through traditional 'official outlets', such as municipal corporations, universities, cathedral chapters and magistrates: 'Access to these channels was crucial'.[11] By the mid-nineteenth century it had ceased to be so. It was accepted that group pressures might properly be applied directly to government office-holders. And both constitutional theory and actual power relationships concurred in the location of the prime point of access.

The period between the first Reform Act of 1832 and the second of 1867 was the golden age of the private member of the House of Commons. Party discipline, greatly weakened during the 1830s, was almost negligible during the 1860s. Governments dependent on parliamentary majorities for office had virtually no means of coercing support. Certainly, cabinet still had the major hand in the formation of policy, and parliament recognized this in 1852 by agreeing to give government business precedence on three, instead of two, days a week. But ministers were still obliged to defer heavily to backbench opinion, in an age when parliamentary majorities were typically narrow, and their influence was frequently outweighed by constituency pressures and the personal interests of private members. As for the civil service, ministerial (and hence parliamentary) dominance was still fairly easily maintained at a time when bureaucratic tasks were 'sufficiently light and straightforward for one man to master and personally supervise the work of a department if he felt so inclined'.[12]

[11] Samuel Beer, *Modern British Politics*, p. 17
[12] John P. Mackintosh, *The British Cabinet*, p. 140.

In these circumstances, 'pressure groups usually concentrated on returning or interesting Members rather than on direct attempts to influence the government'.[13] Constituency election campaigns, formal petitions to parliament and lobbying private MPs: these were the standard pressure group tactics—supplemented, where appropriate, by mass meetings and demonstrations. Deputations to ministers were not uncommon; but parliament was the focus of pressure group attention.

Trade union leaders were no different when they took to political action. Thus it was only after a series of massive demonstrations on the electoral reform issue that the union-sponsored National Reform League in 1867 sent deputations to see Derby, the Prime Minister, and Disraeli, government leader in the House of Commons (having earlier interviewed Gladstone, the Liberal leader). On the other great legislative issue of the time, in their view, union leaders mounted one ministerial deputation in 1864 urging reform of the law of master and servant; but they thereafter relied on public meetings and, above all, direct lobbying of parliamentarians before finally achieving their goal by means of a private member's bill. Their use of deputations appears, otherwise, to have been confined to matters specifically within the *administrative* competence of ministers. There was a union deputation, as early as 1861, to the War Office protesting against soldiers being used as strike-breakers; another raised the Polish question with Palmerston in 1863; and a third asked Gladstone, then Chancellor of the Exchequer, for access to the Post Office Savings Bank in 1864. The Home Secretary received union deputations concerned about police action against demonstrations in both 1864 and 1866. Another put the union case on the Sheffield outrages to him in 1866, and the following year he discussed the composition of the Royal Commission on Trade Unions with two more. But on greater issues, it was to sympathetic backbenchers that union leaders looked with most hope, as one of them indicated when he fulsomely credited their parliamentary 'friends' with 'energy, pluck, perseverance, high character, pure motives, and the desire to improve the condition of the labouring classes'.[14]

[13] ibid., p. 94.
[14] Howell, *Labour Legislation*, vol. II, p. 461.

The Reform Act of 1867 reinforced the unions' political friendships by putting electoral sanctions within the reach of urban skilled workers. Tory politicians quickly acknowledged this by their 'efforts to collect demonstrations of gratitude to the Derby-Disraeli Ministry for its Reform Bill', culminating in a 'surprisingly successful "working men's" assembly . . . in the Crystal Palace'.[15] Union leaders were no less conscious of this new factor, and in the general election of 1868 urged unionists to register as electors and to press candidates on the issue of legal recognition for trade unions.

This was the backdrop against which the TUC took its first hesitant steps on to the stage of British politics. It was founded by men more used to standing in the wings. But they had been gathering themselves for a less retiring role. As one historian has commented of the union deputation that confronted Gladstone in 1864: 'Such confidence, a generation earlier, would have been unthinkable'.[16] By 1868 the passage of the Reform Act and of the Master and Servant Act had strengthened their confidence; and their interest in political action had been sharply intensified by the certain prospect of parliamentary legislation on trade unions which would either confound or confirm their hopes for the future. Spurred to act at the national level, they found their attention turning to the question of trade union coordination at that level.

[15] Maccoby, *English Radicalism 1853–86*, p. 101.
[16] Magnus, *Gladstone*, p. 161.

3

The Politics of Deference
1868–1889

THE emergent TUC drew strength from the way in which the Reform Act apparently stimulated both the political expectations of trade union leaders and the responsiveness of government office-holders. Circumstances also provided it with specific political goals of pressing importance to the unions at large. Significantly, these goals were modest, by later standards, and did no great violence to orthodox conceptions of the proper role of government. In addition, the TUC's spokesmen approached government office-holders with a sense of awe which acknowledged their own social inferiority.

GOVERNMENT

During the 1870s and 1880s there was a striking expansion in the scope of domestic public policy, despite the continuing preoccupation of political leaders with foreign and imperial affairs and, increasingly, the special problem of Ireland. The tone was set by the epoch-making Education Act of 1870 and succeeding measures in the same field. Legislative steps to protect tenant-farmers were equally indicative of the trend. So, too, was a series of measures, starting with the Trade Union Act of 1871, which extended state protection to industrial labour.

The differences between the two established parties, when in office, were not great in the case of social reform and economic intervention. A Gladstonian government could be assailed as 'the most Socialistic . . . seen in England since Wat Tyler'.[1] But Gladstone, in turn, could accuse Disraeli's ministry of creating an atmosphere in which 'the nation is perplexed with fear of change'.[2] An electioneering Arthur Balfour provided

[1] Quoted in Philip Williams, 'Public Opinion and the Railway Rates Question in 1886', *English Historical Review*, vol. 67, 1952, p. 57n.
[2] Quoted in K. B. Smellie, *A Hundred Years of English Government*, p. 125.

the key when he spoke of the Liberals' new-found 'zeal for social reform', and claimed that it 'followed too closely upon the alteration of the franchise, and had too near a bearing on the acquisition of votes'.[3] The charge was equally applicable, although he denied it, to his own party.

The second Reform Act of 1867 had increased the size of the national electorate by a massive 88 per cent; the third, of 1884, increased it by 67 per cent: an electorate totalling a little more than one million in 1866 had soared to 4.4 million by 1885. The 'masses', to use Gladstone's term, now dominated the electorate. The outcome was a marked shift in the style and content of British party politics.

General elections began to centre more explicitly on the persons and policies of major political figures, with the implication that the electorate, and not simply parliament, made or broke governments. And so the convention, initiated by Disraeli in 1868, that a government defeated in the House of Commons seeks a dissolution and, if defeated at the ensuing election, resigns without meeting parliament.

Party organization outside parliament became tighter. The affiliation of local Conservative associations to a National Union dates from 1867, and was initiated explicitly for the purpose of facilitating the recruitment of working-class supporters. Joseph Chamberlain's Birmingham Caucus, reorganized in the same year for the same purpose, inspired the formation of the National Liberal Federation ten years later.

Electioneering practices changed. Gladstone became the first leading politician to stump the country with his station-stop speeches on a train journey to his Midlothian electorate in 1879. For the Conservatives, Lord Salisbury and Sir Stafford Northcote followed his example the following year. Extension of the franchise, as Chamberlain told Gladstone, meant that 'the platform has become one of the most powerful and indispensable instruments of Government'.[4]

Above all, social issues, with 'little political prestige' previously, now became essential items in the vote-catching baggage of politicians.[5] Disraeli suddenly discerned a need 'to advance

---

[3] Quoted in S. Maccoby, *English Radicalism, 1886–1914*, p. 114.
[4] Quoted in J. H. Grainger, *Character and Style in English Politics*, p. 109.
[5] John Vincent, *The Formation of the Liberal Party, 1857–1868*, p. 243.

boldly, in search of working-class support, into the field of Social Reform'.[6] His government of 1874–80 produced the greatest single burst of legislation in the field during the nineteenth century. The Liberals trod the same path.

The new policies included some of special concern to the trade unions. A Liberal government gave them legal recognition through the Trade Union Act of 1871, but simultaneously limited their right to strike through the Criminal Law Amendment Act's anti-picketing provisions. The Conservatives temporarily remedied those provisions in 1875 by way of the Conspiracy and Protection of Property Act—a measure which Disraeli predicted 'will gain and retain for the Tories the lasting affection of the working classes'.[7] His government also produced a liberating Employers and Workmen Act and a Summary Jurisdiction Act in which the unions were strongly interested; supported a union-backed bill which issued as the Trade Union Amendment Act of 1876; and introduced another on compensation for industrial injuries that lapsed with the dissolution of parliament. The last matter was taken up in the Employers' Liability Act of 1880 by the succeeding Liberal government, which legislated as well on other union-promoted matters such as bankruptcy, patents, safety on ships, the payment of seamen's wages and amendments to the Employers and Workmen Act. The Conservative government of the late 1880s supported a private member's Truck Bill promoted by the unions, and withdrew two of its own bills on seamen and on workers' compensation in the face of union opposition to them.

George Howell, first secretary of the TUC, was later to claim that 'the influence of labour leaders' was reflected, between 1868 and 1889, in the passage of 69 statutes on diverse matters ranging from industrial regulation to parliamentary reform and company law.[8] The claim is questionable in detail, but there can be no doubt that the general political influence of union leaders was enhanced by the new electoral significance of the working class. The local branch organization of the unions meant that they penetrated the electorate to a degree

---

[6] Quoted in Asquith, *Fifty Years of Parliament*, vol. 1, p. 28.
[7] Quoted in Paul Smith, *Disraelian Conservatism and Social Reform*, p. 217.
[8] Howell, *Labour Legislation*, vol. II, 472.

then matched only by the two groups locked on the liquor question ('The Trade' and the temperance societies), the nonconformist churches and the insurance companies with their growing army of collectors. But the unions alone were exclusively working-class in character. The politicians, who might well have doubted the ability of union leaders to manipulate the working-class vote, could scarcely have doubted that they articulated the aspirations of many working-class voters. It was not possible, in other words, to ignore them.

The signs of political acceptance of the trade unions during the 1870s and 1880s were infrequent and muted, by later standards, but dramatic by earlier standards. One sign was the extent to which union officials were able to gain direct access to government leaders. Prime ministers during the period were virtually unapproachable. Conservative ones were totally so. 'Of all things in the world', one of Disraeli's fictional characters remarks, 'I dislike a deputation . . . receiving a deputation is like sham marching: an immense dust and no progress'.[9] True to this youthful opinion, he himself twice declined union requests for an interview. Salisbury, his Conservative successor, appears never to have been asked for one. Gladstone, in the first flush of supreme office, may have received a union deputation about low-paid workers in 1868; he certainly saw one urging recognition of the French Provisional Government two years later. But he refused to see another about the labour laws in 1873. The next (and, apparently, last) time he saw one, as Prime Minister, was in 1884 when the occasion provided useful publicity in support of his electoral reform bill.

Lesser ministers of both parties were more accessible. In 1871 the Liberal Home Secretary, Henry Bruce, received the first deputation mounted by the TUC, on the government's Trade Union Bill; and his Under-secretary saw another about the Criminal Law Amendment Bill. The following year each of them also discussed the Payment of Wages (Truck) Bill with TUC deputations. 1873 was even more remarkable. The Attorney-General and the TUC secretary met several times on the subject of the Criminal Law Amendment Act. And Bruce's successor as Home Secretary, Robert Lowe—'the last of the

---

[9] *Sybil: or The Two Nations* (1954), pp. 352–3.

genuine Benthamites'[10] and an outspoken critic of trade unionism—astonished TUC leaders by responding to a letter about the Trade Union Act with an intimation that he would welcome a deputation. Lowe, who had the reputation of being somewhat cavalier with deputations in general, further surprised them by making 'the interview a conversational one, informal, as compared with most deputations'.[11]

Disraeli's ministers, if not quite as forthcoming as Lowe, seem to have been accessible enough. In 1874 TUC deputations met the Chancellor of the Exchequer and the Home Secretary about the Trade Union Act, and the Lord Chancellor and the President of the Board of Trade about the patent laws. The next year, two others were seen by the Home Secretary and the Chancellor of the Exchequer, respectively, on the subject of trade union legislation. By the end of the 1870s, it appears, relevant ministers were receiving an annual TUC deputation carrying relevant Congress resolutions—a practice that was to persist for many years. During the 1880s at least, ministers of both parties appear to have seen a number of other union deputations as well: for example, an impressive trio of Conservative ministers (the Chancellor of the Exchequer, the Home Secretary and the President of the Board of Trade) interviewed Sheffield union representatives in 1887.

Below the ministerial level, direct dealings with union leaders seem to have been infrequent, and correspondence the usual means of communication. On the other hand, by the 1880s, the TUC was claiming a cordial working relationship with both the Chief Inspector of Factories and the head of the Board of Trade's Marine Department.

Government recognition of the unions also took other forms. In 1870 one of the Junta, Robert Applegarth, became the first trade union official to sit on a royal commission, the Royal Commission on the Contagious Diseases Acts. The Disraeli government later appointed Alexander Macdonald, then TUC chairman and one of the first two working-class MPs, to its Royal Commission on Labour Laws. It rejected union claims for representation on commissions concerned with agriculture and the criminal code. But another Conservative government

[10] A. V. Dicey, *Law and Public Opinion in England*, p. 253.
[11] Howell, *Labour Legislation*, vol. II, p. 326.

placed two unionists on the Royal Commission on Trade.

Perhaps even more striking, as a form of recognition, was the Liberal appointment of a union leader to a factory sub-inspectorate in 1881—an event hailed by the TUC as 'the entrance into the Governmental system of the country of a bona fide workman'.[12] By the end of 1886 four more union officials were sub-inspectors, and another occupied a position in the newly-created Bureau of Labour Statistics in the Board of Trade. Conservative governments had appointed at least another two unionists to factory sub-inspectorates by 1890, and appear to have had some hand in the appointments of seven former miners who became mine inspectors in the last six years of the 1880s. The factory and mine inspectors of an earlier age had been characterized by their disapproval of trade unionism.[13]

Recognition of a similar type followed union complaints about magistrates' behaviour in cases arising from industrial disputes: during 1885–6 the Liberals elevated six union officials to the magisterial bench. And 1886 also saw the appointment of Henry Broadhurst, TUC secretary, as parliamentary Under-secretary of State to the Home Office in Gladstone's third and shortest-lived government.

In retrospect, a few ministerial deputations, a handful of appointments to royal commissions, magistracies and minor administrative positions may not seem to amount to much. Even Broadhurst's under-secretaryship was humble enough in political terms ('My own opinions on large questions of policy were, I confess, never sought for by the chiefs of the party'[14]). Nevertheless, they signified a new era in British political relationships. At that time, university men competed for factory inspectorates, and magistracies comprised a rung in the honours system to which many aspired. Moreover, all these appointments, and not only Broadhurst's, would have been inconceivable to the union officials and the party leaders of Palmerston's day.

The social attitudes involved are exemplified in Lord Granville's astonishment when he discovered, through a chance

[12] TUC, *Parliamentary Committee's Report*, 1881, p. 1.
[13] See David Roberts, *Victorian Origins of the British Welfare State*, p. 169.
[14] Henry Broadhurst, *Henry Broadhurst, M.P.*, p. 186.

encounter in Regent Street in 1878, that Gladstone had attended a meeting of working men.[15] Similarly, six years later Sir George Trevelyan, as a Liberal minister, could be 'startled by the daring of the suggestion' that working men should be placed on magistrates' benches.[16] The point is underlined by the earlier difficulty the TUC's leaders had in obtaining access to the lobby of the House of Commons. As it was touchingly put in the minutes of the TUC's executive body: 'Persons only interested in pecuniary schemes are allowed admission why not us?'[17] Both the Speaker and the Sergeant-at-Arms declined to extend free access to the TUC. Its spokesmen, as a result,

> had to send in our names to members, and they had to come into the Central Hall and pass us into the Lobby. Sometimes the member sent for was not in; sometimes I fear that the member was not . . . desirous of seeing us . . . In which case we got no reply . . . and we felt at a disadvantage compared with other bodies . . . On the whole members were courteous . . . but it was the waiting, the loss of time, the weariness of the thing.[18]

Only after a direct appeal to the Prime Minister was the TUC eventually given unfettered access to the lobby by being placed on the Speaker's 'list'.

Political recognition of the unions both reflected and, probably, affected changing social attitudes to trade unionism. There was, according to Howell, a marked shift in press opinion from the mid-seventies. 'Instead of "slogging articles" against . . . trade unions . . . there was tenderness of treatment': 'Labour leaders were no longer tabooed'.[19] Alfred Marshall and his wife remarked in the late 1870s that the unions, once led mainly by 'ignorant, rude men', now included most of the more 'intelligent and steady workers' and had leaders who frequently displayed a sense of responsibility.[20] Others evidently shared this view. The delegates to the TUC's Congress of 1872 were accorded a mayoral banquet and the Nottingham 'townspeople threw open their houses . . . in a way that was most generous and *surprising*'[21]—a reception that was to be

[15] See Smellie, op. cit., p. 135.   [16] Broadhurst, op. cit., p. 135.
[17] Parliamentary Committee, *Minutes*, 19 March 1872 (*PC Mins.*, hereafter).
[18] Howell, *Labour Legislation*, vol. I, pp. 227–8.
[19] ibid., vol. II, pp. 369–70, 389.
[20] Alfred Marshall and Mary Paley Marshall, *The Economics of Industry*, pp. 189–90, 192, 198.
[21] Howell, 'Trades Union Congresses and Social Legislation', *Contemporary Review*, September 1889, p. 8. Italics added.

repeated elsewhere. When Broadhurst entered parliament in 1880, he was embarrassed by numerous invitations to functions of the social élite.

Such indications of the changing social status of union leaders were doubtless prompted often by sympathy, paternalism, courtesy or curiosity. But the emergence of unionism as a political force was scarcely a negligible factor. Certainly, this was plainly the consideration which persuaded a social reformer such as Samuel Plimsoll, concerned with the safety of seamen, to enlist union support for his cause. Other Liberals with less specialized political interests turned their attention in the same direction. Several addressed Congresses of the TUC, including A. J. Mundella (who presented a paper on industrial conciliation and arbitration to the first Congress in 1868), Sir Thomas Brassey in 1877 and John Morley in 1878. Joseph Chamberlain drew Howell and Robert Applegarth into his National Education League founded in 1869, and subsequently forged ties with other unionists like W. J. Davis. Gladstone associated with labour leaders in his Eastern Question Association during the late 1870s, and often conferred with Broadhurst on this cause both at his London house and at the TUC office. In 1885 he invited Broadhurst to lunch at Hawarden, his country home. Twelve months earlier, the Liberal leadership had publicly acknowledged its trade union connections when Lord Rosebery, accompanied by the Earl of Aberdeen, addressed the TUC's annual Congress. The 1886 general election, was followed not only by Broadhurst's under-secretaryship, but also by a dinner which Rosebery gave 'as a compliment to the Labour Party'.[22] By this time, too, the Conservative leadership was more than mildly interested in the issue of working-class candidates. The result was that union leaders, for whom it had once been 'almost impossible to find a Member of Parliament who cared to ask a question in the interest of labour', were confronted by the late 1880s with 'a great many members contending as to which shall be the first to render a service of this kind'.[23] As this suggests, political recognition of the trade unions might still be confined and partial, but it was incomparably greater than a generation earlier.

[22] Broadhurst, op. cit., p. 301.   [23] *TUC Report*, 1887, p.16.

TRADE UNIONS

Union leaders in the 1870s and 1880s were predominantly Liberal in sympathy, tending to identify with the party's Radical wing. Their expectations of government reflected this association.

'We do not ask for State aid', the TUC leadership insisted, 'we ask only for the removal of State obstructions to freedom and equality and prosperity'.[24] Otherwise, it was up to organized labour to 'increase its dignity and importance' by 'showing self-reliance . . . in trade matters, by refusing State assistance . . . and keeping a firm grip on all that it has gained'.[25] Distrust of state intervention and faith in independent unionism formed the core of what the Lib-Labs, as they came to be known, stood for. Both were reflected in the terms in which George Shipton and John Burnett advised a parliamentary committee to oppose legislation protecting men (women, as 'the creatures of circumstance', were different) in sweated occupations: 'the matter is . . . rather one for the workers than for the Legislature', the solution being union organization.[26]

Lib-Lab political programmes, accordingly, tended to be limited to policies designed to clear legal and other 'brambles from our path'.[27] Nevertheless, the economic depression of the late 1870s and 1880s forced many Lib-Labs at least to question what one traditionalist union leadership described as 'a state of society in which can exist, side by side, practically illimitable wealth and downright starvation'.[28] By the mid-eighties, even a Conservative union official like James Mawdsley could doubt the likelihood of 'improvement . . . so long as the present state of society continued to exist'.[29]

Socialism, as yet, had little influence at the level of union leaderships. The TUC carried a resolution advocating land nationalization in 1882, rescinded it the following year, rejected a similar resolution in 1885, and adopted another in 1886 urging the nationalization of land royalty rents. But this owed

[24] ibid., 1884, p. 14.   [25] ibid., 1887, p. 16.
[26] Quoted in Helen F. Hohman, *The Development of Social Insurance and Minimum Wage Legislation in Great Britain*, p. 365.
[27] *TUC Report*, 1886, p. 18.
[28] Quoted in Alan Fox, *The National Union of Boot and Shoe Operatives, 1874–1957*, p. 192.
[29] Quoted in Webb, *The History of Trade Unionism*, p. 379.

more to the Radical strain of social reform than to Socialism. Non-unionist Radicals, in fact, were the initiators of many union-supported policies. The TUC's first formal legislative programme was largely based on a paper which Henry Crompton, a lawyer, had presented at the Congress of 1873. Similarly, its interest in protective legislation for seamen was inspired by Samuel Plimsoll, and its concern for codification of the criminal law by Sir James Stephen.

But even the relatively limited political aims espoused by the unions involved a wide range of political tactics. By 1874 union leaders had lobbied MPs, sent letters and deputations to cabinet ministers, canvassed parliamentary candidates, organized public meetings and demonstrations and, in some cases, stood for parliament themselves. The focus of their attention, however, was the legislature. 'It is in the House of Commons', a TUC president emphasized in 1886, 'that we must win for our fellow-workers those triumphs which are destined . . . to bless them in the future'.[30]

This concentration of attention was undoubtedly influenced by a perception of parliament's role which was closer to the reality of the 1850s and 1860s than that of the 1870s and 1880s. Yet it was relevant enough. Party discipline was still relatively weak. Although the extent to which parliament as such determined the fate of governments during the later period is debatable,[31] and although there was a distinct trend towards voting divisions on strict party lines, non-party voting remained common. Thus, in 1883, two criminal law reform bills of union interest were abandoned by the Gladstone government in the face of parliamentary opposition. In addition, much legislation was still initiated by private members. Union leaders could scarcely have been unimpressed by the fact that both the Trade Union Amendment Act of 1876 and the Employers' Liability Act of 1880 originated as private member's bills.

Nevertheless, union leaders were well aware of the value of securing ministerial support to strengthen their case in parliament. The point was underlined by changes in House of Commons procedures during the 1880s, when the obstructionist tactics of the Irish Nationalists led to the introduction of the

[30] *TUC Report*, 1886, p. 25.
[31] Cf. Mackintosh, op. cit., p. 480; and Ivor Jennings, *Cabinet Government*, p. 480.

'closure', the 'guillotine' and a number of other devices which restricted the freedom of backbench parliamentarians and strengthened cabinet control. In 1887 the TUC executive could not recall a parliamentary session in which 'the opportunities of private members for bringing forward their Bills and Motions have been so curtailed. . . . Nearly the whole Session has been taken up by the Government'.[32] Union leaders' attention was also directed towards the executive arm of government by their interest in some distinctively administrative matters, such as the composition of the factories and mines inspectorates. Nor had they failed to register the emergence of delegated legislative powers in areas of interest to them: thus the TUC comment on the 'discretionary power' which the Factories and Workshops Act of 1878 vested in the Home Secretary.[33]

Union leaders, accordingly, could not ignore ministers and their departments. They found communication by way of correspondence easy enough but, initially, ministerial deputations were another matter. Their diffidence is seen in the TUC executive's astonished reaction, mentioned above, to Robert Lowe's initiative in this respect. The way in which the executive reached a decision to ask his Conservative successor for an interview provides a further illustration. In 1875 the TUC leaders wanted to ascertain the government's intentions in the matter of labour legislation. They made numerous attempts to do so through 'friends and advisers, both in and out of Parliament', before contemplating an interview with the Home Secretary. Their friends and advisers were doubtful: 'The idea of a deputation was not at first favourably received, as it was feared that we were unduly pressing the Government and possibly prejudicing our own case'.[34] Only after much hesitation did they finally decide to press the point—with total success. Thereafter, this procedure was employed with much less agonizing.

There was one other form of consultation with government which was of particular concern. The 1871 Congress, boldly for its time, pointed out that commissions investigating labour matters 'never include' working-class members, and urged that

[32] *TUC Report*, 1887, p. 12.   [33] TUC, *PC's Report*, 1878, p. 3.
[34] ibid., 1875, p. 3.

'working men should always form part of such Commissions'.[35] When Alexander Macdonald accepted a seat on the Royal Commission on Labour Laws three years later, however, he was forced to resign from the TUC chairmanship by colleagues who interpreted the commission as a Tory delaying tactic. There was a similar flurry when a later Conservative government appointed a TUC executive member, Thomas Birtwistle, to the Royal Commission on Trade in 1885, and then added a second unionist, C. J. Drummond, after the TUC asked for more. The real problem, as Broadhurst later admitted, was that both Birtwistle and Drummond were Conservatives.

But parliament was still the focus of attention. Union leaders' attempts to influence it took three principal forms: exerting pressure on sitting MPs, providing campaign support for sympathetic election candidates, and nominating working-class candidates.

Lobbying MPs was the primary tactic. This was how union leaders obtained sponsors for their private member's bills, had parliamentary questions put to ministers, and recruited parliamentary support for bills they favoured and strengthened opposition to bills they did not. Occasionally, they resorted to the ancient device of a formal petition 'in order to impress Parliament';[36] and 'meetings, lectures, publications, annual congresses' were also employed to the same end.[37]

Union electoral activity was encouraged by the passage of the second Reform Act. During the general election of 1868, 'all the best known men in the labour movement were engaged in promoting the return of the Liberals all over the country'.[38] The election of 1874 evoked less enthusiasm. Many union leaders, alienated by the Liberal government's refusal to revise its Criminal Law Amendment Act, virtually opted out of the campaign. But, once the Conservatives had resolved that issue, most of them worked in the Liberal cause during the elections of the eighties.

Concerted moves to secure the election to parliament of men with working-class backgrounds—'direct representation' as it came to be known—began with the 1868 election. All three

[35] *TUC Report*, 1871, pp. 87–8.
[36] TUC, *PC's Report*, 1883, p. 1.
[37] Howell, *The Conflicts of Capital and Labour*, p. 145.
[38] Howell, *Labour Legislation*, vol. II, p. 338.

unionist candidates were defeated. The following year saw the formation of the union-sponsored Labour Representation League, ostensibly independent but in fact with strong Liberal leanings. Its first candidate, at a by-election in 1870, was narrowly defeated; and the two (of fourteen) trade union candidates who won in 1874 owed their success to the miners' unions rather than the league. By 1880, when Broadhurst joined these two in parliament, the league was effectively defunct. The number of trade union MPs (strictly defined) rose to nine in 1885, before dropping to six the next year when the TUC founded the Labour Electoral Committee (later renamed the Labour Electoral Association). The LEC was firmly associated with the Liberal party, but proved no more viable than the league.

In 1889 there were only eight distinctively trade union members in the House of Commons, despite the extent to which the obvious obstacles to direct representation had been reduced by this time. In terms of sheer voting power at least, working men were fairly regarded as 'masters of the situation';[39] and the introduction of the secret ballot (1872), together with the extension of polling hours (1884), enhanced their ability to exercise that power. As candidates for parliamentary office, on the other hand, working men were still seriously handicapped. Despite restrictions on election expenditure (1883), they could feel disadvantaged by 'the practice of systematic canvassing . . . whether by personal calling, letter, or circular'.[40] There was also the problem of providing salaries for MPs without independent means. But above all loomed the obstacle of working-class attitudes to working-class candidates.

In the afterglow of the 1884 Reform Act, the TUC leaders had acclaimed and savoured 'our enormously increased political power'.[41] One year and two general elections later, they knew better. Working-class voters, they lamented, had failed to appreciate the necessity 'to elevate . . . the men in their own ranks'.[42] And later again, Broadhurst was to reflect that 'working men have never been enthusiastic about having representatives of their own class in the legislative assembly'.[43]

---

[39] *TUC Report*, 1886, p. 16.
[41] *TUC Report*, 1885, p. 13.
[43] Broadhurst, op. cit., p. 286.

[40] *PC Mins.*, 5 November 1889.
[42] ibid., 1886, p. 16.

This, it seems, was the handicap imposed on aspiring working-class politicians in 'a lord loving country'[44]—or, in Bagehot's more measured phrasing, a 'country of respectful poor' in which the 'mass of the . . . people are . . . politically deferential'.[45]

Perhaps the TUC leaders should not have been surprised. For they and their colleagues were not altogether immune, formal Radicals though many of them were. A Yorkshire delegate to the first Congress of 1868 was proud of being 'a trade union man' because it taught him not only 'to benefit himself' but also 'to be useful and respectful to his employers'.[46] Later, George Howell described as 'the only notable event' of the 1877 Congress, 'the appearance of Mr Thomas [later Lord] Brassey, M.P., whose addresses . . . gave an important character to the sittings of the Congress'.[47] And W. J. Davis waxed lyrical about the social event of the 1881 Congress: 'Everything was of a sumptuous character, as the Lord Mayor of London gave orders that there should be no difference in any particular between his receptions to the *elite* of society and the Trades Union Congress'.[48]

Henry Broadhurst's autobiography throws a closer light on the social attitudes of a Lib-Lab trade union leader of the time. A stonemason by trade and the TUC's secretary from 1875 to 1890, Broadhurst entered parliament in 1880. He was acutely conscious of the fact that his political activities from the late seventies brought him into 'close contact with a class of people whom I otherwise should never have met'.[49] The climax was three days he spent as house-guest of the Prince of Wales, an event to which he devotes a whole chapter ('My Visit to Sandringham'): 'I left Sandringham with the feeling of one who had spent a week-end with an old chum of his own rank in society . . .'.[50] The awe pervading this and numerous other references to contact with social notables is crystallized on the last page of the book, which ends with an account of Gladstone's funeral.

[44] Quoted in Cecil Woodham-Smith, *The Reason Why* (1958), p. 16.
[45] Walter Bagehot, *The English Constitution*, p. 238.
[46] Quoted in Edmund Frow and Michael Katanka, *1868 Year of the Unions*, p. 25.
[47] Howell, *The Conflicts of Capital and Labour*, p. 449.
[48] W. J. Davis, *British Trades Union Congress*, vol. I, p. 89.
[49] Broadhurst, op. cit., p. 88.
[50] ibid., p. 153.

Within the Abbey my place was on the north side of the grave. On my immediate right was the late Lord Chief Justice, and on my left Lord Justice Rigby. Behind sat the Lord Chancellor, and as the Duke of York retired from his post of pall-bearer he brushed against me.[51]

The other side of the awe was a sense of inadequacy. At Sandringham, owing to 'difficulties in the matter of dress', Broadhurst preferred to take dinner alone in his room (his wife, throughout his career, 'steadfastly refused to take part in the frivolities of fashionable people').[52] When he joined Gladstone's ministry in 1886, he had himself excused from the customary presentation to the Queen because, as a man 'scarcely emerged from a life of vicissitudes and hardships', he thought that in court dress (to which he had no objection in principle) 'I could not fail to look supremely ridiculous . . . at least to my own eyes'.[53]

Broadhurst's social uneasiness carried over into the more strictly political sphere. There was pride in his conclusion that working-class MPs had 'earned a reputation for their class of solid and abiding worth to the commonwealth', but the compulsion to defend them revealed something more: 'Here and there [among them] may be found eccentricities, but no boorishness, little if any vulgarity, and no disordered minds'.[54] Predictably, Gladstone's offer of a place in his ministry evoked an agonizing self-appraisal.

I left Mr Gladstone's house without any of those feelings of exhilaration . . . which the gift of office is generally supposed to awaken in the breast of the politician . . . I lived my life over again. . . . The lowly beginning of my career . . . the privations, the wanderings, and my varying fortunes . . . I realized as I had never done before the irretrievable loss which the lack of education in my early days involved. Visions of humiliation arising from the duties of my new office and my meagre capacity and endowments rose before me. . . . The next twenty-four hours were passed in a tormenting alternation of desire and reluctance.[55]

One way of compensating was whole-hearted identification with Gladstone—'the great Chieftain', 'our beloved leader', 'the greatest Englishman of the century'. Another was to demonstrate an interest in middle-class concerns: 'I took great pleasure in my success [concerning court arrangements in his electorate], which entirely disproved the theory that a Labour

[51] ibid., p. 312. [52] ibid., pp. 150, 212. [53] ibid., p. 206.
[54] ibid., p. 293. [55] ibid., pp. 188–9.

representative could be of no service to the general and commercial interests of his constituency'.[56] In all this there is ample
confirmation of Engels' sour comment on 'the bourgeois
"respectability" which has invaded the very blood and bone'
of English working-class leaders.[57]

Yet, if the memoirs of an old man give little hint of it, there
had been some iron in the soul of a younger Broadhurst.
Talking to his own people, he had spoken of the 'humiliation'
TUC leaders 'had to go through in the House of Commons and
its lobbies'; and had urged the election of 'men of their own
order', so that they could speak in parliament 'without cringing
and bowing to the upper classes'.[58] Even the aged Broadhurst
could regard the appointment of unionists to state administrative posts as a means of reducing 'the preserves of the
privileged classes'.[59] In these views, he presented the other side
of the Lib-Lab coin—the belief that position and influence
should not be merely a matter of birth or wealth or educational
opportunity.

There was thus an edge to the deference of union leaders
like Broadhurst. They might be over-eager for respect, and
gain too easy a 'satisfaction with the tone of the speeches in the
House', simply because 'not one word was said . . . which
could hurt the susceptibilities of the most sensitive workman'.[60]
But they were correspondingly touchy and quick to perceive
slights: hence the TUC president's sneer at those 'men of light
and learning who are continually telling us . . . that the working
classes can be better represented by men of wealth and social
position than by men who are comparatively uneducated and
poor'.[61] More important, they were also very ambitious. Thus
the TUC leadership was not content merely to hail the first
unionist appointment to a factory inspectorship as a 'breach . . .
in the ancient fortress of Civil Service exclusiveness'; it went
on to assert that 'we must not rest satisfied with this instal-
ment'.[62] Similarly, when the first working-class magistrates

[56] ibid., p. 105.
[57] Quoted in Robert Michels, *Political Parties*, p. 318.
[58] Quoted in Davis, op. cit., pp. 58–9.
[59] Broadhurst, op. cit., p. 136. For a different and simpler analysis of Broadhurst's character, see Bauman, *Between Class and Elite*, pp. 128–31.
[60] TUC, *PC's Report for 1875*, p. 5.
[61] *TUC Report*, 1886, p. 25.
[62] TUC, *PC's Report*, 1881, pp. 1–2.

were appointed: 'This movement must not be permitted to rest here; we must have men on most of the magisterial benches of the United Kingdom'.[63] And the TUC's president looked still higher after Broadhurst's elevation to Gladstone's ministry: 'I shall not be satisfied until we have a representative of unionism within the charmed circle of the Cabinet'.[64]

These ambitions, however, related less to the working class at large than to the 'men of a trade'. Union leaders were not untouched by the plight of the 'less fortunate in life', and professed to be 'painfully aware of the seething mass of suffering amongst the very poor'.[65] But their attitude was less one of compassion than of 'a slightly contemptuous pity':[66] thus their smug depiction of Bradlaugh's bill (against wage-payments in public houses) as 'a useful social measure, its purpose being to do for unskilled labour what the Unions have done for the trades'.[67] For democrats though union leaders understood themselves to be, they were not equalitarians. They stood too close to the unskilled labourer, and had struggled too hard to distinguish themselves from him, for that. As unionists, moreover, they emphasized quality rather than quantity. Trade unionism, for them, 'did not consist so much of numbers as of compactness and discipline. A well-regulated body of men could not estimate their power'.[68] Unskilled workers, with a few exceptions, seemed incapable of discipline.

This view, of course, was to change. But in the meantime established union leaders could draw confidence both from the widening gap they saw between themselves and the working-class mass, and from the recognition they were wringing from formerly remote political notables. One sign of their new confidence was a decreasing dependence on middle-class advisers. In 1883 Frederic Harrison read a paper to the TUC's annual Congress but, against precedent, was refused admission to the debate on another issue; and after 1884 the practice of inviting middle-class sympathizers to present papers at Congress was abandoned altogether. Union leaders no longer found it necessary for their annual gatherings to be legitimized in this way.

[63] *TUC Report*, 1885, p. 13.   [64] ibid., 1886, p. 25.
[65] ibid., 1884, p. 15.   [66] Fox, op. cit., p. 2.
[67] *TUC Report*, 1882, p. 11.   [68] ibid., 1877, p. 9.

TRADES UNION CONGRESS

The Congress convened in Manchester in June 1868 was distinguished by its sponsors' intention that it was to initiate a continuing series of annual gatherings representative of English trade unionism as a whole. Congress endorsed this aim. It elected a committee of five to arrange the next Congress with the Birmingham Trades Council. The Birmingham Congress, in August 1869, decided to ask the London Trades Council to convene the third Congress. It also appointed a committee of six London delegates 'to watch' the parliamentary passage of a Mines Regulation Bill.[69] The London Congress did not meet until eighteen months later, in March 1871. It set up another committee of five, with two tasks: to keep an eye on the Trade Union Bill then before parliament, and 'to draw up a code of rules for the regulation of future Congresses'.[70] The outcome, at Nottingham in January 1872, was the creation of a 10-member (increased to 11 in 1874) body entitled 'the Parliamentary Committee', which then elected Alexander Macdonald as its chairman. The enabling resolution implied that the new committee was assured of existence only until the next Congress, but it was to endure as the TUC's executive organ.

The Parliamentary Committee's specified functions were to take 'any action that may be necessary to secure the repeal of the penal clauses of the Criminal Law Amendment Act, the Truck Act, the getting of a proper Compensation Act, and to watch over the interest of labour generally in the proceedings of Parliament'.[71] This went well beyond the intentions of those who had convened the first Congress in 1868. They had conceived it as a working-class version of the Social Science Association, at which papers on topics of interest to trade unionists would be read and discussed. The union cause was to be advanced by any attendant publicity rather than by action on the part of Congress—although even the first Congress had departed from that conception to the extent of adopting resolutions advocating specific legislative reforms.

Organization

The TUC's formal arrangements were rudimentary up to 1872. The first four Congresses were organized by the relevant local

[69] ibid., 1869, p. 219.　　[70] ibid., 1871, p. 86.　　[71] ibid., 1872, p. 38.

trades council, a different honorary secretary being elected each time. At the first two Congresses each delegate had paid an equal share of the expenses involved. A fee of 10*s.* per delegate was fixed at the third in 1871; and the elected committee was expected to meet expenses from the £14.16*s.* (plus £2 from an undisclosed source) left after Congress costs had been met. This was little enough, even by contemporary standards, for a gathering consisting, in 1868, of 34 delegates from an unrecorded number of organizations claiming over 100,000 members; in 1869, of 47 delegates from 40 bodies with 250,000 members; and in 1871, of 57 delegates from 49 organizations purporting to cover 289,000 members.

Expenses mounted with the formation of the Parliamentary Committee in 1872. George Howell was appointed as its paid secretary. The position carried a salary ranging, erratically, from £97 to £132 a year until 1881, when it was fixed at £200—although Howell was given a 'testimonial' of £250 after his retirement in 1875, and his successor another of £1,200 in 1884. The treasurer first received an annual honorarium of £10 in 1874, and of £15 thereafter.

Throughout the period, apart from the Congress delegate fee of 10*s.*, the TUC was dependent on voluntary financial contributions. The only formal pressure to contribute was a requirement that election to the Parliamentary Committee depended on a contribution from the candidate's organization. The TUC's annual income from this source was £2 in 1871, but thereafter fluctuated between £287 in 1872 and £802 in 1889. The full Parliamentary Committee met infrequently, especially during the 1870s, because of financial stringency. It made continual appeals for funds throughout the period.

George Howell had to dip into his salary to meet the cost of occasional clerical assistance, the rent of his office, heat, lighting and other expenses. Henry Broadhurst, his successor, was relieved of liability for rent and other office expenses, but had to find his own furniture. From 1877 he received an allowance, usually less than £20 a year, for clerical assistance. Like Howell, he had to rely on voluntary help for such things as the drafting of bills and legal interpretations.

Eligibility for membership of the TUC was broadly conceived initially, but soon modified. There was no formal system of affiliation. The 1872 Congress rejected a challenge to the admission of delegates from the Labour Representation League, the Artizans' Club and the Peace Association. The next Congress, however, decided to restrict representation to trade unions and trades councils. The total membership officially covered in this way reached a peak of 1,191,922 in 1874; it then declined to 463,899 in 1881, before rising to 885,055 in 1889. The number of organizations officially represented at Congress rose to 153 in 1874, dropped to 92 in 1879 and then climbed to 171 in 1889. Both sets of figures involve double-counting. No allowance was made for overlapping memberships between trades councils and individual unions; and union branches, which commonly sent their own delegates when Congress met in their locality, were counted as distinct organizations. The looseness of the TUC's structure in its first 20 years is summarized in the fact that, although voting was by show of hands on a one-man-one-vote basis, no limit was set to the number of delegates from a particular body so long as it paid their expenses and the Congress fee.

Concerns

From the start, the TUC concerned itself with matters of government policy. There were moves, during the later 1870s, to involve it in industrial affairs. The Parliamentary Committee produced a plan for the federation of trade unions, in response to a discussion at the 1874 Congress, but the next Congress turned it down. The 1877 Congress rejected a proposal to authorize TUC intervention in industrial disputes, but instructed the Parliamentary Committee to explore the possibility of intervening in union demarcation disputes; it reported unfavourably at the next Congress. In 1879, however, it urged the need for closer organization. Congress narrowly carried a resolution advocating the formation of a federation, but the proposal was subsequently shelved in the light of the limited union response to a draft constitution circulated by the committee.

In the 1880s the TUC leaders flirted with international involvement, if without much conviction. They sent delegates to two Paris conferences, in 1883 and 1886. Under Congress pressure, they reluctantly convened, in 1888, another in

London at which the Continental delegates all supported the Socialist John Burns, instead of the TUC nominee, in the election for chairman. They declined to be represented at a Paris conference the following year.

Government policy thus retained pride of place in the TUC's concerns throughout the period. By later standards, the causes it espoused were limited. A 'programme of Parliamentary Action for the Session of 1874',[72] the first which the Parliamentary Committee submitted to Congress, listed eleven items. No fewer than seven involved the elimination of legal disabilities applicable either to employees specifically (relating to picketing, the right to strike, workers' compensation and contracts of employment) or to working-class people in general (the imprisonment of small debtors and the summary jurisdiction of magistrates). Three items involved regulatory extensions (affecting seamen, women and children); and one the admission of workmen to juries. But all the non-industrial items (magistrates' jurisdiction, small debtors and jury service) were excluded from the list that the TUC later submitted to candidates in the 1874 general election.

The programme for 1877 omitted the legal reforms achieved in the interim, and included three new items (relating to the Factory Acts, seamen's contracts of employment and reform of the patent laws). Codification of the criminal laws, certification of steam engine and boiler operators, and a proposal for more factory inspectors were added to the programme for 1879. The 1880 programme, the last to be submitted to Congress in this form, included four new planks, one concerning the land laws and the others electoral reform. Most of the items which the TUC circulated to parliamentary candidates in 1885 had not been in the 1880 programme: they concerned safety on railways, mines inspectors, land royalties, education, working-class magistrates, the payment of MPs and three new electoral reform issues (those in the 1880 list having all been realized).

These lists are not exhaustive, since the TUC took up other policy issues during this time. Nor do they indicate precisely, in all cases, the point at which Congress initially adopted particular policies. But they do indicate the major public policy concerns of the TUC. There were, of course, variations

[72] TUC, *PC's Report*, 1873, p. 9.

in emphasis. During the early 1870s, the removal of legal impediments on strike action was central. When this issue was resolved in 1875, its place was taken by reform of the law governing compensation for industrial injuries. With the achievement of this aim in 1880, the emphasis shifted to constitutional and general law reform.

Notably absent from these policy aims is any reference to either the 'Irish question' or the foreign policy issues which, together, formed the principal watershed between Liberal and Conservative during the period. The TUC leadership consistently resisted the urgings of longstanding middle-class advisers to involve itself seriously in these policy areas. It similarly refrained from an outright affirmation of Liberal support. Lib-Labs were dominant in the Parliamentary Committee and in Congress, but in both cases the Conservative minority was significant enough to impose, in the interests of unity, an officially non-partisan political stance. 'With party differences in the strictest sense of the term', the Parliamentary Committee intoned, 'we . . . have nothing to do'.[73]

But, later in the 1880s, when it insisted that 'Congress is a non-political body . . . confined to strictly trade questions', and condemned 'the recent tendency to drift into political and controversial subjects',[74] the committee was reacting to a new force. The influence of unionists with Socialist convictions began to be felt in the TUC from 1886. Their proposal for general legislative imposition of the eight-hour working day provided the touchstone. At the 1889 Congress, the 'old guard' carried the day with ease against these 'new men', on this issue and on others. The Socialists' day was still to come.

Tactics

From 1869 (when Congress resolutions dealing with education and cotton supplies were posted to the appropriate ministers), the TUC communicated directly with government by way of correspondence, sending 'memorials' and copies of resolutions to ministers and writing to senior officials in their departments. From 1871, when all 57 delegates to the third Congress saw the Home Secretary, it also sent deputations to ministers, at first

---

[73] PC, *Address to the Officers of Trade Societies and Trades Councils*, 1885, p. 3.
[74] *TUC Report*, 1888, p. 13.

only occasionally and then, from the late 1870s, on a regular basis following the annual Congress.

For the most part, however, these dealings were treated as a subsidiary tactic. The proceedings of ministerial deputations were sometimes detailed in circulars to unions, but the Parliamentary Committee's annual reports to Congress almost invariably made little of them. On the other hand, parliamentary events and the committee's related activity were usually recounted with a wealth of detail in the annual report.

From 1871 the tactic of circulating parliamentary division lists was frequently employed by the TUC, subsequent action being left 'to the judgement and concerted action of the trade societies in those constituencies whose members spoke and voted against us'.[75] From 1873 it sent out draft petitions on particular issues for transmission through local MPs. From 1874 it circulated policy lists for submission to parliamentary candidates, urging that any 'withholding his adhesion should be opposed'.[76] But, always, the emphasis was on lobbying parliamentarians.

This emphasis was evident from the time of the 1871 Congress. Its meeting hours were rearranged to enable delegates to spend an evening lobbying MPs about the government's Trade Union Bill. Every MP was subsequently sent a letter on the subject. Congress also instructed delegates to press their local member to support a Mines Regulation Bill.

The Parliamentary Committee, formed the next year, followed suit. In 1875 its secretary, over a considerable period, 'was almost daily in the Lobby consulting members' about the repeal of the Criminal Law Amendment Act;[77] and every other member of the committee accompanied him for two of those days. From 1873 it issued 'special notices' (later referred to as 'whips') to all MPs, informing them when matters of concern to the TUC were to be raised in the House, and asking for their support.

Parliamentary Friends

The TUC leaders relied heavily on the good offices of particular MPs. During the 1870s their 'Parliamentary friends', the term

[75] Quoted in Davis, op. cit., p. 22.
[76] TUC, *Preliminary Notice, Sixth Annual Trades Union Congress*, p. 4.
[77] Howell, *Labour Legislation*, vol. II, p. 367.

used in TUC reports, included A. J. Mundella, Thomas Hughes, Samuel Morley, Auberon Herbert, Thomas Brassey, W. H. Smith, Eustace Smith, Hinde Palmer, Jacob Bright and Charles Hopwood. Mundella and Hughes, for example, worked closely with the TUC and acted as its parliamentary spokesmen when the Trade Union Bill was under consideration in 1871. Again, the Trade Union Amendment Act of 1876, originating as a private member's bill prepared by the Parliamentary Committee, was the outcome of the joint efforts of Mundella, Brassey, Morley and Bright, in the House of Commons, and Lord Aberdare in the House of Lords—each of whom played their respective roles in response to an approach from the committee.

Friends were also important, initially, in relation to direct dealings with ministers. Thus it was Mundella who arranged the TUC's first ministerial deputation in 1871. Two years later the Parliamentary Committee publicly acknowledged that the unexpected invitation to see Robert Lowe, the Home Secretary, was primarily due to 'one of our oldest and staunchest Parliamentary friends'.[78]

The TUC leaders had friends of their own kind in parliament with the election of Macdonald and Burt in 1874; not only were both unionists, but Macdonald had been chairman of the Parliamentary Committee from its inception. They nevertheless continued to rely on their middle-class friends in the case of major issues and technical matters. But Broadhurst's election in 1880 was of a different order. His political standing was more considerable than either Macdonald's or Burt's. Unlike them, too, he did not regard membership of the Parliamentary Committee as incompatible with parliamentary office. Apart from a few months in 1886, when he was in Gladstone's ministry, he retained the TUC secretaryship. His dual role enabled him to handle the TUC's lobbying work more expeditiously than had previously been possible. Equally important, when he put questions or contributed to debates in the House, he could claim to be acting less as an intermediary than as the direct representative of the TUC. His election, accordingly, diminished the TUC's dependence on middle-class parliamentary friends.

[78] TUC, *PC's Report for 1873*, p. 5.

Broadhurst's parliamentary position was reinforced in 1885 when he was joined by W. Crawford, another member of the Parliamentary Committee who also chose to retain his seat on it. In 1886 Congress, which had first approved the direct representation strategy in 1869 (although it had no official connection with the Labour Representation League formed the same year, despite substantial overlapping in membership), confirmed the importance attached to this strategy by creating the Labour Electoral Committee—while, at the same time, keeping it independent of the Parliamentary Committee. But there was no intention of breaking away from established political structures. Direct representation was regarded as no more than an important extension of the lobbying tactic. Broadhurst later implied this when he described the TUC as having 'fulfilled the functions of the Radical wing of the Liberal Party'.[79] The point is that, in discharging these functions, the TUC's reliance on middle-class parliamentary friends had been significantly reduced by the late 1880s with the entry into parliament of Broadhurst, Crawford and other trade unionist MPs.

Internal Authority

The TUC was under challenge from the start. As a gathering inspired by provincial antagonism to the London trades, the first Congress was ignored by most London union leaders. The second Congress was attended by one delegate from the London Trades Council, but the more select Junta kept their distance. The decision to hold the third Congress in London gave the initiative to the London Trades Council, with the result that Congress met six months later than intended—and then only after vigorous urging from provincial trades councils.

The Junta, in the meantime, had taken it upon themselves to organize the presentation of the union case in support of the government's Trade Union Bill. Initially, there was some friction between them and the committee (although it included three of their close associates) which the 1871 Congress appointed for the same purpose. The Junta's Conference of Amalgamated Trades disbanded once the bill was enacted. But they continued to question the TUC's authority. At the

[79] Broadhurst, op. cit., p. 77.

1873 Congress they moved, unsuccessfully, to dissolve the year-old Parliamentary Committee and transfer its political functions to the London Trades Council. Although three of the five Junta leaders secured election to the committee at this Congress, their campaign continued until the secretary of the London Trades Council, George Shipton, also accepted election to it in 1875.

As this challenge faded, however, another emerged. The repeal of the Criminal Law Amendment Act in 1875 resolved the last of the urgent legislative issues which had fired union leaders from the late 1860s. To many, it looked like the end of the road for the TUC. The Parliamentary Committee reported in October 1875 that 'the work of emancipation is full and complete'.[80] Howell, the principal author of its report, simultaneously tendered his resignation because the 'great work which I allotted to myself as your Secretary . . . has been accomplished'[81]—although years afterwards, he was to ascribe his resignation to ill-health. The chairman of the next Congress acknowledged there were those who thought that 'the questions which led to [the] establishment [of the TUC] have passed away, and that we do not want any more congresses in the future'.[82] And even ten years later, despite some undoubtedly useful achievements, the TUC leadership was still on the defensive against those who 'would have us believe that the work of our Congress is about done'.[83] A body which feels the need to justify its existence at this level is plainly uncertain of its internal authority.

This lack of assurance is reflected in the composition of the TUC's ministerial deputations, in which Parliamentary Committee members were almost invariably swamped by individual union representatives. The committee went out of its way to ensure that all interested unions were represented. Reinforcing this practice was the apparent belief that ministers were impressed by weight of numbers. TUC reports of the period repeatedly extolled deputations as 'large and representative' or 'large and influential'. Even on a narrowly sectional issue like the expansion of the mines inspectorate, a deputation to the Home Secretary in 1884 numbered more than eighty. The same year,

[80] TUC, *PC's Report for 1875*, p. 6.
[82] *TUC Report*, 1876, p. 4.
[81] ibid., p. 16.
[83] ibid., 1886, p. 18.

on the larger issue of electoral reform, no less than 240 union officials exchanged compliments with Gladstone, to the accompaniment of much cheering.

Broadhurst, who described this deputation as 'sufficiently numerous', also referred to the difficulty of selecting speakers: 'it was essential to keep the numbers down, and yet *every interest had to be represented*'.[84] As this comment implies, union leaders did not conceive of the Parliamentary Committee's members acting as their sole spokesmen. Nor did the committee. Its limited pretensions are further indicated by the little or no guidance it provided, as a body, on resolutions considered at Congress. (All resolutions were submitted by either unions or trades councils, and the order in which they were introduced was decided by lot.) Moreover, it exercised virtually no discretion as to the nature of the claims it submitted to government or the manner in which they were presented. TUC deputations simply submitted to ministers all relevant Congress resolutions as adopted, usually with supporting speeches from representatives of the sponsoring unions or trades councils.

Outside Congress, the Parliamentary Committee's role was in any case circumscribed by limited resources. It could afford to have the full committee meet only occasionally, most business being handled by the 'London committee' consisting of the chairman, vice-chairman, secretary and any readily available members. One other consequence was that, on sectional matters, 'whenever possible unions themselves were expected to draft bills or [parliamentary] resolutions and to do their own lobbying, while the Committee gave them general support'.[85]

There was, of course, a clear acknowledgement by unions of a minimal coordinating authority reflected in their acceptance that the TUC was the appropriate body to organize deputations and lobbying campaigns on issues of general concern. On sectional issues also, it was frequently asked to help union lobbyists and union-arranged deputations, usually by sending Parliamentary Committee members along. But in many cases its assistance was entirely marginal, or was rebuffed altogether. In 1872, for instance, the TUC leaders 'soon saw that they were

[84] Broadhurst, op. cit., p. 125. Italics added.
[85] H. A. Clegg *et al.*, *A History of British Trade Unions since 1889*, vol. I, p. 252.

unwelcome' when they offered to support the cotton unions' campaign for nine-hour day legislation covering women and children factory workers.[86] And as late as 1887, they were again obliged to withdraw from the field, leaving it to 'our friends engaged in the cotton trade' to press for an expansion of the factory inspectorate.[87]

Nevertheless, there were other occasions when the cotton unions did welcome TUC intervention. The miners, too, made use of it, most notably in relation to their eight-hours bill. And it appears that in other cases the Parliamentary Committee was sometimes invested with principal responsibility for sectional issues, such as proposed legislative protection for wool-sorters and boiler 'enginemen'.

The TUC's involvement in the cotton unions' promotion of their Cotton Cloth Factories Bill, in the late 1880s, is particularly significant. Of all unions, the cotton unions had least need of support in influencing parliament. Electoral considerations meant that they could call on the services of some thirty MPs from Lancashire constituencies. The miners, in comparison, were less well-endowed; in addition, their eight-hours bill was much more controversial, both inside and outside the unions. Together, however, 'coal and cotton' took pride of place among the trades on the score of political weight. The fact that both chose to enlist the TUC's support for sectional purposes is especially noteworthy for this reason. It indicates that the TUC's internal authority, if small by later standards, was not entirely negligible.

There are also signs that the TUC leaders themselves had some sense of authority. For one thing, although the Parliamentary Committee may have been, for the most part, 'the unadventurous servant of Congress',[88] it was not completely servile. Occasionally, the committee took the initiative. Sometimes, if rarely, this involved positive action—as exemplified in the campaign of the mid-1870s for labour law reform, and in the 1886 decision to send a delegate to a Paris conference without, as in the past, awaiting Congress approval. More often, it involved the avoidance or blocking of action—as when the committee declined an invitation to a later Paris conference

[86] *PC Mins.*, 9 April 1872. [87] *TUC Report*, 1887, p. 15.
[88] Clegg *et al.*, op. cit., p. 250.

(on the ground that it lacked Congress approval) and organized two union polls on the eight-hour day issue in such a way as to favour the anti-legislation school of thought.

The members of the Parliamentary Committee, in any case, had ample reason to regard themselves as a cut above the general run of union leaders. They were, in their own right, all figures of importance in the trade union world. One or two of them carried some weight outside that world. Broadhurst, as secretary and the most prominent working-class MP in the Liberal ranks, led the field: during the 1880s he clearly attracted, to the TUC, the attention of unions with policy aims requiring state action. For the rest, there was the prestige inevitably flowing to the member of a select body heading a national organization with which the bulk of unions and major trades councils were associated. The standing of the men who contested Parliamentary Committee elections from 1873, and the swift emergence of the convention that there should be no more than one representative of a single trade on it, attested to that prestige.

But the most striking indication of the TUC's standing among unionists in general was the struggle that erupted in the late 1880s when the new men of the left sought to harness it to the Socialist cause. Both sides in this struggle plainly saw it as a valuable prize. And the mounting intensity of the struggle in later years confirmed that, despite the shortcomings in its internal authority, the TUC occupied a unique position in the structure of British trade unionism at the end of its second decade.

External Authority

The TUC was a body of some note outside trade union circles from the time of the 1872 Congress. Press coverage of that Congress, and its successors, was wide and often detailed. Employers paid their tribute in 1873 by forming, in open emulation, the National Federation of Associated Employers of Labour. 'Electioneering politicians' came to watch Congress as one 'barometer of working-class opinion'.[89] The TUC's initial middle-class advisers (notably Mundella, Hughes and Herbert inside parliament, and Frederic Harrison, E. S.

[89] G. M. Trevelyan, *English Social History*, pp. 368–9.

Beesly and Henry Crompton outside it) were soon joined by others anxious to mobilize support for policy lines of their own. Liberal patricians thought it worth serious cultivation by 1884 when Gladstone saw his first TUC deputation, as Prime Minister, and Rosebery addressed Congress. Conservative politicians, with less to hope for from a body dominated by Lib-Labs, found it useful on occasion—as exemplified in the TUC secretary's encounter with J. K. Cross, then Home Secretary, in 1875 during the parliamentary debate on a key clause in the government bill repealing the Criminal Law Amendment Act.

Mr Cross left the House, and I went to meet him in the Lobby. He . . . said, 'You have seen Mr Lowe's [Liberal] amendment; I cannot accept that'. I replied, 'Why not put down one of your own, covering the same ground?' 'Who is to draft it?' he asked. 'Mr R. S. Wright', I replied. He said, 'I have his in my pocket—do you think it would be acceptable?' I replied that . . . anything suggested by Mr Wright would carry great weight. He . . . then returned to the House and moved his now historic amendment.[90]

Earlier, moreover, the Conservative government had withdrawn its Friendly Society Bill, which would have superseded the Trade Union Act of 1871, after the TUC had registered the unions' opposition.

Nevertheless, all this adds up to an external authority of decidedly modest proportions. Government leaders, prime ministers apart, could accept TUC requests for interviews readily enough, infrequent as they were. With the single exception of Robert Lowe in 1873, none of them went out of their way to consult the TUC. There was little reason why they should. Its concerns, for the most part, were of marginal importance in the total scheme of government interests: the relative inaccessibility of prime ministers is indicative of this. By the same token, it had no real bargaining power in the case of governments which were neither involved in the detail of industrial relations nor dependent on the unions' administrative support in other areas. So far as the TUC had any political bargaining power, it was limited to the level of the backbench MP who was either a union man himself or held a constituency in which unionist votes were important. Even in these cases, particular trade unions tended to carry greater

[90] Howell, *Labour Legislation*, vol. II, pp. 374–5.

weight, whether as the source of a unionist-MP's salary or as the assumed mouthpiece of an electoral segment.

The TUC's utility to government leaders rested on the assumption that it articulated the pressing aspirations of at least most trade unionists and, possibly, of working-class voters at large. It was, in these terms, a convenient source of electoral information. But even then, there was no reason for them to confine their dealings with the unions to the TUC. For one thing, the TUC itself did not claim exclusive consultative rights; for another, the evidence soon suggested that it had no substantial control over the disposition of working-class votes.

In the end, of course, there is the critical fact that the TUC was granted audience and had its claims heard by ministers of the crown. It was not, in other words, ignored by government. In addition, members of the Parliamentary Committee figured among the recipients of the patronage which governments, Liberal governments in particular, dispensed to union officials in the form of inspectorates and magistracies. And while there is no record that the TUC itself was ever formally asked to make nominations for such appointments, it seems that a number of them may have been made on the recommendation of Henry Broadhurst—who was himself offered two appointments of this kind, both of which were declined. It is probable that, in large measure, such external authority as the TUC possessed during the 1880s depended on its secretary's unique position as the most distinguished trade-unionist parliamentarian of his day.

An Embryonic Political Authority

Like George Howell, his predecessor, Broadhurst was an ardent Gladstonian Liberal with a tinge of Radicalism. This meant, among other things, that he conceived the TUC's role as that of a Liberal 'ginger-group' with the task of directing the party's attention to matters of special working-class interest—but otherwise accepted the Liberal cause as the Grand Old Man declared it. Such a conception not only entailed reliance on the Liberal Party (rather than the TUC) as the main political vehicle of trade union aspirations. It also placed narrow limits on the scope of the TUC's concerns and functions, especially since it was associated with the view that only a restricted range of matters of special working-class interest fell within the proper province of governmental action.

Broadhurst, in short, seems to have had no great interest in asserting the TUC's authority as a political spokesman, either in relation to government or to the unions. And if he had no such interest, as the dominant figure on the Parliamentary Committee from the mid-1870s to the end of the 1880s, it is highly unlikely that other committee members would have had more. For union leaders in general, the TUC was a moderately useful institution once the legal obstacles to trade unions and their industrial methods had been surmounted in the mid-seventies.

Nor did the politicians, whether on the back or the front benches, have much interest in augmenting the TUC's authority. The Conservatives, if somewhat casually until the Irish storm blew Joseph Chamberlain into their laps, were more concerned with cultivating trade unionists at large. The Liberals, while ready to pay ritualistic homage to steady allies, were under no compulsion to give really serious attention to the Lib-Lab deferentials who dominated the TUC's leadership. For ministers of both parties, there was no occasion for hard bargaining with the TUC.

This is not to deny that the TUC discharged a political function of value to both government and the unions. The point is rather that this function, after the mid-1870s, was largely marginal to the principal concerns of both.

4

Expanding Horizons 1890–1905

A 'gale of novel aspirations and resentments' swept through British trade unionism in the 1890s.[1] One product was a greater readiness to look to state action for the achievement of union aims. On the side of government, too, there was a new concern with industrial relations. With the turn of the century, the *Taff Vale Case* created a political issue of the first magnitude for union leaders. By this time, however, the TUC no longer stood alone at the head of the trade union movement. Alongside it were the General Federation of Trade Unions and the Labour Representation Committee. Both threatened the TUC's hegemony.

GOVERNMENT

Conservative governments ruled Britain for all but three years (August 1892 to June 1895) up to the last weeks of 1905. Although not noted for social reforms, the period saw several legislative innovations of close union interest.

The scope of safety and health regulation, in terms of both industrial coverage and subject-matter, was significantly extended by three Factory Acts. Two of them (1891 and 1901) were Conservative-initiated. So were other measures tightening health and safety controls in the mining, cotton and railways industries.

The Factory Act of 1891 also sought to protect some workers against underpayment, a provision which the Liberals extended four years later. But the more notable innovation concerning wages was the House of Commons' Fair Wages Resolution of February 1891. This recommended that labour employed under government contracts should be paid wage rates prevailing in the relevant trade and district, a policy subsequently followed

[1] E. H. Phelps Brown, *The Growth of British Industrial Relations*, p. 154.

by government departments and many local authorities. The resolution was accepted by both parties.

A second generally-agreed resolution, moved by a leading member of the Conservative opposition in 1893, urged that the state should, in effect, establish itself as a model employer. The Liberal government subsequently introduced the eight-hour working day in state dockyards and ordinance factories. It also moved towards regulating male working hours on the railways.

It was the Conservatives, however, who introduced the greatest single legislative innovation in the form of the Workmen's Compensation Act of 1897, which abandoned two principles that had emasculated earlier legislation. One was the 'contracting out' principle allowing an employee to relieve his employer of liability for industrial accidents and diseases; the other was the principle that compensation was payable only when negligence could be proved on the part of somebody other than the victim. This measure, although applicable only to certain industries, justifiably earned the TUC president's description as 'one of the most revolutionary of the laws relating to labour that the century has . . . given birth to'.[2]

Both Conservative and Liberal governments acted to alleviate unemployment other than through the Poor Law. A circular authorizing local authorities to provide work, first issued by Joseph Chamberlain in 1886, was re-issued annually during 1891–3 and again in 1895. London local authorities were authorized to operate labour exchanges in 1902–5; a system of local committees was organized to provide work in London, and then extended to other cities under the Unemployed Workmen Act of 1905; and the Aliens Act of 1905 discouraged foreign labour.

Of particular significance, however, was the active concern of government with the settlement of industrial disputes. A. J. Mundella, the TUC's old ally, set the precedent in 1893 as Liberal President of the Board of Trade. His unsuccessful personal intervention in a Hull dock strike was formally unofficial but, as Gladstone himself told parliament, had the government's 'great sympathy and goodwill'.[3] Mundella tried

[2] *TUC Report*, 1898, p. 30.
[3] Quoted in Clegg *et al.*, op. cit., p. 81.

again, and failed again, to settle an English coal stoppage later the same year. Gladstone consulted cabinet, then asked the parties to meet under the chairmanship of Lord Rosebery, the Foreign Secretary; the offer was accepted and a settlement followed. This 'doubtful step',[4] as *The Times* described it, was the first official intervention by a government seeking to settle an industrial dispute by mediation. Before the Liberals lost office, there were two other successful interventions. Asquith, then Home Secretary, settled a London cabdrivers' strike in 1894, and the Permanent Secretary of the Board of Trade ended the boot industry lockout of 1895. Officials of the Labour Department, which Mundella had created within the Board of Trade in 1893, also appear to have taken an active concern in other disputes.

The interest of the succeeding Conservative government was reflected in the Conciliation Act of 1896 which authorized the Board of Trade to try to bring industrial combatants together on its own initiative, to appoint an arbitrator on the request of both parties to a dispute, and to appoint a conciliator on the request of one party. It was a modest measure, a 'mere skeleton', but it broke new ground and provided 'the very slight legislative base' for governmental involvement in industrial disputes during the next twenty years.[5] Shortly after its enactment, the Act was invoked by the union involved in the Penrhyn quarry dispute. The President of the Board of Trade, C. T. Ritchie, was rebuffed by Lord Penrhyn, and so were the departmental officials who followed him: the strikers acknowledged defeat some months later. Before then, Ritchie had fared better in December 1896 when his personal intervention led to the settlement of a railways dispute But the failure of his Penrhyn intervention impressed him more. He refused a union request for his personal intervention in a more serious railways dispute in 1897. He also appears to have left the big engineering dispute, which broke out earlier that year, entirely to his departmental officials. But there was no doubt of his continuing concern with the general problem. He later explored the possibility of a system of conciliation boards, representative of both unions and employers, to deal with issues likely to lead to

[4] Quoted ibid., p. 108.
[5] Lord Askwith, *Industrial Problems and Disputes*, p. 78.

stoppages; but the scheme was rejected by employers' groups in 1899. And although he and his successors steered clear of personal involvement, the Board of Trade's Labour Department continued to act in the field.

The department's conciliators and arbitrators were mainly outsiders, particularly barristers like George Askwith. It dealt with 209 disputes in the eleven years to the end of 1906. It had its successes; but its failure to mediate an early settlement of the Taff Vale railway dispute in 1900 was more portentous. The department's careful published reports on industrial disputes, as well as on unemployment, indicated government's entrenching interest in the field more clearly, perhaps, than anything else.

The trade union presence was also acknowledged by the appointment of union officials to advisory and administrative positions. The Conservatives were least generous, but in 1891 they appointed six trade unionists to the Royal Commission on Labour, one to the Royal Commission on Mine Explosions, and another, Thomas Birtwistle, to the factory inspectorate. During the Liberal interregnum, Thomas Burt became Parliamentary Secretary to the Board of Trade; Broadhurst, temporarily out of parliament, was made a member of the Royal Commission on the Aged Poor; 'no less than 70 working men' were made magistrates;[6] and a dozen or more union men were appointed Inspectors' Assistants, a new grade in the factory inspectorate which Asquith created in order to get round prescribed age and examination requirements. During the Conservative decade from 1895 there seem to have been a few unionist appointments to the magistracy and the factory inspectorate. Two union officials were members of a royal commission on railway accidents, but the unions were refused representation on the Royal Commission on Trade Disputes and on the proposed authority to administer the Port of London.

Another form of ministerial acknowledgement was the reception of trade union deputations. Meetings between ministers and TUC deputations, in particular, appear to have become more common from the early 1890s. So were ministerial refusals. The principal reason was the TUC's new concern with the working conditions of certain state employees. Liberal

[6] *TUC Report*, 1893, p. 18.

ministers, the first to be approached, had no objection to dealing with the TUC on the issue. Their Conservative successors
at the Admiralty, the War Office, the Colonial Office and the
Post Office were for a time less compliant and, between them,
rebuffed many requests for similar dealings; not until 1904,
largely owing to changes in ministerial personnel, were they
all agreeable. On other matters, the TUC was refused ministerial interviews on four occasions. Arthur Balfour declined to see
deputations about the political status of postal employees and,
as Prime Minister, about old age pensions; and two of his
ministers refused to discuss, in one case, unemployment and, in
the other, the administration of the legislation governing
factories and workers' compensation.

Moreover, there are indications in the TUC's reports that
Conservative ministers, at least, preferred to deal with union
claims by way of correspondence. Certainly, neither the
Liberals nor the Conservatives went out of their way to consult
the TUC when in government: the only recorded occasion of a
ministerial initiative in this respect occurred in 1899 when the
President of the Board of Trade invited the TUC secretary to
talk with him about the minister's proposed system of conciliation boards. There were also some complaints from the
members of TUC deputations about 'the indignities that
Ministers imposed upon them',[7] chiefly in relation to the time
allotted them. But, in general, they seem to have been given a
courteous reception—if little else, as one of them alleged:
'When deputations waited on Ministers, they were smothered
in smiles, but nothing practical came of interviews'.[8]

Nevertheless, the fact remains that direct dealings between
ministers and union leaders, if the TUC's experience is any
indication, were distinctly more frequent from the early 1890s.
This was a striking development because it occurred at a time
when the tide of public opinion was running strongly against
the unions. Employers, stirred by the spreading unionization
of unskilled workers and the mounting militancy of the skilled,
were combining to resist the claims of this 'cruel organization',
as Lord Salisbury described the unions.[9] The sufferings of

[7] ibid., 1905, p. 111.
[8] Quoted in Davis, op. cit., vol. II, p. 152.
[9] Quoted in S. Maccoby, *English Radicalism, 1886–1914*, p. 172.

striking unionists' families evoked public sympathy. Oxford dons, on more pragmatic grounds, could support the union case in the great engineering dispute of 1897–8. But at Cambridge, Alfred Marshall declared that the striking engineers must be crushed; and he mirrored public opinion more accurately, as both the Webbs' and later judgements confirm.[10] In addition, urban employers were a rising influence in the Conservative party.

Even in these circumstances, Conservative ministers met trade union leaders and, sometimes, made policy concessions. Their eye, it is apparent, was on the working-class votes they saw behind the unions. Thus, from the early 1890s, they made great electoral play with the issue of old age pensions, chiefly through Chamberlain, their Liberal Unionist ally. His Workmen's Compensation Act of 1897, as well as lesser measures, reflected the same inspiration. The Boer war and the subsequent campaign for tariff reform diverted the attention of Chamberlain, and others, from this policy area during the later years of Conservative rule. But Balfour's Bismarckian comment of 1895 indicated its electoral weight for many Conservatives: 'Social legislation . . . is not merely to be distinguished from Socialist legislation, but is . . . its most effective antidote.'[11] Another indication is the contrasting political fortunes of the coal and cotton unions.[12]

The cotton operatives secured substantial legislative concessions from Conservative governments of the period; the miners relatively little. Both were electorally concentrated and highly unionized. The miners were predominantly Liberal in sympathy. They also returned several of their own men to parliament, all of them allied with the Liberals. The cotton operatives, on the other hand, did not have one of their own in parliament until 1902, and they were much more evenly divided in their party sympathies. This disunity, an obstacle to the achievement of direct parliamentary representation, strengthened their hand when it came to dealing with Conservative governments anxious to hold the Lancashire constituencies.

[10] See Webb, *The History of Trade Unionism*, p. 485; and Clegg *et al.*, op. cit., pp. 166n., 249.   [11] Quoted in Ralph Miliband, *Parliamentary Socialism*, p. 37n.
[12] The following analysis is derived from Clegg *et al.*, op. cit., esp. pp. 245–7, 271–5.

But the Liberals' interest in the unions was much greater by the turn of the century. Electorally, their support among industrial workers, outside Lancashire, was more substantial. Their links with the unions had traditionally been more extensive owing to the Lib-Lab complexion of most union leaderships; and they had unionist-MPs on their side of the house. Liberal leaders did not neglect these sources of support in their policy-making, but they made no concerted effort to cultivate union leaders as such until the dependability of their working-class support appeared to be endangered. The threat came from an independent party based on the unions which emerged in 1900 as the Labour Representation Committee. The pattern of Liberal relations with the TUC about this time tells the story.

Sir Charles Dilke, returned to parliament in 1892 by a mining constituency, quickly became the principal intermediary between unions and the Liberal leadership. In 1898, when the movement to form the LRC was mounting, his activities took a new turn when he initiated a meeting with TUC leaders to discuss possible labour legislation. In 1899 he invited them to meet a number of other MPs to consider the possibility of 'some more definite and concerted action' on labour questions: it was agreed that by contacting Dilke, when appropriate, the TUC 'might expect valuable assistance from members of various shades of political opinion'.[13] Later that year the TUC's annual Congress passed the resolution that paved the way for the eventual formation of the LRC. Shortly after the Congress, TUC representatives discussed the resolution with Asquith. Just a week before the LRC was founded, they again met Asquith, who 'expressed himself as being in entire sympathy' with their aims, and undertook to discuss with them any bills on labour matters.[14] A month later, he chaired a meeting of union officials and thirty MPs concerned with parliamentary tactics in relation to the Conservative's Factory and Workshops Amendment Bill. Thereafter, until 1905, there was an unprecedented surge of dealings between union officials and prominent Liberals including, in addition to Asquith and Dilke, Sir Robert Reid, R. B. Haldane and the Leader of the Opposition, Sir Henry Campbell-Bannerman himself. The

[13] *TUC Report*, 1899, p. 39.   [14] ibid., 1900, p. 36.

Taff Vale judgement, and the Conservative government's inactivity on the issue, were particularly productive in this respect; but there was consultation on the other issues as well. The significant aspect of the whole episode is the sudden interest which Liberal leaders acquired about 1900 in direct cooperation with the unions.

Earlier, moreover, government reactions had signalled the emergence of another and, ultimately, equally important extension of the trade unions' political significance. What was involved was the changing character of industrial conflict. Government attempts to mediate the settlement of strikes and lockouts began, as we have seen, in the 1890s. The London dock strike of 1889 had provided the first British example of a large-scale stoppage with widespread impact outside the industry concerned. The stoppage of Hull port workers in 1893 reinforced the point: it was smaller in scale, but for a time seemed likely to spread to other ports, and it raised the spectre of violence. All these elements were later brought together and heightened in the coal dispute of the same year, 'by far the largest dispute the country had ever seen'.[15] It involved 300,000 miners, lasted 14 weeks, created tensions culminating in the deaths of two miners when troops opened fire, and forced factory closures and slow-downs owing to coal shortages. The elements of scale, violence and outside impact (if to a lesser degree than in 1893) were again critical in the engineering dispute of 1897–8, regarded by contemporaries as 'the greatest struggle between Labour and Capital' in British history.[16] The South Wales coal strike of 1898 added military to civil repercussions by forcing the Navy to cancel its annual manoeuvres owing to a shortage of high-grade steam coal—and *The Times* thundered about 'a national calamity' and its fears for Britain's future security in times of 'public peril'.[17]

These, of course, were exceptional stoppages. Most, as in the past, were localized, peaceful and unnoticed. But the exceptional disputes made the political point. This was shown by the initial ministerial interventions, by the Conciliation Act of 1896, by the subsequent involvement of the Board of Trade's

[15] Clegg *et al.*, op. cit., p. 107.
[16] Quoted in Phelps Brown, op. cit., p. 162.
[17] Quoted in Clegg *et al.*, op. cit., p. 174.

Labour Department, and by the Conservative President of the
Board of Trade who told a TUC deputation in 1898 that the
disputes of 'the last few years' had convinced him that 'some
remedy ought to be found to put an end to these conflicts'.[18]
Trade union industrial action thus became a concern of
government. For the time being, its impact on union-government relations was marginal. But that was to change.

TRADE UNIONS

The late 1880s and early 1890s have customarily been celebrated as the years of the 'new unions'. They were also years
which saw the total trade union membership more than double,
to 1.5 million, between 1889 and the end of 1892. By the turn
of the century it was more than two million, remaining at
about that figure until 1906. The new unions played a relatively small part in this growth pattern once their initial
impetus was stemmed by employer resistance and economic
conditions: they accounted for less than one-tenth of all union
members in 1900.

However, the attention paid to the new unions owes less to
their size than to the assumption that they represented a new
kind of unionism. The characteristics conventionally attributed
to them include, among others, an unskilled membership, a
militant outlook, a tendency to seek legislative solutions to
industrial problems, and a belief in Socialism. In fact, as Clegg,
Fox and Thompson have shown,[19] none of these features was
common to all the new unions. The only major thing to
distinguish them, as a group, was their newness—especially in
the sense that they organized workers in occupations which had
previously either escaped or proved resistant to unionization.

They were also the source of a highly significant structural
innovation in the form of the 'general' union recruiting across
occupations and industries, although not all of them took this
form. They were involved, along with 'old' unions, in three
other major organizational developments of the time: a sharp
rise in the number of full-time officials; a trend to executive
bodies drawn from the whole membership instead of (for
financial reasons) from a union's headquarters locality; and

[18] *TUC Report*, 1899, p. 33.   [19] See Clegg *et al*, op. cit., esp. pp. 92–5.

the creation of coordinating inter-union federations in specific industries. Alongside these developments, and often prompting them, there was another affecting both old and new unions— the trend to national agreements incorporating collective bargaining procedures for settling pay rates and working conditions. At the start of the period only cotton weaving was covered in this way; by 1905 national agreements were operative in a number of industries. Wider negotiating areas meant widened areas of industrial conflict, and greater strains on union strike funds. The General Federation of Trade Unions, formed in the aftermath of the national engineering dispute of 1897–8, originated as an attempt to insure against the financial risks of large-scale industrial action by establishing a central strike fund.

Those of the new union leaders who professed to be Socialists, and not all of them did, had a great deal to do with the GFTU's foundation. Their Socialism, and that of their fellows in the old unions, was of a relatively sober brand by Continental standards, particularly once the responsibilities of administrative office had taken their toll. Thus by the late 1890s, even a staunch Lib-Lab could write of the 'steady fusion between . . . the old and new unionism'.[20] What was also reflected in this fusion was an acceptance by Lib-Lab unionists of policy aspirations that they had earlier tended to think of as either utopian or improper.

Socialism in the broadest sense won a famous, if superficial, victory in 1894 when the TUC's annual Congress overwhelmingly accepted Keir Hardie's amendment to a resolution advocating nationalization of land. The amendment added the words: 'and the whole of the means of production, distribution and exchange'.[21] The previous Congress had agreed, in similar vein, that a proposed political fund should be available only to parliamentary candidates pledging support for 'the principle of collective ownership and control of all the means of production and distribution'.[22] Tom Mann sensibly doubted that many of those voting for such proposals (and they included Henry Broadhurst) saw them as anything more than 'the mere expression of a pious opinion'.[23] But on more concrete issues,

[20] Quoted ibid., p. 304. [21] *TUC Report*, 1894, p. 55.
[22] ibid., p. 46. [23] Quoted in Clegg *et al.*, op. cit., p. 258.

there was in train a genuine shift in non-Socialists' attitudes towards the proper province of state action.

The shift was evident, if least widespread, in the case of the eight-hour day issue. Congress in 1888 had declared against an eight-hours bill for railways and coal mines. In 1889, it backed a bill confined to underground mineworkers, while rejecting general legislation on the issue. In 1890, by a small majority, it supported legislative imposition of the eight-hour day throughout industry; and it reaffirmed this decision by a much larger majority the following year. The strength of the divisions that remained were reflected in the inability of either the coal or the cotton unions to present a united front even on eight-hours legislation applying to their own industry alone.

On other issues, however, the divisions were either relatively slight or soon faded. Recurring periods of economic depression and massive unemployment (accompanied in 1902–4 by a fall in real wages), and crushing strike defeats affecting both old and new unions, swung Lib-Lab union leaders inexorably towards government intervention. Thus the 1894 report of the TUC's Parliamentary Committee records that the committee applauded Rosebery's mediation of the 1893 coal dispute, asked the relevant minister to urge local authorities to provide work for the unemployed, and sought the government's help in maintaining wage rates by raising with the Secretary of the Treasury the issue of the wages paid to employees of government contractors. On wider issues, too, union leaders during the period displayed a growing inclination to accept a more generous conception of the state's responsibilities, as in the case of working-class housing and old age pensions.

Associated with this expanding conception of government's role was an increased interest in political action. That interest, reinforced as it was by the great strike failures of the 1890s, was jolted into intense concern in 1901 when the House of Lords handed down the Taff Vale judgement which threatened to make the strike weapon unusable. Legislation was the only possible remedy. There were differences among union leaders about the precise form of the remedy, but the judgement united them on a political issue to a degree and with an intensity of purpose unknown for a quarter of a century. Nor was this all that the Law Lords unwittingly achieved. They also succeeded in infusing new life into a faltering political party whose demise they would have doubtless welcomed.

The parliamentary record of the unions up to this time had not been encouraging. By the end of the decade there were eleven unionist-MPs, only three more than in 1890. With one or two exceptions, they owed their success to official Liberal support—which was given sparingly because the final word was left, as in the case of the Conservatives, to local party associations. The Liberal-aligned Labour Electoral Association, formed under TUC auspices in 1886, faded from the scene in the mid-nineties. Its latter-day competitor for official union support, the Independent Labour Party, had emerged in 1893 with a programme disdaining alliances with the major parties. The ILP secured some impressive voting figures in the general election of 1895, but no seats. In the same year, Lib-Labs arranged amendments to the TUC's standing orders which at once excluded many of the ILP's members from Congress and increased the voting strength of its opponents. The ILP offended the imbedded party loyalties of most trade unionists by professing to be both Socialist and independent.

By the end of the decade, however, memories of the Liberals' limited concessions when in office, the Conservatives' generally stiff reaction to union policy proposals, the mounting problems of depression and unemployment, and the success of the employers' industrial counter-attack had all helped to sway union opinion towards an independent electoral strategy. The outcome, but only by a five-to-four majority, was the call by the 1899 Congress for a conference 'to devise ways and means for [*sic*] securing the return of an increased number of labour members to the next Parliament'.[24]

At the conference in February 1900, barely a quarter of the country's trade union members were represented alongside three Socialist groupings, the ILP, the Fabian Society and the Social Democratic Federation. The conference agreed on the principle of independent political action, constituted the Labour Representation Committee and rejected an SDF proposal to commit it to a Socialist objective. The LRC's functions were confined to giving moral support to candidates (otherwise nominated, promoted and financed by affiliated bodies) who

[24] *TUC Report*, 1899, p. 65.

undertook to join the Labour group in parliament if elected.

These modest aims disarmed trade union critics and induced the disaffiliation of the Marxist SDF in 1901, but initially provided little incentive for unions to affiliate with the LRC. At the end of its first full year, only 41 unions claiming 353,000 members were affiliated; at the end of its second, the tally was 65 unions with 455,000 members—still short of the 550,000 represented at the 1900 conference. But the tide turned in 1902–3 when affiliations almost doubled to 127 unions covering 847,000 members.

This dramatic change of fortune was an outcome of the Taff Vale decision and the realization that the Conservative government was unwilling to remedy it. The climate of opinion thus created also enabled the LRC's position to be strengthened in other ways. In 1903 it set up a Labour Members' Maintenance Fund (financed—compulsorily from 1904—by affiliated unions) and stipulated that its endorsed candidates should pledge, if elected, both to stand apart from other parties and to vote in accordance with parliamentary caucus decisions. By the end of 1905, professed Lib-Labs still dominated the 15-member trade union group of MPs; but Ramsay MacDonald, LRC secretary, and Herbert Gladstone, Liberal chief whip, had clinched their secret electoral agreement which paved the way for the LRC's emergence as a serious parliamentary force the following year.

In the meantime, the difficulties of parliamentary action by other means had continued to mount. In 1890 the TUC complained that 'the opportunities for legislation by private members seem to grow less and less'.[25] They were lessened still further by procedural alterations in 1896 and 1902, which enabled a single opponent to cripple a private member's bill with ease. But it was the growing ability of cabinet to monopolize parliamentary time that came to be monotonously blamed for the repeated failure of union-sponsored bills. Occasional successes, as in the case of children's working hours in 1899, only underlined the point that 'it is almost impossible to get any useful Bill through the House unless the Government allows it to pass by withdrawing its opposition'.[26] Cabinet control was strengthened not merely by procedures but also by hardening

[25] ibid., 1890, p. 23.   [26] ibid., 1899, p. 31.

party discipline. At the turn of the century, very few divisions in the House of Commons were not the subject of a formal party vote.

Nor did it escape trade union leaders that the discretionary powers of the executive arm of government were increasing outside parliament as well. A sharp expansion in the delegation of regulation-making powers to ministers was reflected in industrial measures, notably the various Factories Acts. In addition, there was the growing administrative involvement of government officials, with and without express legislative authorization, in areas of intense union concern like unemployment and industrial disputes.

These considerations may well account for an apparent tendency on the part of some union leaders to give greater emphasis to direct dealings with government. The TUC Parliamentary Committee's report to the Congress of 1893 was the first, since its inception, to refer explicitly to a general round of post-Congress deputations to ministers; and its subsequent reports also made rather more of such deputations than in the past. At the same time, many union leaders were not overly impressed with the technique. In 1897 the Parliamentary Committee acknowledged 'a divergence of opinion as to the utility or otherwise of these annual deputations to Ministers'.[27] The next year's Congress confirmed this by narrowly adopting a resolution declaring, in effect, that they were pointless. The committee, nonetheless, continued to mount deputations. Three years later (ironically enough, in the report which also recorded the Taff Vale judgement), it was able to claim that its recent deputations had met with 'more success than usual'—a comment which was held to answer a charge from the floor that they were 'obsolete'.[28] But the criticism continued.

There was, on the other hand, much less disagreement about the utility of parliamentary action. The legislature remained the focus of attention for union leaders in general. Their interest in direct representation, if on varying terms, is one reflection of this. Another is the importance they continued to attach to traditional lobbying procedures. Thus the 1898 Congress resolution disowning ministerial deputations stipulated, instead, that a statement of the TUC's legislative

[27] ibid., 1897, p. 18.   [28] ibid., 1901, pp. 56–7.

proposals should be sent to all MPs 'for a plain "yes" or "no" answer'.[29] Shortly afterwards, but independently of this action, the Parliamentary Committee's role as lobbyist was enhanced, as we have seen, by the development of an unusually close working relationship with prominent Liberal parliamentarians through Dilke and later Asquith. The Irish Nationalists, too, proved more cooperative than before. One result was the Balfour government's defeat in a parliamentary vote on a union-sponsored amendment to its Factories Bill of 1901.

The Taff Vale judgement, in any case, was bound to turn union leaders to parliament once it became clear that Balfour was going to be of no help. Above all, there was the fact that despite the growth of cabinet control, 'the prestige of the House [of Commons] as the forum in which . . . national issues were debated' was still very considerable by the standards of a later generation.[30] But if the emphasis remained where it had been for the unions since the 1870s, on lobbying MPs and securing direct representation in parliament, there was nevertheless at least a marginal shift towards dealing with government outside parliament by 1905. Ministers and their officials were less remote than they had been to union leaders who had become more accustomed to direct contact with them. This was one aspect of a more pronounced shift in union attitudes and expectations.

During the 1890s union officials took in their stride developments of a kind that had evoked expressions of wonder and delight from them in earlier years. Thus TUC leaders, in 1892, sedately recorded their 'satisfaction' with Birtwistle's appointment as a factory inspector and Burt's inclusion in Gladstone's ministry.[31] Their consultative claims were larger: in 1891 they pressed on the minister concerned 'the necessity of selecting fully one half' of the Royal Commission on Labour's membership 'from the representatives of Labour' (and lodged an 'emphatic protest' when this was denied).[32] Their ambitions were greater in relation to administrative appointments: in 1893 they claimed 'the leading positions' in the Board of Trade's new Labour Department for 'recognized Trades Unionists' against 'outsiders'.[33] Their protests, unlike the

[29] ibid., 1898, p. 68.   [30] Ronald Butt, *The Power of Parliament*, p. 96.
[31] *TUC Report*, 1892, pp. 24–5.   [32] *PC Mins.*, 3 March and 15 April 1891.
[33] ibid., 1 February 1893.

pained reproofs of the past, acquired an aggressive edge. The 1896 Congress took the unprecedented step of directing that an amendment to the Queen's Speech should be moved protesting against the refusal of the Postmaster-General and the First Lord of the Admiralty to receive TUC deputations. Another refusal from the First Lord evoked a letter condemning his action as 'unworthy of a British Minister'.[34]

The sharper tongue and larger pretensions may have owed something to the rise of Socialists in the ranks of officialdom. But the union leaders of the time were still predominantly non-Socialist with a heavy Lib-Lab leavening. Typically, as in the past, they were class-conscious like the Socialists, but in a different way, perceiving wide class distinctions below as well as above themselves. They might not have dreamed of the total elimination of social distinctions, or shared the aggressive class-consciousness and pride in working-class origins professed by trade union Socialists—although their rhetoric was sometimes similar. But by the turn of the century, their kind had travelled a long way since the working-class voter had first become a factor to be reckoned with in British politics.

They had presided over the continuing expansion of trade unionism, despite economic recession and industrial setbacks. (It is, perhaps, a symptom of their pride in this that, from the early 1890s, TUC reports almost invariably used the term 'trade-unionists' in preference to the earlier 'working men'.) They had seen the elevation of their colleagues to elective positions in parliament and a variety of local government bodies. They had sensed the political muscle of the working-class vote: 'as Parliaments approach the close of their natural existence they are much more disposed than at other times to consider the claims of labour'.[35] They had observed or received personal appointments to magistracies and factory inspectorates and royal commissions. And they had become more used to dealing at close quarters with both ministers and back bench MPs. There was ample reason for greater assurance in these experiences.

At the same time, while the face that union leaders presented to the political world was more confident than before, it still seems to have concealed a sense of inferiority. One indication

[34] ibid., 14 December 1898.   [35] *TUC Report*, 1891, p. 27.

of this is the social fawning evident in a solemn and unique decision of the Parliamentary Committee—that 'the following newspaper clipping should be pasted in the minute Book': the clipping, headlined 'A Compliment for Mr W. J. Davis— Received by the Prince of Wales', gave an account of an inconsequential conversation after a meeting which both had attended.[36] Nor were all the new unionists immune from a compliment sweetened by the status of its donor. Thus Will Thorne's recalled reaction to a congratulatory remark from a TUC president: 'I felt like turning a somersault with joy, for . . . I was more than delighted with such recognition from a man . . . who was the leader of a long and well-organized body of skilled workers'.[37] And Philip Snowden, an acute observer in some things, saw the diffidence of union leaders as helping Ramsay MacDonald's early career as LRC secretary: 'They regarded him as a superior person and their "inferiority complex" treated him as such'.[38]

TRADES UNION CONGRESS

The Liverpool Congress of 1890 marks a watershed in the TUC's history if only because it was the last which Henry Broadhurst attended as secretary. It was also the scene of his greatest defeat. For its resolution advocating a general eight-hour day imposed by legislation involved a proposition which the preceding Dundee Congress had rejected. Moreover, only three of the Parliamentary Committee men who had dominated the Dundee Congress were members of the committee elected at Liverpool. John Burns, one of the new members, claimed a resounding victory for 'us Socialists'.[39]

But the victory was far from unqualified. The Socialists had been unable to prevent the adoption of a new system of representation and voting which gravely disadvantaged them at future Congresses. Nor could they prevent Charles Fenwick, one of the most conservative Lib-Labs, from succeeding Broadhurst as secretary. The Parliamentary Committee, despite the turnover in personnel, was still firmly in the grip of Lib-Labs;

[36] *PC Mins.*, 1 May 1902.
[37] Will Thorne, *My Life's Battles*, pp. 156–7.
[38] Viscount Snowden, *An Autobiography*, vol. 1, p. 93.
[39] Quoted in Webb, *The History of Trade Unionism*, p. 409.

and that grip remained unshaken in the years that elapsed before Congress next met at Liverpool in 1906.

Political Outlook

Officially, the Parliamentary Committee remained neutral on the issue of party and, in its secretary's words, 'knew no politics at all'.[40] Time and again, however, the preference of its Lib-Lab majority shone through its annual reports. Thus the Conservative government's connection with the important Factories Act of 1891 went virtually unacknowledged, while the Liberal government's corresponding measure was later greeted with warm tributes. There was no rebuke, only a passing reference, to the same government's faint-hearted abandonment of a workers' compensation bill which the TUC had urged above all others from the time the Liberals won office. Yet the Conservatives' far bolder Workmen's Compensation Act, while conceded to be 'new and startling legislation', was otherwise welcomed in the most grudging terms[41]—and only a year later was totally ignored in an attack on the government: 'It must be obvious to everyone who has watched the proceedings of Parliament during the last two or three years that it is useless to expect any active measures of industrial reform from the [present] House of Commons'.[42]

Most of the TUC's leaders were little better disposed towards the Socialists, but they had to tread more warily. Their public reaction to the ILP's intervention in the 1895 general election was carefully unspecific. 'We are sorry to believe . . . that among the working classes there are too many "faddists", and each "fad" has got its followers, and, as a result, the working class vote . . . is broken up into factions.'[43] Their antagonism was also reflected in the steps taken to reduce the influence of ILP supporters at Congress.

In 1892, following the Liverpool decision, the TUC abandoned the practice of allowing affiliates to decide the number of their Congress delegates which, in turn, had determined the fees they paid. Instead, entitlements to delegates and liability for fees were to be related to an organization's membership. In addition, the delegate entitlement of trades councils was

[40] *TUC Report*, 1896, p. 28.
[42] ibid., 1898, p. 39.
[41] ibid., 1897, p. 18.
[43] ibid., 1895, p. 26.

limited to unionists not otherwise represented through individual unions. These changes drastically cut the representation of
the trades councils and the new unions in which the Socialists
were strongest. Their position was further eroded by three
decisions of the 1895 Congress. Trades councils were excluded
altogether from affiliation; Congress delegates were required to
be either full-time union officials or currently working at their
trade (a decision which got rid of Keir Hardie at the cost of
losing Broadhurst as well); and the system of delegate voting
was replaced by the 'card vote' enabling a union's votes,
equivalent to the number of its members, to be cast in one
block—a device which enhanced both the voting weight of the
older and larger unions, and their leaders' ability to control its
use.

However, the 'victors of the *coup d'état* of 1895 were not the
"old guard" of 1889.'[44] Above all, they tended to be less
rigidly opposed to state intervention than their counterparts of
the Broadhurst era. In any case, they soon found that curbing
the influence of some Socialist ideas was more difficult than
cutting the Socialists' voting strength in Congress. An attempt
to dilute Keir Hardie's socialization amendment of 1894 was
defeated at the 1896 Congress, and the next adopted a resolution restating the amendment. In the later 1890s, moreover,
the Socialists of the ILP were deliberately more restrained in
their approach to the unions. This was one factor helping to
disarm Lib-Lab opponents of their campaign for independent
parliamentary representation.

Political Activity

The Parliamentary Committee continued to devote much
attention to parliament. Promoting private members' bills and
parliamentary resolutions comprised the bulk of its work. The
direct fruits of these labours were not impressive. In 1890 it
reported that its secretary had successfully steered through a
Seamen's Union bill on load-lines. Nine years elapsed before
it was able to celebrate the passage of another private member's
bill (on juvenile working-hours in the cotton industry)—and
that a bill for which it was not directly responsible. Otherwise,
the TUC's own bills seem invariably to have been caught up in

---

[44] Clegg *et al.*, op. cit., p. 262.

'the slaughter of the innocents', a phrase used in its reports with monotonous regularity to describe measures which received only a first reading before lapsing with the end of the parliamentary session.

The Parliamentary Committee was officially responsible for up to a dozen or more bills each year. Its first task was to arrange for a parliamentarian to take charge of each bill. Usually, no great difficulty was encountered in doing so. On only one occasion, it seems, was a TUC bill (in 1891, on the qualifications of 'enginemen') accepted by a Conservative. In 1905 the committee went to the length of writing to all MPs asking whether, if successful in the private members' ballot for parliamentary time, they would introduce the TUC's bill to remedy the Taff Vale decision: 20 agreed.

Lobbying in support of TUC bills, once their sponsor had secured a favourable placing in the ballot, was usually left to the secretary and MP-members of the Parliamentary Committee. The secretary was himself an MP for all but one year in the 1890s, but not between 1900 and 1906. Neither was any other committee member during 1900–2, and for much of that period Dilke's services were heavily relied on in this connection. On a few occasions the committee descended on the parliamentary lobbies *en masse*. Nor was its lobbying confined to its own bills, parliamentary questions and resolutions. It was similarly active, sometimes mounting a mass lobby for the purpose, in relation to bills and resolutions promoted by individual unions or emanating from Liberal or Conservative sources.

Apart from direct personal approaches, the committee sometimes 'issued a whip' by circularizing all MPs on matters considered specially important. It tried, particularly during the later 1890s, to induce the affiliated unions to lobby and write to MPs about TUC bills, but apparently without much success. It circulated parliamentary division lists, and sometimes called on trade unionists at large to exert pressure on their local MPs. Now and again it directly approached union bodies in the constituencies of particularly troublesome MPs, such as those 'who habitually blocked . . . night after night' its bill on 'engine-men'.[45] From 1902, it put a great deal of effort

[45] *TUC Report*, 1897, p. 19.

into arranging demonstrations and union conferences with an eye to impressing MPs and ministers.

These activities were consistently given pride of place in the Parliamentary Committee's annual reports. Of course, the TUC leaders were acutely conscious of the growing difficulties of parliamentary action—and, almost certainly, more so than most other union officials less intimately involved in the national political scene. This partly explains why they tended, in practice, to place rather more emphasis than their colleagues on dealing directly with ministers. It showed up in their annual reports. Although still treated as a secondary line of action, in terms of space, the proceedings of ministerial deputations were the subject of increasing attention. The trend was first evident in the report of 1893 which, unlike its predecessors as we have seen, made something of the post-Congress interviews with ministers.

Another early indication of this shift in emphasis was a procedural change which implies that the TUC leadership was taking the deputation technique rather more seriously. Up to 1895, although deputations on other issues often dealt with a single minister, Congress resolutions were usually handled by a so-called 'omnibus' deputation which met all the relevant ministers at once. But in that year 'a new departure was taken,' and the TUC leaders 'made their arrangements with the respective Ministers separately, at different times and on different dates', because they had concluded that the old method was 'almost next to useless'.[46] The new deputations were still tagged with the 'omnibus' label, but only because they usually carried a number of Congress resolutions. There was an unexplained reversion in 1897 to the old 'omnibus' form; but thereafter it was the general rule for ministers to be seen on their own.

Apart from the difficulties of parliamentary action, there was a more positive reason for the change of emphasis. This was the Parliamentary Committee's growing concern with administrative, as distinct from legislative, issues. The House of Commons' Fair Wages Resolution of 1891 was particularly important. By 1895, Congress was being assured that 'there has not been a single month in which your Committee has not

[46] ibid., 1896, p. 20.

been . . . making most strenuous endeavours to press on the Government' violations of the resolution.[47] Up to the end of the 1890s, the committee arranged, or tried to arrange, far more deputations on this matter than on any other. Moreover, when the 1898 Congress temporarily debarred ministerial deputations on its resolutions, and directed that they were to be sent instead to MPs, the committee had no difficulty in defending its subsequent decision to arrange six deputations on Congress resolutions involving clear-cut administrative matters. There was obviously no better way of communicating such matters. The committee's procedural preferences in relation to administrative issues are indicated by its instruction that the secretary was to try, 'if possible, to arrange a [ministerial] deputation . . . failing which, to get the question raised in the House of Commons'.[48] But the same order of preference was very often applied in the case of legislation as well.

This is not to say that TUC leaders had great expectations of the policy outcomes from deputations. There were occasional successes to be claimed, such as pay increases for naval dockyard workers, amendments to factories legislation and a measure making foreign shipowners liable to workers' compensation. For the most part, however, the best that could be said of deputations was that they were 'on the whole . . . fairly satisfactory' and, hopefully, 'will be productive of good'.[49] In the end, what it came down to for the TUC leadership was the fact that, 'expensive, cumbrous, and generally unsatisfactory' as ministerial deputations admittedly were, nobody had 'been able to devise any better process of bringing their labour grievances before the Government'.[50]

Internal Authority: the Affiliated Unions

The Parliamentary Committee's position in the TUC structure was strengthened during the period. Its income was placed on a regular basis from 1892 when the fees paid by affiliated unions were tied to their memberships. Its membership, and representativeness, was increased from 11 to 13 a year later. In 1894 it was empowered to compress related union proposals into 'composite' resolutions for Congress consideration. From 1900

[47] ibid., 1895, p. 22.
[49] ibid., 1903, p. 49.
[48] ibid., 1899, p. 33.
[50] ibid., 1897, p. 18.

it settled, if still only by ballot, the order of items on the Congress agenda; but, much more important, it was also authorized to exclude propositions outside the 'generally accepted . . . objects and aims of Trades Unionism'.[51] The position of Congress president, formerly filled by a union official of the town in which Congress met, was allotted to the chairman of the outgoing Parliamentary Committee from the same year.

There were also improvements in the committee's secretarial support. Sam Woods, elected secretary in 1894, initially devoted much more time to his duties than either Fenwick or Broadhurst. A full-time clerk was employed from 1896, and the part-time position of legal adviser was created in 1900. The office was shifted to more suitable rooms in 1903, a typewriter purchased and a telephone installed. By this time, however, ill health and overwork had sapped Woods's efficiency. The clerk had also developed deficiencies (the minutes refer to 'the foul smell in the office')[52] and was sacked, his replacement being chosen from a field of 998 applicants. On Woods's retirement in 1904 the secretaryship, formerly subject to annual election, was made permanent and its incumbent was required to forgo other positions except that of MP.

Outside the structure of the TUC itself, there were other innovations in the Parliamentary Committee's role. It entered the field of litigation from 1896 when it sought to alter judicial doctrine on picketing by strikers. In 1894, it breached its long-standing 'rule never to interfere in disputes between two societies'[53] by agreeing to arbitrate a jurisdictional dispute between two tailors' unions; and from the turn of the century was regularly involved in similar inter-union disputes.

The committee's traditional functions of lobbying and mounting ministerial deputations were also in demand. It was frequently asked to help with private members' bills advanced by particular trade unions. Sometimes such bills were placed in its hands, as the result of either a Congress resolution or a direct approach from the unions concerned: seven of the twelve bills which the committee allocated to MPs in 1898, for example, were sectional in character. More often, however, unions handled their own bills and amendments to government

[51] ibid., 1900, p. 70.   [52] *PC Mins.*, 13 October 1903.
[53] ibid., 18 February 1890.

bills, and simply asked the committee for support. Sometimes all they wanted was a TUC whip issued to MPs; at other times they sought the committee's active involvement in lobbying or in deputations.

Apart from Congress resolutions of a specifically sectional nature, general resolutions sometimes required the committee to handle sectional claims. The key case was a resolution of 1892, the first of a series following the House of Commons' Fair Wages Resolution. It advocated union wage rates and the eight-hour day for the manual employees of government and its contractors. This resulted in the committee, at the instance of concerned unions, taking up with government a great many detailed claims relating to alleged infringements of the Fair Wages Resolution. The committee's activities in this respect encouraged the postal unions, denied government recognition themselves, to ask it to take up a number of their grievances in 1896. Again, in 1903, the Royal Army Clothing Workmen's Union asked it to negotiate wage and other claims with the War Office.

Sectional issues of this kind had previously not figured at all in the Parliamentary Committee's concerns. They added substantially to its workload, and its meetings were much more frequent from the mid-nineties. They provided it with numerous opportunities to play a leading, rather than merely supporting, role on issues of central importance to the unions concerned. In doing so, they reflected a trend that was evident also in the committee's role in relation to lobbying and deputations.

In the case of lobbying, the trend is illustrated by two events, both related to government bills concerned with the regulation of conditions in factories. In 1890 and in 1900, the full Parliamentary Committee met representatives of the cotton unions and a number of MPs. The 1890 meeting was convened jointly by the committee and the cotton unions; the 1900 meeting was arranged by the TUC secretary alone. At the 1900 meeting, unlike that of 1890, it was agreed that the committee would be solely responsible for subsequent dealings with the MPs, and that the unions would notify the TUC secretary of any amendments they wished to press. This acknowledgement of the committee's role as lobbyist came from the, politically, most influential group of unions in the country.

In the case of ministerial deputations, the trend is illustrated by the changing composition of TUC deputations. Traditionally, all interested unions were entitled to be represented. Nor were any limits placed on the number of representatives: unions were simply informed of projected deputations and asked to 'get their delegations appointed as early as possible'.[54] Deputations, as a result, were typically large. The Home Secretary, for example, received deputations numbering over 200 members in 1893, 250 in 1895 and just on 200 in 1896. This practice was discontinued only after the 1898 Congress temporarily banned ministerial deputations altogether. As we have seen, the Parliamentary Committee ignored the ban in the case of some administrative issues. The deputations it mounted on this occasion were small, and consisted wholly or largely of its own members. Subsequently, the TUC leaders made no attempt to re-established the general-invitation system. The significant point of the new system was that, as they themselves put it, 'if found necessary at times it might be convenient for the Committee to invite persons from outside who are specially interested in the questions to be discussed' by a particular deputation.[55] In other words, they claimed the right to issue selective invitations. This claim was challenged at the 1905 Congress, but without success. In the meantime, the membership of TUC deputations was often confined to the Parliamentary Committee; and when individual union representatives were included, it seems usually to have been because of the technical nature of specific issues.

The Parliamentary Committee's changed role in relation to lobbying and deputations suggests an enlarged internal authority. Changes in its relationship with Congress pointed in the same direction. It continued, as in the Broadhurst era, to ignore or obstruct occasional Congress directives—but, it appears, with more boldness. Thus it dragged its feet in the case of Congress resolutions about eight-hours legislation for miners, a general eight-hours bill and the creation of a political fund. Following the 1898 Congress, it ignored one resolution purporting to deny it the power to propose resolutions of its own; it declined to act on six resolutions, on the ground that they were inconsistent with each other; and it moved to arrange a number

[54] ibid., 15 October 1896.   [55] *TUC Report*, 1901, p. 40.

of ministerial deputations despite Congress's ban. Above all, however, it began to give a stronger lead to the affiliated unions. At one level this was reflected in procedural changes. By 1901, as we have seen, it was empowered to consolidate similar resolutions for Congress consideration and to exclude those it considered beyond the proper scope of trade union concerns; and its chairman presided over Congress. There was also a growing tendency for resolutions on major matters of general interest, whatever their source, to be introduced by a committee member. At another, more significant level, the committee's new initiative was reflected in the way it developed its own concerns and procedures without prior Congress authorization. Its abandonment of the old 'omnibus' form of deputation was one example. Another was its decision to confine TUC deputations largely to its own members. In particular, in the words of the Congress chairman in 1905, there was the 'entirely new . . . departure' of the 'past two or three years' when the committee, instead of 'simply . . . carrying out the decisions of Congress . . . have taken the initiative on several matters of importance'.[56] Among the matters on which the committee appears to have acted, either without Congress instruction or beyond the requirements of Congress resolutions, were unemployment, housing, workers' compensation, the Taff Vale decision, the corn tax introduced in the 1902 Budget and the admission of indentured Chinese labour to South Africa. Its initiatives were also reflected in its unprecedented enthusiasm for demonstrations and special union conferences from 1902.

All these changes add up to the conclusion that, by 1905, the Parliamentary Committee carried appreciably more weight among the affiliated unions that it had fifteen years earlier. There were, of course, limits to its authority; and the limitations took two forms. In the first place, its ability to control either Congress or individual unions was far from assured. Thus the 1903 Congress firmly directed the committee to amend its Taff Vale bill in order to give trade unions complete immunity from liability for damages, instead of merely qualified immunity. Again, the committee encountered persistent difficulty in enforcing its decisions in inter-union disputes; the important Amalgamated Society of Engineers disaffiliated in 1899 rather

[56] ibid., 1905, p. 47.

than accept one such decision. In the second place, by 1905 the scope of the committee's authority, in the sense of the range of matters it related to, was more restricted than it had been, or had seemed likely to become, during the 1890s. This was largely an outcome of the way in which, around the turn of the century, the TUC shed functions that it had either exercised in some form, or might well have claimed to exercise. The principal functions involved were connected with industrial disputes, international trade union affairs and electoral organization.

In the case of industrial disputes, the Parliamentary Committee initially avoided involvement. In 1890 it declared that it 'had no power' to donate money from its funds to striking brick workers.[57] Three years later it declined even to issue an appeal on behalf of the Hull dockers, asserting that its policy 'has always been one of strict neutrality in Labour disputes'.[58] Within a few months, however, the miners' lockout induced it to discard this policy and make an appeal for funds. When the engineering dispute broke out in 1897, the committee not only issued an appeal but, on the instruction of Congress, collected and disbursed funds. It was relieved of this function by the formation of the General Federation of Trade Unions in 1899.

The GFTU was originally conceived solely as a means of channelling financial support to unions involved in industrial disputes. But it also relieved the TUC of its international function. One aspect of this function was foreign strikes. Long before it discharged the same role in relation to domestic stoppages, the Parliamentary Committee collected and forwarded £678 in support of the Australian maritime workers' strike in 1890; and at the end of the decade it gave similar support to Austrian and Danish strikers. The other aspect was international trade union conferences. Despite their unhappy experiences of the 1880s, the TUC leaders were obliged by Congress to send delegates to the Brussels conference of 1891. Five years later they were associated with the International Socialist Workers and Trades Union Congress held in London, an experience which left them wondering whether it was 'wise and prudent' for the TUC 'to identify itself with Congresses of this character'.[59] Subsequently, the GFTU eagerly accepted

[57] *PC Mins.*, 18 February 1890.   [58] ibid., 3 May 1893.
[59] *TUC Report*, 1896, p. 23.

the burden, and helped form the International Conference of Trade Union Secretaries in 1901. The Parliamentary Committee was content to restrict itself to its customary (since 1894) exchange of 'fraternal' delegates with the American Federation of Labour. Thus it told a deputation of Amsterdam railway strikers that it would 'be pleased to endorse' any appeal for funds made by the GFTU.[60] It was equally happy merely to support a later LRC appeal on behalf of 'the Russian strikers'.[61]

As for electoral organization, the Parliamentary Committee, no doubt with the failure of the Labour Electoral Association in mind, put up no great opposition to the creation of the LRC. Like the GFTU, the LRC took over a function which carried a high risk of disruption for a body as broad-based as the TUC. In both cases, as Phelps Brown points out, it is probable that the TUC 'preserved its unity by establishing a separate channel to carry each of these disturbing currents away'.[62] At the same time, it had also narrowed the scope of its potential authority among the unions.

But this was not all that was implied by the formation of the LRC and the GFTU. For it was not only functions the TUC did not want that had been transferred to them. They had also been conceded a share in functions which the TUC was supposed to have retained. And that concession, potentially, was the more vital because it posed a threat to the very existence of the TUC.

Internal Authority: the LRC and the GFTU

Both the LRC and the GFTU originated, effectively, in resolutions of the TUC's annual Congress. In each case, too, the Parliamentary Committee played the leading part in the inaugural arrangements. It convened the 'Special Federation Congress' that formally constituted the GFTU in January 1899, and it acted as the GFTU's 'Provisional Committee' until July of that year.[63] According to its own minutes,[64] it decided unilaterally to convene the conference of February

---

[60] ibid., 1903, p. 50.
[61] *PC Mins.*, 13 February 1905.
[62] Phelps Brown, op. cit., p. 248.
[63] *PC Mins.*, 24 January and 7 February 1899.
[64] ibid., 6 December 1899. But cf. A. M. McBriar, *Fabian Socialism and English Politics*, p. 309.

1900, which founded the LRC; and its decision was endorsed at a meeting with other interested bodies when a delegate from the Social Democratic Federation, seconded by Bernard Shaw of the Fabian Society, also moved 'that the invitations to the Conference and the arrangements thereof generally be left in the hands of the Parliamentary Committee'. But it showed no desire to preserve an organic connection with either of the new bodies. Neither of them, as their functions were formally defined, impinged on its traditional political functions of lobbying MPs and interviewing ministers. This, however, was to change.

In 1904 Ramsay MacDonald, the first official LRC spokesman to address the TUC's annual Congress, coined a metaphor that was to become the stock-in-trade of his successors in the same role. He and a colleague, he said, 'had been described as fraternal delegates'; the LRC, however, 'was neither sister nor brother to the Congress, but its child', and they were there 'to offer their filial respects'.[65] A TUC leader responded to these blandishments with the hope that 'the lusty child of Congress would not turn out to be a disobedient child'.[66] The edge to this remark was almost certainly intentional. By this time the LRC and the GFTU had not only demonstrated their capacity for survival, but had expanded both their affiliated memberships and their functions. The LRC, initially limited to giving moral support to approved candidates, now administered a political fund, selected constituencies for its candidates and exacted from them a pledge to abide by caucus decisions. The GFTU had extended its concerns beyond the administration of a strike fund to include union recruitment, amalgamations and representation at international labour conferences. In neither case were the TUC's functions directly affected. But the enhanced stature of the two 'filial' bodies helped to strengthen claims which both had begun to make on the TUC's traditional functions.

George Howell, in common with many others, had early seen the GFTU as 'a rival body . . . which it is expected will supersede the Congress'.[67] As it happened, the LRC, founded

[65] *TUC Report*, 1904, p. 100.
[66] ibid., p. 101.
[67] Howell, *Trade Unionism New and Old*, 4th ed., pp. 238–9; as written in 3rd ed. of 1900.

after he wrote those words, was to throw out the more serious challenge. The TUC leaders acknowledged Howell's point in 1900 by securing an undertaking that the GFTU would 'confine itself to purely trade matters and leave political questions outside its work';[68] and the GFTU's secretary re-iterated the undertaking in an address to Congress, after referring to 'a fear expressed that the Federation would come into rivalry with the Congress'.[69] But that was before the Taff Vale decision. At first, the GFTU executive deferred to the Parliamentary Committee on the matter, and sent a deputation which 'thanked the Committee for receiving them and with-drew' on being informed of the committee's planned action.[70] Within a few months, however, their relationship had changed. The change was signified by a joint meeting between the two executives on the Taff Vale issue. The willingness of the TUC leaders to participate may well have been inspired by a recognition of the more pressing threat posed by the LRC, and their need for support in meeting it.

The threat had been implicit from the time the LRC was formed with the aim of creating a cohesive parliamentary 'Labour group'. That aim, if realized, was plainly bound to affect the TUC in its role as lobbyist. But up to 1902 the threat was easily assumed remote, partly because of the LRC's un-impressive beginnings, and partly because of the way in which the TUC improved its parliamentary links in the preceding three years.

The TUC secretary, Woods, in March 1899 convened a meeting of nine unionist-MPs, including himself. They agreed to operate as a group on labour issues, appointing Woods and John Burns as 'a sub-committee' and Fenwick, the former TUC secretary, as whip.[71] Within a few weeks, however, the Parliamentary Committee was moving to by-pass the group. The meetings with Dilke and Asquith followed. The outcome on the eve of the LRC's formation was, as we have seen, an under-standing which assured the committee of direct access to the Liberal leadership. For a time, the committee seems to have relied almost exclusively on this connection. After Woods and

[68] *TUC Report*, 1900, p. 41.
[69] ibid., p. 80.
[70] *PC Mins.*, 5 February 1902.
[71] *TUC Report*, 1899, p. 39.

W. C. Steadman, the committee's only other MP-member, lost their seats in the general election of October 1900, it was Dilke whose services were most heavily called on, instead of a unionist-MP. But there was a shift in this emphasis in 1902, and there were signs of it even before the committee acquired another MP-member, Richard Bell, towards the end of that year.

It was the Parliamentary Committee's reaction to a complaint from Keir Hardie which first suggested that the TUC leaders had registered the implications of the mounting surge in the LRC's fortunes following Taff Vale. Hardie's charge, that the committee had ignored Labour MPs, evoked a decision that the TUC secretary 'arrange for a meeting of Labour MPs alone to confer with the committee at least once a year on Labour legislation'; and a promise that 'in future all literature issued from the [TUC] Office should be sent to the Labour MPs'.[72] A month later, there was a decision to invite them to sit on the platform at future Congresses. The committee's sense of insecurity was underlined by the almost simultaneous launching of a Lib-Lab campaign for the formal incorporation of both the LRC and the GFTU in the TUC. Congress subsequently rejected moves in this direction, while accepting another proposal that all three bodies 'should have their offices in the one building, with the object ultimately of founding a National Labour Institute'.[73] But it was soon evident that this idea, too, was still-born.

The Parliamentary Committee changed tack shortly after the 1902 Congress. In a letter stressing that 'your body is an offspring of the Trades Union Congress',[74] it invited the LRC and GFTU executives to discuss 'concerted action . . . during the next session of Parliament' on the Taff Vale issue.[75] The outcome was a joint sub-committee with the task of drawing up a suitable bill in conjunction with Edmond Browne, the TUC's legal adviser. This was a significant concession. It acknowledged the right of the LRC and the GFTU to concern themselves with a function (the drafting and promotion of a bill on a general labour matter) which the TUC had formerly claimed as its prerogative. The concession was confirmed by

[72] *PC Mins.*, 30 April 1902.   [73] *TUC Report*, 1902, p. 75.
[74] ibid., 1903, p. 52.   [75] *PC Mins.*, 18 December 1902.

the appointment of another joint sub-committee to organize a national conference on the bill.

Nevertheless, the Lib-Labs on the Parliamentary Committee continued to resist the LRC and its supporters on other fronts. In January 1903, they moved to arrange 'the usual meeting' with Labour MPs, without reference to either the LRC or the GFTU; and they rejected a proposal that the MPs 'should be asked to appoint one of their number' to introduce the TUC's forthcoming ministerial deputations, preferring to make their own choice.[76] At the LRC's annual conference in February, they sponsored an unsuccessful motion which would have permitted the affiliation of the National Democratic League, a predominantly Lib-Lab body. In April they rejected an LRC request for quarterly meetings with both the LRC executive and Labour MPs, 'to discuss political report and future policy'.[77] And although joining with the LRC and GFTU executives in another meeting about the Taff Vale bill in June, they were to assert themselves even on this issue six months later.

The occasion was provided by Browne, the TUC's legal adviser, who had arranged a meeting on the bill with the Liberal MP and lawyer, Sir Robert Reid. Reid had suggested that the three full executives should attend. Browne, accordingly, wrote to all three. The Parliamentary Committee reacted angrily. Browne's letters to the other two executives were condemned as 'quite unauthorised'. It was decided that 'the Committee alone' should see Reid, and that 'afterwards' the LRC and the GFTU would be 'invited to render all help to the Bill after completion'.[78] The committee's irritability, on the day of this decision, is reflected in its reception of an invitation to send two fraternal delegates to the LRC's next annual conference: 'After a somewhat lively discussion, the matter dropped without any Resln. being passed'.[79] The committee stuck to its guns on the issue of the Reid interview, relenting only to the extent of inviting some Labour MPs along and convening the joint sub-committee on the Taff Vale bill soon afterwards. But is accepted the LRC's conference invitation, and later returned the courtesy.

[76] ibid., 13 January 1903.   [77] ibid., 7 April 1903.
[78] ibid., 20 January 1904.   [79] ibid.

The Congress of 1904 was the first to which the LRC sent fraternal delegates, a privilege the GFTU had enjoyed since 1902. Two other incidents at this Congress throw light on the TUC's new relationship with the LRC. The preceding Congress had specifically confirmed its competence to deal, like earlier Congresses, with items relating to the LRC's constitution. In 1904, however, the agenda committee, with the reported support of 'the majority, if not the whole, of the Parliamentary Committee', declared all such resolutions to be 'outside the jurisdiction of Congress':[80] its recommendation was accepted. The second incident was the adoption of a resolution empowering the Parliamentary Committee to endorse parliamentary candidates, provided they had first been endorsed by *either* a trade union, the LRC or the GFTU. Thus while the first incident confirmed the LRC's independence of the TUC, the second confirmed the TUC's independence of the LRC by authorizing it to endorse Lib-Lab candidates regardless of their acceptability to the LRC. But there was a sequel to the endorsement resolution, and it was more revealing.

The LRC soon moved on the issue. The TUC leaders agreed to attend a joint conference, including the GFTU, at Caxton Hall in February 1905. The outcome was an agreement which, while still permitting the TUC to endorse Lib-Lab candidates, otherwise bound it to the LRC's chariot wheels. Briefly, the LRC was allowed to withhold support from TUC-endorsed candidates who did not subscribe to its platform, but the TUC was committed to supporting *all* LRC-endorsed candidates. The Parliamentary Committee, in other words, could not discriminate against Socialists in the way that the LRC could discriminate against Lib-Labs.

The Caxton Hall conference was notable for another reason as well. Although the minutes of the conference itself are silent on the point, the TUC's records indicate that it was the occasion of a preliminary agreement about forming a tripartite body to facilitate consultation on general policy matters. There had already been cooperation on such an issue. In December the Parliamentary Committee had responded with uncharacteristic alacrity to a GFTU request for discussions about unemployment, and their joint deputation saw the

[80] *TUC Report*, 1904, p. 91.

Prime Minister shortly before the Caxton Hall conference. Three months after the conference, the committee responded to an LRC approach on the same issue by inviting it to a meeting already arranged with the GFTU. The President of the Board of Trade subsequently received a deputation representing all three, and the committee accepted an invitation to cooperate in an LRC-organized demonstration about unemployment. But the proposal for a standing consultative committee on policy matters in general was evidently a horse of a different colour.

The Lib-Labs on the Parliamentary Committee were now much more wary of centralization, even in this mild form, than in 1902 when they had floated the idea of amalgamating with the LRC and the GFTU. Their caution was reflected in the three members they chose to represent the TUC on 'the Joint Committee formed at the recent Caxton Hall meeting'.[81] One was David Shackleton, an MP who had joined the Parliamentary Committee in 1904: he was also immediate past-chairman of the LRC, but closer to the Lib-Labs than the Socialists. The others were both die-hard Lib-Labs, W. J. Davis and Richard Bell (also a former LRC chairman). The joint committee produced two major recommendations when it met in May. The TUC leadership accepted one suggesting that the three secretaries consult regularly on political issues. But it deferred, until after the next Congress in September, the more important proposal for the formation of a 'National Labour Advisory Board'.[82] As a result, the new body did not hold its inaugural meeting until the end of November 1905, when it adopted the title of 'The Joint Board'.

The Joint Board, as Ben Tillett was to put it a decade later, 'came into being because there were warring sections in our movement'.[83] It could not have come into being had the doyen of those sections, the TUC, been more than merely reluctant to countenance its formation. The TUC's seniority was symbolically acknowledged in the appointment of its chairman to the board's chairmanship. But there the acknowledgement stopped. The LRC and the GFTU each had precisely the same representation on it as the TUC. There could scarcely be a more

[81] *PC Mins.*, 9 March 1905.   [82] ibid., 27 July 1905.
[83] *TUC Report*, 1916, p. 319.

concise indication of the way power relationships in the labour movement had changed since 1900. The TUC's relations with its 'offspring' were now enclosed in a formal structure which implied, unequivocally, that they were each entitled to an equal voice in matters of mutual concern.

For all three participating bodies, of course, the Joint Board involved at once a reduction in independence and an expansion in function. None was as completely master in its own house as it could formerly claim to be; each could look forward to the possibility of sharing in the functions of the others. But it was the TUC that stood to lose the most and gain the least. This was evident from the start. The first policy matter considered by the board was the question of labour representation on the Royal Commission on the Poor Law. In earlier times, this would have been the business of the TUC alone. Through the board, it became the business of the LRC and the GFTU as well. Moreover, even when membership of the board enabled the TUC to encroach on the preserves of the other participants (as it later did), the TUC was recovering rather than gaining ground—because its leaders alone could look back to a time when they and their predecessors had been the sole repository of such authority as the unions at large had entrusted to a national inter-union body. For the LRC and GFTU leaders, on the other hand, the board was more obviously a means of gaining fresh ground and an enhanced stature in the labour movement.

The LRC, in more direct competition than the GFTU with the TUC, is accurately described as the TUC's 'junior partner' and as 'far from being the movement's sole political arm' in 1905.[84] What is more significant, however, is that by this time the TUC was no longer, as it had been in the 1890s, 'the movement's main political instrument'; nor was its secretary's office any longer 'the one real centre of the trade union world'.[85] The Joint Board symbolized that fact. So that although it is true that 'the Parliamentary Committee's reputation stood higher in 1905 than in 1900',[86] among the unions, its capacity for independent action as a union spokesman was reduced. For the time being, its internal authority was substantially

[84] Clegg *et al.*, op. cit., pp. 381, 383.   [85] ibid., pp. 249, 251.
[86] ibid., p. 372.

unimpaired. But it was to be a different story before the next ten years were out.

External Authority

In 1891 Salisbury became the first Conservative Prime Minister to receive a TUC deputation. During the 1890s and up to 1905, many other ministers of both parties (including another Conservative Prime Minister) also agreed to see TUC deputations. When the Parliamentary Committee decided to abandon the old 'omnibus' form of deputation in 1895, it appears to have encountered no difficulty in arranging separate interviews with ministers about Congress resolutions. And if, as we have seen, it was refused such access on a number of occasions, all but four of these rebuffs were ministerial re-actions to the novel claim that an outside body like the TUC was entitled to deal with the working conditions of government employees. In any case, the TUC had won its point on this issue by the end of the period. Apart from direct dealings of this sort, both Liberal and Conservative governments appointed TUC leaders to a number of temporary advisory bodies, including royal commissions. From 1893, also, the Board of Trade regularly sent observers to the annual Congress.

Ministerial recognition of the TUC was echoed in other political quarters. After the TUC's policy 'manifesto' was sent to MPs, in accordance with the 1898 Congress instruction, the Parliamentary Committee was 'literally . . . besieged' by MPs asking 'what they are expected to do'.[87] More important, the leaders of the Liberal opposition took an active interest from 1899 in fostering consultative arrangements with the committee.

Neither government nor opposition, however, confined their favours to the TUC. In 1896, for example, while a TUC deputation put its views on workers' compensation to the Home Secretary, it was some 200 members of the Birmingham Trades Council who were treated to a special conference with a number of Conservative MPs—including that most notable Birmingham parliamentarian, Joseph Chamberlain, then Chancellor of the Exchequer and subsequently author of the Workmen's Compensation Act of 1897. Burt, given a place in two Liberal ministries, was never a member of the Parliamentary

[87] *TUC Report*, 1899, p. 31.

Committee. Birtwistle, who was a member, owed his factory inspectorship of 1892 entirely to his expertise as a cotton union official. Most Parliamentary Committe members on royal commissions and other advisory bodies shared the representation of labour with others from individual unions or, later, the LRC. Thus the TUC's one representative appointed to the Royal Commission on the Poor Law, in 1905, was accompanied by another from the LRC, as well as Beatrice Webb of the Fabian Society; and it was refused any representation at all on the Royal Commission on Trade Disputes, set up in the wake of the Taff Vale decision. And while the Liberals consulted closely with the TUC from the turn of the century, they had no hesitation in negotiating also with the LRC once its survival seemed assured.

Nevertheless, there was a distinct and quite dramatic change in both the scale and the intimacy of the TUC's dealings with political notables after 1889. The policy outcomes of these developments were not wildly impressive, even if its own claims of success are accepted without qualification. There were a number of administrative concessions, one or two minor pieces of legislation and some amendments to government bills. There was nothing to match the Conspiracy and Protection of Property Act of 1875, or even the Employers' Liability Act of 1880—for the TUC had little to do with Chamberlain's Workmen's Compensation Act of 1897. But the consultative developments were a more accurate portent of the future.

For one thing there was the nature of some of the issues involved, and the importance attached to them by established political leaders. Of greatest significance for the near future was the Taff Vale decision. This converted trade unionism into the kind of major political issue that it had been during the late 1860s and early 1870s. Because the TUC was the principal union spokesmen on this issue, if not in as unqualified a sense as in the past, its position was enhanced in the eyes of government and opposition politicians. As far as the more distant future was concerned, it was the extension of TUC-government consultation to new types of issues which was significant. Ministerial recognition of the TUC's right to take up such matters as the political rights and working conditions of some government employees was not easily won. But it was won, and it was won despite the traditional policy of both Liberal and Conservative ministers against dealing with 'outsiders', even as officials of unions covering government employees. There was also the tentative intrusion into the TUC-government relationship of the strike-settlement issue. In 1898, as we have seen, the idea of a system of union-employer conciliation boards was floated by Ritchie, President of the Board of Trade. This proposal, which he first raised with a TUC deputation seeing him about other matters, subsequently inspired the only ministerial initiation of consultation with the TUC (other than Lowe's in 1873) up to 1905.

It is evident, too, that the emergence of the LRC, potentially threatening though it was, initially helped strengthen the TUC's external authority by creating the possibility that it might be used as a counterweight. This was a consideration of particular importance for the Liberals, whose electoral base was more vulnerable than the Conservatives' to the LRC's appeal. Moreover, the TUC's style and outlook were more congenial to established politicians. Unlike the LRC with its heavy Socialist lacing, the TUC had acquired the aura of 'a British institution of the utmost respectability'[88]—an institution which could be offered, and which accepted, represent-ation on the august Imperial Institute presided over by the Prince of Wales. The continuing Lib-Lab domination of the Parliamentary Committee meant that, however fiery Congress might sound, the TUC leadership remained cautious in utterance and respectful in approach to its social and political betters. It also meant, in contrast to the LRC's proclaimed aim of parliamentary independence, a stronger attachment to the Liberal party.

A Delicate Political Authority

The TUC diverted the issues of coordinated industrial action and direct parliamentary representation away from its juris-diction by helping found the GFTU and the LRC. In doing so, it elected to confine itself to its traditional role and proce-dures, acting on predominantly socio-industrial issues by lobbying parliamentarians and sending deputations to minis-ters. These issues came to include not only grander policy

[88] G. M. Trevelyan, *British History in the Nineteenth Century*, pp. 398–9.

matters, like the Taff Vale decision and unemployment, but also a wider range of administrative detail than before.

As 1905 ended, the TUC was still recognized on both sides as the pre-eminent intermediary between unions and government office-holders. Its traditional methods of action were still seen as being of immediate relevance to the policy problems of common concern to both. Its political authority was founded on this, and stood higher than ever. Before long, however, the fragility of that foundation was to be exposed by the LRC's electoral successes and by the unions' growing reliance on the strike weapon. Indeed the implication of these developments for the TUC's authority was already foreshadowed in the existence of the Joint Board. And a delegate to the 1905 Congress was expressing a common view when he told his members that the TUC 'is dying of old age. It has done its work, and I think good work, but the organizations it has been the means of creating will in the near future take up the work'.[89] This was the ground, too, on which the leaders of the Amalgamated Society of Engineers justified their opposition to re-affiliating with the TUC: the LRC and the GFTU had rendered it redundant. In the event, of course, these judgements were to be falsified—but not before the TUC, after enjoying a brief upsurge in fortune, had undergone a severe decline.

[89] Amalgamated Society of Carpenters and Joiners, *Monthly Report*, No. 515, November 1905, p. 527. I am indebted to Phillip Deery for this reference.

5

Advance and Challenge
1906–1914

THE general election of January 1906 swept into power a
Liberal government inclined to social reform. It also produced
a Labour party of parliamentary substance. The first of these
changes initially worked in favour of the TUC's intermediary
role. But when the government's interest in reform slackened,
the competing claims of the Labour party took their toll. Other
factors helped to diminish the TUC's political authority as the
first world war approached.

GOVERNMENT

The election returns, which killed Joseph Chamberlain's
campaign for tariff reform, gave fresh impetus to the less
personalized movement towards state intervention in other
areas. Public policy extensions during the next few years
involved a number of innovations in legislative principle. They
included workers' compensation for industrial diseases (1906);
compulsory medical inspections of school children (1907);
government-financed old age pensions (1908); statutory
working-hours for adult males, in coal mines (1908); a national
system of state labour exchanges (1909); trade boards to fix
minimum wage rates in sweated industries (1909); a subsidized
health insurance scheme, compulsory for manual workers
(1911); subsidized unemployment insurance, applying compulsorily in certain major industries employing more than a
fifth of all adult male workers (1911); and statutory recognition of the minimum wage principle outside the sweated trades,
in coal mining (1912).

These innovations are now generally acknowledged as com-
pleting the foundations of the welfare state in Britain. They
occurred during a period that was remarkable for ferocious
controversy on the great constitutional issues of Irish home rule,

votes for women and the powers of the House of Lords. It was also a period marked by intensified government concern with trade unions and their activities.

Legislative policy concessions provide one indication of this concern. The Trade Disputes Act of 1906, reversing the Taff Vale and other judgements, is the most clearcut case: the critical influence of union pressure was openly displayed in the parliamentary manoeuvres which preceded the government's amendment of its original bill.[1] Much the same sort of connection is evident in the case of the Workmen's Compensation Act of 1906, the Trade Union Act of 1913 (authorizing union political expenditures), the measures applying the eight-hour and minimum wage principles in coal mining; and also in some other government concessions ranging from a new Fair Wages Resolution in 1909 to the later amendment of the National Insurance Bill which would otherwise have excluded unions from the administration of health insurance. Similarly, Liberal ministers moved quickly in 1906 to reverse Conservative refusals to deal with civil service unions and to establish procedures facilitating the enforcement of the old Fair Wages Resolution.

Another indication of government concern was the incomparably wider opportunities for union representation on formal consultative bodies. Unionists were included in many new advisory bodies concerned with such things as labour exchanges, workers' compensation and national insurance. They were also appointed to bodies with substantial administrative powers like the Port of London Authority and some fifty local committees concerned with health insurance. Sometimes the unions were conceded the right of direct nomination, a notable departure from the established practice of making such appointments either by way of personal invitation or from lists of nominees submitted by the unions.

But it was in connection with *ad hoc* dealings that the heightened government interest in the unions was most strikingly revealed. Union-government relations in this area were closer than before, and contact was more frequent at the level of both ministers and senior civil servants. Not that ministers were invariably or uniformly receptive to union approaches for consultation; but their occasional reluctance

[1] See Clegg *et al.*, op. cit., pp. 393–5.

seems usually to have been overcome by union persistence. More significantly, some ministers displayed an unprecedented enthusiasm for consulting union leaders. This was reflected, above all, in ministerial initiations of consultation and in a ministerial preference, on occasion, for more intimate dealings than had previously been the rule.

Lloyd George, both as President of the Board of Trade and as Chancellor of the Exchequer, invited the TUC to discuss major policy issues with him on at least four occasions. Winston Churchill asked the TUC to form a standing committee to advise him about labour exchanges. His successor at the Board of Trade, Sidney Buxton, renewed the request and later invited selected union leaders to discuss current industrial unrest on two occasions. There was a similar pattern of government initiative in the case of senior civil servants, especially those at the Board of Trade. These initiatives are startling. Before 1906, as we have seen, there had been only two comparable ministerial initiatives in the history of British trade unionism.

The initiatives of these Liberal ministers, moreover, were associated with a preference for private, small-scale meetings. Their predecessors, and most of their colleagues, were content with the quasi-public proceedings (often attended by journalists) of formal deputations. W. J. Davis, a veteran union deputationist, stated the consequences: 'It is customary . . . to put your case to [ministers], listen to their reply, and thank them for receiving you . . . *no Cabinet Minister will permit any discussion* . . . You simply state your case, and they make a public declaration'.[2] Informality and frank discussion, it is well established, are primarily a matter of privacy and small numbers. The preference of some ministers on some occasions for both these things suggests a desire for genuine negotiation. Significantly, that preference was most evident in relation to government proposals concerning labour exchanges and national insurance.

On the issue of labour exchanges, Churchill publicly acknowledged his anxiety to 'cooperate . . . in the closest and frankest terms' with the unions.[3] In the case of unemployment

[2] *TUC Report*, 1906, p. 117. Italics added.
[3] Quoted in Clegg *et al.*, op. cit., p. 402.

insurance, he was equally outpsoken about his belief that 'no such novel departure . . . could possibly be taken without much further consultation and negotiation with the trade unions'.[4] Buxton was even more specific about the importance he attached to union cooperation when he promised union leaders a part in both the advisory and the administrative aspects of unemployment insurance, as a means of catering to 'the susceptibilities of Trade Unionists'; and appealed for their 'benevolent sympathy' for the scheme.[5] Buxton's remarks, like Churchill's, imply a serious bargaining element in the government's relationship with the unions. The point is confirmed by a civil servant's recollection of some of Lloyd George's dealings with them: 'I have seen him, when he wanted some kind of action . . . to which they were reluctant to agree, cajole and flatter their tough and hardened representatives'.[6]

There were three main reasons why Liberal ministers paid so much attention to the unions. First, they were more sensitive than their predecessors to the unions' capacity as electoral spokesmen. Second, they were more dependent on union cooperation for the successful administration of certain policies. Third, they were more closely concerned with the consequences of industrial unrest.

The LRC's showing in the 1906 general election, although largely a product of the electoral compact with the Liberals, impressed both Liberal and Conservative leaders. Balfour spoke of 'a new era'.[7] Campbell-Bannerman, with the resources of government behind him, reacted with what he described as his 'two sops for Labour', measures on trade disputes and workers' compensation.[8] But he and his colleagues did not depart from the Gladstonian tradition of limited and inexpensive reform until after the renamed Labour party's unexpected by-election victories of mid-1907, when it won the Liberal seats of Jarrow and Colne Valley against both Liberal and Conservative opposition. Subsequently, and not long before he introduced the Old Age Pensions Bill, Lloyd George wrote to

[4] Winston S. Churchill, *Liberalism and the Social Problem*, pp. 271–2.
[5] PC, *Fifth Quarterly Report*, March 1910, p. 44.
[6] Lord Salter, *Memoirs of a Public Servant*, p. 61.
[7] Quoted in Halevy, op. cit., vol. VI, p. 92.
[8] Quoted in Bentley B. Gilbert, *The Evolution of National Insurance in Great Britain*, p. 203.

his brother: 'It is time we did something that appealed straight to the people—it will, I think, help to stop the electoral rot'.[9] The decisions to legislate on unemployment and health insurance followed soon after. Churchill, too, eager to 'thrust a big slice of Bismarckianism over the whole underside of our industrial system', thought that the prospective insurance and labour exchange schemes would not only 'benefit the State, but fortify the party'.[10] The Liberals, as Dangerfield has put it, may have 'advanced upon social reform with noisy mouths and mouse-like feet'[11]—but advance they did, impelled by the implicit threat of the Labour party and the forcefulness of their two most imaginative ministers, Churchill and Lloyd George.

Nor were the Conservatives unaffected. The climate was such that, as a union delegate put it, 'Conservatives and Liberals alike are constrained to talk about social and industrial reform'.[12] The Conservative majority in the House of Lords was used to obstruct many other government bills, but there was little frontal opposition in either house to the Liberals' labour-oriented measures. Thus in the case of the health insurance scheme, which had evoked an uproar in middle and upper class circles, Asquith could fairly describe the Conservatives' parliamentary performance 'as that of a Party willing to scratch and yet afraid to kill'.[13] On the other side of the house, Austen Chamberlain was envious: 'Confound Ll. George. He has strengthened the Government again. His Sickness scheme *is* a good one'.[14]

The government's strategy succeeded, although there were other factors involved as well. The Labour party was effectively confined to the role of Liberal camp-follower. And so were the unions, 'the most powerful element in the labour world', as Churchill called them when he sought to wheedle them into acknowledging that 'we have done more for Trade Unionists than any other Government that has ever been'.[15]

The Liberals' innovative social reforms also injected a new element of administrative dependence into union-government

[9] Quoted in William George, *My Brother and I*, p. 220.
[10] Quoted in Gilbert, op. cit., p. 253.
[11] George Dangerfield, *The Strange Death of Liberal England*, p. 26.
[12] *TUC Report*, 1911, p. 202.
[13] Asquith, op. cit., vol. II, p. 121.
[14] Austen Chamberlain, *Politics from Inside*, p. 338.
[15] Churchill, *Liberalism and the Social Problem*, pp. 157–8.

relations. Earlier, the unions had been involved in the administration of legislation governing such things as industrial safety and workers' compensation, but primarily as channels of information peripheral to the formal administrative structure. The labour exchange and national insurance schemes, in particular, required a much closer involvement.

The labour exchanges depended for their viability on the readiness of employers and workers to use them. Buxton, like Churchill before him, frankly admitted that the scheme 'would be hopeless and would not work at all' if it was not 'acccptcd generally and generously' by the unions.'[16] The problem was that many unionists feared that the exchanges might facilitate the employment of strike-breakers and workers willing to undercut union wage rates. They had to be conciliated. Thus, the ministerial request for a special TUC committee to be consulted on administrative planning details; the local advisory committees with union representation; the appointment of a union official, Richard Bell, as Superintendent of Employment Exchanges; the inclusion of another official in the three-man committee deciding all but the highest full-time exchange appointments; the offer to make exchange rooms available for union meetings; and the offer to keep union 'vacant-books' in the exchanges.

The unions were drawn even more deeply into the national insurance schemes relating to health and unemployment, contingencies already covered by many unions. In both cases, they were incorporated as official administrative agencies. In the case of unemployment insurance, this was less an administrative necessity than a means of conciliating union opinion, since the existing state labour exchanges could have handled the scheme on their own. Health insurance, however, was another matter because of the scale of the operation—12 million contributors, as against 2 million in the unemployment scheme. Contributions could be easily collected through the post office system. But, by contemporary standards, an immense administrative outlay would have been required if the government alone had undertaken the distribution of benefits. Lloyd George, as he told union leaders, was anxious to avoid

[16] PC, *Fifth Quarterly Report*, March 1910, p. 43; see also Churchill, *Liberalism and the Social Problem*, pp. 264–5.

having 'to set up a huge salaried staff'; he wanted, instead, 'to utilise the Trade Union machinery', along with that of the friendly societies and insurance companies.[17]

But it was the Liberal government's concern with industrial peace which gave rise to the most dramatic public indications of a new relationship with the unions. Following a flurry of ministerial interventions in some industrial disputes during the mid-1890s, as we have seen, government involvement in this area was left to officers of the Board of Trade's Labour Department. Under the Liberals, for a time, ministerial interventions became almost commonplace.

The trend was set by Lloyd George in 1907 when he intervened in disputes affecting the railways, engineering and cotton industries. The following year, his interventions in other engineering and shipbuilding disputes were taken up by Churchill, his successor as President of the Board of Trade. Churchill took similar action in relation to the coal and cotton disputes of 1909. His successor, Buxton, in turn tried to avert the South Wales coal strike of 1910 and took a hand in the boilermakers' lockout. The next two years witnessed an extraordinary spate of ministerial interventions. In 1911 the London dock strike drew in both Buxton and John Burns, President of the Local Government Board; and the railway dispute attracted the active attention of Buxton, followed by the Prime Minister himself and Lloyd George, then Chancellor of the Exchequer. In 1912 the Prime Minister and three senior cabinet members intervened in the coal dispute; while no fewer than six ministers, including Asquith, involved themselves in the Port of London strike.

One of the factors behind this trend was the scale of industrial unrest. Not only was the period characterized by a dramatic increase in stoppages, but they tended to be wider in scope than before: thus Lloyd George's initiating intervention was in response to the first-ever threat of a *national* railway strike. The industrial location of disputes was important. Of the thirteen cases attracting ministerial action, seven concerned either the railways, the coal mines or the Port of London, in which major stoppages had a special political impact. There was also, particularly from the summer of 1910, an accompanying

[17] *TUC Report*, 1911, p. 75.

note of violence struck by riots, lootings and military shootings. The atmosphere had become so ominous by 1912 that gunsellers could not meet the demand for revolvers; and a phlegmatic and experienced industrial observer later wrote of a 'time of revolution in 1911 and 1912'.[18] Here was reason enough for ministerial involvement. For ambitious ministers, there was the added incentive of publicly displaying their pacifying talents. 'Whatever happens', Lloyd George wrote on the eve of his first intervention, 'I am coming out on top in this business'.[19] And he did, becoming as a result 'the most popular man in the country', according to one newspaper.[20] The kudos he gained from this and other early interventions could hardly have failed to lay temptation in the way of his colleagues. Only after their failure to settle the Port of London strike in 1912 was the Prime Minister finally converted to non-interventionism, and instructed his ministers accordingly. As it happened, there were no further disputes of similar substance before the outbreak of war.

The significance of these ministerial interventions was twofold. On the one hand, they underlined what had already been reflected in the activities of the Labour Department's officers— government acceptance of a responsibility for industrial peace which extended beyond merely the preservation of law and order. On the other hand, they brought ministers into direct contact with the power of industrial labour, and in circumstances which revealed inadequacies in the government's resources. 'Mr Churchill', a union leader responded to a threat of coercion, 'you cannot put 600,000 men into prison'.[21] Mr Churchill, despite his threat, did not try to. Similarly, an irritated Prime Minister, who walked out of a meeting with union leaders on the eve of a major railway stoppage ('Then your blood be on your own head' was his parting remark),[22] very soon after found it advisable to send his more supple Chancellor of the Exchequer back to the negotiating table. Ministers, in other words, were involved in a bargaining relationship with unions which meant that it was often easier

[18] Askwith, op. cit., p. 488.
[19] Quoted in George, op. cit., p. 212.
[20] Quoted in Philip S. Bagwell, *The Railwaymen*, p. 270.
[21] Quoted in Askwith, op. cit., p. 131.
[22] Quoted ibid., p. 164.

for them to solve the immediate problem by forcing employers to make concessions.

There were social implications to the new union-government relationship inspired by the political, administrative and industrial developments of the period. The status of union officials, as we have seen, had been enhanced before 1906 not only by their growing representation on a variety of elective bodies, but also by a trickle of appointments to industrial inspectorates in the Home Office and advisory positions in the Board of Trade. The trickle became a flood. When Churchill moved to the Home Office, for example, he promptly created two posts of Labour Adviser and 30 sub-inspectorates, filling them all with union men. During the six years to the end of 1912, the appointments of 'active union workers' numbered 117 to the Board of Trade (in charge of both labour exchanges and trade boards), 124 to positions connected with national insurance, 48 to the Home Office and 85 to other branches of the civil service.[23] Moreover, in order to make most of these appointments, Liberal ministers were prepared to sacrifice the hallowed principle of recruitment by competitive examination.

There is no doubt that a social chasm still separated union officials from the recognized leaders of society and state. Nevertheless, it had closed far enough for the Earl Marshal to invite the TUC to send two representatives to Westminster Abbey for the coronation in 1911, and for J. H. Thomas to 'put through my first telephone call to Buckingham Palace' in response to a royal request for information on the 1911 railway strike.[24] There is no doubt, too, that class antagonism was sharpened by the rising ambitions of labour, as one union official has strikingly illustrated in his recollections of an Oxford in which, with the foundation of Ruskin College, the two nations of Britain in microcosm were brought uniquely face to face.[25] But this is not to say that 'the world of Edwardian England' was in fact one in which 'it would have been unthinkable to suppose that the Liberal Home Secretary of 1910 [Churchill] . . . would one day invite the Bristol carter [Ernest Bevin] . . . to become Minister of Labour and National

[23] Halevy, op. cit., p. 447.
[24] J. H. Thomas, *My Story*, p. 34.
[25] See Frank Hodges, *My Adventures as a Labour Leader*, pp. 28–31.

Service'.[26] It was, after all, a world in which a comparable event had already occurred. John Burns, former trade union official, strike leader and professed revolutionary—'the man with the red flag' in the Trafalgar Square riot of twenty years earlier—became President of the Local Government Board in 1905 and the first man of working class origins to enter a British cabinet. Nor was it a world adequately typified as one in which 'it would never have occurred to the party leaders of 1910 that, by mid-century, governments . . . would consult the trade-union leaders as a matter of course and court their support'.[27] Government leaders, if not altogether as a matter of course, did go out of their way to consult the unions and court their support on more than one occasion. The nine pre-war years of Liberal rule, in other words, wrought a change in government attitudes which was much more redolent of the mid-twentieth century than of the nineteenth.

TRADE UNIONS

The passage of the Trade Disputes Act in 1906 removed the legal limitations on the strike which had focused union attention on political action since the Taff Vale case. But there was not the same sharp decline in political emphasis that had followed the comparable legislation of 1875. For union leaders in general now had a larger conception of the state's role. They also had higher expectations fostered by an emergent Labour party and a friendly Liberal government with expansive ideas. Nevertheless, while their expectations were met to an unusual degree by legislative action, legislation seemed incapable of solving the major problem confronting the trade unions during the period. The problem was a fall in real wages which was not fully arrested until 1914. The key to that problem, it came to be widely thought, was industrial action. To many unionists, influenced by syndicalist ideas, it seemed to be the key to much more as well. Either way, the relevance of conventional political techniques was placed in question.

Initially, the results of the 1906 general election provided a triumphant vindication of conventional political action. There

[26] Alan Bullock, *The Life and Times of Ernest Bevin*, vol. I, p. 27.
[27] ibid., p. 26.

were 47 members of the new House of Commons, as against 15 in the old, who were formally associated in some way with the labour movement. When the Labour Representation Committee renamed itself the Labour party, 30 of them (including 23 active trade unionists) formed the parliamentary Labour party. The 17 Lib-Labs formed themselves into a separate trade union group, but cooperated with the party until the group collapsed in 1909 when the Miners' Federation and most of its MPs affiliated to the party.

The party's aspirations to parliamentary influence were soon shattered. Only once, in relation to the Trade Disputes Bill, was it in an effective balance-of-power position. Its leadership came to be seen as lacking imagination and drive, and suffered from the inevitable contrast with a Liberal government identified with the vigour of Lloyd George and Churchill. The general election of January 1910 not only reduced the party's representation to 40, but underscored its dependence on the Liberals. The second general election of 1910, in December, changed nothing. Labour representation increased by two, but by-elections had reduced it to 37 by the outbreak of war.

The Labour party's leadership was from the start regarded with suspicion by confirmed Liberal and Conservative unionists. Before long it faced even more vociferous criticism from the left wing of the unions. By 1910 the attack had acquired doctrinal depth from syndicalist notions associated with the Industrial Workers of the World in America, and imported into England largely *via* Australia and Tom Mann. The syndicalist charge that parliamentary politics was futile and corrupting caught the tide of rising disillusion with the Labour party's performance. The Osborne judgement of 1909, cutting at union political expenditures, added fuel to the fire. Above all, the policies of the Liberal government, welcome though they often were, did not directly touch the critical problem of falling real wages in a period of fairly sustained economic prosperity.

For many unionists preoccupied with the wage problem, the syndicalist emphasis on massive use of the strike weapon had its appeal. That appeal was enhanced by early indications that government itself could be brought on to the union side by major strike threats. During the railway crisis of 1907, Lloyd

George told the companies that they 'must give way' because 'there must not be a strike on any account';[28] and his public actions had spoken as loudly as his private words. The following year Herbert Samuel, speaking for the government, publicly stated that the eight-hour day for coal miners was essential because otherwise 'it means a coal strike'.[29]

Industrially, 1908 was the most disturbed year for a decade. But it and 1909 were only the stormy prelude to one of the most turbulent periods in British industrial history, which began in the summer of 1910. Of 1911–13, the *Board of Trade Labour Gazette* commented, 'there has never before been a series of three consecutive years marked as a whole by such widespread industrial unrest'—and, significantly, in 'the great majority of cases the workers were at least partially successful in obtaining their demands' on wage issues.[30]

What was demonstrated during these years, to the satisfaction of many unionists, was not merely the efficacy of the strike weapon. There was also the apparent fact that the bigger a strike, the surer it was of success, especially if it involved a key industry. Thus the TUC leadership's conclusion that the coal miners' strike of 1912 provided 'a most striking object-lesson as to the strength which organized labour can command'.[31] Crucial to this conclusion was the assumption that if a strike was serious enough, government could be forced to intervene and impose a settlement favourable to the unions. That lesson was drawn not only from the miners' dispute, but also from the railway and transport strikes of 1911; and, as we have seen, there were earlier supporting examples as well.

It was in this form that the syndicalist thesis of large-scale industrial action, as a political weapon, was received into the conventional wisdom of British trade unionism. The associated emphasis on closer union organization was furthered by the formation of the National Transport Workers' Federation in 1910, by the amalgamations producing the National Union of Railwaymen in 1913, and by the grand plan, drawn up the next year, for a Triple Industrial Alliance uniting these two

[28] Quoted in George, op. cit., p. 212.
[29] Quoted in Halevy, op. cit., p. 241.
[30] Quoted in M. B. Hammond, *British Labor Conditions and Legislation During the War*, p. 30.
[31] *TUC Report*, 1912, p. 65.

organizations with the Miners' Federation. The mainspring of these developments was the belief that an accession of industrial strength was involved. In the case of the Triple Industrial Alliance, for example, it was thought that the combined strength of its constituents would carry such weight that 'in practice the need for collective strikes would rarely or never arise' because the mere *threat* of a concerted strike by the alliance would be enough to bring in government, 'more or less as a protagonist of labour', when employers proved intransigent.[32]

However, despite this emphasis on industrial action, most union leaders were far from accepting the syndicalist view that strikes were the *only* worthwhile form of union action. After a long debate on the merits of the syndicalist thesis, the 1912 Congress overwhelmingly affirmed its 'continued support of independent working-class political action'.[33]

In the meantime, union leaders had by no means neglected parliamentary activity. Union-sponsored private members' bills were introduced in each parliamentary session of the period: the TUC alone was responsible for as many as twenty in 1912. Increasingly, they were entrusted to Labour parliamentarians, rather than Liberals. A similar tendency was evident in cases where unions sought parliamentary expression of their views on other bills, or wished to lobby across party lines. At the same time, there seems to have been a pronounced decline, at least among the TUC leaders, in the emphasis placed on parliamentary action as against direct dealings with government. This was reflected in the attention given ministerial deputations in the TUC's annual reports which, as we have seen, had traditionally accorded parliamentary activities much greater prominence. The report for 1906 was the first in which accounts of deputations were predominant, an emphasis that was maintained throughout the period. By 1914 the report, while dealing with deputations at considerable length, barely mentioned parliamentary activities.

The accessibility of ministers, their readiness to make concessions, and the lacklustre performance of the parliamentary

---

[32] G. A. Phillips, 'The Triple Industrial Alliance in 1914', *Economic History Review*, 2nd series, vol. XXIV, no. 1, 1971, p. 65.
[33] *TUC Report*, 1912, p. 279.

Labour party, all help explain why the shift in emphasis should have occurred about this time. In addition, there was the widening gap between constitutional theory and practice relating to the respective roles of parliament and government. Closer cabinet control of parliament was reflected, procedurally, in more frequent and tougher use of the closure and the guillotine. The expanding volume of government business progressively limited opportunities for other business, despite moves to lengthen the House of Commons' working hours and institute the beginnings of the present standing committee system. By 1910 the government was taking up 'most of the time . . . allotted to private Members'.[34]

The Liberal government's legislative vigour had two other related features. Its new departures in domestic policy impinged on a wide variety of interest groups. Ministers, for the most part, preferred to settle their differences with such groups by direct negotiation, rather than following the traditional practice of leaving the articulation and accommodation of group views largely to the parliamentary arena. The consequence was that parliament, given tighter party discipline, tended to do little more than register agreements so reached. Secondly, the government's incursions into novel and complex areas of social policy raised considerations (flexibility, technical difficulty and economy of parliamentary time) held to require parliamentary delegation of regulation-making powers. The practice, as we have seen, was far from new, but it 'takes on something of its modern scope with the social legislation of the Liberal Government 1906–14'.[35] The technical and other complexities of the new legislative ventures, as well as delegated legislative powers, thrust not only ministers but also civil servants into weightier policy-making roles. The formulation, and sometimes even the inspiration, of measures directly concerning the trade unions owed as much to Llewellyn Smith, Beveridge, Aves, Morant and Braithwaite as to their more famous ministerial superiors; and, in a field which formal legislation barely touched, the name of Askwith is inseparable from such coherent policy as the government could boast on industrial disputes.

[34] *The Labour Year Book*, 1916, p. 327.
[35] Smellie, op. cit., p. 173.

Politically perceptive trade union leaders reacted accordingly. They were well aware, for example, that parliament's enactment of the Labour Exchanges Act in 1909 had not settled matters: 'the success or failure of the Exchanges will depend absolutely upon the manner in which the regulations . . . are framed'.[36] In other words, they saw success or failure as depending on decisions still to be made by a minister and his civil servants. And being concerned above all with success or failure, they were infinitely more interested in those who made effective decisions than in those whom ancient constitutional theory assumed ought to make them.

This focus on the executive side of the governmental structure suited them for reasons of personal prestige as well. Their self-esteem had been titillated at the outset of the Liberal revival when Campbell-Bannerman included John Burns in his first cabinet; and the TUC leaders celebrated 'the appointment, for the first time in the history of this country, of a representative of Labour to Cabinet rank'.[37] The later expansion in their direct dealings with government, and particularly the extent to which ministers initiated consultation, similarly provided them with 'a source of considerable satisfaction'.[38] For such dealings emphasized their own role, whereas parliamentary action emphasized that of Labour MPs. There was, too, the scale on which union officials and members were admitted to the civil service, the topic on which W. J. Davis dwelt most lovingly in his address to a German trade union conference in 1914: 'it has removed the stigma that all lucrative offices were perquisites for rich men and their friends'.[39] These developments could scarcely have failed to boost the self-confidence of union leaders, and encourage them to treat ministers and civil servants with more assurance than in the past. It was not only the syndicalists who could now conceive of the trade unions approaching government as something more than suppliants.

TRADES UNION CONGRESS

The TUC was initially strengthened by its involvement in the developing relations between trade unions and government

---

[36] *TUC Report*, 1909, p. 55.
[38] ibid., 1909, p. 55.

[37] ibid., 1906, p. 52.
[39] ibid., 1915, pp. 197–8.

during the period. But, throughout, its position was under challenge from the Labour party; and towards the end of the period, it began to look as though the party was destined to triumph.

The TUC shared in the electoral success of 1906. Of the 51 candidates it officially endorsed, 31 were elected[40]—two more than the successful endorsements of the LRC. Eight of the Parliamentary Committee's thirteen members gained seats, and another won a by-election later in the year. MPs remained in a majority on it until 1910. Although only three of them initially declined to accept the parliamentary Labour party whip, 'all were Lib-Labs in spirit',[41] sharing both a suspicion of the party's Socialist element and a strong sense of their own autonomy as trade union leaders. One of them was of singular importance.

David Shackleton began a remarkable career as a 'half-timer' in a weaving shed at the age of nine. He became secretary of the Darwen Weavers' Association 22 years later, in 1894, and in 1902 won a Lancashire parliamentary seat. A year later he was a member of the LRC's executive, and in 1905 its chairman. In 1904 he was elected to the TUC Parliamentary Committee, became its chairman in 1907 and was re-elected the following year. In the meantime, after Keir Hardie defeated him by one vote for the chairmanship of the parliamentary Labour party in 1906, he was elected deputy chairman, and later acted as chairman when Hardie fell ill. He was generally expected to succeed Hardie in 1908, but declined nomination, leaving the field to Arthur Henderson. Shackleton nevertheless continued to play a leading role in the parliamentary party, and a dominating one in the TUC, until late in 1910 when he left Westminster and the labour movement for Whitehall—and, eventually, a permanent secretaryship.

Shackleton's record is unique. His nearest counterparts, Arthur Henderson and Ernest Bevin, do not match him in terms of formal position, though it is arguable that their influence was as great in their heyday. Essentially Lib-Lab in outlook, Shackleton identified primarily with the TUC rather than the Labour party with its heavier Socialist lacing: he refused to nominate for the party leadership in 1908 because of

[40] *PC Mins.*, 31 January 1906.   [41] Clegg *et al.*, op. cit., p. 392.

difficulties with the Socialist wing. This commitment, given his personal standing, seems to have been a major factor in the competitive struggle which broke out in earnest between the TUC and the party once the 1906 general election was over. The party began to make significant gains at the TUC's expense only after his departure.

The Challenge of the Labour Party

Party spokesmen were not reluctant to acknowledge the TUC as its progenitor. However, when Henderson brought the greetings of its 'youngest and most innocent and most *independent* child' to the 1907 Congress,[42] he was also asserting the autonomy of the party. The party's annual conference of 1908 made the same point more bluntly when it determined that members of the Parliamentary Committee were ineligible for election to the Labour party executive. But autonomy was merely the minimum claim. Henderson later made this clear when he asserted that 'the legislative and administrative work of the Labour Party would be to give effect to the resolutions of the Congress'.[43] His audience was well aware of the implication of this remark. It was that the TUC's *raison d'être* had substantially disappeared with the Labour party's emergence as the labour movement's specialized political organ, and with the creation of the General Federation of Trade Unions as its specialized industrial organ. The Congress Henderson addressed was asked to accept the logical consequence of this proposition in the form of a resolution instructing the TUC leadership to discuss with the party and the GFTU the question of amalgamation. The motion's seconder went straight to the point: 'the time was ripe for the dissolution of the Congress'.[44] Congress itself disagreed—on this occasion by a substantial majority, but only narrowly (by 779,000 card votes to 750,000) two years later in 1910.

Short of the ultimate solution, some form of amalgamation, those who sided with Henderson pinned their hopes on the ostensibly more modest solution of firmly demarcated spheres of action. The problem with which they were concerned, 'overlapping' as it came to be called, was to prove endemic to

---

[42] *TUC Report*, 1907, p. 177. Italics added.
[43] ibid., 1908, p. 161.   [44] ibid., p. 153.

the TUC's relationship with the party. But it was never more controversial as an issue than during these years when the Labour party's ambitions were essentially those of a pressure group rather than those of a party intent on office.

One approach to the problem of overlapping was in terms of the type of policy topics appropriate to each body. This, for the party's spokesmen, yielded the conclusion that the TUC should confine itself to 'industrial' matters, leaving 'political' issues to the party. Early in 1907 they moved to achieve this aim by asking the Joint Board to try 'to systematize the agendas' of conferences of the TUC, the GFTU and the party, 'with a view to preventing overlapping and possible confusion of decisions'.[45] The TUC leaders concurred with the board's decision to form a committee on the matter, and referred to it the proposed agenda of the next Congress. But they were less compliant when the party requested the deletion from the agenda of items dealing with such things as education, housing, land law, municipal trading, factory inspectors and nationalization of natural resources. The request was rejected *in toto* on the ground that none of the items was 'outside the scope of [the TUC's] usual work'.[46]

The party persisted. It prompted the Joint Board to set up another investigating committee, which again failed to function. The party's executive then proposed a joint meeting with the Parliamentary Committee. This was delayed until the end of 1907, after Shackleton had seized the opportunity provided by a Congress speaker (opposing a resolution on the House of Lords) to assert publicly that 'this movement of ours embraces reforms applying to the whole community'.[47] He was no less uncompromising in the privacy of the joint meeting. He and his TUC colleagues, he said, would have no truck with 'any proposition limiting their power to put on the Congress Agenda any resolution sent in by affiliated societies'.[48]

The party leaders tried another tack. They succeeded, with the TUC's agreement, in having the Joint Board's constitution amended to enable it to 'consider and decide' disputes on matters about which there was 'some doubt or difference . . .

[45] *PC Mins.*, 5 March 1907.   [46] ibid., 16 May 1907.
[47] *TUC Report*, 1907, p. 160.   [48] *PC Mins.*, 19 December 1907.

as to which body they properly belong'.[49] But their victory was wholly symbolic. The Congress that was informed of the changes in the Joint Board's constitution was also told that it 'would not be wise' to limit the TUC's control of its own agenda, and that the TUC retained the right to handle 'any question of public importance'.[50]

But the overlapping controversy was not only about the allocation of policy topics. It was, above all, a dispute about the use of particular methods of action on behalf of the trade unions. It centred on competing claims to the role of principal union spokesman in parliament and in direct dealings with government.

Who Acts in Parliament?

It was the Labour party's function, Henderson affirmed at the 1906 Congress, 'to give legislative expression to the needs of Congress on the floor of the House of Commons'.[51] He spoke at a time when the TUC's leaders were deeply involved in parliamentary manoeuvres. They had re-introduced their own anti-Taff Vale bill, in response to rumours of inadequacies in the government's forthcoming Trade Disputes Bill. They had consulted their old ally, Charles Dilke, lobbied other Liberals and convened a meeting of Labour and Lib-Lab MPs. Dilke shared the role of main TUC spokesman with Shackleton during the committee stage of the government bill. Within days of Henderson's Congress speech, the TUC leaders decided on another meeting with Labour and Lib-Lab MPs, but diplomatically invited the Labour and Lib-Lab whips 'to sign the notice' of meeting.[52] Later, however, these formal niceties were brushed aside when they convened a similar meeting on housing and old age pensions. The party executive promptly complained that the invitations had been issued 'in the name of the Parliamentary Committee only'.[53] Not long afterwards, as we have seen, it made its request for deletions from the next Congress agenda—its long list including four items on wage issues, because they involved proposals of parliamentary action, and one on old age pensions from which the executive wanted

---

[49] *TUC Report*, 1908, p. 122.
[51] ibid., 1906, p. 144.
[53] ibid., 11 February 1907.

[50] ibid., pp. 85, 153.
[52] *PC Mins.*, 8 September 1906.

the following words excised: 'and trusts that the P.C. will take every opportunity of pressing this scheme's acceptance on Parliament'.[54]

The point of these exchanges surfaced briefly at the 1907 Congress. A delegate protested that the TUC's annual report incorrectly gave the impression that the Trade Disputes Act and the Workers' Compensation Act stood to the credit of the TUC rather than the Labour party. That, the Congress chairman replied, was 'quite a matter of opinion'; but tactfully suggested that 'the result is due to all the forces acting together'.[55] Henderson's tone was less generous, though still diplomatic: he thought the report reflected the party's 'splendid work'.[56] But it was Shackleton, addressing the party's conference some time later, who displayed the surer grasp of diplomatic acidity when he thanked 'the Labour Party most heartily for the support it had given the Parliamentary Committee in their work in Parliament'.[57]

The virtual collapse of the Lib-Lab trade union group, early in 1909, deprived the TUC leadership of a useful parliamentary counter to the Labour party. But two of its MP-members, including the secretary, stood firm against accepting the Labour whip. And it continued to deny the party's claim to exclusive control of parliamentary action. Hence the complaint of the parliamentary party's chairman, in mid-1909, that the TUC leaders had been 'both unfair and unwise' in proposing amendments to the Labour Exchanges Bill without his knowledge.[58] By this time, however, the focus of union attention had shifted decisively away from parliament to cabinet ministers and their departments.

Who Deals with Government?

Part of Shackleton's justification for rejecting the Labour party's proposal to cull the 1907 Congress agenda was that the TUC had a distinctive character and role. 'The Labour party', he told the party executive, 'is naturally antagonistic to every Government: the Parliamentary Committee are in a somewhat different position', and accordingly had to retain

[54] ibid., 16 May 1907.   [55] *TUC Report*, 1907, p. 137.
[56] ibid., p. 177.   [57] ibid., 1908, p. 114.
[58] *PC Mins.*, 11 July 1909.

the 'right to approach Ministers'.[59] His view, as elaborated in the committee's report to the 1908 Congress, was that the TUC could therefore 'approach with greater freedom, and, from some points of view, greater influence, the various Ministers of State, in order to call attention to the wishes of the Trade Unions'.[60]

Shackleton's claim to independence was asserted in practice. The TUC and the party had cooperated in two Joint Board deputations in 1906, and had made a joint submission to the Royal Commission on the Poor Law in 1907. But otherwise the TUC had acted on its own in arranging deputations to ministers and senior civil servants, and in submitting evidence to a variety of departmental committees. The party executive did not openly question this practice until 1909, although there is the hint of a challenge in its earlier claim that the party had shown its value not only by 'its shop-window work', in parliament, but also by 'interviewing Ministers'.[61]

The attack was launched at a meeting of the Joint Board's constituent executives in July 1909, after the TUC had twice seen Winston Churchill, at his invitation, about the Labour Exchanges Bill. Henderson protested that 'the policy of the movement' on the bill should first have been decided by the Joint Board. Shackleton replied that the party itself 'was frequently compelled to act without consultation'. Henderson then proposed that the board should 'consider how far separate action . . . can be avoided' in such cases. Shackleton retorted that 'if the resolution meant that the Parliamentary Committee had got to consult the Labour Party before taking any action they were not going to do it'.[62] He was presumably assured that Henderson's motion did not mean this, because it was carried unanimously. It was then agreed that the Joint Board should handle future dealings on the labour exchanges. Shackleton arranged talks between Board of Trade officials and the Joint Board, which was also involved in later discussions with Churchill.

The July agreement, however, neither typified relations between the TUC and its Joint Board partners, nor established

[59] ibid., 19 December 1907.
[60] *TUC Report*, 1908, p. 85.
[61] Eighth Annual Labour Party Conference, *Report of the Labour Party Executive for 1907*, p. 38.
[62] *PC Mins.*, 11 July 1909.

a pattern for dealings with government on other matters. A more accurate indication of those relations was provided shortly afterwards by the Parliamentary Committee's response to a Joint Board request for help in organizing a public meeting on old age pensions: the TUC leadership decided instead to arrange a public meeting of its own on the same subject, adding loftily that 'should the Joint Board decide to cooperate . . . the Committee will welcome such cooperation'.[63] A few weeks later, in similar vein, there was the calculated contempt with which Shackleton brushed aside objections to discussions between the TUC and Churchill about unemployment insurance. In response to Henderson's complaint that the TUC had acted without informing the Joint Board, Shackleton blandly replied that 'he had no authority to place any information before the Joint Board'.[64] And he calmly repeated this statement, almost word for word, when Keir Hardie heatedly reiterated Henderson's complaint. Shortly afterwards, the Joint Board finally got round to discussing the July resolution about avoiding 'separate action'. It ended by shelving the matter.

There was some sympathy on the Parliamentary Committee for the party's disquiet. Some time later the committee resolved that, in the case of future legislation, 'all necessary information as to the negotiations will be willingly communicated by the Committee'. Nevertheless, the same resolution not only re-affirmed the TUC's determination to negotiate with the Board of Trade at its own discretion, but also justified the Joint Board's exclusion on the ground that 'the Board of Trade are unwilling to deal with the Joint Board [because it] has affiliated with it an independent and possibly opposing political party'.[65]

The argument for the importance of the TUC's independence in this respect was given its most coherent public expression by Shackleton at the last Congress he attended as a trade union official.

In the course of our negotiations with the Government from time to time . . . the advantage has been manifested of having a Trade Union body as

[63] ibid., 30 August 1909.   [64] ibid., 6 October 1909.
[65] ibid., 23 February 1910.

distinct from a political body. Our feeling is that if there is not that distinctive Trade Union element we shall always be in the position of fighting
the Government of the day; and we are desirous of being able to continue
our negotiations with any Government, apart from the fight that goes on
in the country between the three parties.[66]

The Party Gains Ground

Shackleton's departure from the TUC, at the end of 1910, was
a watershed. He left a gap which none of his Parliamentary
Committee colleagues had the talent and force of character to
fill in quite the same way. The committee had also lost Richard
Bell to Whitehall, a year earlier, and was soon to lose, through
death, its secretary, W. C. Steadman—both of them dogged
Lib-Labs who, as MPs, had refused the Labour party whip.
These losses weakened the element in the TUC's leadership
most strongly committed to an independent role.

The observer, writing on the eve of the war, who thought
that 'despite the advent of the Labour Party, the Parliamentary
Committee of the Congress steadily refuses to abandon *any* of
its political activities', was wrong.[67] Even before Shackleton's
departure, the committee appears to have ceased endorsing
by-election candidates (it had, for example, endorsed five
during 1907); and there is no indication in its reports or
minutes that it granted any endorsements in either the January
or the December general elections of 1910, although in the
second case its acting-secretary was authorized to do so. More
important, despite its earlier insistence on the point, the TUC
leadership had by 1914 abandoned all but a minor part of its
former parliamentary activities. In particular, its traditional
lobbying function was reduced to a minimal level after 1910.
Thus, it still maintained a list of private members' bills, but no
longer looked beyond Labour MPs for sponsors. Similarly, it
still fed questions into parliament, but mainly through its new
secretary, C. W. Bowerman; and he, unlike his predecessor,
was a member of the parliamentary Labour party.

It is noteworthy, too, though less surprising, that the TUC
leaders also conceded a major role to the Labour party in
relation to industrial and inter-union disputes. Traditionally,
as we have seen, they preferred to steer clear of industrial

[66] *TUC Report*, 1910, p. 121.
[67] C. M. Lloyd, *Trade Unionism*, p. 201. Italics added.

disputes, apart from occasional appeals for financial help. They were more active in the case of inter-union disputes, but still found it difficult to enforce decisions. Even before Shackleton's departure, they did not oppose the party's involvement in either type of dispute through the medium of the Joint Board. The board had intervened in a Clydeside stoppage in 1906 and in an inter-union dispute in 1907, although its constitution did not authorize such action until 1908. In the same year it played a major role in negotiations arising from a shipbuilding lockout on the north-east coast. The board, as such, does not seem to have been directly involved in the great strike wave of 1910–12; but Labour party representatives played a leading part after 1910. Thus, while TUC leaders also participated in discussions on the eve of the 1911 railway strike, they left the later negotiations to Henderson and Ramsay MacDonald. Nor did they object to the party leaders' much closer involvement in the coal mining and Port of London stoppages the following year.

The Dublin transport strike of 1913 provided the one exception. Congress, stirred by reports of police brutality, directed the Parliamentary Committee to intervene. The committee collected funds and organized food supplies, as well as trying to settle the strike. For some time it obstructed the party executive's suggestion that the Joint Board be brought in, but eventually agreed to the appointment of a board delegation (three TUC members, two party members and one GFTU member) which remained in charge until settlement negotiations broke down. The following year, the Joint Board convened a national union conference on the London building trades dispute: there was no opposition from the TUC.

In the case of inter-union disputes, the TUC leaders had protested in 1911 when the Joint Board decided to hear one dispute they claimed for their own. But it was their lack of reaction three years later, when Henderson stepped in to settle a dispute originally submitted to the TUC, which was more typical.

It was not only the TUC that accepted Joint Board and Labour party involvement in industrial and inter-union disputes. So did the GFTU, even though industrial disputes were one of its principal constitutional concerns. Its leaders appear to have been more than willing to share this responsibility after they had burnt their fingers in the cotton industry lockout of 1908.

Holding the Line

The GFTU was also the loser in the case of the one expansion that occurred in the TUC's functions before the war. Apart from the annual exchange of fraternal delegates between the TUC and the American Federation of Labour, the GFTU had monopolized international activities. The TUC moved into the field in 1913 when its delegates were accepted, alongside the GFTU's, at the inaugural conference of the International Federation of Trade Unions. Nor did the TUC encounter any problems when it subsequently invited the union centres of Canada, France and Germany to send fraternal delegates to Congress. This development, although involving a function of marginal significance in itself, had a prestige-value of some importance at a time when the TUC's *raison d'être* was more widely questioned than ever before.

The party leaders moved in again soon after Shackleton's departure. At a meeting of the three executives, held on their instigation, they revived a 1906 Congress proposal (eventually killed by the Parliamentary Committee) that the offices of the TUC, the GFTU and the party should be located in the same building to facilitate 'consultation'.[68] They also urged the immediate merging of the three annual conferences. The TUC and GFTU executives preferred to refer both mátters to the Joint Board, which was asked to report back: there is no record that it ever did. Later, the TUC leadership pursued a policy of masterly inactivity in relation to a 1911 Congress instruction that it combine with the party executive to establish a 'central body'.[69] The next Congress rejected an identical resolution.

The party leaders then narrowed their attack on the overlapping problem. Henderson, admitted to a Parliamentary Committee meeting, suggested that the party should confine itself to 'urgent political questions', and leave 'industrial matters' to the TUC. Davis, the chairman and an old Lib-Lab, pointedly commented that it was often difficult to distinguish

[68] *PC Mins.*, 25–6 April 1911.   [69] *TUC Report*, 1911, p. 257.

between political and industrial questions. Bowerman, the secretary, argued more aggressively that the party had taken over matters formerly dealt with by the TUC. His minutes record that others present supported his charge that 'the Labour Party should "put its own house in order", the Congress never having deviated from its recognised procedure'.[70]

In the meantime, the friction over direct dealings with government continued. The day before the three executives discussed the party's proposal for a merger of their annual conferences, the TUC leadership considered a letter from Ramsay MacDonald, newly-elected chairman of the parliamentary Labour party. He complained that he had been left in the dark about a series of discussions on health insurance between TUC and government representatives. His complaint was brushed aside. On the same day, however, the TUC leaders decided to make a protest of their own against the Joint Board's recent appointment of W. A. Appleton, GFTU secretary, to act as trade union advisor on health insurance to the Chancellor of the Exchequer. The TUC's board representatives had agreed to Appleton's nomination because they had understood that the minister did not want a parliamentarian, this ruling out the TUC secretary (the TUC chairman was ineligible because he lived outside London). The board declined to rescind the decision, even though 'it was eventually admitted that a statement had been made at the previous meeting' that the minister preferred a non-MP; and the implication of deception was spelt out when the TUC leaders reiterated their protest, insisting that their representatives had 'agreed to the nomination of [Appleton] under a misapprehension'.[71]

Predictably, in the shadow of this shabby episode, union officials closely aligned with the party were later to express their displeasure at 'the lack of united action on the part of the National Committees' in negotiations relating to the National Insurance Act.[72] Predictably also, the TUC leaders smartly resurrected Shackleton's argument when the party executive asked if it might join a deputation to the Prime Minister about a royal commission on industrial insurance: they turned down

[70] *PC Mins.*, 18 June 1913.   [71] ibid., 24–6 April 1911.
[72] ibid., 8 October 1912.

the request, pleading 'the difficulty of arranging such a joint deputation . . . in view of the fact that the Parliamentary Committee stand on neutral ground politically'.[73]

There were, however, occasions and issues on which the Parliamentary Committee was prepared to share the deputizing function. Thus it joined with the party and GFTU executives in three deputations to the Prime Minister on the issue of legalizing union political expenditures; and it acceded to the Joint Board's submission of proposed legislation on union amalgamations to the Prime Minister. But the committee continued to cling to the principle that, at least on matters raised by Congress resolutions, it was exclusively responsible for transmitting them to government.

MacDonald, in the guise of fraternal delegate, poured scorn on the ministerial deputation as a method of action. 'Can you afford year by year . . . just to pass resolutions and send them up to Whitehall? No. You have to get the men standing in the House of Commons and making speeches in the House of Commons.'[74] Some members of the Parliamentary Committee agreed. Most, however, preferred to identify themselves with the view expressed by their colleague, W. Mullin, who claimed that ministerial deputations, 'these practical talks' as he called them, were the means by which 'every new measure affecting the working classes, before it reaches the House of Commons, is influenced and moulded'.[75] But the importance of the deputation technique was not merely a matter of its questionable effect (*pace* Mullin) on government policy. It was also a matter of the TUC's survival. A. G. Walkden, not then a member of the Parliamentary Committee, put his finger unerringly on the point:

The only purpose of this Congress is to get together once a year to formulate our demands as representatives of organized labour and to seek interviews with the heads of the Government Departments in support of those demands. If we did not have that procedure there need not be any Congress at all; the work could be done by the Labour Party.[76]

The TUC's insistence on its right to deal independently with government was thus the crucial element in a defensive strategy. By making so much of ministerial deputations in their

[73] ibid., 20 November 1912.   [74] *TUC Report*, 1912, p. 213.
[75] ibid., 1911, p. 49.   [76] ibid., 1913, p. 173.

reports of these years, the TUC's leaders were highlighting the one political function of substance that they still commanded. The problem, after 1911, was that this function mattered less to both unions and government.

Internal Authority

The TUC's affiliated membership passed two million in 1912. The Parliamentary Committee, its representation broadened in 1906 by an increase in size from twelve to sixteen (excluding the secretary), handled an expanding volume of business during the period. Monthly meetings, occupying two or more days, became the rule. In 1913 it moved into the field of international trade union representation, without serious opposition. Throughout, the committee played a major role in direct dealings between its affiliates and government.

Congress resolutions concerning government policy were almost invariably transmitted by way of ministerial deputations, consisting wholly or largely of Parliamentary Committee members. There were one or two old-style mass deputations (the Home Secretary was confronted by a sixty-member one in 1910). But the standard pattern, in the case of Congress resolutions, was a deputation consisting of all the committee's members and up to a half-dozen or so union representatives. Frequently, the committee members were unaccompanied. This was normally so when, as often happened, the TUC dealt with ministers on matters other than those raised directly by way of Congress resolutions. The committee also took full responsibility for submissions to a number of royal commissions and departmental committees of inquiry.

On matters of sectional concern that were not the subject of Congress resolutions, deputations arranged by individual unions were commonly introduced to ministers by TUC leaders who sometimes took part in ensuing negotiations. On occasion they made the arrangements for union deputations to be received. More often, they acted on behalf of particular unions, a service which they provided with particular frequency at the request of unions encountering difficulties with employers holding contracts from the Admiralty, the War Office, the Post Office and the India Office.

These are all symptoms of liveliness and indications of authority. But, particularly towards the end of the period, they were overshadowed by other features which shed a quite different light on the TUC's internal authority.

In the first place, there was the mounting interest of many trade union leaders in the potential of large-scale industrial action. The TUC was almost wholly irrelevant to this interest. Even when major stoppages involved both affiliated unions and negotiations with ministers, it played an altogether negligible part. Its role was more significant, as we have seen, in the case of the Dublin transport strike of 1913, involving a non-affiliated union; but even then, it eventually preferred to share responsibility with the other constituents of the Joint Board. Pointedly, when the London Trades Council sought support during the building trades dispute the following year, it turned to the Joint Board rather than to the TUC. Again, in a related area, although the TUC was constitutionally concerned with promoting union amalgamations, it had no hand in the most significant developments of the time—the formation of the National Union of Railwaymen, the Transport Workers' Federation and the Triple Industrial Alliance.

In the second place, the Labour party leaders had not only managed to ease the TUC largely out of the area of parliamentary activities by this time; they had also established a stronger claim to an intervening role in industrial and inter-union disputes, both independently and through the Joint Board. Moreover, with Shackleton's departure from the TUC and the almost simultaneous election of MacDonald to the party's parliamentary chairmanship, the TUC lost an irreplaceable personal drawcard while the Labour party gained a leader with an unusual capacity for converting unbelievers and attracting disciples.

In the third place, the TUC's principal function of dealing with government lost its importance in the eyes of many union leaders once the Liberals' zest for reform flagged. For the TUC was then concerned either with administrative issues of peripheral significance to many unions or, in the case of larger issues, with matters that increasingly seemed likely to be more effectively promoted through either the Joint Board or the Labour party alone. It was, for example, the party which was credited (rightly, it appears) with the passage of the Trade Union Act of 1913 which remedied the Osborne judgement's prohibition of union expenditure for political purposes.

This combination of factors fostered a conception of the TUC as the sick man of the labour movement. What was seen to be at stake was not merely the disposal of the one major function the TUC clung to, direct dealings with government. Rather, the question for many was whether there was any point in the continuation of the TUC itself. As early as 1907 the leaders of the Amalgamated Society of Engineers gained their members' approval for a second disaffiliation from the TUC with the argument that 'the old-time functions of the Congress have become obsolete'.[77] Four years later the Amalgamated Society of Carpenters and Joiners also disaffiliated—as one of its officials had predicted it would, 'now the Labour Party was established'.[78] Keir Hardie turned these and other defections to account when he urged closer cooperation with the party (he meant subordination to it) on the TUC leaders: 'Was not the fact that societies had seceded from the Congress a warning that something should be done in order to prevent the Congress from "fissling out"?'[79] Others were more candid; they demanded, not cooperation, but abnegation.

There are at present three bodies professing to coordinate the Labour Movement. The Labour Party is purely political: the General Federation [GFTU] purely industrial. The Trades Union Congress is a highly academic body—a debating society rather than a legislative assembly. Its Parliamentary Committee [was] formed mainly to carry on the work that is now done by the Labour Party . . . The existence of such an ill-defined body is a source of weakness to the Labour Movement, and the Parliamentary Committee must hand over its work and powers to other bodies more fitted to the task.[80]

The TUC stalwart, Davis, might seek to divert such attacks, and lay claim to a distinctive role, by describing the TUC as only 'semi-political' in its concerns.[81] It was a desperate defence. The TUC had not only been dislodged from the

[77] Quoted in Clegg *et al.*, op. cit., p. 408n.
[78] *TUC Report*, 1910, p. 119.   [79] *PC Mins.*, 25 April 1911.
[80] G. D. H. Cole and W. Mellor, *The Greater Unionism*, p. 18.
[81] *TUC Report*, 1913, p. 56.

unique position it had once occupied among the trade unions, but its proponents had to justify its very existence.

On the eve of war, two minor incidents confirmed the threat to the TUC. The Dockers' Union, a TUC affiliate, wanted financial help for a legal appeal to the House of Lords; it turned to the Joint Board. The National Association of Local Government Officers, affiliated to none of the Joint Board's constituents, wanted to know whether 'workmen' as well as 'officials' should be included in its proposal for a superannuation scheme; it also turned to the board rather than the TUC.

The threat came, above all, from the Labour party. The GFTU was on the point of being pushed into the wings as a result of weak leadership, declining membership and the hostility of powerful elements in the trade union movement. The party's challenge was to become even more potent once war came.

External Authority

Government recognition of the TUC reached unprecedented heights in the pre-war period. Campbell-Bannerman set the pattern within days of becoming Prime Minister in December 1905. He wanted a trade unionist for the Conservative-created Royal Commission on the Poor Law, and he turned to the TUC for a nominee. Subsequently, although there were one or two instances of overborne ministerial reluctance, only once was the TUC flatly rebuffed in relation to a wholly trade unionist deputation—and that a marginal case, where it had asked the minister to see officials of a small mining union with whom he had already had some contact.

But it was not simply a matter of the TUC leaders being given access to ministers when and how they wanted it. Even more significant, as an indication of external authority, was the extent to which government initiated consultation with them, and dealt exclusively with them so far as representation of the labour interest was concerned. Equally relevant, were the occasions on which TUC-government dealings clearly involved a serious bargaining element.

Sometimes the TUC was conceded the status of sole union spokesman in dealings which might well have included the Joint Board or either of its other two constituents, the Labour party and the GFTU. Thus when Lloyd George wanted to discuss the implications of the 1910 Finance Act for working-class home-ownership, he invited the TUC to talks with himself, the Cooperative Union and the building societies. Earlier, in 1908, he and Churchill had invited Henderson and Sidney Webb to their initial discussion with the TUC leaders about labour exchanges. But only the TUC was represented on the government-sponsored team which then investigated German labour exchanges and health insurance. Thereafter, Churchill confined negotiations on the labour exchanges to the TUC leaders until they succumbed to party and GFTU pressure by agreeing to work through the Joint Board—although the one labour representative Churchill later appointed to the committee selecting most labour exchange staff was the TUC chairman. Again, he and his successor in office appear to have dealt only with the TUC, on the labour side, when they were negotiating the more complex issue of unemployment insurance; and it was to the TUC alone that William Beveridge, the civil servant primarily concerned, submitted his draft scheme for comment.

In the case of health insurance, however, the TUC was not accorded so singular a role. It was consulted about the legislation and regulations, its advice was sought on administrative details and it was asked to nominate unionists to publicize the scheme. But Lloyd George also entered into intensive negotiations on this aspect of the National Insurance Bill with MacDonald and G. N. Barnes of the parliamentary Labour party. Moreover, both before and after the bill's enactment, he and his colleagues appear to have consulted the GFTU on an equal footing with the TUC, as well as a number of trade unions. Thus the TUC, the GFTU and some individual unions were all represented on the Advisory Committee associated with the English Insurance Commission; and they jointly nominated the union members of local Insurance Committees. Nevertheless, the TUC did play a major part in health insurance negotiations. And its role seems to have been enhanced once the Insurance Commission was formed to administer the scheme, probably because of Shackleton's appointment as the commissioner primarily concerned with the unions. In 1913, for example, the TUC secretary introduced to the insurance commissioners an invited deputation of nine members which included only one GFTU representative.

Government recognition of the TUC's intermediary role was even more emphatic in the less innovatory areas of safety in factories and enforcement of the Fair Wages Resolution. In the former case, soon after the Liberals took office, the Home Office undertook to use the TUC as its channel of communication about all proposals and inquiries concerning regulations. The TUC leadership indicated the importance it attached to this undertaking with its detailed description, in its annual report, of the procedures involved; by 1911 it was laconically listing the regulations issued 'after draft copies had been submitted through the Parliamentary Committee to the societies concerned'.[82] In the case of fair wages, the Admiralty and the War Office early agreed to supply the TUC regularly with detailed information about their contracts and contractors. Moreover, TUC authorization was required for individual unions to be given the details of new contracts and firms invited to tender, and objections had to be channelled through the TUC. The Post Office, the India Office and the Board of Works later entered into similar arrangements.

Industrial disputes were another matter, given the TUC's inclination to steer clear of them. The Dublin transport strike of 1913, which the Parliamentary Committee was propelled into by Congress, provided the occasion for the only direct approach from government in the case of a specific stoppage. Earlier, it is true, five TUC leaders were invited to discuss industrial unrest in general with Asquith and Buxton. All of them were appointed in 1911 to the short-lived Industrial Council, which the government created in the forlorn hope that it might promote the settlement of disputes; but the council also included three other union officials and five Labour MPs.

Despite its qualifications, the recognition which the Liberal government accorded the TUC signified an external authority which, for a time, was far greater than ever before. The competing claims of the Labour party, if anything, strengthened the TUC's hand. For Liberal ministers impressed with the need to negotiate with the unions, the predominantly Lib-Lab

[82] ibid., 1911, p. 136.

complexion of the TUC Parliamentary Committee made it a welcome alternative. This, at any rate, was substantially the story which, as we have seen, Shackleton and his colleagues put about. And on the government side, Churchill at least made no secret of his preference for dealing with the TUC rather than the Labour party.

Nevertheless, while the TUC's external authority reached a new pinnacle during this time, it had plainly declined by the end of the period. The TUC was effectively irrelevant to the government's concern with industrial peace, and Liberal leaders were no longer preoccupied with other domestic policy areas of the kind that had earlier inspired their interest in the TUC. Ministers continued to receive as many TUC deputations as before, and their departmental officers continued to consult it on administrative matters; but the drive had gone. It was not a matter of ministers or civil servants spurning the TUC. It was simply that they, ministers in particular, had lost interest in issues they thought of as falling within the scope of the TUC. After 1911, the TUC leaders received only one consultative invitation from a minister—and that from a junior minister who wanted them to talk with civil servants about accounting procedures in relation to the health insurance scheme. Wartime events were to confirm and intensify this decline in the TUC's external authority.

A Qualified Political Authority

'Gradually losing its old functions, and failing to find new ones, the Parliamentary Committee counted for less and less'.[83] There is much to be said for this assessment of the TUC's standing on the eve of the first world war. Of course, its role as an intermediary between unions and government still counted for something; it remained useful to both sides. Among the unions, although the Webbs might dismiss it as being 'rather a parade of the Trade Union forces than a genuine Parliament of Labour',[84] the annual Congress was still valued at least as a publicity platform—which was all that its founders had claimed for it nearly a half-century earlier. Membership of the Parliamentary Committee was still a mark of distinction to be

[83] G. D. H. Cole, *A Short History of the British Working Class Movement*, p. 412.
[84] Webb, *The History of Trade Unionism*, p. 564.

coveted. The committee was still a major organ of the labour movement; and its representation on the Joint Board was one symbol of that.

On the other hand, the Parliamentary Committee's membership of the Joint Board also symbolized the TUC's loss of the pre-eminence it had once possessed, when it stood alone at the head of the labour movement. And the scope of the board's concerns, not to mention those of the Labour party, underlined that loss. In addition, as England sank into war, the TUC's independent activities related to procedures and issues which were largely of lessening interest to both government and trade unions. The outbreak of war held out the possibility of arresting the decline in the TUC's political authority. But it was a false dawn.

6

The Pressures of War 1915–1918

THE exigencies of total war forced government into a relationship with the trade unions that was characterized by close
dealing and hard bargaining. The Labour party was able to
play a leading role in this. The TUC, on the other hand, was
virtually swept aside.

GOVERNMENT

The war Britain faced, as Lloyd George became fond of saying,
was 'an engineers' war' which had to be fought 'mainly in the
workshops of France and Great Britain'.[1] The dominating
domestic problem throughout the period was the supply and
utilization of industrial labour. Government leaders initially
hoped that major aspects of the problem could be resolved by
negotiation between unions and employers. Only when this
hope proved illusory did they move to develop a comprehensive
labour policy.

The main elements of such a policy were formulated by mid-
1915 in the first Munitions of War Act. The Minister of Munitions was empowered, in relation to undertakings engaged on
war production, to impose 'dilution' requirements ensuring
that skilled tradesmen were employed only on work beyond the
capacity of semi-skilled workers. A system of 'leaving certificates'
was introduced, to limit labour mobility in essential industries.
The diversion of workers from non-essential occupations was
authorized. Strikes and lockouts were prohibited in munitions
industries.

The Act's prohibition of strikes signalized the government's
aim of minimizing production hold-ups. It also indicated the
principal obstacle to an effective labour policy—worker opposition. Moreover, the magnitude of that obstacle was soon

[1] Quoted in Samuel J. Hurwitz, *State Intervention in Great Britain*, p. 261.

to be shown by the inability of the government to prevent strikes simply by declaring them illegal and making strikers liable to fines, imprisonment and 'deportation'. All these penalties were imposed in various cases; but, more often than not, they created greater industrial strife. The lesson was plain for government leaders who quickly came to the view that 'industrial unrest spelt a graver menace to our endurance and ultimate victory than even the military strength of Germany'.[2] Unable to coerce labour's compliance, they were obliged to adopt the more complex strategy of winning its cooperation.

The government's obsession with industrial peace thus enormously enhanced the bargaining position of the trade unions. They had made a free gift of their cooperation in the first flush of patriotic fervour: hence the sudden industrial truce of the war's first months. But by early in 1915, unionists were setting a price on their cooperation. This was signified by the breakdown of union-employer negotiations on traditional union restrictions, and by a serious unofficial strike of Clyde engineering workers. Government recognition of the need to conciliate unionists was symbolized in its convening of the first 'Treasury Conference' with union officials in March 1915. There were also substantial policy concessions which reflected the strength of the position into which wartime circumstances thrust the unions.

Lloyd George tried for full-scale industrial conscription in his negotiations with union leaders preceding the first Munitions of War Act; but he settled for very much less because he felt he could go no further than 'the labour leaders were prepared to go in submitting labour to the control of the State'.[3] Again, when he introduced the bill that became the Munitions of War (Amendment) Act of 1916, his remark that the 'whole of this Bill consists of concessions' was, in large measure, an accurate reflection of union influence.[4] To take a specific issue, the system of leaving certificates was modified and then, in 1917, finally abandoned in open response to industrial unrest; a move to re-introduce it in a limited form (the 'embargoes scheme') foundered as the result of a Coventry

[2] David Lloyd George, *War Memoirs*, vol. IV, pp. 1925–6.
[3] *History of the Ministry of Munitions* (hereafter *Hist. Muns.*), vol. II, part I, p. 10.
[4] Quoted ibid., 4/II/66.

engineering strike. The dilution policy, although eventually operative over a considerable area, was extended piecemeal and with great caution owing to persistent shop-floor opposition. The government's attempt to apply it to non-munitions work in 1917 triggered one of the most serious strikes of the war; and after negotiating with the unions for three months, during which it 'conceded point after point in the hope of securing agreement to dilution on private work',[5] the government dropped the proposal.

There was a similar pattern in relation to wages. Government representatives time and again conceded wage increases, in the face of actual or threatened stoppages, from the time the Clyde strike shattered the industrial truce in February 1915. From then on the task of the government's wartime arbitration tribunal, the Committee on Production, became one of 'endeavouring to prevent stoppages . . . by adjusting wages'.[6] The trend was decisively reinforced in July 1915 when Lloyd George intervened in a South Wales miners' strike and overrode a ministerial colleague to concede all the strikers' main wage demands. Belated government moves to impose a general wage freeze in November collapsed by the spring of 1916. The precedent of ministerial intervention set by Lloyd George, in war as earlier in peace, was thereafter followed for the sake of industrial peace. Appeals on wage claims were 'rife, first to one Minister and then to another, and finally to the War Cabinet or the Prime Minister';[7] and below this level, munitions inspectors became notably prone to the quick concession of local wage claims. Churchill, as Minister of Munitions in 1917, capped the process with 'a rhetorical flourish'.[8] The phrase is that of his colleague, a serving trade union official and Minister of Labour, whose opposition he brushed aside when he decreed a wage-rise for certain skilled time-workers in engineering. In doing so, he inspired a long ripple of industrial strife which spread the increase throughout the munitions industries, and eventually beyond.

The eagerness of government leaders to conciliate the trade unions was also evident in their burgeoning readiness to promote labour representatives, to address labour gatherings and

[5] ibid., 6/II/1.   [6] Hammond, op. cit., p. 79.   [7] Askwith, op. cit., p. 423.
[8] John Hodge, *Workman's Cottage to Windsor Castle*, p. 175.

to enter into consultative arrangements. The Treasury conference of March 1915 was the first major manifestation. Others were Henderson's cabinet appointment two months later; Lloyd George's address (at his request) to the TUC's annual Congress in September; the admission of two more Labour MPs to cabinet rank in December 1916; the conferences involving the Minister of Munitions, the First Sea Lord and the Chief of the Imperial General Staff during April 1917; and the trade union conference attended by the Prime Minister in January 1918. Below this lofty level, there was not only a general expansion in *ad hoc* consultation, but also in the range of both advisory and administrative bodies with 'labour' members of one sort or another. The creation of formal consultative bodies with labour representation was enormously accelerated after Lloyd George became Prime Minister in December 1916.[9]

However, it was in relation to representation in the administration of the war effort that the limitations of labour leaders' influence on government was most precisely demonstrated. There were other indications, such as the tentative nature of state controls on the managements of essential industries, the delays in initiating or developing major policies like food rationing, not to mention the government's two-year persistence with the intensely controversial leaving certificate system. But even more striking was the fact that the 'passion for committees', displayed by wartime ministers,[10] was distinctly bridled when it came to labour representation.

More often than not, ministers had to be prodded to grant such representation. For example, the Committee on Production and the Reserved Occupations Committee, both highly significant bodies set up in 1915, did not include labour members until 1917. Nor did ministers always give way on the point. Despite persistent pressure, the Tramways Committee and the Railways Executive Committee remained free of labour representation. Even when such representation was granted, the selection of members was often made without soliciting a list of nominations from relevant organizations. Hence the TUC's exhilaration at the 'important new departure' of the

[9] Based on data in N. B. Dearle, *Dictionary of Official War-Time Organizations*, *passim*.
[10] Askwith, op. cit., p. 455.

Statutory War Pensions Committee when it informed local authorities that local labour bodies were 'to make their own selection' of their representatives on local pensions committees.[11] This practice, although apparently more common after 1916, did not become universal.

The appropriate contrast is with the corresponding role accorded employers. They were also consulted on labour matters and, to a slighter degree, on questions of social policy. But they were more heavily involved in consultations about broader economic and industrial issues. They were, as a result, represented on a far greater variety of formal advisory bodies than were the trade unions. The pattern was the same in the case of administrative bodies. The unions shared membership with employers on bodies concerned exclusively with the regulation of labour, but not usually on those concerned with the broader reaches of industry and commerce. As for the few exceptions to this rule, the unions' numerical representation was almost invariably smaller than the employers'—which explains the triumphant assertion that the Wool Control Board, formed late in 1917 with equal union and employer representation, created 'a precedent of the greatest possible importance.'[12]

The contrast was even sharper in the case of appointments to full-time government positions. The alacrity with which businessmen were drawn into the war administration, especially the War Office, evoked an early protest from the TUC leaders who claimed that union officials should, 'in fairness', be similarly inducted.[13] Lloyd George ignored this injunction when he staffed the new Ministry of Munitions. It was effectively, as he subsequently boasted, 'from first to last a businessman organization'.[14] Of its 208 'principal officers' during the war, 86 were officially listed as coming from high positions in industry or commerce; and none of the others had a labour background.[15] A succeeding Minister of Munitions told parliament in 1917 that his ministry included men from 'every branch of commerce and industry . . . scientists, lawyers, literary men, commercial men, travellers, soldiers, sailors, and

[11] *TUC Report*, 1916, p. 123. [12] *Labour Year Book*, 1919, p. 172.
[13] *PC Mins.*, 10 March 1915. [14] Lloyd George, op. cit., vol. I, p. 245.
[15] See *Hist. Muns.*, 2/I/260 ff (Appendix VIII).

I know not what besides'.[16] Everything, it seems, except trade unionists. There were some, nevertheless, buried among those of the minister's staff whom he knew not. Shackleton, the former TUC leader, had been first head of the Ministry's Labour Enlistment Complaints Section, and he was succeeded by W. Mosses of the Federation of Engineering and Ship-building Trades. Mosses's appointment was followed by the only substantial influx of labour men to full-time positions, when 66 union officials were appointed to the local committees which were set up under his section to decide disputes about exemptions from military conscription. 'The peculiarity of this scheme . . . lay in the granting of executive powers to the representatives of Labour'.[17]

Outside the Ministry of Munitions, of course, high office was achieved by Henderson and those of his party colleagues given ministerial positions from mid-1915. Shackleton, though he had been a civil servant for almost six years by then, became first permanent head of the Ministry of Labour. And it is worth noting that Robert Smillie of the Miners' Federation was offered, and refused, the important post of Food Controller in mid-1917. There were certainly some other full-time appointments of labour men further down the administrative scale. But the disparity of treatment remained. In the case of the Ministry of Food, for example, the full-time staff included 'a majority of men normally engaged in private trade'.[18] Labour appointees, on the other hand, were almost wholly confined to part-time committee positions.

The reason for the disparity was not simply a matter of expertise. When Lloyd George scoured the business world for Ministry of Munitions staff, he seems to have been primarily concerned with the political aim of winning 'the hearty co-operation of employers', a 'very urgent' problem.[19] But when it came to the 'equally vital' problem of winning 'the good will of the workers',[20] he preferred other solutions. Similarly, in so far as expertise was an issue, although wartime governments followed a general policy of 'administering production controls through agencies headed and directed by business men',[21] they

[16] Quoted ibid., p. 153.   [17] ibid., 6/I/90.
[18] William H. Beveridge, *British Food Control*, p. 73.
[19] Lloyd George, op. cit., vol. I, p. 257.
[20] ibid.   [21] Hurwitz, op. cit., p. 150.

scarcely ever applied the same policy in the case of labour controls and union officials. The one major exception has already been mentioned: the Ministry of Munitions' Labour Enlistment Complaints Section, created in December 1916. The comments of the ministry's official history on the section and its work provide an insight into government attitudes.

The section and its local administering committees were judged an unqualified success. So much so that, if set up 'eighteen months or even a year earlier', they would have avoided 'many of the most serious labour troubles, which disorganized the output of munitions and imperilled the home front'.[22] The explanation of this success is revealing. It was seen as depending on the 'indispensable condition' that the functions of the committees, in particular, were both limited and precisely laid down in such a way as to prevent 'deadlock within the committees [and] conflict with the policy of the Government'.[23] The implication of this, given the less restricted administrative role so often accorded businessmen, is that labour was more likely than management to be at odds with government policy. There is also the associated implication that, as administrators, labour representatives were likely to press their group interests with less restraint than employers. Labour leaders, in other words, were thought to be less susceptible than business leaders to the 'civilizing' influence of office. The point is underlined by the admission that the decision to create the section and its committees was made with the greatest reluctance—because it was feared that 'if administrative powers were given [in this form] to Labour, there was a risk of introducing into the departmental machinery wheels that would not work'.[24]

These comments clearly express the reservations of men, including a heavy lacing of former 'captains of industry', who occupied influential positions in an administrative structure whose values they saw as being radically different from those held by labour leaders in general. Their doubt that trade union officials could 'fit' into that structure is explicable, and understandable, in the light of pre-war social class divisions and the attitudes they engendered. Admitting unionists to office in relatively marginal and sealed-off areas, like labour exchanges and industrial inspectorates, was one thing. Admitting them to the bureaucratic heartland, on an equal footing with those of greater social and educational attainments, was quite a different matter. And the effect of class attitudes is suggested not only by this, but also by the fact that trade union officials themselves, for the most part, gave little sign that they seriously expected to be admitted on the same terms as businessmen.

Yet, if labour's voice in the wartime administration was smaller than that of employers, in formal terms, it was still larger than it had ever been. Above all, union-government dealings embodied a much stronger bargaining element. The principal reason was the extreme sensitivity of the government, and of wartime political leaders generally, to industrial unrest. This was the factor that forced Lloyd George, in December 1916, to concede so much in order to secure Labour's parliamentary support for his coalition: War Cabinet membership for Henderson; five other ministerial posts for Labour MPs; undertakings concerning controls on shipping, mining and food supplies; the introduction of food rationing and the formation of a Ministry of Labour. For the Conservatives, on whom his chances of forming a viable coalition ultimately depended, were convinced that such support was indispensable if any wartime government was to cope with the central problem of labour.[25] Similarly, his later appointment of J. R. Clynes as Parliamentary Secretary to the Ministry of Food was explicitly 'a recognition of the bearing of food problems upon labour unrest'.[26] The importance attached to industrial peace is aptly epitomized in a senior civil servant's recollection of events preceding the revision of the Munitions of War Act in 1916, when labour leaders complained that 'when they had asked for amendments by constitutional methods nothing was done, whereas a strike or a threat of a strike, was electric in its effect'.[27]

TRADE UNIONS

Wartime circumstances at once focused the trade unions' attention on government and narrowed the range of their political

[25] See Lloyd George, op. cit., vol. III, pp. 1061–2.
[26] Beveridge, *British Food Control*, p. 55.
[27] Humbert Wolfe, *Labour Supply and Regulation*, p. 130.

activities. Parliamentary action was of minimal relevance. Government by coalition, with the Labour party's assent from May 1915, stifled serious opposition in a parliament which, in any case, was largely excluded from major policy and administrative areas by the delegation of sweeping legislative powers to the executive. Direct electoral representation also ceased to be a concern following the inter-party agreement not to contest parliamentary vacancies: the Labour party observed this until late in 1918.

Political action, for the unions, was thus confined almost wholly to direct dealings with government. These dealings were complicated by a lack of organizational coordination on both sides.

In the case of government, the haphazard pre-war evolution of industrial and social policy had been reflected in an administrative structure in which responsibility for issues of special concern to trade unions had been divided among the Home Office, the Board of Trade, the Local Government Board, the National Health Insurance Commission, the Admiralty and the War Office. Wartime creations added to this hotchpotch with ministries of Munitions, Labour, Shipping and Air, a Railways Executive Committee and a Coal Controller. Moreover, particularly within the Ministry of Munitions, there was an internal decentralization of authority which allowed quasi-independent supply departments to compete for scarce labour. The Ministry of Labour, when it eventuated, met with little success in its attempts to coordinate labour policies. The outcome was a confusion of administrative responsibilities in the field, which was intensified by the frequently overlapping concerns of the various agencies.

There was, for the unions, both advantage and disadvantage in this situation. As to disadvantage, different agencies often issued contradictory directives, and it was frequently unclear which was the appropriate authority to approach on a specific matter. On the other hand, the multiplication of effective decision-making points in the governmental structure was commonly an advantage, especially in relation to wage issues.

The government's lack of coordination on labour matters was more than matched on the trade union side. The war, as it has been rather grandiloquently put, 'brought clearly into the light of day the general disorganization of the army of Labour'.[28] Broadly speaking, the main fissures cut two ways—between union leaders and members, and between unions of skilled and unskilled workers.

War, and the patriotic sentiment it generated, created a double purpose for most union officials, They dealt with government not only in order to safeguard the interests of their members, but also as a means of cooperating in the defence of the nation. Accordingly, although their bargaining position was immeasurably stronger, they hesitated to exploit it. The industrial truce they initiated soon after the declaration of war testified to this; and subsequently they continued to be 'almost unanimous in repudiating strikes and in doing all in their power to prevent stoppages'.[29] Almost all wartime strikes were unofficial or unauthorized.

The pattern was set by the Clyde engineering workers who, in February 1915, ended the 'miracle' of the industrial truce by striking on a wage issue in defiance of their official union leaders. The Clyde strike also gave birth to a form of independent rank and file organization that was to play an important role in later wartime stoppages. It came to be known as the shop stewards' movement.[30] The movement was confined largely to the engineering industry. Its basic unit was typically the shop committee consisting of worker-elected shop stewards. By the end of the war, in almost every engineering centre, there was also a local 'Workers' Committee' representative of the various workshops in the area. A rudimentary national organization was established in 1917.

The shop stewards' movement was, above all, an expression of rank and file distrust of union officialdom. At its most moderate, the position of its leaders was that: 'We will support the officials just so long as they rightly represent the workers, but we will act independently when they misrepresent them'.[31] At its extreme, their position was as stated in a telegram to a minister: 'Joint Engineering Shop Steward's Committee

[28] G. D. H. Cole, *Self-government in Industry*, p. 49.
[29] *Hist. Muns.*, 4/II/10.
[30] See G. D. H. Cole, *Workshop Organization;* and Branko Pribicevic, *The Shop Stewards' Movement and Workers' Control, 1910–1922*, esp. chaps. IV–VI and VIII.
[31] Quoted in W. A. Orton, *Labour in Transition*, p. 93.

repudiates any interference by the official executives of the workers in the present dispute'.[32]

But the shop stewards' movement was also an expression of a division within the trade union rank and file itself. Although it was influenced by syndicalist ideas about organizing across traditional union boundaries and achieving 'workers' control' of industry, it was dominated by skilled workers and was primarily concerned with immediate industrial issues. Its activities, as a result, were largely restricted to 'efforts which asserted the claims or expressed the grievances of the craft unions'.[33]

The Amalgamated Society of Engineers, the biggest engineering union, was especially vulnerable to pressures generated by the shop stewards' movement, partly because of its structure and partly because its membership provided many of the movement's most vigorous spokesmen. These factors helped to thrust the official leadership of the ASE into a wartime role which ensured that the division of interest between skilled and unskilled workers was a central issue at the level of official inter-union relations.

The independent line which the ASE leaders followed in dealings with government was both a source and a symptom of the unions' inability to present a united front. A recurring pattern of the war years was set in March 1915 when the ASE, with only the Miners' Federation in support, declined to accept the original Treasury agreement on dilution and other matters—and then, single-handed, negotiated a more favourable agreement with government. Similarly, on some later issues such as the extension of dilution to private work, the ASE executive in 1917 rejected an agreement with government which all other relevant unions had accepted, and eventually had its way. Again, on some issues, like the administration of conscription exemptions in 1916, the government negotiated with the ASE an agreement which other affected unions were simply required to accept. Time and again, union leaders urged ministers not to deal with the ASE alone on general matters. The government acceded on one major issue, the administration of conscription exemptions in 1918; but then it

[32] Quoted in *Hist. Muns.*, 6/I/113.
[33] ibid., 6/I/94.

abandoned its stand after the ASE's claim for separate negotiations was endorsed in a ballot of its members. The ASE
carried its lone-wolf role to the extent not only of remaining
unaffiliated to the TUC until the last months of the war, but
of disaffiliating in 1917 from the Federation of Engineering and
Shipbuilding Trades.

The antagonism toward the ASE in official union circles was
quite singular. The Miners' Federation, also a lone wolf on a
number of occasions, was the target of much less resentment.
The reason was that the ASE, in terms of membership, was not
so overwhelmingly dominant in the engineering and shipbuilding industries as was the Miners' Federation in the coal
industry. The heavy representation of other skilled and unskilled unions in engineering and shipbuilding meant that
there was a wide range of unions whose leaders were embarrassed by the ASE's achievement of a special relationship
with government. As they pointed out on one of the occasions
when they had to accept an ASE-negotiated agreement, 'such
treatment' of their unions 'prejudiced their officials in the eyes
of their members and gave the ASE a splendid advertisement'.[34]

Nevertheless, the skilled unions (prestige apart) at least
shared in the concessions which the ASE's recalcitrance won
from government. The unskilled unions were often less fortunate. In the case of conscription exemptions, for example, the
ASE's insistence meant that unskilled workers were drawn on
more heavily than would otherwise have been the case; and
their officials were denied the impressive (if short-lived)
powers of their craft union counterparts to grant exemptions
under the ASE-negotiated 'trade card' scheme. The unskilled
unions, in any case, were sometimes inclined either to side with
government or to express muted opposition on issues of profound disquiet to the craft unions. They could afford to be more
sanguine about the government's dilution policy, for instance,
because that policy was a threat to skilled workers precisely to
the extent that it widened the opportunities of the unskilled
and semi-skilled. The ASE's lone-wolf role, in other words,
exacerbated existing tensions between skilled and unskilled
unions. While other craft union leaders might dislike the ASE's
special relationship with government because it deprived them

[34] ibid., p. 41.

of a more imposing consultative role, it was objectionable to their counterparts among the unskilled unions for the more fundamental reason that it enhanced the influence on government of interests which often conflicted with those of their own members.

These differences among trade union leaders sometimes worked to the disadvantage of government, as when the ASE was able to extract additional concessions by asserting its independence. Sometimes they were an advantage, as when the unskilled unions' agitation against the 'trade card' scheme 'served the Government in good stead' after it had decided to draw more heavily on skilled workers for military service.[35] But it was the division between union officials and their rank and file militants which had the more farreaching implications for the officials' relations with government.

Government recognition was vital to the trade union leaders if they were to maintain their status as labour spokesmen and act to any purpose in wartime. For government, the value of such recognition depended on the extent to which it facilitated the control of labour. This placed union officials in a highly exposed position because it meant, given rank and file unrest, that government might find it more profitable to by-pass them. They were acutely aware of their own vulnerability once the industrial truce broke down. Thus it was they who initially suggested holding the Treasury conference of March 1915, arguing that this would help them secure their members' acceptance of proposed labour controls.[36] Again, the ASE leadership sought concessions on the ground that they were essential 'if we are to maintain our influence with our members' while helping realize the dilution policy.[37]

In the event, although government did occasionally by-pass them and deal directly with shop stewards, it came to accept that the official leaderships provided 'the only handle by which [it] could get a grip upon Labour'.[38] Its dependence on them was reflected in the two aims underlying its general approach to the labour question. One was to prevent alliances between shop floor militants and their union officials. Thus the government consented to the Treasury conference in the expectation

[35] G. D. H. Cole, *Trade Unionism and Munitions*, p. 202.
[36] *Hist. Muns.*, 1/II/37, 39–40. [37] ibid., 6/I/84.
[38] Henry Clay, *The Problem of Industrial Relations*, p. 148.

that the ensuing agreement would 'deprive further labour "unrest" of the official support of the trade union executives'.[39] Thereafter government spokesmen repeatedly emphasized that unofficial strikes constituted a 'revolt . . . directly against the executive authority . . . of the trade unions'.[40]

The second aim was to shore up the internal authority of union leaders. This was more difficult to achieve because the officials were often compromised, in the eyes of many of their members, by their cooperation with government. Contrary to expectations, for example, the Treasury agreement actually strengthened the hand of shop floor militants who could pillory their officials with having 'signed away the strike'.[41] Nor was the ASE's leadership exempted, despite the separate and harder bargain it struck. Arthur Henderson indicated the gravity of the problem when he wrote to the Prime Minister in 1916: 'Through my association with the Military Service Acts and with the Labour Policy of the Munitions Department, I believe I have permanently forfeited the confidence of certain sections of the organised workers'.[42] A shift in the government's policy on unofficial strikes signalled the firming of its conviction that the officials' authority had to be bolstered. Government representatives negotiated with striking shop stewards on a number of occasions up to early 1916. A Clydeside strike in March, leading to the 'deportation' of several shop stewards, was the turning-point. From that time the government followed a 'deliberate policy' of negotiating 'only with the recognized leaders of the trade unions' in the belief that 'to do otherwise would have further impaired their authority, already shaken by [their agreement to] the Munitions of War Act'.[43] Not that the government subsequently found it possible to ignore the shop stewards altogether, especially when it came to applying the dilution policy. By and large, however, it did manage to hold the line in the case of major strikes.

The generally cooperative relationship between union officials and government owed a great deal, on the side of the officials, to patriotism. But there were other factors influencing

[39] Orton, op. cit., p. 41.
[40] *Hist. Muns.*, 6/I/112.
[41] Wolfe, op. cit., p. 120.
[42] Quoted in M. A. Hamilton, *Arthur Henderson*, p. 107.
[43] *Hist. Muns.*, 6/I/38.

them as well. The unions, at the official level, were vulnerable to wartime coercive measures; and government spokesmen were notably assiduous in publicizing, for example, the legal liabilities of union officials if strike benefits were paid in contravention of the Munitions of War Act. More significantly, co-operation also had its rewards. The wage and policy concessions, already mentioned, were important to officials as well as their members. In addition, there were three other consequences of their wartime relationship with government which were of peculiar interest to trade union leaders.

One was the great growth in their membership. Government's wartime recognition of the unions encouraged, and often virtually compelled (as a condition tacitly attached to the award of contracts), their recognition by private employers. The recruitment of members was directly promoted by some government measures such as the temporary 'trade card' scheme, relating to conscription exemptions, and the power conferred on the Seamen's Union in connection with the employment of maritime labour.

Second, there was government's effect on the system of collective bargaining. Pre-war agreements were typically confined to the local or district level. Government's wartime concern with wage-determination, reflected particularly in the activities of the Committee on Production, predictably resulted in a trend to wage settlements on a national basis in a number of industries. This trend to industry-wide bargaining, by shifting responsibility for wage negotiations from the local to the national level of unions, shifted authority in the same direction. It was highly valued by national officials.

The third consequence was the elevation, as union officials perceived it, of their status. The relative intimacy, the frequency and scale of their dealings with government, and above all the bargaining position conferred on them by total war, could scarcely have failed to impress men whose initial expectations were the product of very different circumstances. Beatrice Webb, attending her first Congress of the TUC in three decades, observed that delegates were 'more sophisticated . . . than thirty years ago'.[44] Nevertheless, when Lloyd George addressed them, 'the Parliamentary Committee was obsequious;

---

[44] Margaret Cole (ed.), *Beatrice Webb's Diaries, 1912–1924*, p. 44.

the delegates were flattered by his presence, and showed it'.[45] Similarly, there was the breathless report of an official who attended a meeting with Lloyd George and others: 'for the first time in history a conference of Labour representatives was held whose deliberations were of such importance that the Cabinet of the Government were meeting at 5.30 p.m. to hear the decision this Conference of workers had arrived at'.[46] Familiarity might later have modified these responses. But the mere fact of consultation, quite apart from policy concessions, remained a matter for pride: 'both industrially and politically, we have been called into conference. We have been consulted'.[47] Moreover, this sense of achievement had a personal, as well as a group, meaning—not so much in terms of 'fat allowances for service on Committees'[48] as in the subtler coin of self-esteem. Some of them were awarded honours of the realm (commonly the OBE), a few had social encounters with the King that were lovingly recollected,[49] and others had the offer of a government position which even an Ernest Bevin found most pleasing.[50] There was every reason why men, who found themselves with 'a standing . . . never before attained or even visualised',[51] should have been a little dazzled by it all.

This is not to say that most trade union leaders were transformed, as Miliband has it, into little more than 'agents of the State'.[52] Rather, as he points out more accurately elsewhere, their role was essentially that of 'brokers and intermediaries between the Government and . . . labour'.[53] In other words, they had the complicated function of at once 'urging the Government to make Labour restrictions more palatable and entreating their own members to accept the restrictions necessary for the war effort'.[54] The importance of this function, for government, depended on rank and file disaffection. Thus the cleavage between union officials and their members enhanced, more than it diminished, the negotiating position of the officials. The most telling indication of this was government's special relationship with the ASE, the union

[45] ibid., p. 45.   [46] Quoted in Fox, op. cit., p. 372.
[47] *TUC Report*, 1916, p. 55.
[48] Margaret Cole (ed.), *Beatrice Webb's Diaries 1912–1924*, p. 45.
[49] See Hodge, op. cit., pp. 188–91; Thorne, op. cit., p. 195.
[50] See Trevor Evans, *Bevin*, p. 69; Francis Williams, *Ernest Bevin*, p. 60.
[51] W. Milne-Bailey, *Trade Union Documents*, p. 30.
[52] Miliband, op. cit., p. 53.   [53] ibid., p. 47.   [54] Hurwitz, op. cit., p. 272.

most deeply affected by the shop stewards' movement. In so far as wartime union leaders were 'not merely recognised by State and employers, but treated with deference and respect',[55] they owed it to those of their members whose recalcitrance they condemned.

TRADES UNION CONGRESS

The TUC Parliamentary Committee cancelled the 1914 Congress, scheduled for the naval town of Portsmouth, on the outbreak of war. Before the next regular Congress met in September 1915, the committee appears to have made no move even to explore the possibility of initiating general union discussions on common problems. Its capacity for assuming a coordinating role in any other form was strictly limited. It was ill-equipped for collating and processing information on the new and varied issues thrown up by the war: its full-time secretary was also an MP, up to 1917, and he still had only one clerk to help him. There were also crippling gaps in its affiliation list. Above all, the ASE remained unaffiliated until 1918; other absentees for most of the war included the Workers' Union, the Society of Ironfounders and the National Union of Boot and Shoe Operatives.

The proposal which produced the Treasury conference of March 1915, the first major public indication of the new relationship between unions and government, originated among officials outside the TUC's leadership.[56] The TUC was not even used as the channel for issuing invitations to attend. Its three representatives at the conference were accompanied by others from the GFTU, three inter-union industry bodies and thirty trade unions. The TUC secretary, Bowerman, was the only one of them elected by conference to a seven-member working committee. Arthur Henderson, formally representing the Society of Ironfounders, was chairman of the committee, and its secretary was William Mosses, general secretary of the Federation of Engineering and Shipbuilding Trades. These two alone signed the Treasury agreement. The working committee, with the addition of an ASE representative, was subsequently converted into the National Advisory Committee on

Labour which functioned for some time as the principal union-government consultative body. Although Mosses and one other member, apart from Bowerman, were also on the Parliamentary Committee, it was plainly their other connections that were valued: later, an official publication listed Mosses's union positions without mentioning his TUC office.[57]

This gives some indication of the limited role which the TUC played in wartime dealings between government and the unions. Moreover, despite the enormous expansion in the scope and scale of such dealings, the TUC's independent activity in the field became almost entirely marginal. It might well have been expected, in the light of its pre-war role, to have discharged something of a coordinating function on broad issues. But that function was not only often denied the TUC by individual unions; it was also claimed by other bodies, now more numerous than before and more eager than ever to seize the ear of government.

New Competitors and Old

Inter-union industry organizations, like the National Transport Workers' Federation and the Federation of Engineering and Shipbuilding Trades, devoted most of their attention to government once the war began, though they usually confined themselves to matters specific to their industry. The broader-based Triple Industrial Alliance (better known as the 'Triple Alliance'), was more ambitious, though initially designed to coordinate industrial action. From early in 1916 it took an active interest in general policy matters such as old age pensions, the importation of foreign labour and postwar policies. The Triple Alliance, whose constituents were all TUC affiliates, was widely regarded as a most powerful body: its first deputation to a wartime Prime Minister wrenched a protest from *The Times* at this presumed attempt 'to frighten the appointed Ministers of the Crown'.[58]

In the case of the TUC's oldest competitors, the GFTU does not seem to have significantly strengthened its position with the onset of war. But the Labour party did. It quickly emerged as the principal source of such wartime coordination as the labour movement achieved. This development was facilitated by a

[57] ibid., 6/I/88n.   [58] Quoted in *The Labour Year Book*, 1919, p. 94.

split in the party, on the issue of supporting the war, which toppled Ramsay MacDonald from its parliamentary leadership. Henderson took his place, while retaining the party secretaryship. Throughout the war, he was able to straddle the industrial and political wings of the labour movement in a way that would have been beyond MacDonald. His ability to do so, in a manner reminiscent of Shackleton's role a few years earlier, was partly a matter of personality and partly a matter of his industrial credentials. For in addition to his party offices, he was president and a former full-time official of the Society of Ironfounders, the third largest of the engineering unions. His position was reinforced by his admission to cabinet membership in May 1915, an appointment which carried with it not only prestige but unique access to the highest level of government.

Henderson's election to leadership of the union side in the first Treasury conference indicates the long shadow that he, and through him the party, threw across the trade unions in the early months of the war. In itself, however, it was not long enough to ensure a common union approach on many matters of general concern. The party's limited authority, and still more the TUC's, was reflected in the use made of joint bodies intended to forge a united front on government policy matters.

One was the old Joint Board. In the first months of the war it sponsored the declaration initiating the industrial truce, secured government financial help for unions coping with the surge of unemployment and organized support, at the government's request, for the recruiting campaign. Many of the labour representatives on government committees were subsequently appointed through it. Significantly, the nominating procedure it adopted allowed a great deal of discretion to its chairman— who, for most of the war period, was Henderson. The board's meetings were unusually frequent during the first twelve months of the war, although a great deal of its time was taken up with inter-union disputes and proposals for its own reform, generated by the GFTU's unpopularity with the Miners' Federation.

By the middle of 1916, the Joint Board was flanked by two other bodies concerned exclusively with government policy. The older and more important was the War Emergency Workers' National Committee, usually referred to as either the 'Workers' National Committee' or the 'War Emergency

Committee'. It was formed, the day after war was declared, at a conference convened by Henderson who also became its first chairman. It eventually included representatives of the TUC, the GFTU and the Labour party, as well as of fifteen other industrial and political organizations ranging from the London Trades Council and the National Union of Teachers to the British Socialist party and the Women's Cooperative Guild. The committee concerned itself with an equally varied range of topics including such things as unemployment relief, war pensions, price stabilization, food distribution, rent restrictions and sweated labour on government contracts. Direct negotiations with government formed a major part of its activities; and it was represented on a number of government advisory bodies alongside the TUC and the Labour party. During its early days it met at least twice a week, if less frequently thereafter. It called the first of a number of conferences of industrial and political labour organizations in March 1915. By the end of that year the Joint Board was asking for its advice. By the end of the next, the TUC leadership was publicly referring to it as one of 'the four National Committees',[59] a designation formerly reserved for the executives of the TUC, the Labour party and the GFTU. Apart from anything else, the War Emergency Committee had the advantage of being regarded as 'the most representative Labour body that has ever existed'.[60]

The second wartime creation was the Joint Committee on After-the-War Problems, formed in 1916 with a membership drawn from the four 'national committees', including the War Emergency Committee. It handled such specifically trade union matters as the displacement of munitions workers, general unemployment problems and the question of restoring pre-war union conditions. It also dealt directly with government. Like the War Emergency Committee, although its scope was narrower, this committee was symptomatic of the absence of a single recognized coordinating centre on the trade union side.

The TUC's Counterattack

Nevertheless, there was life yet in the Parliamentary Committee; and, although often suggested, suicide was never seriously

[59] *TUC Report*, 1916, p. 111.   [60] G. D. H. Cole, *Labour in Wartime*, p. 99.

contemplated. In December 1914 its instinct for survival had still been strong enough for it to reject, as 'inopportune',[61] the Labour party's revival of the old proposal that their two annual conferences should be held simultaneously, in the same town and with agendas arranged by a joint sub-committee. Similarly, when it later settled the agenda for the 1915 Congress, the Parliamentary Committee did not agree that resolutions on 'the War and terms of peace' were 'outside the scope of industrial questions treated by the TUC'.[62] By the end of 1915, moreover, the TUC leaders seem to have acquired a new zest for life, for thereafter they abandoned the static defence strategy and moved on to the attack.

Their new aggressiveness, in the face of the competing pressures hemming them in, first surfaced in January 1916. They expressed 'surprise' at Henderson's failure to invite them to a meeting at which the Prime Minister had discussed the Military Service Bill with Labour MPs and the party executive.[63] Mild though this reaction may appear to be, it signalled that the TUC leaders were no longer content to be edged to the sidelines. And it was only the start.

Two months later they struck out again, this time at the War Emergency Committee, with a declaration that its 'status' did not warrant its inclusion in the proposed Joint Committee on After-the-War Problems.[64] They were to lose on that point, but shortly afterwards attacked on another with more success. They rejected a War Emergency Committee proposal for a broad-based national conference on industrial conscription and other matters, asserting that no such gathering should be convened without 'the consent of the three national bodies'.[65] Their subsequent decision (on a 9–5 vote) to hold a special and exclusively trade union Congress forced the abandonment of the original proposal.

In the meantime, the Joint Board had declined in significance largely owing to the campaign against the TUC's oldest competitor, the GFTU. Few of the bigger unions were affiliated to the GFTU, and many were hostile to it because of its craft union orientation. In particular, the powerful Miners' Federation, incensed by an unfavourable decision in an inter-union

---

[61] *PC Mins.*, 10 March 1915.   [62] ibid., 10 June 1915.
[63] ibid., 20 January 1916.   [64] ibid., 15 March 1916.   [65] ibid., 25 May 1916.

dispute, had agitated from 1913 against the GFTU's membership of the Joint Board. After its initial flurry of wartime activity,
the board met only four times between August 1915 and May
1916. It did not meet again until November. In the interim the
TUC's annual Congress, prompted by the miners, resolved that
the GFTU should be excluded from the board. At the November meeting the Labour party representatives accepted the
proposition. This all but disposed of both the GFTU and the
Joint Board.

Nearly nine months elapsed before the board, reconstituted
to represent only the TUC and the party, was again convened
in July 1917; and it appears to have met only once or twice
more by the war's end. Its place was taken by joint meetings
of the full TUC and party executives, which were held monthly
from October 1917. The board, as reconstituted, in fact became
an embarrassment to the party because of its constitutional
competence to determine the *bona fides* of any union applying
for affiliation to either of its constituents. This meant, in the
absence of the GFTU, that the TUC leaders had the power to
veto would-be party affiliates. They subsequently exercised
this power in the case of three unions, piously asserting that
since the TUC 'will not take in any society to whom the Labour
party object, the Labour party must not take in any union to
whom the Parliamentary Committee object'.[66] The party
executive responded by pressing for the board's dissolution,
arguing that it was redundant in view of the agreement on
monthly joint meetings of the two executives—which were not
governed by a formal constitution, and thus left each executive
free in the matter of affiliations. The TUC leadership successfully opposed this proposal, but without showing any interest
in restoring the Joint Board to its former stature.

Meanwhile, the Labour party had given ground in the face
of TUC ambitions for a larger role in the international sphere.
In July 1917 the party announced the names of its delegates to
a Paris meeting about a proposed conference in Stockholm of
Socialist representatives from neutral and belligerent nations,
on both sides. The TUC protested that it should have been
consulted. Henderson explained that the party executive had
acted alone because the TUC 'was not directly affiliated with

[66] ibid., 11 December 1917.

the International movement'.[67] Nevertheless, in the case of an 'Allied Congress' to be held in London the following month, he promised the TUC eight places in the delegation allocated to the British Section of the International Socialist Bureau. TUC nominees were also included in the party's delegations to the Stockholm conference itself and to the next Paris meeting of Allied Socialist parties in early 1918. Moreover, in response to another claim, the party executive agreed that it would not convene an international conference without first consulting the TUC leadership. The Parliamentary Committee's chairman subsequently occupied the chair at the two Allied Labour and Socialist Conferences held in Britain during 1918, the first of these gatherings being formally initiated by the TUC.

The GFTU also suffered from the burgeoning international aspirations of the TUC. To a limited extent, it had already done so before the war, as we have seen. But in September 1918 Samuel Gompers, of the American Federation of Labour, cut through months of TUC-GFTU wrangling when he told TUC and Labour party leaders that he 'would yield to the judgement of the Parliamentary Committee' on the question of whether the GFTU should be admitted to a conference held later in the month.[68] The GFTU was obliged to settle for little more than joint representation with the TUC at all subsequent international conferences. It was to lose even this toe-hold in 1920 when the TUC repudiated the arrangement and secured exclusive recognition as the British Section of the International Federation of Trade Unions.

Earlier in 1918 the TUC leaders had also moved to eliminate another competitor. A rebuke from the War Emergency Committee, for failing to consult it before selecting three TUC representatives on the government's Food Control Council, evoked a declaration that the 'work now done by the War Emergency Committee could be done' as adequately by the TUC and party executives.[69] The committee did not fall at this trumpet blow; but afterwards there was no question of its peacetime continuation, though it took a little time to die. Nor did the Joint Committee on After-the-War Problems long survive the Armistice.

[67] ibid., 25 July 1917.   [68] ibid., 6 September 1918.
[69] ibid., 14 March 1918; 10 April 1918.

But the Labour party remained. And the TUC leaders were determined on their independence. In March 1918 they rejected a longstanding proposal for a joint research department, saying that they preferred to 'develop this work for themselves';[70] and they reaffirmed this position when the party persisted. Three months later, the party's proposal of a joint committee 'to enquire into the possibility of closer cooperation' between the TUC, the party executive and its parliamentary wing, evoked an almost contemptuous response. The Parliamentary Committee replied that it had decided 'not to appoint representatives, leaving it to the [party's] two Parliamentary bodies to deal with the matter'.[71] The following month, it reversed a 1916 decision by refusing to join with the party in publishing an 'International Labour Review' on the ground that it 'had already decided to start a similar publication' on its own account.[72]

Nevertheless, the presidential address to the Congress in September was not altogether off the mark with its reference to 'closer cooperation' between the TUC and the Labour party.[73] They had joined in negotiation for more spacious office accommodation, which they then shared. Despite its earlier disavowals, the Parliamentary Committee had participated in the activities of the new Labour Research Department, if on a strictly limited basis. There was also the party's conciliatory reception of the TUC's claims to international representation. Above all, there were the monthly joint meetings of the TUC and party executives.

The sharp switch in the TUC's attitude after 1915, from apparent passivity to aggressive assertion, is not easily explained. There were factors which almost certainly bolstered its leaders' self-confidence or stirred their antagonism, but they did not fully emerge until later in the war period. One of them was the expansion in the TUC's affiliations. The number of its affiliated unions increased by more than 25 per cent between the end of 1913 and the end of 1918. The influx was greatest during the last two years of the war, and especially in 1918 when it was crowned with the reaffiliation of the ASE.

[70] ibid., 13 March 1918.
[71] ibid., 12 June 1918.
[72] ibid., 10 July 1918.
[73] *TUC Report*, 1918, p. 52.

Another factor was the strengthening of the TUC's administrative resources. Even before the war, its full-time staff of the
secretary and one clerk had been outnumbered three-to-one
by the Labour party's staff. The president of the 1916 Congress
looked forward to the day when the TUC possessed 'its own
block of offices and civil service, commodious and well appointed'.[74] The next Congress, less generous of vision, approved one new full-time position of assistant secretary; but it
was filled by Fred Bramley, a Parliamentary Committee
member who was to prove more forceful and enterprising than
Bowerman, the secretary. Steps were also taken to create
'Statistical and Intelligence Departments', and affiliated
unions with international connections agreed to the formation
of an 'International Department'.

In addition to these developments in its own organization,
the value of an independent TUC was enhanced for many
union leaders by the Labour party's adoption of a new constitution in February 1918. This embodied, for the first time, an
explicit Socialist objective. It also radically altered the party's
structure, giving affiliated unions the power to determine the
composition of the executive committee, and incorporated the
1908 conference declaration that members of the Parliamentary Committee were ineligible for election to the executive.
The Socialist objective was distasteful to many union leaders,
and they were not confined to old Lib-Lab men. They appear
to have had the sympathy of a majority of the Parliamentary
Committee. Two of its members, with the open support of at
least one other, reacted by helping launch a campaign for 'the
formation of a purely Trade Union Party, run under the
authority of the Trades Union Congress'.[75] One of these
members, J. B. Williams, was the subject of a formal complaint
by the Labour party executive: the Parliamentary Committee
discussed the complaint at length, but reached no conclusion.
Shortly afterwards, a joint meeting of the two executives
carried a motion condemning Williams and others, but the vote
(thirteen to four) indicates a high rate of either abstention or
non-attendance on the part of the TUC's eighteen members.
A month later the Parliamentary Committee expressed neither

[74] ibid., 1916, p. 62.
[75] Labour Party, *Report*, Executive Committee, June 1918, p. 17.

opposition nor support when informed of the party's intention to issue a circular attacking Williams's campaign. The matter was resolved in September when Congress rejected a resolution urging the formation of a 'Trade Union Labour Party'. This episode, however, serves to underline the TUC leadership's resistance to the Labour party's competitive claims.

Internal Authority

By the end of the war the TUC had asserted its independence of the Labour party and shaken off some other major claims to inter-union authority. It had also acquired a leading role in international labour affairs, and expanded both its affiliated membership and its administrative resources. But these developments appear to have had little impact on its wartime internal authority—partly, perhaps, because they occurred so late in the period.

The TUC's major problem in this respect was that the utility of its customary political procedures, on which its pre-war authority had largely depended, was even more open to question in wartime than it had been in peace. The official who spoke of 'worn-out methods', that 'should be buried with the battle-axes and bows and arrows of Plantaganet England',[76] had a point. Parliamentary action, as we have seen, was virtually ruled out. The TUC's report for 1916 was the last to include the traditional list of private members' bills, although both the 1917 and 1918 Congresses went through the pre-war ritual of calling for reforms to facilitate the passage of such bills. The Parliamentary Committee's role of mounting an annual round of ministerial deputations on Congress resolutions was also severely circumscribed for some time. The cancellation of the 1914 Congress left it with no resolutions to submit in the early months of the war. There were plenty of resolutions a year later, but most ministers declined to see deputations about them because they did not deal 'specifically with the War'.[77] Although only the Home Secretary still held to this principle by 1917 (and he abandoned it the following year), the Parliamentary Committee early acknowledged the futility of 'even attempting to secure legislative effect' in the case of the great

[76] *TUC Report*, 1917, p. 54.
[77] *PC Mins.*, 19 April 1916.

bulk of Congress resolutions while the war lasted.[78] In addition, there was the glaring fact that the TUC's channels of access to government were infinitely inferior to those available to the Labour party through its ministerial members, especially Henderson from May 1915 until his resignation from the government in August 1917.

The impression of an internal authority which was not merely limited, but actually declining, is confirmed by the composition of trade union deputations involving the TUC. Even those carrying Congress resolutions seem usually to have been dominated to a much smaller extent by Parliamentary Committee members than they were during the pre-war period. In deputations on other matters, at least in the case of obviously important policy issues, the TUC leaders seem normally to have played second or third fiddle. For example, it was the Labour party which arranged a 1916 deputation to the Prime Minister about the government's wages policy: the Parliamentary Committee was casually invited to send along 'one or two representatives'.[79] Shortly afterwards the TUC tagged along behind the Federation of Engineering and Ship-building Trades in a deputation that discussed unemployment benefits with the President of the Board of Trade.

The pattern is the same in the case of representation on formal advisory and administrative bodies set up by government. Henderson, from the start, appears to have been allowed to play the major part in selecting labour representatives. A TUC protest in 1917, at the government's failure to consult it about the membership of commissions of inquiry, led to a Joint Board discussion. The decision reached was that such matters should be 'left in the Chairman's [Henderson's] hands, the *suggestion* being that when Industrial Committees were being set up, the . . . Parliamentary Committee *might* be consulted; in the case of Political Committees, the Labour Party Executive *to be* consulted'.[80] The subsidiary status of the TUC leadership is further confirmed by the composition of the general run of advisory and administrative bodies. The National Advisory Committee on Labour, formed after the first Treasury

---

[78] *TUC Report*, 1915, p. 278.
[79] *PC Mins.*, 17 February 1916.
[80] *TUC Report*, 1917, p. 142. Italics added.

conference, was the model. It included, as we have seen, only one TUC representative. When it was replaced two years later by an enlarged Trade Union Advisory Committee, with more than twenty regular members and a number of occasional members, the TUC's representation was unchanged. Similarly, its nominees were almost invariably a minority of the labour members on bodies concerned with non-industrial matters, such as the Statutory War Pensions Committee and the Consumers' Council created by the Ministry of Food. The one or two exceptions involved relatively minor bodies. Moreover, there were many others, of greater significance, with which the TUC had no formal connection despite their inclusion of other labour representatives.

Above all, trade union leaders were not prepared to entrust to the TUC major issues of immediate importance to them. The nature of Congress resolutions, almost wholly concerned with long-term peacetime aims, was symptomatic of this. The Parliamentary Committee itself, as we have seen, had no illusions about the likelihood of a wartime government giving effect to such aims. On the few occasions when the committee tried to assert itself on more central issues, it was either submerged or brushed aside. In 1916, for instance, it arranged to take up the question of 'substituted labour' with the Manpower Distribution Board, only to find that the trade unions directly concerned had already settled the matter with the Ministry of Munitions. On other occasions it failed to secure effective union acceptance of its position. Thus in 1918 it strongly opposed the Ministry of Food's proposal to provide supplementary rations for heavy manual workers. But it could not hold its affiliates. The 'Triple Alliance . . . as well as many separate unions' supported the proposal,[81] and they carried the day.

The TUC's limited internal authority was not merely a matter of union officials refusing to concede it a larger role on issues of close concern to them. It was also a product of its leaders' apparent unwillingness, except when they felt their position directly threatened by the claims of the Labour party or the War Emergency Committee, to take a firm stand on many contentious issues. Their reluctance even to consider the Whitley Committee's famous first report on joint industrial

[81] Beveridge, *British Food Control*, p. 213.

councils is a case in point. And the young Ernest Bevin, with a fine flourish of his verbal scalpel, spelt out the implications of this at the 1917 Congress. He moved that a special committee should be set up to determine the TUC's attitude to the Whitley Committee's report, since 'it is too big a question for the Parliamentary Committee to undertake in addition to the many other duties they have to perform'.[82]

External Authority

The obvious shortcomings in the TUC's internal authority severely restricted its usefulness to government leaders chiefly concerned with issues beyond the competence of the Parliamentary Committee. The executive of a union like the ASE was of far greater interest to them. Their reaction in the matter of supplementary food rations for heavy manual work was indicative of this.

Not that the government was altogether uninterested in cultivating the TUC. Early in the war the Board of Trade sought its advice on a number of issues concerning national insurance; and, at government request, the chairman of the Parliamentary Committee visited the United States to talk with union officials there. Later, the Cotton Control Board asked the TUC leaders to 'use their influence with Mr Gompers' in order to secure more shipping for the transport of American cotton;[83] and Labour party ministers initiated discussions on some major policy issues including the Whitley Committee report, supplementary food rations and the employment rights of demobilized soldiers. But these were unusual events, as is suggested by the way in which they were dwelt on in the Parliamentary Committee's annual report.

Government leaders certainly regarded the TUC as *one* of the more important labour organizations; but that was all. When they drew it into consultation, and very often they did not trouble to, it was usually in company with other bodies. Thus a Prime Minister, anxious to secure labour support for the recruiting campaign in 1916, asked for it at a meeting which included representatives of the GFTU, the ASE, the Triple Alliance and the Labour party, as well as the TUC. The government's repeated use of large conferences, in its dealings

[82] *TUC Report*, 1917, pp. 227–8.   [83] *PC Mins.*, 14 November 1917.

with the unions, similarly reflects the TUC's inability to secure recognition as the principal union spokesman. The Treasury conference of March 1915 was the first of a series. At the last, held two days after the signing of the Armistice, trade union leaders discussed wages policy and the restoration of pre-war union practices with ministers and employers. The TUC's official representatives appear to have figured no more prominently at this conference than they had at the first. In the interim, moreover, the TUC had not even been invited to many of the multi-union conferences convened by ministers.

Again, when it was accorded direct representation on formal advisory or administrative bodies, the TUC seems more often than not to have been given no opportunity of making its own nominations. Government's usual practice was to issue a personal invitation to a Parliamentary Committee member, leaving it to him to notify his colleagues and seek their approval. What is more surprising is the fact that government made little use of such a broad-based organization in constituting the many local committees with union representation. The TUC seems to have had little to do with most of them. The one exception was the local committees which the Statutory War Pensions Committee asked local government authorities to form; and, in doing so, suggested that they seek the Parliamentary Committee's advice if they were uncertain about which labour organizations they should approach for nominations. This function, while useful, was scarcely of decisive significance to the pensions committee scheme. It is revealing, therefore, that the TUC leadership was so obviously delighted at being 'entrusted . . . with the important task of acting as the medium for dealing with Labour representation' in this case.[84] Such a reaction reflects the low expectations of men who, as a body, did not have a great deal of influence in relation to the major wartime issues which forced government into a bargaining relationship with the trade unions.

A Very Modest Political Authority

The TUC's total role in union-government relations during the war was, at most, decidedly modest. It has, however, been

[84] *TUC Report*, 1916, p. 80.

described in terms which imply a more imposing conclusion: 'At a higher level [than that at which individual unions operated] the Parliamentary Committee had been in constant consultation with members of the Cabinet and heads of Government departments on all manner of subjects affecting the members of the unions during the war'.[85]

Certainly, the committee was busy. But so far as it dealt alone with government, it did so for the most part on relatively routine matters—concerning itself with such things as the submission of union officials' claims for exemption from military service, information about departmental arrangements of interest to unionists and issues relating to the administration of national insurance. The major successes claimed, somewhat doubtfully, for it (legislation on workers' compensation and trade union amalgamations),[86] and by it (the inclusion of union representatives in the Committee on Production),[87] involved matters that were essentially marginal to the dominating mutual concerns of unions and government.

In the case of union-government dealings on larger and more urgent matters, the TUC almost invariably either acted alongside other labour bodies, or was excluded altogether. Moreover, its representative function at this level was not only shared with others, but was usually shared to a degree that reduced its role to something less than *primus inter pares*.

Above all, the Parliamentary Committee's minutes and reports, voluminous as they are, reveal one thing quite clearly. This is that, given the prominence of its formal position in the labour movement, the committee had remarkably little to do officially with the mainstream of wartime negotiations between unions and government. The general point was implied by a speaker at the 1917 Congress, which considered proposals concerning the TUC's administrative facilities. 'The country frequently hears what the miners are thinking and are going to do, and we hear from the railwaymen from time to time, and so on, but it does not readily pick up the idea as to what the Labour movement is going to do'.[88] The time was to come

[85] Roberts, *The Trades Union Congress*, p. 310.
[86] ibid., pp. 287–8.
[87] *TUC Report*, 1917, p. 93.
[88] ibid., p. 344.

when the voice of the TUC leadership would be heard, and listened to, above these others. Meanwhile, it was drowned, on industrial issues, beneath the voices of the separate trade unions and their federations; and, on broader issues, beneath that of the Labour party.

7

In the Shadow of the General Strike 1919–1926

THE war's end sharply diminished the sense of mutual dependence which had drawn government and trade union leaders into a relatively close relationship while hostilities lasted. But there was not a simple reversion to their pre-war relationship. One major reason for this was that, for the better part of a decade after the Armistice, both saw a general strike as a genuine possibility. The currency of this belief also helped rejuvenate the TUC's political authority.

GOVERNMENT

Lloyd George and his coalition emerged from the general election of 1918 with a massive parliamentary majority dominated by Conservatives intent on dismantling the wartime apparatus of state intervention. Food rationing and controls over labour, prices, production and trading were all scrapped by the close of 1921; and private interests had regained the electricity, shipping, coal and railways industries. There were exceptions to this trend, exemplified in the continuation of import duties and modified rent controls, government involvement in housing construction, the extension of unemployment insurance to most wage-earners from 1920 and the introduction of contributory pensions for widows and orphans in 1925. But the overriding postwar theme was one of contracting state activity.

The de-control movement largely ran counter to trade union expectations which wartime government leaders themselves had done much to foster. Union opposition no longer raised the spectre of military defeat, but it could not be ignored. Particularly during the early days of the peace, there was danger in the air. The reliability of the police had been placed in question by the metropolitan police strike of August 1918, and there was mounting unrest in the armed forces. A surge of strikes, includ-ing a big Glasgow stoppage which erupted in violence, partly reflected the continuing influence of extreme left-wing agitation among rank and file unionists. In addition, many trade union officials were displaying great interest in the idea of a general strike.[1] Government leaders were obliged to tread warily. This was reflected in the way they played for time, especially up to the autumn of 1919, with a mixture of concessions and delaying tactics.

In February they convened a National Industrial Conference which diverted the attention of some leading union officials to lengthy negotiations with employers about joint recommend-ations to government on postwar industrial problems. They pressed the de-control policy with caution, retaining the Ministry of Labour, together with control of the railways and coal mining; and retracting a decision to wind up the Ministry of Food. The railwaymen were granted the eight-hour day in the same month, and thereafter engaged in drawn-out wage negotiations. In February, too, the miners were induced to withdraw a national strike threat in return for a royal com-mission into their grievances, a device enabling Lloyd George to separate their momentous demand for nationalization of the coal industry from their wages and hours claims. By mid-year the latter were satisfied, but the government had not had to declare itself on the nationalization issue. Nor had it given firm responses to major proposals issuing from the National Industrial Conference (and in the end, apparently, it never did).

There were further concessions to the unions in the second half of the year. These included a show-piece Profiteering Act, legislative restoration of pre-war union practices and the exclu-sion of compulsory arbitration from the measure that became the Industrial Courts Act. And placatory government an-nouncements about ending compulsory military service and intervention in Russia followed a Triple Alliance decision to

[1] The term 'general strike' is used loosely here to denote a strike directly in-volving workers in *at least* the coal and transport industries, acting in concert and on a national scale. This minimum conception, which put a general strike within the reach of the Triple Alliance, appears to have been widely accepted outside the unions during the period. Moderate union leaders, no doubt anxious to disown implications associated with syndicalism, generally preferred to avoid the term altogether. Thus they chose to diminish the significance of the 1926 general strike by calling it a 'national strike'.

hold a strike ballot on these issues. But there were also signs of a hardening government line during the last months of 1919.

By late summer, booming economic conditions had reduced industrial tensions and eased the movement of demobilized servicemen into civil employment. Differences among union leaders on the issue of a general strike had become more open and pronounced. Administrative arrangements to 'make a general strike innocuous',[2] which the government had quietly set in train at the beginning of the year, were complete: they centred on stores of food supplies and means of distributing them in the event of a total transport stoppage. Early in August the collapse of the second police strike settled, to the government's satisfaction, the issue of police loyalty.

Shortly afterwards, Lloyd George put a finger into the wind and formally rejected nationalization of the coal industry. The miners hesitated, and were lost, when they decided to seek support through the TUC instead of reviving their February strike threat. In September an emboldened government ended seven months of negotiations with the railwaymen by presenting an ultimatum involving the prospect, if prices fell, of a wage reduction for many. The railwaymen did not hesitate. They responded with a national strike. The government reacted warily. It quickly denied, in contrast with its response to a similar strike seven years earlier, that troops would be used to run trains; and for the first time fought a strike by way of a massive publicity campaign. But it did not fight for long. A little over a week later, before the dispute could widen, the Prime Minister accepted a compromise settlement ruling out wage reductions. It is clear that he and his colleagues viewed the railwaymen's action in much the same terms as Beatrice Webb, writing when the strike began: 'The Great Strike—which has been brewing since the close of the war—has happened . . . Never has there been a strike . . . anything like this in magnitude or social significance'.[3] And they were not yet confident enough to test the unions' determination.

During 1920 they continued to play their cards with care, even after the TUC's special Congress in March declared against a general strike in support of the miners' nationalization

[2] Beveridge, *British Food Control*, p. 289.
[3] Margaret Cole (ed.), *Beatrice Webb's Diaries, 1912–1924*, p. 167.

campaign. They tacitly backed down in August, on the issue of intervening in the Russo-Polish war, when threatened with a general strike by a Council of Action uniting all major elements of the official labour movement. Two months later, a threat of strikes in support of a miners' stoppage evoked a sterner reaction, in the form of the Emergency Powers Act which created sweeping anti-strike sanctions; but the day after its enactment, the government conceded the miners' wage claim on a temporary basis. During the pause gained in this way, the government's resolve stiffened.

In the early weeks of 1921, mounting unemployment figures and a plummeting coal export market confirmed that the postwar boom had ended. The government promptly advanced de-control of the coal industry to the end of March, the date on which the miners' temporary settlement expired. The second national coal strike in British history began on the first day of April, after wage negotiations with mineowners had deadlocked. Government representatives intervened a week later when the Triple Alliance called out railwaymen and transport workers in sympathy. Negotiations again broke down. The government deployed troops throughout the country and called up reservists. This time, it was the unions that cracked. At the eleventh hour, on 'Black Friday', a virtual general strike was averted when the strike notices of the railwaymen and transport workers were cancelled after a confused series of events which at least demonstrated that few union leaders were spoiling for a fight with government.

The threat of the general strike had been lifted, if only for the time being. The last stages of the de-control policy could be pushed through with all speed. Government leaders ceased to take an active interest in industrial conflict. They intervened in the engineering lockout of 1922, the biggest dispute of the next three years, only because union leaders asked them to. The limited economic upswing from late in 1923 revived union militancy, and created difficulties for the minority Labour government; but a general strike was not threatened until after the ministry had fallen. Once again, the troubled coal industry provided the issue.

The mineowners determined to reduce wages and other conditions from the start of August 1925. The miners said they would refuse work on these terms. The TUC backed them with a threat to impose an embargo on coal movements. Government intervention followed. The strike was averted when the Prime Minister, less than two days after categorically refusing to do so, agreed on 'Red Friday' to provide a subsidy enabling the maintenance of existing wage rates for nine months while another royal commission went to work. 'We were not ready':[4] this was Stanley Baldwin's justification of his decision, and he argued it both in cabinet and in parliament. But they were ready, and had made elaborate administrative preparations to ensure this, when the 'Red Friday' settlement expired in May 1926. Then they not only chose to meet a general strike head-on, but put the resolve of union leaders to the ultimate test by insisting on unconditional surrender. Their total victory finally dispelled the shadow that the general strike had thrown across the path of British governments since the war.

Strike crises, however, were not the only source of union-government dealings in these years. The postwar process of consultative disengagement was neither as abrupt nor as complete as has been alleged.[5] Many wartime consultative bodies operated for some time after the Armistice, some for a considerable period; and others with labour representation were created, although many of them were temporary bodies.[6] There was a marked slackening in the pace of new creations from 1920, but the unions continued to retain and to be offered representation on formal government bodies, including some with administrative as well as advisory powers. The extension of unemployment insurance in 1920 drew more unions into its administration; and many continued to participate in the national health insurance scheme.

On the side of *ad hoc* dealings, apart from those inspired by industrial stoppages, ministers continued to receive union deputations. Occasionally they took the initiative, as in 1922 when the Home Secretary arranged a series of meetings in search of an 'agreed' measure on workers' compensation. Churchill, as Chancellor of the Exchequer, declined a TUC request for an interview on the ground that 'no practical

---

[4] Quoted in G. M. Young, *Stanley Baldwin*, p. 99.
[5] See V. L. Allen, *Trades Unions and the Government*, pp. 30–1.
[6] See Dearle, op. cit., *passim*.

purpose could be served by a discussion' of the issues in question, because the government's mind was already made up.[7] But ministers were usually more forthcoming. Thus Sir William Joynson-Hicks, long celebrated as a Tory 'Die-Hard', took time out not only to thank TUC representatives 'for coming to him and telling him of their difficulties', but also to assure them that in 'non-political matters, he was only too pleased for them to come and consult with him and he invited them to come as often as they liked'.[8] Even his restriction to 'non-political matters' was not generally applied. A few days later, for example, the Prime Minister and the Foreign Secretary discussed Anglo-Soviet relations with trade union leaders. Similarly, Bonar Law had been prepared to talk about conscription, intervention in Russia and the German blockade in 1919; and Lloyd George followed suit in the case of the Russo-Polish war in 1920 and the 1922 Chanak crisis in the Balkans.

Not that union leaders were conceded all their consultative demands. They frequently complained about being excluded from particular bodies, about being inadequately represented and about being unable to choose their own representatives. Nor did they find less to complain about during the first Labour government's term of office. The TUC was so dissatisfied with the representation offered the unions on the important Balfour Committee on Industry and Trade that it not only refused to submit nominations, but even declined to present evidence to the committee. In only one respect did Labour discriminate in favour of the unions: under pressure, the Prime Minister reversed ministerial refusals to breach tradition by allowing TUC leaders to see the drafts of two industrial bills before they had been introduced in parliament.[9] Otherwise, Labour ministers seem, if anything, to have been less forthcoming than their Conservative counterparts. Years later, Sidney Webb tried to justify their failure to consult the TUC about the Balfour committee. He insisted that even a Labour government could not accept a right of consultation on this issue. 'But that is just it', the TUC secretary records himself as replying, 'the Conservative Government *had* consulted us on

[7] *TUC Report*, 1925, p. 171.
[8] ibid., pp. 121–2, 126.
[9] General Council, *Minutes* (*GC Mins.*, hereafter) 26 March and 9 April 1924.

such matters, and they have done so since. They do not always accept our view, but at least they consult us. You did not even do that'.[10]

Yet, for all their complaints, the consultative status of union leaders was clearly higher than that of their pre-war counterparts. The intense, if sporadic, industrial unrest of the years after the war (and the threat of a general strike was part of this) helps explain the difference. So does the nature of postwar public policy which, despite the successes of the de-control movement, retained a few elements recalling the government's wide-ranging administrative dependence on the unions during the war. There was, for example, a decidedly wartime flavour about both the main problem confronting government leaders, in the discharge of their new responsibility for promoting housing construction, and the way they tried to solve it. The problem was a shortage of skilled building workers. The solution, attempted by Labour as well as non-Labour ministers from 1920, was close consultation with the building trades unions in the hope of securing their acceptance of dilution, piecework and a ban on stoppages.

The difference in consultative status is also likely to have been affected by changes in social attitudes. The war had diminished class distinctions. Wage movements and taxation policies combined to reduce inequalities of income in some measure. Styles of life, manners and dress were less reliable indicators of class than they had once been. Not, of course, that class differences had ceased to matter by the mid-1920s. Their continued political importance was reflected both in the outbursts of 'class hatred' characterizing the 1923 parliament,[11] and in the diary-entry written by a well-placed civil servant shortly before the general strike: 'It is impossible not to feel the contrast between the reception which Ministers give to a body of [coal] owners and a body of miners. Ministers are at ease at once with the former, they are friends jointly exploring a situation'.[12] At the same time, wartime associations had at least ensured that politicians and civil servants were less ignorant of the character and capacity of working-class leaders. And

[10] Lord Citrine, *Men and Work*, p. 270.
[11] C. L. Mowat, *Britain Between the Wars 1918–1940*, p. 155.
[12] Thomas Jones, *Whitehall Diary*, vol. 2, p. 19.

after the war many were impressed, for example, when the varied talents of Robert Smillie and Frank Hodges were displayed in the show-case of the 1919 Coal Industry Commission, or when the 1920 Shaw Inquiry into dockers' wages revealed the formidable intelligence of Ernest Bevin. Later, the *Sunday Times* drew comfort from the fact that members of the first Labour government, about to take office, had 'a sound business experience in the management of the trade unions'.[13] Then there was the discovery made by the King (who wondered, rather unnecessarily, what 'dear Grandmama' would have thought of a Labour government) that J. H. Thomas of the railwaymen, on the testimony of personal contact, was actually 'a good and loyal man'.[14] These kinds of attitudes hint at a climate in which the tone of personal dealings between unions and government is likely to have been at least a little less readily influenced than before by social disparities.

TRADE UNIONS

The unions emerged from the war with swollen memberships and large expectations. Their expectations had been nourished both by the wartime promises of government spokesmen and by a sense of power springing from a belief in the efficacy of the strike. That belief was a dominant element in trade union thought up to 1926. In centred on the notion that the unions held in their hands an ultimate weapon—the general strike. As one union official active in this period recalled three decades later, 'many of us thought that our aims . . . as trade unionists could be readily achieved by industrial action alone. We were . . . much under the influence of ideas derived from syndicalist . . . theories of direct action'.[15] Even otherwise conservative union leaders were affected. In 1920 the cautious J. H. Thomas could boast of the Triple Alliance that the 'existence of such a colossal organization . . . makes possible a national strike by which the whole life of the country could be brought to a standstill'.[16]

---

[13] Quoted in Richard W. Lyman, *The First Labour Government, 1924*, p. 84.
[14] Quoted in Harold Nicolson, *King George V*, pp. 340, 384.
[15] J. Tanner: *TUC Report*, 1954, p. 77.
[16] J. H. Thomas, *When Labour Rules*, p. 42–3.

The general election of December 1918 had encouraged this emphasis. The Labour party won the largest representation on the opposition benches with its 59 members, but it still remained little more than a parliamentary splinter group. The path to independent political power, which it had chosen by leaving the wartime coalition, looked long and stony.

Nevertheless, as we have seen, up to the autumn of 1919 trade union leaders, including those heading the Triple Alliance, succumbed to Lloyd George's shrewdly varied blandishments so far as industrial issues were concerned. On other issues, however, the Triple Alliance leaders were less patient. They were thinking of industrial action in April when they asked the TUC to call a conference about British military intervention in Russia, the continuation of conscription and some other matters. The Parliamentary Committee refused: most of its members agreed with the Labour party's leadership that the general strike weapon should not be employed in support of non-industrial aims. The government's announcement of dates for the ending of both conscription and its Russian adventure came a few days after the Alliance's decision to hold a strike ballot of its constituents' members.

Both the TUC and party leaders were out-of-tune with the prevailing climate of trade union opinion. In September Congress not only, in effect, censured the Parliamentary Committee for rejecting the Triple Alliance's request, but declined to condemn industrial action on 'political' matters. However, eager as they were to affirm their faith in the principle of the general strike, irrespective of issue, union leaders in general tended to be cautious about using it. They responded to the miners' plea for support on nationalization with a decision to hold a special Congress if the government held to its opposition. They displayed little inclination to bring their members out behind the railwaymen's wage strike in September; and when rank and file action threatened to widen the strike, union leaders who had previously spoken in favour of a general strike joined with others to form an *ad hoc* committee which successfully mediated between the railwaymen and government. As for the miners' nationalization demand, the TUC's special Congress in December decided on a publicity campaign instead of a general strike; and four months later, after that campaign had run into the sand, another special Congress voted almost four-to-one against a general strike, tamely opting instead for 'intensive political propaganda in preparation for a General Election'.[17]

They were less cautious, as it turned out, on other issues. In July 1920 another special Congress declared in favour of a general strike if British troops were not withdrawn from Ireland. This decision, however, was hurried and vaguely drafted and would probably have come to nothing even had subsequent events not diverted attention from it. Shortly afterwards, rumours of impending British intervention in the Russo-Polish war provided a much more emotive issue. Widespread local labour demonstrations were capped with the formation of a Council of Action whose spokesman told Lloyd George to his face that intervention would evoke 'not merely political action, but an action representing the full force of Labour'.[18] The issue, although plainly 'political', crumbled divisions within the labour movement in a way that none other had since the Taff Vale judgement. Former opponents of the general strike, such as Arthur Henderson, spoke hotly in favour at a great conference of party and union leaders which unanimously authorized the Council of Action to call a general strike. Britain did not intervene.

But the mood of that moment was not transferable. The miners called off a planned wages strike the following month when their partners in the Triple Alliance withheld active support—although when they eventually launched a national strike in October, the threat of a supporting railway stoppage helped them secure a favourable, if temporary, settlement. But the Emergency Powers Act, brought down at the same time, evoked a comparatively mild reaction among the unions. And later, on 'Black Friday' in April 1921, the miners' Triple Alliance colleagues seized the last-minute opportunity offered them to cancel their declared supporting strikes.

The times, in any case, were distinctly unpropitious. During the preceding three months unemployment had more than doubled. By 'Black Friday', the most dramatic decline that had ever occurred in union membership and funds was already

[17] *TUC Report*, 1920, p. 112.
[18] Quoted in Alan Bullock, *The Life and Times of Ernest Bevin*, vol. 1, p. 137.

underway. So, too, was a tide of wage reductions which industrial action was helpless to stem. It was many months before political action was the source of much hope. The Labour party won 142 seats, and the status of official parliamentary opposition, at the general election of November 1922. Its holding was increased to 191 seats in December the following year. Shortly after the election the Liberals made clear their readiness to support the first, if minority, Labour government in British history.

The Labour government that took office in January 1924 failed, for the most part, to live up to even the more modest hopes of its most active supporters. For them, its back-down on rent restrictions, its tentative measures against unemployment, and the absence of any distinctively Socialist policy initiative, tended to weigh heavier than its admitted achievements in both domestic and foreign policy. Trade union leaders, in particular, were offended by other aspects of its performance which were less readily excused by its parliamentary minority. Ramsay MacDonald started off on the wrong foot with them when he gave only seven of twenty cabinet posts to trade unionists, while allocating five to relatively new party members and two to non-Labour men. The reluctance of Labour ministers to grant the trade unions customary consultative rights, let alone privileged rights, further exacerbated relations. So did their willingness to invoke the Emergency Powers Act against strikers.

The general election of October 1924 ended an unhappy episode for the unions, by cutting Labour's representation to 152 seats and giving the Conservatives an absolute majority. But union leaders had learned something of signal importance. It was well expressed by W. J. Brown of the Civil Service Clerical Association.

In short, they [trade union leaders] had learned this, that even with a complete Labour majority in the House, and with a Labour Government which was stable and secure, there would be a permanent difference in point of view between that Government . . . and the Trade Unions . . . and that difference in point of view did not arise from any wickedness on the part of [either] side . . . but arose from the fact that the Trade Unions had different functions . . . and that the Government . . . would be influenced by all kinds of considerations which were excluded from the Trade Unions' considerations.[19]

[19] *TUC Report*, 1925, pp. 363–4.

The point was implicitly acknowledged, six weeks after the 1924 election, when the parliamentary Trade Union Group decided to confine its membership to MPs directly 'promoted and financed by Trade Unions'.[20] It had been pressed, while the Labour government was still in office, by those convinced of the peculiar virtue of the strike weapon. The proponents of industrial action inevitably included the Communists, who created the militant National Minority Movement in mid-1924, but they were by no means confined to the extreme left. Improving economic conditions and dashed hopes in the Labour government helped swell their ranks. Their hand, although not the only influence at work, was evident in some big strikes while Labour held office and in a successful move to enlarge the TUC's formal industrial powers. After Labour fell, they threw their weight behind efforts to confirm the TUC's independence of the Labour party and to establish a more comprehensive version of the defunct Triple Alliance. They triumphed on 'Red Friday' in 1925.

Baldwin's 'Red Friday' concession inspired a euphoric response. The TUC president thrilled at the thought of 'a glorious week—one that will ever be remembered', and of a 'demonstration of Trade Union solidarity' that had 'given hope to the whole movement'.[21] But it was not a movement that was capable of equal solidarity when it came to using, as distinct from threatening, a general strike. The acid test came in May 1926. And then, union leaders who were constitutionalists at heart suddenly found themselves trying 'to run a revolution in the spirit of a friendly game of cribbage'.[22] The outcome, as after the 'Black Friday' of 1921, was that the miners were left to fight on alone to grinding defeat. But there was one difference. The general strike had finally been put to the test; and had proved ineffective in the hands of British trade unionists. It was the close of an era.

Up to that time, the idea of the general strike had gripped the imagination of trade union leaders to an extraordinary degree. The more cautious, or far-sighted, were aware of its dangers; but they were also tempted by the power it promised.

[20] Quoted in R. T. McKenzie, *British Political Parties*, p. 416n.
[21] *TUC Report*, 1925, p. 68.
[22] G. D. H. Cole, *A Short History of the British Working-Class Movement*, 1937, vol. III, p. 153.

G. H. Stuart-Bunning, TUC president in 1919, was not alone in believing that it 'meant revolution' and 'a desperate gamble with the lives of men, women and children'.[23] J. H. Thomas described it, by implication, as an act of madness which would bring 'disaster and bloodshed upon the country'.[24] Ernest Bevin opposed extending the railway strike in October 1919 because he thought that would lead to 'civil war'.[25] Earlier, Robert Smillie had felt that 'we were beaten and we knew we were' as soon as Lloyd George, having admitted that the Triple Alliance could 'defeat' the government by striking, asked its leaders if they were prepared to accept the constitutional consequences he envisaged.[26]

Yet, shortly afterwards, Smillie led the campaign for a general strike on conscription and intervention in Russia. Bevin did not oppose the Triple Alliance decision to hold a ballot on the matter. Thomas did oppose it; but later on (around the time of his 'disaster and bloodshed' prediction) could write of the general strike as a legitimate weapon of last resort and 'an invaluable lever'.[27] Again, in 1920, at the conference on the issue of British intervention in the Russo-Polish war, Thomas stood shoulder to shoulder with Bevin in advocating the step which, as he candidly admitted, meant 'a challenge to the whole constitution of the country'.[28] There were no dissenting voices. Moreover, the suggestion of a general strike on this issue was first officially raised, not in the heady atmosphere of the conference, but four days earlier at the joint meeting between the executives of the TUC, the Labour party and the parliamentary party, which also set up the Council of Action. And that meeting had accepted the suggestion with 'surprising unanimity', as the official report put it.[29] The pattern was to be repeated in 1921, in 1925, and again in 1926.

The explanation of this paradox seems to be that while union leaders in general saw, and feared, the *possible* revolutionary consequences of the general strike, they had convinced themselves that those consequences were avoidable. For one thing,

[23] *TUC Report*, 1919, p. 52.
[24] ibid., 1920, p. 113.
[25] Quoted in Bullock, op. cit., pp. 108–9.
[26] Quoted in Aneurin Bevan, *In Place of Fear*, pp. 20–1.
[27] Thomas, *When Labour Rules*, p. 43.
[28] Quoted in Snowden, op. cit., vol. II, p. 562.
[29] Quoted in Ralph Miliband, *Parliamentary Socialism*, p. 78.

the latent power of the general strike seemed so immense that it was easily assumed that government, more likely than not, would prefer to concede comparatively modest demands rather than run the risks its use entailed;[30] and by 1926 this conclusion had gathered support not only from the 'Red Friday' and Council of Action episodes but also, as G. A. Phillips points out,[31] from the less obvious example of 'Black Friday' and its aftermath. Secondly (and this was the crucial blindspot), it seems that the possible consequences of the general strike were assumed to be avoidable simply because they were not intended by union leaders themselves. 'We have been told', Bevin remarked as events moved towards the climax of 'Red Friday', 'that this virtually means a revolution'. Then he brushed aside those 'who are always raising the constitutional issue' by blandly insisting that the issue 'won't be raised by those of us who have to lead the strike'.[32] Nine months later, he and his colleagues were trying 'hard to persuade themselves that they had only organized a sympathetic strike'.[33]

The general strike was thus a gigantic bluff because it was essentially a revolutionary technique that could not, in the end, be effectively used by trade unionists lacking a revolutionary purpose. It could, for them, be a source of power only so long as it remained a threat. For a time, of course, the myth of the general strike was unquestionably a source of power; and, as such, helped bolster the self-confidence of union leaders in their postwar dealings with government. There were also less ephemeral factors working in the same direction.

Wartime governments, as we have seen, had conceded consultative rights that often reached right down to the factory floor—sweeping working shop stewards, as one of them proudly put it, 'into the limelight of great events'.[34] Ministers and civil servants might still have been able to dazzle union officials with the authority of office or quickness of wit, though this was less certain once Lloyd George had discredited both for officials who came to rate the man-to-man plainness of a Baldwin more highly. But familiarity, in any case, destroyed the aura which

---

[30] See, e.g., J. H. Thomas, *My Story*, pp. 62–3.
[31] See Phillips, *The General Strike: The Politics of Industrial Conflict*, p. 11.
[32] Quoted in Bullock, op. cit., p. 274.
[33] L. S. Amery, *My Political Life*, vol. II, p. 484; see also Thomas, *My Story*, p. 96.
[34] J. T. Murphy in Arthur Gleason, *What the Workers Want*, p. 185.

remoteness had once given ministers, in particular. The process is precisely illustrated in a union leader's recollections of the time. On his first visit to 10 Downing Street, he felt that 'I was going to meet the great ones of the earth'. Later visits still evoked 'a certain sense of awe', but 'one does not feel the same sense of humility'.[35]

One symptom of the new assurance of union leaders was the notably more matter-of-fact tone of TUC reports of postwar interviews with ministers, especially prime ministers. Another was the more ambitious nature of the claims they made in relation to consultative representation. They were aggressively concerned not merely with representation on advisory bodies, but with its scale and the method of selection involved. Thus Baldwin was told that two union places on a twelve-member committee was 'a very unfair representation';[36] and, as the Labour government's Home Secretary was informed in one case, fair representation could amount to 'one-half of the members' of an investigating committee.[37] Similarly, union leaders indignantly protested when it was revealed that labour representatives comprised only 140 of the 809 members of committees responsible for recommending magistrates' appointments—and barely 700 of almost 10,000 magistrates.[38] They also demanded to be consulted about all advisory positions allocated to the labour interest on the ground that they had been too often filled, in the case of local Employment Committees, by 'some social worker or . . . small shopkeeper';[39] and in the case of magistrates' selection committees, by men who had either 'seceded from the [Labour] party, or are working men Tories or Liberals'.[40]

Nor were they disposed to accept offers of formal consultation at any price. The TUC leaders declined to join a cabinet-created body inquiring into the trade depression in 1921, because of the 'narrow scope' of its terms of reference.[41] Two years later they rebuffed repeated government requests to make nominations to the National Council for the King's Roll, concerned with the training and employment of ex-servicemen, because they disagreed with the council's aims.

[35] Hodges, op. cit., p. 91.
[37] *GC Mins.*, 24 September 1924.
[39] ibid., 1925, pp. 398–9.
[41] *PC Mins.*, 6 January 1921.
[36] *TUC Report*, 1925, p. 170
[38] See *TUC Report*, 1924, p. 271.
[40] ibid., 1924, p. 271.

And, as we have seen, they boycotted the Labour government's Balfour Committee on Industry and Trade on the ground of lack of prior consultation and an inadequate allocation of members.

Confidence, of course, on its own was not enough to achieve the unions' policy aims. Peacetime released opposing political pressures which the war had either diverted or repressed. The groundswell of commercial and industrial interests eager for a return to 'limited government' was powerful and obvious. Also influential, if less obvious, was the restoration of the *ancien regime* within the structure of government itself. During the war it had been relatively easy for unions to pick off free-spending departments that were largely independent of each other. But with 'the Armistice guns the Treasury's winter ended; stage by stage, trying its strength against the new departments, it crept back to its old position of dominance and of making finance the lever for the control of policy'.[42] And the slide into economic depression from 1920 made assurance double sure that the lever would be tilted against the usually expensive ambitions of the unions.

Nor, in the end, were the sanctions available to the unions capable of tilting the lever the other way. Their two major attempts to influence government by threatening to withhold administrative cooperation were unsuccessful. On the first occasion, in 1920, the issue was the admission to the enlarged unemployment insurance scheme of friendly societies which, it was thought, would impair the unions' ability to recruit non-unionists newly covered by the scheme. But withdrawal from the scheme, it was soon realized, could mean the loss of existing union members; and the threat was quickly dropped.[43] The issue on the second occasion, in 1922, was a Treasury decision to cut the grants to bodies administering unemployment insurance. Although the unions secured some concessions of detail, the Treasury's principle was preserved and applied.

Only in the case of the general strike did it seem, for a time, that British trade unionism had found 'a punch mated to its bulk'.[44] But it was in the hands of men who thought of it as a superior bargaining technique, rather than a means of beating

[42] Beveridge, *British Food Control*, p. 304.
[43] See *TUC Report*, 1920, pp. 211, 241.
[44] Gleason, op. cit., p. 20.

a ruling class to its knees. It was also a weapon that lacked versatility; it was too blunt to be threatened, let alone used, on all but the most exceptional issues.

The collapse of the 1926 general strike left trade union leaders politically disarmed for the near future. They retained, however, the wider experience and greater social assurance which they had gained during and since the war. There was no sanction in this, but it continued to mould their vision of the possible, and their relations with both government and business leaders. There was no going back to the pre-war world despite their loss of the sanction that, for a time, had seemed to make all the difference.

TRADES UNION CONGRESS

The TUC's role in the general strike reflected a militancy, on the part of its leadership, which was notably lacking seven years earlier. In April 1919 the Parliamentary Committee was asked to convene a special Congress to consider taking industrial action on conscription, conscientious objectors, the German blockade and intervention in Russia. The committee opted, instead, for a talk with the Lord Privy Seal, in the absence of the Prime Minister; and afterwards decided (by seven votes to five) that Bonar Law's response, although 'not . . . entirely satisfactory', was 'satisfactory enough to justify . . . refusing to call a special conference'.[45] It later re-affirmed this decision (by six votes to four) when the Labour party officially added its voice to the clamour among the unions.

At the annual Congress in September, the decision was defended primarily on the ground that the TUC had no formal policy on the general strike issue and there was no relevant 'precedent'.[46] Congress, unconvinced, rejected both the committee's report on the matter and a resolution opposing political strikes. At the same time, however, it re-elected almost all the old members of the committee, while denying representation on it to the miners who had provided the militant spearhead. Nothing, it seemed, had changed. But during that same

[45] *PC Mins.*, 28 May 1919.
[46] *TUC Report*, 1919, p. 52.

fateful autumn, which Keynes saw as 'the dead season of our fortunes',[47] there was an event which was to prompt developments that helped transform the fortunes of the TUC.

The Choice is Made

The national railway strike was launched not long after the Congress. The TUC's vice-chairman and secretary quickly interviewed the Prime Minister. But it was an *ad hoc* Mediation Committee which successfully moved to contain and then settle the strike. This committee was formed at a conference convened by the Transport Workers' Federation, and only later was it augmented by two TUC representatives.

For those who initiated and led the Mediation Committee, the railway strike confirmed the inadequacy of the trade unions' standing organizational arrangements in relation to major cases of industrial action. Once the strike had ended, they turned their attention to the question of a permanent body capable, in such cases, of coordinating the approach of the unions at large. The General Federation of Trade Unions, though formally concerned with industrial action, was insufficiently representative and its membership was declining. The industrial coverage of the Triple Alliance was strictly limited. The trade union committee emerging from the government-sponsored National Industrial Conference had shown an inclination to move into the industrial field, but it did not include either the Amalgamated Society of Engineers or the constituents of the Triple Alliance. Only the TUC possessed a sufficiently comprehensive membership. The Mediation Committee accordingly recommended that the Parliamentary Committee's powers should be extended 'to enable it to become the central coordinating body of all future Trade Union activities'.[48]

But drastic surgery was thought to be necessary before the TUC's executive could become, in the current phrase, the 'General Staff' of the trade union movement. The matter was taken up by a special Coordination Committee consisting of representatives from the Mediation Committee, the Parliamentary Committee and the trade union side of the National

[47] J. M. Keynes, *The Economic Consequences of the Peace*, p. 278.
[48] *PC Mins.*, 8 October 1919.

Industrial Conference. The Coordination Committee was subsequently authorized, by the TUC's special Congress of December 1919, to formulate proposals for replacing the Parliamentary Committee with a 'General Council' equipped with broader powers and a more elaborate administrative structure.

Almost two years were to elapse before the General Council became a reality. In the meantime, the TUC leaders displayed less reluctance than before to associate themselves with industrial action. Up to the December Congress their only notable interventions had been in the August police strike, when they saw the Home Secretary and appealed for strike funds; and in the railway strike, mainly through their representation on the Mediation Committee. Within a few days of that Congress, however, they were mediating an iron-moulders' dispute and, later, another in the furnishing trades. They plainly had no stomach for a general strike on the coal nationalization issue; but, then, neither did the special Congress of March 1920. Similarly, they were evidently content when the next special Congress in July, while advocating a general strike against military involvement in Ireland, omitted to direct them to take action on the resolution. But earlier, they had taken a militant initiative of a different sort by threatening a union boycott of the unemployment insurance scheme if friendly societies were admitted to its administration. And, later, they joined with the Labour party in the Council of Action which threatened a general strike if Britain intervened in the Russo-Polish war. They again took a militant initiative in October 1920 by convening a union conference to consider action in support of the striking miners, although the strike ended soon after. Later, too, they intervened in a dispute involving Belfast shipbuilding workers; and, during the sequel to 'Black Friday', offered their good offices to unenthusiastic miners' leaders.

Thus, by September 1921 when it was replaced by the General Council, the Parliamentary Committee had become distinctly more venturesome. It had also witnessed the demise of once-important competitors. The Triple Alliance disintegrated on 'Black Friday'. Three months later the committee representing the trade union side of the National Industrial Conference was wound up, when all hope failed. The General

Federation of Trade Unions did not die, but it was conclusively eclipsed. In 1919 the TUC leadership ignored a government suggestion that a GFTU member should be included in the delegation to the conference which gave birth to the International Labour Organization. The following year the TUC-GFTU wartime agreement, providing for equal representation on delegations to bodies like the International Federation of Trade Unions, was amended to give the TUC seven delegates and the GFTU three. However, the 1920 Congress repudiated the agreement, claiming exclusive representation on the IFTU and rejecting any association with the GFTU in the international field. The GFTU fought back, without success. But, alongside the first General Council of the TUC, there was still the Labour party.

The Party Moves In

For most of 1919 the Parliamentary Committee appears to have had little official contact with the Labour party leadership. No joint meeting of the two executives, frequent as they were during the later war years, seems to have been held. There was only one attempt to arrange a joint deputation to a minister, and that did not eventuate because of disagreement about the nature of the case to be put. The strains in their relationship surfaced most obviously in the TUC's reaction to a government request that it nominate nine labour representatives to attend the founding conference of the ILO. The Ministry of Labour, which issued the invitation, specifically suggested the inclusion of Arthur Henderson; but his name was not on the list sent in by the Parliamentary Committee. Only after persistent pressure, from both the minister and the party executive, did the committee eventually relent. Henderson, as the party's fraternal delegate to the September Congress, thus had ample reason to appeal for 'greater cooperation'.[49]

The railway strike, which broke out shortly afterwards, was a turning-point in TUC-party relations, as well as much else. Henderson was a member of both the Mediation Committee and the Coordination Committee. His hand, at least, was evident in the Coordination Committee's resolution, adopted by the special Congress of December 1919, which instructed the

[49] *TUC Report*, 1919, p. 312.

Parliamentary Committee to negotiate with the Labour party and the Cooperative movement about forming joint research, legal advice and publicity departments 'in order to avoid overlapping in the activity of working-class organizations'.[50] Not long before, in November, there had been an indication of improving relations when the TUC and party executives mounted their first joint ministerial deputation of the year; it raised the issue of unemployment benefits with the Minister of Labour.

The highpoint of their collaboration during 1920 was the formation of the Council of Action which threatened a general strike on the Russo-Polish war issue. But their closer relations were signified in other ways as well. The party was invited to join the TUC's inquiry into the cost of living. There were a number of meetings on the proposal for joint departments. The Parliamentary Committee's report, presented to the Congress of September 1920, was unusually generous in its acknowledgement of the party's parliamentary work. The same Congress adopted re-organization proposals which, while falling short of the party leaders' ideals, promised them joint departments and consultation on all future Congress resolutions 'requiring political action', in order that a joint decision might be made 'on methods for furthering them'.[51]

During the next twelve months, before the formation of the General Council, the tide continued to flow in the same direction. There were frequent joint meetings between the TUC and party executives. Together, they appealed for funds in support of the miners after 'Black Friday', protested against the Safeguarding of Industries Bill, and set up a committee to devise means of combatting unemployment. They persisted with the proposal for joint departments, even after the Cooperative movement lost interest. They also discussed the possibility of reviving, in some form, the defunct Joint Board.

The 1921 Congress not only elected the first General Council, but endorsed the formation of four joint departments—an international affairs department being added to the three originally recommended. It also approved the creation of a National Joint Council on which the parliamentary Labour party had equal representation with the TUC and party

[50] ibid., 1920, p. 311.   [51] ibid., p. 268.

executives. The inclusion of the parliamentary party was one departure from the model of the old Joint Board. There were others as well. The formal statement of the NJC's powers left no doubt that what was intended was a purely consultative body: it was denied the Joint Board's power to 'decide' matters of joint concern and to determine unions' *bona fides* and interunion disputes. Significantly, too, while the Joint Board's chairman had latterly been a representative of the party, that position on the NJC was allocated, *ex officio*, to the General Council's chairman—the secretaryship going to the party secretary. In addition, it was specified that the combined representation of the two party groups, in the case of joint conferences, was not to exceed the membership of the General Council.

The Labour party leaders had doubtless hoped for more. But they had gained enough since 1919 to encourage Henderson's belief that 'we are going to make the political and the industrial not two separate movements, but in a very real sense two sides of the one movement'.[52] His belief was apparently vindicated shortly afterwards when the Prime Minister invited the General Council alone to discuss unemployment with him. The TUC leaders not only accepted a suggestion from Henderson that they should be accompanied by members of the party executive on that occasion, but later agreed that the party and the TUC should be equally represented in the delegation which took up the Prime Minister's offer of further discussions.

In the same month, October 1921, the NJC was formally constituted, as also were the committees governing the proposed joint departments (although the legal committee never met and no legal department was formed). Moreover, the NJC soon began to play a larger role than its formal constitution envisaged. It took over from the TUC negotiations with the Ministry of Labour about administrative grants under the unemployment insurance scheme. It intervened, at Henderson's instigation, in the big engineering stoppage of 1922; and again, the same year, in a shipbuilding dispute after the General Council itself had decided that the matter should be 'placed in the hands' of the NJC.[53] Subsequently, too, the 1922 Congress referred to it many resolutions of 'a purely and distinctly political character'.[54] And during the next twelve months it was the NJC

[52] ibid., 1921, p. 327.   [53] *GC Mins.*, 4 April 1922.   [54] *TUC Report*, 1922, p. 401.

which handled the major statements and representations on such matters as unemployment, health insurance and foreign affairs. During the same twelve months, however, there were signs that the TUC leaders had neither forsworn independent political action nor enjoyed an entirely harmonious relationship with their party counterparts.

Slackening Bonds

Despite the 1922 Congress's referral of 'political' resolutions to the NJC, the General Council still sent its own deputations to see the Prime Minister, about unemployment, and other ministers on matters raised at Congress. But the issue of the council's relations with the Labour party leadership was raised much more sharply in two less public episodes.

Within a few days of the Congress, the Chanak crisis brought Britain to the brink of war with Turkey. The TUC chairman proposed a special meeting of the NJC. Henderson and Sidney Webb, for the party, thought the matter should be left to the Joint International Committee. The General Council thereupon sent a deputation of its own to the Prime Minister; and later it flatly rejected Webb's claim that the JIC had exclusive right 'to deal with the Eastern situation'.[55] The second episode centred on the question of whether Arthur Greenwood, following his election to parliament, should continue as paid secretary of the Joint Research and Information Department. The General Council thought he should resign. The party executive thought he should stay. After five months of wrangling, the TUC leaders decided to drop the matter: they had just learnt that the party executive not only had 'somewhat misunderstood' the nature of their objection, but had previously declined an offer to resign which Greenwood had made at the time of his election.[56]

At the 1923 Congress there was no mention of either the Chanak or the Greenwood incident. Soon afterwards, the party executive again proposed that the annual conferences of the two bodies be synchronized. Again, the TUC leaders declined. But there was a more specific echo of Chanak and Greenwood in their counter-proposal of a formal inquiry into the 'staff and

[55] *GC Mins.*, 21 September 1922.
[56] ibid., 22 August 1923.

general administration' of the joint departments.[57] The echo was there again, a month later, when the General Council made its annual selection of its representatives on the Joint International Committee only after 'considerable discussion' (a phrase employed with decent rarity in its minutes) about the committee's functions.[58]

The formation of the Labour government in January 1924 provided the council with another opportunity to assert itself. The new ministry included Margaret Bondfield, the council's chairman, and two other members, J. H. Thomas and Harry Gosling. Bondfield was quickly told that she ought to step down from the chairmanship; and then it was decided that all three should vacate their seats on the council. The TUC leaders also moved for a fresh investigation of the joint departments. They were reported as having forced W. W. Henderson, a newly-elected MP and Arthur Henderson's son, to resign from the secretaryship of the Joint Press and Publicity Department—although they subsequently agreed that he could retain the position. Their doubts about the joint administrative arrangements were reinforced by the disclosure that specialist advisory committees, associated with the Joint Research and Information Department, had been dealing with government departments 'on their own initiative, without the endorsement' of either the TUC or the party.[59]

Nevertheless, the General Council maintained quite close relations with the party executive during 1924. The NJC was not as active as it had been the previous year. But that was largely compensated by a revival of the wartime practice involving regular meetings between the two full executives. At the same time, when the party executive suggested that 'joint business equally affecting' them both should be dealt with jointly, the General Council shrugged off the proposal with the laconic declaration that 'the present practice with regard to joint business be continued'.[60] And overshadowing all, as a source of disaffection, was the TUC leaders' inability to gain privileged access to Labour ministers on the basis of their connection with the party.

[57] ibid., 26 September 1923.
[58] ibid., 31 October 1923.
[59] ibid., 23 April 1924.
[60] ibid., 25 June 1924.

The TUC leadership's alienation, in this respect, was given muted expression in the opening passages of the General Council's report to the 1924 Congress.

Unfortunately, there are those who . . . take the mistaken view of regarding the political Labour Movement as an alternative, instead of an auxiliary to the Trade Union Movement . . . Political organization, far from being an alternative to the Trade Union Movement, is its natural corollary.[61]

The immediate purpose of this statement was to support the council's claim to larger industrial powers. It also supported another departure which reflected more directly on the TUC-party relationship. This was the 'Industrial Workers' Charter', which Congress adopted unanimously. The charter, for the first time, incorporated in the TUC's formal 'objects' a list of specific public policy aims, ranging from education and housing to pensions and public ownership. In addition, the relevant resolution directed the General Council to launch a 'vigorous campaign in all parts of the country with a view to mobilizing public opinion' behind the charter[62]—an instruction which authorized a political campaign conducted independently of the Labour party.

There were also implications for the TUC-party relationship in another section of the General Council's report. It noted that the council had arranged a conference of trades council representatives earlier in the year, the first formal link between them and the TUC since 1895. A similar conference was later to consider proposals for standing consultative arrangements. Officially, the TUC's initiative in this respect was justified on the ground of the need for coordination. But Walter Citrine later admitted that the TUC leadership was also anxious to ensure, in the case of the many trades councils which had operated as both local union centre and party branch since 1918, that 'proper industrial Committees are established so that Trade Union work would be transacted solely by responsible Trade Union delegates'.[63]

Shaking Free of the Party

The Labour government fell shortly after the 1924 Congress. Ranks closed for the general election. The TUC, as in the

[61] *TUC Report*, 1924, p. 81.   [62] ibid., p. 351.
[63] Citrine, *The Trade Union Movement of Great Britain*, p. 61.

previous two elections, appealed for a Labour vote from trade unionists. Unlike 1923, it did not issue a joint manifesto with the party; but again placed its staff 'at the disposal' of the party.[64] Moreover, it not only issued its usual appeal for union donations to the party's campaign funds but, apparently for the first time, contributed £1,000 from its own resources. The cracks reappeared once the election was over.

There was, first of all, a petty dispute about the special leave to be given full-time staff members of the TUC, the party and the joint departments, in acknowledgement of their electioneering work—an issue that had caused no trouble after the previous election. Then the TUC leaders refused to take part in a joint investigation of tariff policy. Barely a year before they had joined with the party executive to issue a statement on tariffs; but they now thought that this was 'necessarily an industrial matter' which should be left to them.[65] A public allegation that TUC funds were being used for political purposes gave them an excuse for requesting a staff report on the joint departments. Citrine, then assistant secretary, produced a highly critical report in May 1925. It was shelved for the time being. But Beatrice Webb caught the drift. The TUC leaders, she wrote, 'are apparently deciding to break up their present connection with the Labour Party'.[66]

A month later, the General Council publicly signalled its intentions. First, it decided to convene an exclusively trade union conference on unemployment, a topic which had almost invariably been handled jointly with the party since the war. Second, it invited the party leaders to attend but denied them the right to speak. Third, it affirmed that any resolutions emanating from the conference would be submitted to the Prime Minister by a deputation representing only the TUC. There was, however, a more critical step to be taken at the annual Congress in September 1925.

The General Council's report to Congress went straight to the point; and the point was the dismantling of the joint departments. 'The general feeling . . . is that . . . if [its] work is to be effectively carried on the General Council must have entire control of its own Publicity, Research and International

[64] *GC Mins.*, 16 October 1924.   [65] ibid., 25 March 1925.
[66] Margaret Cole (ed.), *Beatrice Webb's Diaries, 1924–1932*, p. 60.

Departments'.[67] It was also claimed that the premises shared with the party were no longer adequate. The debate on these recommendations was restrained by the presence of the press. There were no explicit references to the points made in Citrine's May report about excessive cost, lack of staff control, salary anomalies and parliamentarians-cum-staff members. Bramley, the secretary, canvassed support primarily on the ground of the TUC's enlarging functions which he described as being 'too big, too various, and too distinctly Trade Union to make it possible for them to be developed as one-half of joint departments'.[68]

In April 1926 the General Council became the master of its own administrative arrangements, apart from a shared library. By this time, too, it had effectively achieved something similar in relation to the trades councils. It had secured agreement on a set of model rules requiring councils that doubled as Labour party branches to refer all industrial questions to a separate and exclusively trade unionist committee. Within a few months the number of subscribing trades councils had more than doubled, to 395, on the previous year. They were now organically linked with the TUC through a permanent Trades Councils Joint Consultative Committee and an annual conference.

Not that the TUC leadership severed all ties with the party. Their new offices were still in the one building, as a result of Bevin's offer to extend Transport House in order to accommodate them. The NJC and a half-dozen specialist joint committees survived the destruction of the joint departments and their associated consultative bodies. There were, it appears, further meetings between the two full executives—although they were irregular, like those of the NJC. Party representatives accompanied at least three TUC deputations to ministers between the end of the 1925 Congress and the general strike. Moreover, on the day it decided to issue the general strike notices, the General Council also invited MacDonald and Henderson to attend the daily meetings it planned to hold throughout the strike-period.

Nevertheless, there is no question that their relations had cooled in comparison with two years earlier. The joint departments had been a fertile source of friction. But the first Labour

[67] *TUC Report*, 1925, p. 85.   [68] ibid., p. 359.

government's term of office was certainly more productive in this sense. Above all, it had shattered the illusion that a special relationship with the Labour Party guaranteed a special relationship with a Labour government. The TUC secretary put the matter in a nutshell.

The Labour Party cannot have it both ways. If when [it is] in office we are to be detached from the Labour Movement, we cannot be treated as an integral part of that movement when Labour is out of office. During the period the Labour government was in office, we were not taken into consultation at all by the Prime Minister.[69]

In addition there was the fact that the TUC leaders' concern with conventional political action had been displaced, in some measure, by their interest in the political use of the strike weapon.

The Emphasis on Industrial Action

It was widely accepted that the point of reorganizing the TUC, and replacing the old Parliamentary Committee with a General Council, was to give British trade unionism a central body capable of coordinating strike action. The aim, in Bevin's words, was to 'develop the industrial side of the Movement as against the "deputizing" or "political" conception'.[70] True to this aim, the constitution adopted in 1920 required the General Council to 'keep a watch on all industrial movements', 'coordinate industrial action', 'promote common action on general questions', and 'assist any union which is attacked on any vital question of Trade Union principle'.[71] But the constitution contained no powers to match these new functions. And union leaders proved reluctant to confer such powers.

The 1921 Congress overwhelmingly rejected a motion which would have given the General Council express power to intervene in serious industrial disputes. The council subsequently sent a circular to affiliated unions, in which it pleaded for wider powers. It took the issue to the 1922 Congress, with a proposal that would have required unions in dispute to consult with it and would have authorized it to levy affiliates in support of striking unions. The proposal was heavily defeated. So was a

[69] Quoted in V. L. Allen, 'The Reorganization of the Trades Union Congress, 1918–1927', *British Journal of Sociology*, vol. XI, 1960, p. 36.
[70] Quoted in Bullock, op. cit., p. 111.
[71] *TUC Report*, 1921, p. 425.

similar resolution at the 1923 Congress. In the meantime, as we have seen, it was the NJC that intervened, with TUC support, in the engineering and shipbuilding disputes of 1922; and there had been no TUC complaint about Ramsay Mac-Donald's intervention in the agricultural workers' strike of 1923.

But in 1924, the year of the first Labour government, the pattern changed. Within eight months the General Council was claiming to have been 'called upon to intervene' in six 'important disputes' and a number of lesser ones.[72] Perhaps the Congress of that year was impressed. At any rate it granted an extension of power which, apart from its omission of authority to levy affiliates, was substantially the same as that rejected in 1922 and 1923.[73] Affiliated unions were now formally obliged to keep the TUC informed about disputes. The General Council was empowered to initiate consultation with affected unions if a major stoppage seemed likely; and if its intervention was accepted by the unions, the council was to give them such support as it considered necessary in the event of a stoppage.

Subsequently, Congress's grant seemed handsomely justified by the TUC's role in the woollen industry lockout and, above all, the triumph of 'Red Friday'. But the 1925 Congress was not prepared to accept a motion from the floor which would have empowered the General Council to call for sympathy strikes and impose a levy on affiliated unions. Yet when the crunch came in May 1926 it turned out that, irrespective of formal powers, the TUC's authority among the trade unions was sufficient to enable its leaders to launch the greatest industrial action in British history.

Internal Authority: the Debit Side

In 1924, when the General Council asked once again for wider industrial powers, the delicacy of the manoeuvre was reflected in the council's anxiety to reassure the unions that such powers 'can be safely exercised'. 'In any efforts of a mediatory nature which the Council has undertaken it has always been a primary condition that the disputing ... unions should first have indicated their acceptance of the Council's assistance'.[74] The

[72] ibid., 1924, p. 126.
[73] See Phillips, *The General Strike*, pp. 17–20, for a discussion of conflicting interpretations of this *volte-face*.
[74] *TUC Report*, 1924, p. 82.

formal extension of powers that it was given on this occasion maintained the emphasis on consultation and mutually acceptable decisions. The real limitation on its role of industrial coordinator, the attitudes of union leaders, thus remained enshrined in the TUC's constitution.

Some union leaders, deeply committed to coordinated industrial action, were unhappy about this. Their discontent generated moves to form an enlarged version of the old Triple Alliance covering unions in the coal, electricity, engineering, iron and steel, and all transport industries. By late 1925 they had formulated a constitution involving highly centralized control of national stoppages. But waning support prevented the new alliance from being formally established, and put to the test. Instead, it was the TUC that was tested.

The miners stopped work on 1 May 1926. On the same day a conference of TUC affiliates handed the management of the dispute to the General Council. The implications of this decision were largely ignored, only Bevin pointing to the possibility that 'you may have to cease being separate unions . . . [and] become one union with no autonomy'.[75] But the miners, at least, had already qualified Bevin's proposition. Their officials had conferred privately beforehand with the TUC leaders, when they were told that the General Council must have 'control' of the dispute, with 'the responsibility for the future conduct of negotiations'. The council's minutes record Herbert Smith, their president, as replying that 'they understood that the position was that all negotiations would now be carried on through the General Council, but that they, as the Miners' Federation, would be consulted'.[76] The understanding which the miners' executive recorded, on the other hand, was more stringently phrased: 'no settlement would be reached without the miners' consent'.[77] And cabinet papers record the concurrence in this of the council's chairman, who admitted to government leaders that 'we cannot negotiate independently of them [the miners] absolutely . . . we cannot take the decision'.[78] Smith's rider, thus interpreted, imposed a constraint on the TUC leadership which turned out to be critical.

[75] Quoted in Bullock, op. cit., p. 302.
[76] *GC Mins.*, 1 May 1926.
[77] Quoted in Phillips, *The General Strike*, p. 116.
[78] Quoted ibid., p. 326.

It was a matter of time. The general strike was to start from the night of Monday, 3 May. Early on Sunday, the TUC's negotiating committee and the Prime Minister tentatively agreed on a formula that would have postponed the strike for up to a fortnight. The committee said it would consult the General Council and the miners, and report back to cabinet by noon that day. It then discovered that the miners' leaders had dispersed outside London; they did not reassemble until a little before midnight. Their discussion with the General Council was interrupted by a summons from the Prime Minister. He presented an ultimatum: if the general strike orders were not withdrawn, the government would break off negotiations. The TUC leadership had no alternative but to launch the general strike.

The explanation of the abrupt hardening in Baldwin's position appears to be that, some time between 11 p.m. and 1.00 a.m., cabinet learned of the *Daily Mail* compositors' refusal to set a leading article attacking the TUC. This news, in the phrase of one minister, 'tipped the scale'.[79] The delay arising from the TUC's obligation to consult the miners had helped provide the cabinet hawks with the lever needed to push their colleagues over the edge.

The miners again demonstrated the limits of the TUC's authority when the general strike ended. After consulting them, the General Council decided to call a halt despite their opposition. They refused to accede and, as all other strikers straggled back, embarked on a further six months of hopeless struggle. The miners' recalcitrance harshly illuminated the TUC's limitations as industrial coordinator, for theirs was the one case that mattered above all others.

Nevertheless, while the general strike laid bare the constraints to which the TUC was subject, it also provided an indication of an internal authority that was appreciably greater than it had been a few years earlier.

Internal Authority: the Credit Side

The General Council's formal industrial powers were not much more substantial than those of the old Parliamentary Committee. They did, however, reflect a significant change in union

[79] Amery, op. cit., p. 483.

attitudes to the TUC. The Miners' Federation provides the illustrating case. Its leaders had been prepared to work through the TUC in relation to their nationalization claim during 1919 and 1920. But they refused its offer to help in their dispute, following 'Black Friday'; and later, at the 1921 and 1922 Congresses, they voted against proposals to extend its formal industrial power. But by 1924 they had been converted, and supported the similar proposal which that year's Congress accepted. Their conversion was even more convincingly demonstrated in July 1925, when the miners' executive presented itself before the General Council to ask for support in the current coal industry dispute. The council agreed, and 'Red Friday' followed. Nine months later, when the council intervened in the dispute that culminated in the general strike, it again did so at the request of the miners' leaders.

By this time, moreover, there had been a notable change in the General Council's status as an intervenor. Before 1925, its role was confined to that of mediator rather than participant. But that year, in the case of both the miners' dispute and the woollen industry dispute, it was accepted as a direct party to the negotiations. And in May 1926, there was a further development in its role: it dealt *alone* with government before and during the general strike.

In the end, of course, the function of industrial coordinator provided a transient source of authority that was buried under the wreckage of the general strike. But there were other sources which, if less imposing, were more reliable.

The General Council retained the formal political functions of its predecessor—and continued to face much the same criticism in this respect. In the year of the council's formal conception, the Webbs wrote of 'futile annual deputations' presenting 'crude resolutions',[80] and Congress itself unanimously condemned the practice as 'now almost obsolete'.[81] At the time of the council's birth, the TUC chairman complained that the deputations of the preceding year had 'resulted . . . in greater barrenness than usual'.[82] But the annual round of ministerial deputations continued. By 1924, indeed, the council was plainly eager to boost their importance. Its report of that year recorded

[80] Webb, *The History of Trade Unionism*, p. 570.
[81] *TUC Report*, 1920, p. 268.   [82] ibid., 1921, p. 58.

discussions with ministers at a length that, for some years past, had been reserved for prime ministerial encounters. Moreover, council members dominated all but one of the numerous deputations which the TUC arranged between 1923 and April 1926.

On the other hand, there was no attempt to revive the TUC's pre-war claims to a direct parliamentary role. That role was left to the Labour party. But there were links other than through the party's official machinery. The number of MPs in the General Council's membership did not fall below four during 1923–6; and by 1926 TUC officers were attending meetings of the parliamentary Trade Union Group, at the group's invitation. The council signalled its changed priorities in 1923 by debarring its secretary from holding a parliamentary seat.

Outside the political field, the TUC's traditional interest in union amalgamations was maintained, although it seems to have had little or nothing to do with the more important post-war developments in this respect. In the case of inter-union disputes, however, the General Council handled more than its predecessor. Equally noteworthy, it displayed a tendency to investigate them with more care, a practice that was eventually to lead to the formulation of principles and a body of case-law which strengthened its role in this area.

There were also extensions in the TUC's structure and activities. The General Council inherited a Trade Boards Advisory Council, created in the Parliamentary Committee's dying moments, and formed a special department to deal with trade board issues. From 1921 it took over the functions and establishment of the Women's Trade Union League. The 1923 Congress, the first presided over by a whitecollar unionist, authorized the formation of a joint consultative committee with whitecollar unions.

Of more immediate importance were the steps taken from early in 1924, as we have seen, to bring the trades councils into an organic connection with the TUC. This move, initially designed largely to break the Labour party's grip on local union organization, found a target further to the left following the formation of the Communist party's National Minority Movement later in 1924. The NMM, a vehicle for the party's campaign against established union leaderships, won a fair degree of support among the trades councils. The General Council responded, in January 1926, with a ruling that no trades council with NMM associations would be recognized by the TUC—a threat that proved remarkably effective.[83] But, so far as the General Council's internal authority is concerned, what is even more remarkable is the fact that both its ruling against the NMM and its earlier decision to create formal links with the trades councils were made without prior approval from Congress.

Congress not only accepted these initiatives; it also enlarged the General Council's potential for independent action on another and much wider plane. It did this by adopting, as we have seen, the Industrial Workers' Charter in 1924. Most of the charter's aims had been the subject of individual Congress resolutions, some of them on many occasions. Usually, however, executive action on any one of them had required the authorization of a resolution at the preceding Congress. The charter changed this by giving these aims permanent force. In doing so, it gave the General Council both the time and the incentive to formulate the detailed terms of specific policies and to explore their administrative requirements. In addition, it left the council free to determine the timing and the method of action employed in the case of a particular policy.

The implications of the Industrial Workers' Charter, on their own, are enough to point the contrast between the internal authority of the General Council and its predecessor. The Parliamentary Committee, for the most part, substantially discharged its functions once it had acted on the resolutions of each annual Congress. Its lack of standing was strikingly illustrated when the issue of its own reform was placed, by Congress, in the hands of the Coordination Committee on which its own representatives were in a minority. In contrast, by May 1926, the General Council had both initiated and won Congress acceptance of proposals for wider industrial powers, for the Industrial Workers' Charter, and for separate administrative departments—not to mention its activities relating to strikes and trades councils.

[83] See Roderick Martin, *Communism and the British Trade Unions*, pp. 96–9.

The Significance of the General Council

For more than two years after the election of the first General Council in 1921, there seems to have been little change in the TUC's standing among the unions. The change, when it came, was reflected in the expansion which has been traced above in the TUC's industrial and political roles. It has customarily been associated with such factors as a revival of industrial militancy, disillusion with the first Labour government, and a weakening of the conservative element in the General Council's membership (the importance of the latter consideration being the subject of particular dispute).[84] But one factor that has been neglected in this respect is the developments in the TUC's administrative structure.

One of the stated justifications of an enlarged TUC executive body was that the new General Council would be able to make more use of sub-committees than the smaller Parliamentary Committee. The council quickly spawned an elaborate sub-committee system. Its report for 1926 (compiled after the disappearance of committees associated with the abolished joint departments) listed a total of 40 sub-committees: six confined to council members, 18 with affiliated union representation, eight constituted jointly with the Labour party, and eight with other bodies—and the list seems to have overlooked one or two others. Some, it is true, were moribund. Nevertheless, during 1925, there were nearly 400 meetings of committees containing General Council members. These circumstances are typically those in which a full-time staff becomes indispensable as a means of briefing busy part-time committee members, keeping minutes, and providing the other forms of background coordination that are inevitable as filing systems proliferate and an organization loses its infant simplicity.

This had been foreseen. The 1920 Congress approved an increase in affiliation fees on the understanding that it would be used for staff expansion. The TUC's full-time staff at that time comprised the secretary, the assistant secretary, a 'confidential secretary' and two typists. The initial expansion was primarily an outcome of the formation of the joint departments shared with the Labour party. But around the same time there

[84] See especially Phillips, *The General Strike*, pp. 17–19, 69–70.

were developments with a profound bearing on the quality and allegiance of future staff members.

There was an unsuccessful move at the 1921 Congress to by-pass the aging Bowerman, who had been both an MP and TUC secretary for a decade. But a year later, when he was seventy-one, Congress resolved that its full-time officials should retire at seventy. Bramley, his most likely successor, shortly afterwards indicated the way the wind was blowing when he announced his resignation as prospective Labour candidate for the Reading constituency. The TUC leadership, though only by 14 to 13 votes, subsequently stipulated that the secretary should 'devote his whole time to the work of the General Council';[85] and the 1923 Congress endorsed this decision. The TUC was to have no more MP-secretaries. For the first time it had laid first claim to the working time and allegiance of its senior full-time official.

The principle was applied down the line. After Bramley's promotion, short-listed candidates for the assistant secretary-ship were told that 'the terms of the appointment would not allow them to stand as Parliamentary candidates'.[86] At this point the General Council bureaucratized its administrative structure by taking the decisive step towards creating a career service within it. Simultaneously, it also took a critical step on the issue of staff quality. For, from the five candidates it interviewed for the assistant secretaryship, it selected Walter Citrine.

Citrine, as time was to show, combined the talents of a gifted administrator with a single-minded identification of his personal fortunes with those of the TUC. He soon had to shoulder most of the secretary's duties, owing to Bramley's failing health. He was appointed acting secretary on Bramley's death, in October 1925, and formally elected to the position after the general strike. Citrine early displayed ambitions for the General Council which had to be restrained by 'older and probably wiser heads'.[87] But he and Bramley made common cause from the start, and had a hand in the developments that signalled an enlarging of the TUC's internal authority from the beginning of 1924. Bramley played a major role in relation

[85] *GC Mins.*, 28 February 1923.   [86] ibid., 7 January 1924.
[87] Citrine, *Men and Work*, pp. 86, 144.

to industrial disputes, at least during the early part of 1924. Citrine helped initiate the action taken to link up with the trades councils. They would certainly have thrown their weight behind the Industrial Workers' Charter and the claim for strengthened industrial powers which the 1924 Congress accepted. Both of them were obviously guiding spirits in the moves leading up to the 1925 Congress decision to dismantle the joint departments.

The ambition of the bureaucrat was plain in the great emphasis which the General Council's report for 1925 placed on the need for staff expansion. His initiative was reflected in Citrine's memorandum of January 1926, which raised neglected questions of policy and preparation relating to the possibility of a general strike. Both were evident in the way the General Council in 1924 took on the task of fostering regular and frequent exchanges of information, not only with trades councils, but also with individual unions and their federations. Functions of this kind are the staple diet of full-time officials. The functions involved in supporting an elaborate committee system and in adding flesh to a policy skeleton, like that of the Industrial Workers' Charter, provide something more: they increase the opportunities and strengthen the capacity of staff members to influence policy decisions formally taken by their part-time superiors.

The new TUC constitution of 1921, as Roberts has said, changed little 'in a fundamental sense'.[88] By 1926, however, there had been a fundamental change. For by then the TUC's structure incorporated a nuclear bureaucracy. There were only seven small 'departments'—finance, organization, international, trade boards, women's group, research, publicity. But they were headed by officials whose professional commitment was unequivocally to the TUC. It was this, rather than the formation of the General Council, which was of greatest significance for the future of the TUC.

External Authority

The coming of peace initially made little difference to the TUC's standing in relation to government. In January 1919, it was only as an afterthought that the TUC was invited to the

[88] Roberts, *The Trades Union Congress*, p. 358.

Paris talks about the projected ILO; the Labour party's representatives were already there. It was invited less casually to the National Industrial Conference the following month, but was accorded no special representation or role. Later, however, there were signs of a shift in ministerial attitudes. In August the TUC alone was asked to nominate labour representatives for the Washington conference on the ILO. During 1920, at the request of the government, it nominated two members of an advisory committee on industrial production, three to the Coal Industry Advisory Committee, and convened a conference of building unions for the Minister of Health to attend. Nevertheless, the TUC's official representation on post-war government bodies remained very limited, particularly during these two years. And government leaders seeking formal representation of the general labour interest often failed to distinguish between the TUC and the Labour party.

The same problem arose, if to a lesser degree, in the case of *ad hoc* consultation. The TUC leaders thus found cause for serious complaint when the Minister of Labour neglected to consult them about the Wages (Temporary Regulation) Act and other matters in 1919. But their position was to improve in this respect. Two years later, it was them alone that the Prime Minister invited to a 'confidential chat' about unemployment.[89] Moreover, they usually had no difficulty in gaining access to ministers. This was strikingly illustrated in 1922 when they wanted to see the Prime Minister about the Chanak crisis. The TUC secretary's morning telephone call was transferred, in Lloyd George's absence, to Austen Chamberlain, the Lord Privy Seal. He agreed to pass on the request, and rang back that afternoon to say that the Prime Minister would see the General Council the next morning.[90]

The Chanak incident illustrated two other things as well. One was government's willingness to recognize the TUC's right to consultation even on foreign policy issues. The other was the sensitivity of government leaders to the threat of a general strike. For, inevitably, the TUC's Chanak initiative raised echoes of the Council of Action episode when there had been an explicit general strike threat on the same issue of war or peace.

[89] *GC Mins.*, 5 October 1921.   [90] ibid., 20 September 1922.

The leaders of the first Labour government had the advantage of being untouchable, so far as a general strike was concerned. For the most part, they gave the TUC, like the trade unions at large, only the small change of consultation. Ramsay Mac-Donald, during 1924, seems to have been the only Prime Minister of the interwar years with whom the TUC secretary did not have so much as five minutes' conversation.[91] But it was a different story when Baldwin returned to office.

In 1925 TUC spokesmen saw Baldwin at least twice, on other matters, before their involvement in the July negotiations with him about the coal industry dispute. By then they were, potentially, leaders of a general strike. An indication of the authority this gave them in government eyes, during the period to the general strike of May 1926, is the level, frequency and intimacy of their dealings with ministers—which included, at the Prime Minister's instance, a private meeting at Chequers on 25 April with Arthur Pugh, chairman of the General Council.[92] But that authority was qualified in two particularly noteworthy ways. In the first place, government leaders were more confident of withstanding a general strike than they had been in 1925 because of the preparations they had made for coping with such an emergency.[93] In the second place, they were aware of the constraints imposed, above all by the miners, on the TUC's negotiating freedom: indeed, they may well have over-estimated the severity of those constraints.[94] Despite the qualifications, however, the fact remains that up to 3 May, and the government's ultimatum, its negotiations with the TUC involved a bargaining relationship in the strict sense of the term.

A Rising Political Authority

The limited political authority with which the Parliamentary Committee emerged from the war was underlined at the government-convened National Industrial Conference. In April 1919 the conference adopted recommendations which had been

[91] See Allen, 'The Reorganization of the Trades Union Congress, 1918–1927', p. 36.
[92] See Thomas Jones, op. cit., pp. 22–3.
[93] See Phillips, *The General Strike*, p. 132.
[94] See ibid., pp. 117, 119; and Middlemas and Barnes, *Baldwin*, p. 405.

signed, on behalf of the trade union side, not by the TUC leaders at the conference, but by Arthur Henderson whose official status was simply that of a delegate from the Society of Ironfounders. The parallel with the Treasury conference of 1915 is precise and obvious.

It has been claimed that the Parliamentary Committee which gave way to the General Council, in September 1921, was 'treated by all Governments as the authoritative spokesman of the opinions of organized Labour'[95]—a claim that implies corresponding treatment by the trade unions. This is questionable. The key example is the one occasion in the Parliamentary Committee's postwar life when it acted entirely alone in threatening retaliatory action on a major policy matter. The issue was the government's proposal to bring friendly societies into the administration of unemployment insurance. The committee threatened that the trade unions would withdraw from the scheme if this were done. The National Conference of Friendly Societies was initially impressed: it asked whether 'a deal' was possible.[96] But it soon discovered, along with a watching government, that the threat was empty because the unions themselves rejected the committee's initiative.

This, rather than the imposing standard of 'the authoritative spokesman', is what the General Council's authority in May 1926 is to be measured against. The benchmark, simply stated, is a Parliamentary Committee with a relatively narrow range of functions and formal powers; a body overshadowed, politically, by the Labour party and, industrially, by the Triple Alliance. The reality of 1926 was a General Council which had not only out-lasted the Triple Alliance and asserted its independence of the Labour party, but had greatly expanded its functions and formal powers. Above all, it had negotiated with government leaders as a body explicitly authorized by the unions at large to launch and control the biggest strike in British history.

Even then, the General Council was not 'the authoritative spokesman' of the unions—as the miners, above all, were to show. But it was certainly the most authoritative spokesman

[95] Roberts, *The Trades Union Congress*, pp. 356–7.
[96] *TUC Report*, 1920, pp. 209–10.

they possessed. And by May 1926 the council had acquired a political authority which far outstripped that of the old Parliamentary Committee. The question that hung over its head, before the month was out, was whether that authority could survive the collapse of the general strike.

8

Profit from Disaster 1927–1937

THERE was not much room for optimism in trade union circles by the beginning of the 1930s. The general strike was no longer a credible weapon. The unions' political position had been gravely weakened by the impact of the great depression on their industrial strength. It was further undermined by Labour's crushing electoral defeat in 1931. Paradoxically, however, these circumstances at once forced and enabled the TUC leadership to rebuild the General Council's political authority on more enduring foundations.

GOVERNMENT

The Baldwin government's Trade Disputes and Trade Union Act of 1927 symbolized its release from the constraints formerly imposed by the threat of a general strike. The Act, among other things, restricted picketing, outlawed sympathetic strikes against government, and substituted 'contracting in' for the 'contracting out' principle in relation to union political funds. Under the same government, however, there was a drift towards state intervention in industry which hinted at a less subservient future for the unions. It was this government which nationalized electricity transmission at the end of 1926 and created, in the Central Electricity Board, the first state business agency wholly appointed by and responsible to a minister. It also converted the BBC into a public corporation and moved to promote a national film industry.

The second Labour government, of 1929-31, carried the process further. It inaugurated the first statutory cartel arrangement (in the coal industry), sponsored producer-controlled agricultural marketing boards, and moved to train young unemployed workers and regulate working conditions in road transport. But it was the later Conservative-dominated

National governments that initiated the more radical departures in response to economic depression.

With the abandonment of the gold standard in September
1931, government assumed responsibility for exchange rates
and took a hand in the regulation of credit. In 1932 it discarded
free trade and instituted a comprehensive system of protective
tariffs, later adding quotas on agricultural imports. Supplementary policies proliferated: the provision of capital investment loans and direct subsidies; organized marketing and
guaranteed agricultural prices; the promotion of cartel
organization in a widening range of industries; some extension
in the scope of public ownership; and efforts to promote
economic recovery in particularly hard-hit regions. In the field
of industrial relations, there was legislation to enforce collective
bargaining agreements in the cotton weaving industry and to
encourage the granting of annual paid holidays. The Unemployment Act of 1934 widened eligibility for relief, and the Factories
Act of 1937 was of considerable concern to the unions.

Implicit in the more important of these measures was government's assumption of a measure of responsibility for the state
of the national economy. This prompted what Beer has
described as 'a system of quasi-corporatism in which industry
and government were brought into regular and continuous
contact'—although, he adds, the trade unions were excluded
from 'such governmental "recognition".'[1] Nevertheless, the
consultative relationship between unions and government was
rather closer than this qualification suggests.

It is true that the Baldwin government's dealings with the
unions declined sharply following the general strike. But this
seems to have been almost wholly a result of union preferences.
There is no record of ministers refusing to see union deputations.
Nor did they try to reduce the unions' representation on formal
consultative bodies: on the contrary, they provided further
opportunities.

Ministers in the succeeding Labour government received
relatively more TUC deputations—though they did not always
give them a warm welcome and, for a time, at least one senior
minister fobbed off requests for a deputation. Similarly, while
usually giving the unions a seat on relevant consultative bodies,

[1] Beer, op. cit., pp. 278, 298.

they flatly refused to do so in the case of the new London Passenger Transport Board, an administrative body, and admitted a union representative to the Export Credits Advisory Committee only in response to persistent pressure. Union leaders, in any case, were more eager for consultation with the Labour government. They also expected more from it, and were correspondingly aggrieved by the reluctance of ministers to provide early briefings on legislative plans. But in one other respect their consultative status was substantially advanced: they were admitted to an advisory role at the higher reaches of economic policy. Most notably, they were given representation on the Economic Advisory Council, the Macmillan Committee on Finance and Industry, the Colonial Development Advisory Committee, the Export Credits Advisory Committee and the May Committee on National Expenditure.

'In the old days of the Liberals and the Tories,' Bevin complained in the mid-1930s, 'there was some consultation as to policy, but since 1931 Labour had been treated like an outcast.'[2] This remark, made to a ministerial go-between, reflects the professional bargainer's instinct for hyperbole. For during this period trade union leaders were, if anything, treated more softly than in 'the old days.' There were rebuffs, but nothing to match Philip Snowden's behaviour, during the Labour government's last months, when he repeatedly warded off TUC requests for an interview. An ailing Ramsay MacDonald declined to see one TUC deputation, because his 'time was fully occupied'; and Baldwin, also as Prime Minister, declined to see two more, pleading 'pressure of work' in one case and a pre-emptive parliamentary decision in the other (although he also offered, each time, to make another minister available).[3] Both of them, however, received TUC deputations on other occasions—as also did the Home Secretary who refused to break precedent by discussing specific prison sentences, and the Minister of Health who rejected one deputation request on the ground of inappropriate timing. Indeed, in each year during 1932–7, National ministers saw more TUC deputations (on matters other than industrial disputes) than their predecessors had in any year, except 1925, since the war. Nor were they

[2] Quoted in Bullock, op. cit., vol. I, p. 592.
[3] *TUC Report*, 1935, p. 195; 1936, p. 125; 1937, p. 192.

above initiating dealings. Baldwin privately consulted Citrine about rearmament in 1935 and during the abdication crisis the following year. Different Ministers of Labour sought more formal meetings with the TUC on at least six occasions. At lower levels also there was extensive consultation which seems to have been prompted as often from the departmental as from the union side.

National ministers were less inclined than their Labour predecessors to concede the unions a voice at the higher reaches of economic policy formulation. Nevertheless, they did admit them to a consultative role in economic and industrial matters which was perceptibly weightier than in the 1920s. Thus union leaders were included in bodies like the Transport Advisory Council and the Royal Commission on the Distribution of the Industrial Population; and their representatives accompanied the British delegations to the 1932 Imperial Economic Conference in Ottawa and, in 1933, to the World Monetary and Economic Conference in London. And National ministers were prepared to enter into exchanges on broader policy matters. For example, union leaders on a number of occasions discussed with the Prime Minister or the Foreign Secretary, or both, rearmament, the Spanish civil war, the Sino-Japanese war and other foreign policy issues.

National ministers were also less inclined than their Labour predecessors to allow direct union nominations to consultative bodies, preferring the old practice of making their own selection from union-provided lists of candidates. Similarly, they were more anxious to ensure that unionist appointees acted in a personal rather than representative capacity. But these were marginal matters. What was of much greater importance was the extent to which the unions' claims to formal representation were conceded. This was implied in the TUC's demand, in 1935, that 'all Boards or Commissions . . . set up in connection with marketing or the organization of industries shall include trade union . . . representation'[4]—a resolution which, as its mover explained, was concerned solely with bodies exercising substantial administrative powers. Eleven years earlier, another Congress had adopted a similar resolution; but on that occasion the demand had been limited to purely advisory bodies. The

[4] ibid., 1935, p. 391.

shift in emphasis reflected the fact that government leaders had in large measure conceded the claim of the 1920s.

This was one of the reasons why, by 1937, Bevin was declaring that the 'industrial policy of [our] opponents has changed': 'The old bitter hostility ... has gone. It is a new technique which is being introduced.'[5] In addition to more assured consultative links, the 'new technique' involved some substantial concessions—including, as we have seen, legislation relating to cotton industry agreements, road transport wages, annual paid holidays and factory conditions; and regulations revising unemployment relief scales and extending industrial health and safety controls. It is also of significance that the first purely 'trade union knights' were created at this time. Citrine (who declined a similar offer in 1932) and Arthur Pugh were both given knighthoods in 1935; and Bevin was given the opportunity of refusing one.

Economic depression and, eventually, the possibility of war both thrust government into an interventionist role which forced it to pay deeper attention to economic interests, including the trade unions. Baldwin acknowledged this in 1935: 'the days of non-interference by Governments are gone,' he said, and the 'new era ... calls for the greatest measure of statesmanship, on the part ... of those who are responsible for the conduct of business and of the Trade Unions.'[6] 'Statesmanship', in this context, obviously meant a readiness to cooperate with government.

In part, this emphasis on cooperation sprang from the government's need for technical information in relation to many of its policies. Apart from the field of industrial health and safety, however, the unions appear to have had comparatively little to offer in the way of technical information. Nor was their administrative participation in the health and unemployment insurance schemes as important to government as it had once been. In 1921 organizations other than state employment exchanges, mainly unions, had covered more than 4,000,000 workers in relation to unemployment insurance; ten years later the figure was less than 900,000, and continued to decline.[7] The

[5] Quoted in Bullock, op. cit., p. 599.
[6] Quoted in Young, op. cit., p. 197.
[7] *TUC Report*, 1932, p. 109.

trend was similar in the case of health insurance. But there were other administrative issues on which union cooperation was clearly at least useful to government, as in its moves to re-organize the cotton industry or to construct a cost of living index by surveying 30,000 working-class households. Sometimes such cooperation could be thought essential: thus the inclusion of union representatives in the administration of unemployment relief from 1934 was widely regarded as 'vital . . . for the par-ticular purpose of securing public confidence' in the working of new arrangements strongly opposed by the unions.[8]

Nor was the emphasis on union cooperation entirely absent at loftier policy levels. The importance Baldwin attached to union officials as opinion leaders is indicated by the steps he took to sound out Citrine on the abdication crisis before it broke into the open. Even more to the point is his reaction, late in 1935, when Mussolini's Abyssinian adventure shook the Labour movement's faith in disarmament as a feasible policy. 'Here, at last,' his biographer wrote, 'was the thing which Baldwin had always said was vital to any policy of armament and defence—the cooperation of the Unions.'[9] And he invited Citrine to discuss rearmament a few days after the TUC's annual Congress registered the first official shift in labour opinion. Although, for reasons which are not clear, Baldwin did not follow up his agreement with Citrine and move openly to consult the unions on the issue, some two years later govern-ment leaders did move to seek the unions' cooperation on the central political issue of the time.

TRADE UNIONS

At the last Congress before the general strike, Beatrice Webb had sensed a 'feeling of elation and bursting self-confidence'; at the next she found an atmosphere of 'apathy tempered by pessimism'.[10] The Congress president, who asked delegates to avoid 'hysterical denunciations or sensational threats', also appealed for 'a calm discussion of Trade Union principles and policy'.[11] It was a significant appeal. For Citrine, writing just

[8] A. L. Fleet in Vernon and Mansergh (eds.), *Advisory Bodies*, pp. 316, 336.
[9] Young, op. cit., p. 204.
[10] Margaret Cole (ed.), *Beatrice Webb's Diaries, 1924–1932*, p. 115.
[11] *TUC Report*, 1926, p. 70.

before the general strike, the urgent problems had been 'more those of structure and machinery than of policy and methods of action'.[12] The strike's failure had reversed the priority. Hence the president's appeal; and hence Bevin's confession that trade union leaders, for the moment, found themselves in a 'vacuum'.[13]

The vacuum was partially filled a few months later with the introduction of the Trade Disputes and Trade Union Bill. As the president of the next Congress indicated, after the Bill's enactment, many drew comfort from the thought that 'this Act is just what our movement required to unite its ranks'.[14] But of greater importance in filling Bevin's vacuum were the discussions, begun early in 1927, between certain industrialists and trade union leaders. These led to the so-called Mond-Turner talks, which opened in January 1928. By then, moreover, major union leaders had formulated their solution to the problems of policy and method left in the wake of the general strike.

This solution was set out in a *Manchester Guardian* article, 'The Next Step in Industrial Relations', published under Citrine's name in November 1927.[15] Trade unionism, it was argued, had reached the end of a stage in its evolution in which union functions had been confined largely to 'the politics of industry', the regulation of wages and working conditions. In the next stage, union functions had to be extended into 'the economic sphere', and especially into 'the field of industrial administration'. What this required was a general recognition that trade unions had a part to play in promoting 'efficiency, economy, and scientific development in the productive system'; and an acceptance by unions themselves that they ought to be actively concerned with, among other things, 'eliminating waste and harmful restrictions, removing causes of friction and avoidable conflict, and promoting the largest possible output' —with the aim of ensuring 'a rising standard of life and continuously improving conditions of employment'.

The Mond-Turner talks, between TUC leaders and prominent industrialists, provided an opportunity for pressing this

[12] W. M. Citrine, *The Trade Union Movement of Great Britain*, p. 106.
[13] Bullock, op. cit., p. 393.
[14] *TUC Report*, 1927, p. 62.
[15] Reproduced in Milne-Bailey, *Trade Union Documents*, pp. 431–8.

policy. They also provided a timely source of hopeful action for major union leaders who expected little or nothing from a government that had defeated their general strike and brought down the Trade Disputes and Trade Union Act. Thus Bevin, on the question of a survey of unemployment: 'Whom can you meet to discuss it with? Government Departments who do nothing? No, I would rather sit down with some considered policy on a problem of that character facing the capitalists themselves across the table.'[16] But before long government was again the focus of their attention.

The second minority Labour government took office in June 1929, after a general election at which 287 Labour MPs were elected. The international economic crisis broke a few months later. By this time, moreover, the Mond-Turner talks had been converted into more formal and less promising discussions with the main employer organizations.

The Labour government achieved something in relation to such things as pensions, road transport, unemployment insurance and miners' working hours. But it was unable to repeal the Trade Disputes and Trade Union Act, there were inadequacies in its unemployment relief policy, and it failed even to introduce long-prepared bills on important aspects of factory regulation and workers' compensation. These shortcomings were all held against it among the unions. On the other hand, as we have seen, it was responsible for one innovation of great importance to them. It admitted their leaders to formal advisory bodies concerned with issues of high economic policy. This innovation was reflected in the TUC's submissions to the Macmillan Committee on Finance and Industry which deplored the fact that union leaders had not been consulted before the restoration of the gold standard in 1925, and claimed that 'decisions of this kind . . . should not be taken without consultation with the Trade Union Movement'.[17] The point is that this claim had not been advanced in 1925. Its novelty was underlined by a justificatory preface to the TUC's submissions, which was intended 'to show the very close and direct interest we have in such problems as that with which the [Macmillan] Committee . . . is concerned'.[18]

---

[16] *TUC Report*, 1928, p. 450.   [17] ibid., 1931, p. 275.
[18] ibid., p. 265.

The ambitions fostered in this way survived the Labour government's collapse in August 1931. In contrast to the period after 1924, there was no pronounced swing to industrial action. Soaring unemployment, if nothing else, saw to that; and even when conditions improved from 1934, unemployment remained high. On the other hand, trade union leaders in general acquired a new interest in the Labour party, despite its near-annihilation at the 1931 general election (46 seats) and its painfully slow electoral recovery (only 154 seats at the general election of 1935). Their interest in the party was generated by the opportunity they were given to play a more influential role in its affairs as a result of the depleted ranks and reduced calibre of its leadership. This could have diverted their attention from dealings with government had they shared the sentiments of the doctrinaire Socialists whose position in the party had also been enhanced. But too many of the major union leaders concurred with Citrine, who was not prepared 'to waste my time. . . discussing ultimate Socialist objectives of a theoretical nature'.[19] They were inclined towards a pragmatic political stance and the pursuit of immediate concessions from government, irrespective of party. The attitudes of National government leaders and the continuing interventionist trend in public policy encouraged them in this.

'Economic planning and social control of the mechanism of industry and trade', a TUC president triumphantly announced in 1935, 'are principles which capitalist Governments and employers' organizations [now] recognize and accept.'[20] Nor was it only capitalists whose conception of the state's role had been enlarged. 'I do not think Free Trade and Protection is a thing that a Socialist can get over-enthusiastic about', Bevin calmly remarked in 1932.[21] Barely a year earlier, that comment would have brought down on his head the wrath of Snowdenite free-traders whose influence had then been weighty enough to persuade the TUC to exclude a revenue tariff from its proposals on the financial crisis. Similarly, only after 1931 did the campaign for legislation prescribing a universal maximum working week secure the widespread support which prompted Will Thorne's delight at 'the tremendous change' in union

[19] Citrine, *Men and Work*, pp. 300–1.
[20] *TUC Report*, 1935, p. 70. [21] ibid., 1932, p. 374.

attitudes on the issue.[22] And during the six years to the end of 1937, events in China, Germany, Austria, Abyssinia and Spain, especially Spain, made foreign affairs of consuming interest to union officials. In these circumstances, they could scarcely ignore even National government leaders whom many of them deeply distrusted.

Their attempts to influence government policy during this period placed unusual emphasis on public campaigns, involving mass meetings and demonstrations, a technique that was used with particular intensity in relation to the new unemployment relief scales and household means test of 1935–6. Even more emphasis was placed on parliamentary action, which was employed in a much more calculated fashion than for many years past. Through Labour MPs, the House of Commons was utilized as a public platform in support of union claims, and the parliamentary committee rooms for detailed negotiations on government bills of union concern. Union leaders organized parliamentary silences, too, as when the Home Secretary indicated to them that a particular bill might be forthcoming if it 'could be regarded as non-controversial':[23] they made the necessary arrangements, informed the minister, and the measure went through. There was also something of a revival of interest in private members' bills. These were used mainly to publicize claims, but sometimes to test the climate with an eye to the possibility of 'agreed' legislation.

The principal emphasis, however, was on direct representations to government. Dealings with both ministers and civil servants were more frequent during the 1930s. So were union submissions to commissions, departmental committees and other bodies inquiring into matters ranging from unemployment relief and law court procedure to electricity distribution and cycling accidents.

Union leaders also displayed a heightened concern for formal involvement in the administration of government policy, especially in relation to unemployment relief. The TUC urged before one committee of inquiry that the unions at large 'should be asked to take over for their members the administration of State Unemployment Benefit from the [Employment] Exchanges, including the placing of workers';[24] and that the

[22] ibid., 1934, p. 405.   [23] ibid., 1938, p. 214.   [24] ibid., 1930, p. 121.

worker-members of the administrative Courts of Referees should normally be union nominees. The same claims were later resubmitted to a royal commission, together with new proposals for an 'Unemployment Benefit Board' (including union 'nominees') to determine the conditions under which benefits were paid, and an associated system of local advisory committees.[25] Major union leaders were eager enough for such involvement to accept it even in connection with policies about which they had serious reservations. Thus they hotly opposed the first National government's introduction of the means test for unemployment relief, but accepted representation on an 'Anomalies' Advisory Committee. Similarly, they agreed to participate in appeal tribunals and local advisory committees set up under the Unemployment Assistance Board (created in 1934) despite their strong objections both to many of the board's policies and to its lack of trade union representation.

By this time, too, the unions had an official policy on the selection of their representatives on government bodies. Their first comprehensive statement on the issue was a product of the unpopular Blanesburgh report on unemployment insurance, whose signatories included three 'Labour representatives'— one of them a member of the TUC General Council. The council, acting on the 1927 Congress's appeal for measures 'to guard against such people in future', issued a memorandum which the next Congress endorsed.[26] The memorandum stipulated that government should seek nominations from 'the unions directly concerned' when bodies dealing with a specific industry were involved. Otherwise, the TUC was to be relied on in one of three ways. In the case of administrative bodies requiring technical qualifications, government should at least 'secure the General Council's approval'. When 'Labour' or 'the workers' movement' was to be represented on either administrative or advisory bodies, the council should be invited to submit a list of names, 'the final selections by the Minister to be made from them'. The TUC claimed 'the right to nominate a person for the appointment' only in cases where 'organized Labour as a whole' was to be represented on 'Administrative Boards' or on government-sponsored delegations to international conferences.

[25] ibid., 1931, p. 165.
[26] ibid., 1927, p. 283; 1928, p. 203.

There was as this statement suggests, for all its vaguenesses, a sense of purpose evident in the way the unions turned towards government from the beginning of the 1930s. For some union leaders, in fact, that purpose was more coherent and far-sighted than is readily apparent from official policy statements. In essence, it was a cautious, Anglicized version of the corporate state. It was given its most elaborate exposition in *Trade Unions and the State*, written by W. Milne-Bailey, secretary of the TUC's Research and Economic Department, and published in 1934. In this book the varied strains of the once-famous English political pluralists and the less elegantly formulated, though more moving, aspirations for 'workers' control' were synthesized in a conception of 'functional decentralization' that was both comparatively modest and notably ambitious. The modesty lay in the conception's assumption of the established political framework and its independence of the way 'industry may evolve from the point of view of ownership'.[27] The ambition was reflected in the theme of 'systematic' and pervasive group-government consultation. Ministers were to be 'assisted by advisory bodies', and government as a whole kept continuously in touch with 'the chief economic institutions' by way of a representative 'National Economic Council'—the specific underlying claim being that 'the Unions will actively participate' when the interests of their members were 'most directly and concretely affected', while on 'general policies and the wider economic issues ... the Trade Union Movement will have a recognized consultative and advisory role'.[28]

This conception of state-trade union relations was not immured in the pages of Milne-Bailey's book. It was echoed in the speeches of men like Bevin and Citrine, in specific union claims for consultation and in union publications, such as the TUC study courses for rank and file unionists.[29] It was also accompanied by a notable change in the style and terms of the unions' approach to government, which was summed up in one way by Bevin: 'Those [the 1920s] were the days of advocacy. Ours [the 1930s] is the day of administration.'[30]

---

[27] W. Milne-Bailey, *Trade Unions and the State*, p. 354.
[28] ibid., pp. 351, 377, 379.
[29] See TUC, *Trade Unionism: A General Survey in 12 Lessons*, p. 37.
[30] Quoted in Bullock, op. cit., p. 600.

What this involved, above all, was a carefulness and reflectiveness which contrasted with the more casual practices of the past. Thus the precision with which TUC-sponsored claims on government came to be formulated and presented. Citrine instituted the careful preparation and the briefing sessions which distinguished the TUC's deputations of the 1930s. As he later affirmed: 'We have long gone past the stage when [we] can go to a Government Department with a general case. We must always have the details to support any points we put forward.'[31]

It involved, in addition, a disposition to compromise on old issues of representation and to acknowledge the corresponding rights of opponents. In the case of formal government bodies, there was thus an emphasis on representation *per se*, without overmuch worry about whether it was 'fair' in numerical terms; and an acceptance of the view that unionist-members of advisory bodies should be regarded not as 'delegates', but as having 'a free hand to do what seems best in the circumstances'.[32] In the case of opponents, there was an eagerness both to join forces with employers in approaching government, when possible, and to assure ministers that the unions did not presume to claim exceptional treatment on the score of consultation. As Citrine once told Sir John Simon: 'What the Home Secretary did for the [TUC] he had to do for the comparable body among the employers. The General Council did not ask for special favours.'[33]

Conciliatory though their approach was, however, major trade union leaders were still prepared to talk toughly to government, as their actions in relation to unemployment relief and military conscription amply demonstrated. Nor had their long-term policy ambitions diminished: it was during 1931–6 that the TUC, for example, first moved beyond the easy sloganizing of the past to work out detailed schemes of industry nationalization with the Labour party.

One consequence of the new approach was that the public face of the unions was a good deal more prepossessing than it had been during the earlier 1920s. The impression of union moderation was strengthened by the contrast with Labour

[31] *TUC Report*, 1939, p. 314.
[32] ibid., 1928, pp. 203, 405–6.
[33] ibid., 1936, p. 133.

party extremism, publicly illustrated by the TUC leadership's smothering reaction to the call of the 1933 party conference for a general strike in the event of war.

A 'responsible' image was important to union leaders who wished to deal with government, but had little to throw into the bargaining scales other than the claim to speak for a sizeable public. There was, in this, a notable similarity with the 1870s. But there was also a crucial difference in union attitudes to government, a difference exemplified in Bevin's response to an unofficial request for help with a recruiting campaign: 'It was not for us to appeal or be suppliants; it was for them [government] to come to us and for the first time to recognize Labour as equals.'[34] Such assurance would have been incomprehensible to the union leaders of the 1870s. Moreover, it was not misplaced in the 1930s, as was to be shown a year or two later when a Prime Minister took the first significant step towards meeting Bevin's point under threat of war.

TRADES UNION CONGRESS

Some union leaders thought the general strike had proved the necessity to strengthen the TUC's formal industrial power. They moved, unsuccessfully, to do so at the 1926 Congress. Some opposed the move because they thought that the strike, if anything, had proved the reverse. Others opposed it because they were not sure what the strike had proved. Bevin spoke for them: 'We do not know quite what line to take'.[35] It was J. R. Clynes, a spokesman for the second group, who unwittingly foreshadowed the future in a scornful reference to the past. 'Only a few years ago', he remarked, 'the General Council was a sort of marching brass band at the head of the Trade Union Movement. . . . It advertised, it sent deputations, it timidly consulted Ministers.'[36]

In the meantime, while Bevin collected his thoughts, the TUC was safe from the worst effects of demoralization. Most of the more influential union leaders were identified with the General Council's handling of the general strike; and a special

[34] Quoted in Bullock, op. cit., p. 592.
[35] *TUC Report*, 1926, p. 383.
[36] ibid., pp. 384–5.

conference of executives endorsed its conduct by an almost three-to-one majority. The inevitable onslaught from the extreme left, and the Conservative government's Trade Disputes and Trade Union Bill, also induced a closing of ranks. In any case, the TUC had no serious competitor on the industrial side of the labour movement.

But when it came to developing the TUC's position, as distinct from protecting it, perhaps the most critical factor was the interest in it shared by two men of rare ability, Bevin and Citrine. Citrine, from the time he became secretary, had been clear that his aim was 'to make the TUC indispensable to the affiliated unions; to establish a leadership which they would be willing to follow'.[37] And for Bevin, as one who worked closely with him observed, the TUC 'held in [his] affections and ambitions a special place'.[38]

Intellectually, Bevin and Citrine stood head and shoulders above their colleagues on the General Council. Otherwise, their qualities were complementary and reinforcing—Bevin imaginative, passionate, a powerful orator impressing by simplicity of expression and force of personality; Citrine cool, methodical, relying on the persuasiveness of carefully assembled data and logical exposition. Each of them had a power base of significance. Bevin controlled the votes of the massive Transport and General Workers' Union, Citrine the more subtle resources of the TUC's administrative structure. Temperamentally incompatible, their mutual antipathy was such that they rarely discussed an issue before it was raised in open forum. But their views made them allies in practice. 'I cannot now recall', Citrine later remarked, 'a single issue of first-class importance on which we seriously differed. On tactics, yes, but not on basic policy.'[39] In a partnership whose main instrument was the General Council, these two dominated the trade union movement for more than a decade.

The Brass Band Tunes Up

As late as July 1927, Citrine had lingering hopes that the role of industrial coordinator might still be within the TUC's reach.

[37] Citrine, *Men and Work*, p. 238.
[38] Francis Williams, *Ernest Bevin*, p. 128.
[39] Citrine, *Men and Work*, p. 240.

But he had also concluded by this time (and Beatrice Webb's record of a conversation with him confirms his own recollection) that what was more likely to lead 'towards more power for the TUC' was a broadening of the unions' policy concerns.[40] Bevin had evidently reached much the same conclusion: at the 1927 Congress he advanced resolutions advocating a European customs union and instructing the General Council to investigate the consequences of tariffs and of international cartels. Shortly afterwards, Citrine published the *Manchester Guardian* article (mentioned earlier in this chapter) predicating a widening policy vision on the part of the unions. Its argument was reproduced in the General Council's report to the 1928 Congress on the Mond-Turner talks.

At the same time the formal powers of the General Council in relation to policy formulation were expanded. The council asked the 1927 Congress for the power to provide 'coordination on general questions'.[41] This recommendation was notable for its brevity, its vagueness, the way it was buried in the body of the council's lengthy annual report—and for the fact that not once was attention drawn to it during the Congress. It was automatically endorsed when the report, as otherwise amended by Congress, was formally adopted. Citrine waited for some weeks before publicly disclosing, in his *Manchester Guardian* article, the great importance of the recommendation. He interpreted it as empowering the General Council 'to undertake negotiations on general basic principles . . . to coordinate the policy of the unions on general questions . . . [and] to formulate its ideas in a concrete and practical form for the guidance of the organized movement'.[42] Not surprisingly, these farreaching implications of 'coordination on general questions' had escaped many Congress delegates. Spurred on by the General Council's unilateral decision to enter the Mond-Turner talks, J. T. Brownlie led the attack on Citrine's interpretation at the 1928 Congress, claiming that the phrase did not authorize the council 'to create on its own initiative a policy for the unions'.[43] At the previous Congress, the General Council had complained that it had 'never been empowered to deal with . . . basic

---

[40] ibid., p. 238; see M. Cole (ed.), *Beatrice Webb's Diaries 1924–1932*, pp. 147–8.
[41] *TUC Report*, 1927, p. 112.
[42] Quoted in Milne-Bailey, *Trade Union Documents*, p. 433.
[43] *TUC Report*, 1928, p. 418.

principles'.[44] But now it justified its assertion of power on the basis of not only the new provision, but also an older standing order—and then, for good measure, blithely claimed such power simply 'by virtue of its position as the elected Executive Body' of the TUC.[45] This inconsistency was of no help to Brownlie, whose challenge was defeated.

So far as formal powers went, little more was to be gained. By 1932, references to 'the progress your General Council has made in formulating Congress policy on fundamental issues' excited no comment.[46] Congress, of course, retained the power to reject or modify the outcomes of such progress. But the TUC leadership's right to initiate policy was no longer open to question.

The General Council also tightened its grip on the communication of policy following the general strike. All but two of some 30 deputations that saw ministers under TUC auspices during 1927–31 consisted either wholly or predominantly of council members. The union side of the Mond-Turner talks was drawn exclusively from this source. There was a similar trend, it appears, in the case of *ad hoc* dealings at lower levels. And the 1928 Congress, as we have seen, approved a memorandum concerning representation on formal consultative bodies which specified that the General Council should select appointees intended to represent the trade unions in general.

Underpinning these developments were changes in the administrative structure and resources of the TUC during the five years before the first National government took office. A Social Insurance Department was created in 1928, with an associated standing advisory committee representative of interested unions and the Labour party as well as the General Council. A National Women's Advisory Council and a Non-Manual Workers' Advisory Council, both set up in 1930, drew a wide range of unions into a close relationship with the council. In 1929 a standing Economic Committee was formed, consisting wholly of council members and linked to the renamed Research and Economic Department. By late 1930, moreover, the TUC's full-time staff had been expanded to some 40 members. This

facilitated greater specialization, as illustrated by the recruitment in that year of Sir Thomas Legge, formerly Chief Medical
Inspector of Factories. At the level of General Council members,
the new committees on economic policy and social insurance
fostered a degree of specialization in relation to two complex
and increasingly emphasized policy areas.

Greater efficiency was also achieved in the sense of economiz-
ing the time of the TUC's busy part-time leadership. Well-
briefed committees are likely to require fewer and, perhaps,
shorter meetings. The abolition of many TUC-party joint
committees, rather than staff expansion, largely explains the
dramatic drop in General Council and committee meetings
(from 379 to 220) during 1925–6. But in 1927, Citrine's first
full year as permanent secretary, there was a further decline to
about 135 which was proportionately as large. (Citrine's touch
is also evident in the reorganization of the council's minutes at
this time, standardized subject headings being introduced and
a detailed running index compiled.) In the same year, at Bevin's
instigation, the council effectively agreed that ministerial
deputations carrying Congress resolutions should normally be
limited to 'not more than 5 members . . . instead of the whole
Council being summoned, as previously'.[47]

The administrative developments of these years had more
subtle consequences as well. The greater expertise of staff
members facilitated informal consultation, especially on technical matters, with appropriate government officials. Almost
certainly, too, it enhanced their role in the initiation and
formulation of policy as the TUC's policy concerns became
wider and more complex. One indication of this is that the
practice of including one or two staff members, other than
Citrine, in some ministerial deputations dates from this time.
And it was Milne-Bailey, then head of the Research Department, who first suggested the creation of the Economic Committee. This committee was of particular significance. Bevin
and Citrine both took a close interest in it; and it was soon
recognized as the doyen of the General Council's committees,
with wide-ranging interests extending far beyond the 'matters
of international economic importance' which were initially
specified as its field of concern.[48]

[47] *GC Mins.*, 28 September 1927.   [48] *TUC Report*, 1929, p. 257.

Uneasy Alliance

Most of the Labour party leaders had covertly opposed the general strike. But apart from Ramsay MacDonald, who could not resist one public I-told-you-so, they avoided rubbing salt in the TUC's wounds. Several of them attended the Congress of September 1926, for the first time since the traditional exchange of 'fraternal delegates' was abandoned at the party's instigation in 1923. The practice itself was revived in 1927 when MacDonald's presence as fraternal delegate was hailed by himself and the General Council as 'a testimony to the growing unity' of party and unions.[49]

It was a hastily patched and superficial reunion. At the same Congress, for example, union officials voiced their resentment of the allegedly greater weight given party membership when it came to securing appointments to government advisory bodies. And up to the advent of the second Labour government, the unity fell well short of a genuine working alliance. Certainly, the TUC and party leaders cooperated in the big public campaign against the Trade Disputes and Trade Union Bill: as MacDonald emphasized, 'we are both struck by that Act'.[50] But the National Joint Council, prodded into life during this campaign, was convened only once thereafter; there were few signs of activity on the part of the surviving joint policy committees; and there were no joint deputations to Conservative ministers. The General Council and the party executive continued to hold joint meetings, but not very frequently, and the council at least does not seem to have attached much importance to them.

A major obstacle to close cooperation was the TUC leadership's determination to expand its independent policy concerns. This exacerbated the perennial problem of 'overlapping'. Snowden, for one, made no secret of his unhappiness with 'the stream of purely political manifestos from the . . . TUC'.[51] Henderson, as usual, was more circumspect. He told Congress that they should try 'to harmonise our . . . respective policies' in order to 'avoid confusion in the minds of those we represent'; and suggested an enlivened and enlarged National Joint Council (including the Cooperative Movement) to operate 'not so

[49] ibid., 1927, pp. 58, 354.   [50] ibid., p. 354.
[51] M. Cole (ed.), *Beatrice Webb's Diaries, 1924–1932*, p. 151.

much for the purpose of deciding policy, as for framing a common understanding of policy'.[52]

The TUC leaders, however, showed no interest in reviving the NJC until the accession of the Labour government made cooperation more attractive. Then it was the turn of the party's leaders to lose interest—helped no doubt by the fact that the reconstitution of the NJC, in early 1930, not only continued the Cooperative Movement's exclusion but strengthened the TUC's representation by giving it six seats against three each for the party executive and the parliamentary party. The NJC rarely met during the Labour government's term of office.

On the other hand, joint meetings of the two executives were more frequent; there were a number of joint deputations to ministers; some specialized joint committees were reactivated, and others were created. The General Council also seems at this time to have formed quite close links with the Labour parliamentarians' Consultative Committee, which provided a liaison between ministers and backbenchers. And its five MP-members were primarily responsible for resuscitating the Trade Union Group in parliament at the end of 1929. Above all, the TUC's direct relationship with the second Labour government was distinctly closer than it had been in the case of the first.

Before the 1929 election, according to Hugh Dalton, MacDonald had to be 'persuaded' to consult the TUC leaders about the party's platform.[53] But afterwards, in sharp contrast with 1924, he went out of his way to sweeten relations by inviting the full General Council to dine at 10 Downing Street. He subsequently took part in more business-like meetings with council members, both inside and outside the Economic Advisory Council of which he was chairman; and, as late as the first half of 1931, received formal TUC deputations on at least six occasions. The frequency and range of the TUC's dealings with his ministers were also greater than under the first Labour government.

There was, nevertheless, a great deal of friction in the TUC-government relationship. Much of it was inevitable, given the policy ambitions of the TUC leadership and the political constraints to which the government was subject. But personal

[52] *TUC Report*, 1928, pp. 379–80.
[53] Hugh Dalton, *Call Back Yesterday*, p. 183.

antipathies, clumsiness and inconsistency were also involved. The new government's refusal of the General Council's request for 'some liaison' (on the ground that it would give colour to charges of 'outside dictation') engendered resentment on both sides—in the case of the council, because its rightful reward was withheld; in the case of the government because the TUC had made, in Sidney Webb's phrase, such 'an arrogant claim'.[54] There was a recurring pattern of TUC pressure and ministerial resistance on the issue of access to bills before their introduction in parliament. Nor was there any lack of other sources of friction.

TUC leaders, early aggrieved by the ministry's inclusion of fewer unionists than in 1924, found a later cause for complaint in the government's tendency to emphasize service to the party, at the expense of trade union qualifications, when appointing magistrates. Bevin angered party leaders with a response in kind by ensuring that the TUC monopolized representation on the new *Daily Herald*'s board of directors, set up in conjunction with Odhams Press. There were particular difficulties with some ministers. Ironically, two union officials, one a former General Council member, were among the chief culprits. Bondfield, as Minister of Labour, became notorious for her lack of tact in dealing with deputations; and Clynes, as Home Secretary, was told that the TUC found information from his department harder to come by than under his Conservative predecessors. TUC leaders were also infuriated by ministerial inconsistency in relation to union members of advisory bodies: sometimes they were asked to suggest names, at other times they were not.

The consultation issue was brought to a head when the government decided late in 1930 to set up a royal commission to look into unemployment insurance. The General Council was not consulted; and the government muffed subsequent moves to discuss the commission's terms of reference and to secure TUC representation on it. The council not only lodged a 'very strong protest', in the particular case, but seized the opportunity to complain of 'a number of incidents' which had

[54] Snowden, op. cit., vol. II, p. 762; quoted in R. Bassett, *1931: Political Crisis*, p. 36.

caused it 'perplexity and uneasiness'.[55] It agreed to give evidence before the commission only after a talk with the Prime Minister. But the real climax in the TUC's relations with the second Labour government came later. It came in the form of a financial crisis which was converted into a political crisis of the first magnitude—largely, it seems, because of the lack of sympathy between government and TUC leaders.

Crisis and Consequences

The financial crisis was sparked by the report of the May Committee on National Expenditure, published on the last day of July 1931. On 20 August the Labour party executive and the TUC General Council, at a meeting with cabinet, were told of the proposals for economies to restore confidence in sterling which the government was considering. The party executive subsequently avoided taking a stand; it left the decision to those of its members who were in cabinet. The General Council was less amenable: 'we felt', Citrine later recalled, 'that we must oppose the whole thing'.[56] That decision was the first of two decisive events which broke the government.

Cabinet, on the 21st, overrode the TUC's objections when it agreed on economies amounting to some £56 million. The leaders of the opposition parties were informed. They insisted on their prior understanding that there would be economies totalling £78 million, including heavier cuts in unemployment benefits. This was the second decisive event.

The unanimity of cabinet began to crack. The focal issue was a proposal to cut unemployment payments by ten per cent. On the 23rd, a cut of this magnitude was rejected outright by a substantial cabinet minority which included Henderson, William Graham (both members of the inner cabinet) and Clynes. It was agreed that the government had no alternative but to resign.

Henderson was the key. Without him, the minority would have lacked someone of the stature of MacDonald and Snowden. His alignment with the minority ensured the fall of the government; it might well have survived some resignations,

---

[55] *GC Mins.*, 17 December 1930; and see Robert Skidelsky, *Politicians and the Slump*, pp. 262–70, for a detailed account of this episode.

[56] *TUC Report*, 1931, p. 82.

but not his. And Henderson was clearly sensitive to labour-oriented opinion outside the cabinet room. It was he who first insisted that the TUC and the party should be consulted, as they had not been before 20 August. He was silent throughout the joint meeting at which the TUC's decision was announced. But 'no man present', Bullock comments, 'was more impressed by what he heard'.[57] At least it is unlikely that he and his cabinet allies would have found it politically justifiable to dig in their toes, with the government's survival at stake, if the TUC had adopted the non-committal position of the party executive. After the event, moreover, he was to leave no doubt about the importance he attached to the TUC's support.

Henderson invited Bevin and Citrine to a discussion with party officials and some MPs when it was known that Mac-Donald was to head a National government. They decided to convene a joint meeting of the three executives, including the parliamentary party's Consultative Committee—a decision that was publicly announced by Citrine. The joint meeting later issued a manifesto which effectively endorsed the TUC's stand and, by implication, was critical not only of the party executive's conduct but even of those ex-ministers who had in the end formed the dissident cabinet minority. Two days after, the General Council attended a full meeting of the parliamentary party; this was 'an innovation', suggested by Henderson, 'to mark unity'.[58] He subsequently assured the TUC that there was going to be more 'consultation with the industrial side', and a year later claimed that 'close cooperation has been distinctly achieved'.[59]

Two events justified this claim. The General Council had invited the party to send two representatives to its Economic Committee: Hugh Dalton and Herbert Morrison were appointed. The National Joint Council had not only been formally required to meeting monthly, but was in fact doing so. By the time of the 1933 Congress, moreover, the Economic Committee and the party's Policy Committee had held a number of joint meetings, while the party executive and the parliamentary party each had a representative on the TUC's

[57] Bullock, op. cit., p. 484.
[58] Dalton, *Call Back Yesterday*, p. 277.
[59] *TUC Report*, 1931, p. 403; 1932, p. 345.

Workmen's Compensation and Factories Committee. These arrangements were operative for the remainder of the 1930s.

The gem in this consultative crown was the National Joint Council, which was renamed the National Council of Labour in 1934—a change intended to indicate a wider conception of its role. A more precise indication is the major issues it dealt with. In 1934 they included foreign affairs, unemployment legislation, industrial assurance and cotton trade policy; in 1937, international policy, the 'Spanish problem', electricity supply, unemployment, pensions, nationalization of coal mines and rent restriction legislation. Joint meetings of the full executives of the constituent bodies, abandoned in 1931 after the TUC had damned them as 'more or less ineffective',[60] were resumed in 1934, but confined their attention almost wholly to defence and foreign policy. The NCL, which also expended much time on such issues, seems to have been capable of handling all matters other than the most controversial. These, during the 1930s, tended to fall under the defence and foreign policy headings; and the NCL often formally initiated the joint executive meetings that dealt with them.

Dalton, in 1937, could reasonably talk of the 'harmonised working between the industrial and the political sides of our movement, which has been a happy feature of the post-MacDonald era'.[61] What he did not say, however, was that this 'happy feature' had been achieved at the cost of conceding the TUC's leaders a voice in the party's affairs that they had not even approached since the days of David Shackleton.

The General Council Ascendant

With the fall of the second Labour government, there was a quite radical change in the relationship between the TUC and the Labour party. It was a change which altered, in the TUC leaders' favour, their relative standing both inside and outside the labour movement.

For a time, at least among those in the movement, the TUC's intransigence of August 1931 gave it something of a moral ascendancy. Citrine was capitalizing on this when, 'in common fairness', he purported to excuse the party executive's failure

[60] *GC Mins.*, 30 September 1931.
[61] *TUC Report*, 1937, p. 258.

to take 'an independent decision' in August by pointing out that half its members had been 'in one form or another . . . inside the Government'.[62]

The ascendancy gained in this way was reinforced by two other factors which largely explain why it was substantially maintained throughout the 1930s. One was the outstanding calibre of the General Council's leading members, Bevin and Citrine. Their personal standing in the labour movement was enhanced by Henderson's resignation as the party's parliamentary leader, in 1932, and as its secretary in 1934: for his successors (J. S. Middleton as secretary and George Lansbury, followed by Clement Attlee, as leader) carried much less weight. The second factor was the strength of the party's militant wing during the decade. This placed its leadership under continuing strain and contributed to an image of division and quarrelsomeness. The TUC, in contrast, presented a relatively disciplined front.

The result was a relationship in which, for the first time since the Labour party's very early years, the TUC tended to be the dominant partner. Its leaders, in these circumstances, might have been expected to embrace their partner more closely than they had formerly been inclined to. That, in fact, is precisely what they did. For the striking feature of the TUC-party relationship of the 1930s is not merely that the two coordinated their activities to an unusual degree, but that the TUC's leadership was so enthusiastic about it. One symptom of this was the praise, notably fulsome by earlier standards, which the General Council publicly lavished on the parliamentary party at various times during these years. Another, more significant symptom was the concern the TUC leadership now showed for the party leaders' old bugbear of 'overlapping'. Thus we find Citrine justifying new consultative arrangements by describing them as an attempt 'to avoid traversing the same ground'; and pressing the point that 'it was much less confusing to have some collaboration in this form than to have the state of things that existed previously, when practically no collaboration took place'.[63] Henderson might well have spared a wry grin for this faithful echo of speeches he had been making for almost thirty years.

[62] ibid., 1931, p. 83.   [63] ibid., 1932, pp. 369–70.

Nevertheless, the TUC's ascendancy is easily exaggerated. It was not pronounced enough to justify the description of the Labour party, at this time, as 'the General Council's Party'.[64] There were often differences of view between the two; and these were not always resolved, especially when it came to ensuring that the parliamentary party toed the TUC line. To take one small example: it was a strictly qualified ascendancy which left, to a General Council unhappy with the parliamentary party's performance on the Spanish question, only the alternative of instructing its secretary to 'explore the possibilities of establishing contacts with the Trade Union Group in the House'.[65] But it is the defence controversy, centring on the issue of rearmament, which best indicates both the scope and the limits of the TUC's ascendancy.

This controversy stirred strong passions in a labour movement heavily influenced by pacifism, a belief in the war-making proclivity of capitalism, a distrust of National government leaders and, for a time, by the conviction that the principal threat of Fascism was a *domestic* seizure of power. The TUC's annual Congress of 1933 could thus declare its opposition to both Hitler and British war preparations; the party conference could add a proposal for a general strike in the event of war. The TUC leaders subsequently quashed the general strike proposition but secured a joint statement which, while reiterating support for general disarmament, guardedly admitted the possibility of British military action behind the League of Nations. Congress and the party conference both endorsed this. Then came the government's proposal to increase air force expenditure in the light of German rearmament. The parliamentary party, in a decision which Bevin and Citrine had vigorously opposed at an earlier joint meeting, decided in May 1935 to vote against the proposal. And the TUC leadership formally conceded that 'the responsibility of deciding on the action to be taken should rest with the [parliamentary] Party, after they had the views of the General Council before them'.[66]

Again, on the broader issue four months later, when the Italians were poised to invade Abyssinia, TUC pressure helped

[64] Henry Pelling, *A Short History of the Labour Party*, p. 71.
[65] *GC Mins.*, 24 March 1937.
[66] ibid., 22 May 1935.

to secure a joint declaration of support for 'any action' against Italy consistent with the principles of the League of Nations. But on the specific matter of British rearmament, as raised by the White Paper of March 1936, the parliamentary party again decided on opposition after three days of joint meetings during which Citrine complained that 'the advice of the General Council had been turned on one side'.[67] Shortly afterwards the party also opted for total opposition to the defence estimates.

The National Council of Labour was unable to produce its customary agreed statement on defence in 1936. Congress formally ignored defence; the party conference adopted an ambiguous resolution. But in July 1937, against the opposition of Attlee, Herbert Morrison and Arthur Greenwood, Dalton led a move in the parliamentary party which resulted in a decision to abstain from voting on the defence estimates. An agreed statement on defence emanated from the NCL a week later, and was endorsed by Congress and the party conference. The issue at stake, though obscured by the phrasing of the statement, was posed sharply enough in the debate on it. The labour movement had officially accepted the principle of rearmament.

Bevin and Citrine had 'worked steadily' with Dalton, from 1934 to late 1937, to achieve this success.[68] The pace of change was hardly enough to sustain the charge, common to these years, of a TUC 'dictatorship',—or even to justify Laski's more modest estimation of the TUC's 'immense influence . . . over the Labour Party'.[69] Influence, of course, there was; and there were ample signs of it. Apart from anything else, the party's defence policy *was*, eventually, changed. But it was surely the absence of a *dominating* ('immense') influence that was reflected in the savagery of Bevin's well-known verbal attack on Lansbury, then parliamentary leader and pacifist opponent of rearmament, at the 1935 party conference. At a more petty level, there was a similar flavour to the General Council's attempt to have Aneurin Bevan disciplined for inveighing against it in parliament; and the same is true of its unprece-

[67] ibid., 4 March 1936.
[68] Hugh Dalton, *The Fateful Years*, p. 65.
[69] Harold J. Laski, *Parliamentary Government in England*, p. 169.

dented decision, at Bevin's prompting, to impose a time-limit on the Congress speech of a fraternal delegate who happened to be Lansbury. Nor was the confidence to be expected from a truly dominating partner evident in the qualification which Citrine added to his early statement of the council's new-found concern with 'overlapping'. Neither the TUC nor the party, he said, was 'committed to one another's ... decisions. All we hope is that ... the policies emanating from them will not be contradictory'.[70] Four years later he was still holding to the point when he told party representatives, apropos defence policy, that the TUC leaders 'had not yet ... sacrificed their right to follow such policy as they may determine if ... consultation ... failed'.[71] He might just as well have announced the TUC's inability to dictate terms to the party.

Given this inability, there was one overriding reason why Citrine should have proclaimed the TUC's independence. Bevin, much earlier, had stated it in one way when he remarked that 'the difference between a politician and an industrial leader is this: our political party is working for change, but the industrial leader has every day of his life to deal with facts as they are'.[72] One implication of this distinction between the primary interest of the unions (in immediate policy concessions) and of the party (in acquiring political office) was later spelt out by Citrine. The trade union movement, he said, 'cannot base its fortunes on one political party. We ... have .. to go on trying to do something when we have no Labour Government'.[73] This, for the TUC, meant dealing with non-Labour governments when there seemed an immediate advantage in doing so. At times, too, it could mean bypassing the party during a period when their working relations were unusually close. Thus the General Council, on learning the terms of a new Factories Bill, effectively ignored the party while preparing its submission to government in consultation with affected affiliates; and similarly, on learning that the party was going to suggest a joint deputation to the Prime Minister about annual leave legislation, the council decided on an immediate deputation of its own.[74] For there was the sneaking suspicion, which

[70] *TUC Report*, 1932, p. 369.   [71] *GC Mins.*, 4 March 1936.
[72] *TUC Report*, 1928, p. 448.
[73] Miners' Federation of Great Britain, *Report*, Annual Conference, 1935, p. 123.
[74] *GC Mins.*, 3 September and 23 December 1936.

Bevin confided to an associate in moments of depression, that the TUC leaders might have carried more weight with National governments if they had not been 'so closely tied to the Labour Party'.[75]

Internal Authority

The TUC's standing among the trade unions after August 1931 was strengthened not only by its enhanced position in relation to the Labour party, but also by its administrative resources. One aspect of those resources is reflected in the General Council's 1933 decision to donate £2,000 to a 'Help for Austria' fund, plus a further £3,000 on account—a far cry from the pre-war days when the old Parliamentary Committee had lengthily pondered the purchase of a single typewriter. Above all, there is the more sophisticated administrative structure which a less straitened budget could support.

This made it possible for the TUC, through its Research and Economic Department, to provide unions with data in support of their claims on employers. By 1937 the demand was such that the department was unable 'to devote as much time as in most years to matters of policy and general interest'.[76] But the expansion in full-time and specialist staff showed up to most advantage in dealings with government, which were increasingly concerned with the terms and detailed administration of often highly technical regulations in such fields as unemployment relief, industrial health, industrial safety and workers' compensation. The Unemployment Act of 1934, for example, involved TUC staff members in complicated and protracted negotiations with civil servants about the terms of a multitude of regulations spawned by this measure. Moreover, at this level of operation, the TUC officials seem to have been able to act pretty much at their own discretion. They often consulted particular unions in the case of industrially specific regulations; but even then, took the major responsibility for dealing with their government counterparts. They also dealt with many individual grievances and minor administrative claims on government which were funnelled to them by affiliated unions.

Considerable discretionary power is also evident in the way

[75] Williams, op. cit., p. 202.
[76] *TUC Report*, 1937, p. 197.

the General Council handled dealings at higher levels of government. Between 1932 and 1937 it sponsored some 50 ministerial
deputations, apart from those mounted jointly with the Labour
party. Most of them consisted either wholly or mainly of General
Council members. Almost invariably one of those members was
the principal spokesman. This was a role that Citrine usually
filled in the more important deputations; and the practice of
having other staff members in attendance became increasingly
common. What is particularly striking, however, is that only
some of these deputations had the traditional task of presenting
Congress resolutions. Most were arranged as the need arose,
and in the absence of specific instructions from Congress.
Moreover, when it came to Congress resolutions, the General
Council selected those it wanted to take up directly with ministers, and left the rest to be dealt with by way of less imposing
procedures. The result was that almost all the deputations
carrying such resolutions each presented only one, instead of
the traditional string. In the case of other issues handled by
ministerial deputations, the manner in which interested unions
were consulted by the council—when they were consulted at
all—tended to leave it with the last word because it normally
relied on direct communication with each union, rather than
the conference method.

There was a similar pattern in the case of representation on
formal government bodies. As late as 1931 the General Council felt obliged to point out, in relation to one committee, that
it was confining nominations to its own membership 'in this
particular case'; and to justify an identical decision in another
case 'on grounds of time'.[77] However, the council seems to have
come to terms with its conscience. For it subsequently applied
the same principle, without making excuses, whenever it was
asked for nominations to government bodies of any consequence.

The TUC was also involved in the industrial field during the
1930s, and on a much greater scale than in the period immediately after the general strike. The information service it
provided, in relation to sectional industrial claims, has already
been mentioned. It continued to take a hand in deciding inter-
union jurisdictional disputes. It convened a number of union

[77] *GC Mins.*, 21 August and 22 December 1931.

conferences on the problems of particular industries, in the early years of the decade. It promoted union recruitment campaigns, a concern culminating in moves during 1937 which resulted in the formation of a short-lived National Union of Domestic Workers, with a TUC-appointed national organizer and Citrine as temporary secretary. Another, related failure was its 1932 attempt to revive a scheme for organizing the unemployed which it had first tried to launch four years before, after breaking with the Communist-controlled National Unemployed Workers' Committee Movement; in 1935 the project was finally abandoned in the face of competition from both the NUWCM's successor and unions who preferred to organize their own unemployed members. The TUC was also called on by unions involved in a number of industrial disputes, usually to intercede with employers unwilling to negotiate and sometimes to sponsor financial appeals for strikers. Even the Miners' Federation once asked for its help with a local colliery dispute. But one of its most signal failures occurred in this connection. During the cotton industry stoppage of 1932 it organized a network of local 'TUC Cotton Fund Committees' and a system of 'TUC vouchers', which strikers could redeem in cooperative society shops; and raised more than £58,000. Emboldened by this feat, which it hailed as having 'broken new ground in the sense that the TUC has been the coordinating body of a great national fund',[78] the General Council floated the idea of a permanent central strike fund financed by regular contributions. Its negotiations with a reluctant General Federation of Trade Unions, whose one remaining function of importance was the management of a strike insurance fund, dragged on for several years. The council finally lost patience, circularized affiliated unions on the issue in 1938—and was slapped in the face with a response that overwhelmingly favoured the traditional practice of *ad hoc* appeals.

The limitations of the TUC's industrial role underline the importance, to its internal authority, of the striking development that occurred in its political role during this period. For its political role had become a more substantial source of authority than before. To union leaders at large, dealing with

[78] *TUC Report*, 1933, p. 91.

government was now a more important peacetime activity, primarily because of the way both their own policy concerns and those of government had been affected by economic depression. In addition, the TUC's claim to act as the unions' political spokesman was strengthened by three factors—the slump in the prestige of the other major claimant to that role, the Labour party; the General Council's initiative in broadening the unions' vision of their policy concerns; and the technical complexity of many of the issues arising from those concerns, a factor which placed a premium on the council's relatively sophisticated administrative resources.

The TUC's political role was also a more reliable source of authority than even an expanded industrial role would have been likely to provide. It meant that the General Council was 'more . . . concerned with general principles and long-time results . . . than with immediate details of the workshop'.[79] In other words, the council was concerned primarily with matters which, although important to union leaders, bit less deeply into what they saw as their vital interests than would have been the case had the council grasped at a larger industrial role. By pressing more softly on the nerve of union autonomy, the TUC's political role was less susceptible to challenge. To this extent, it provided a more secure foundation for an internal authority that, by the end of 1937, was much more impressive than Ben Turner could have had in mind ten years earlier when he told Sir Alfred Mond that the General Council possessed 'a certain moral authority in the Trade Union Movement . . . even though it fell short of . . . direct executive authority'.[80] For, by this time, the council not only handled issues of considerable substance in the eyes of union leaders, but effectively monopolized dealings with government at least in the case of matters concerning the unions in general. Equally significant, it acted as much more than merely a communicating intermediary. It usually had the major hand in formulating policy on general issues, and often on sectional matters as well.

External Authority

After the general strike, Conservative ministers continued to treat the TUC as the principal trade union body for consultative

[79] Milne-Bailey, *Trade Unions and the State*, p. 106.
[80] *Minutes*, first meeting of Mond-Turner talks, 12 January 1928.

purposes. So did their Labour successors, who had more frequent dealings with union leaders. Neither complied consistently with the TUC's demand that, 'in the first instance', all approaches about union representatives for advisory bodies 'should be made to the General Council for their submission of a list of names'.[81] But both, in the case of major advisory positions, appear to have confined personal invitations to members of the council and its staff.

There was, as we have seen, one particularly significant innovation introduced by the second Labour government: the a lmission of the TUC into consultation on areas of economic policy from which it had formerly been excluded. Thus the appointment of General Council members to such bodies as the Economic Advisory Council, the Macmillan Committee on Finance and Industry, and the catalytic May Committee on National Expenditure—not to mention the calling in of the full council during the financial crisis of August 1931. All these were unprecedented events which represented a considerable extension of the TUC's external authority. Succeeding National governments were not so forthcoming in this respect. But otherwise, their readiness to deal with the TUC leadership was scarcely less and, if anything, was by 1937 perhaps rather more pronounced.

A note attached to the General Council's minutes, shortly after the Labour government fell, contains a list of five government bodies which included council members who had been officially appointed or suggested by the council. A similar list for 1937 contains eleven bodies, seven of them new. Altogether, 17 different bodies figure in the lists compiled annually between 1931 and 1937. And the lists are not exhaustive. There were also at least one committee of inquiry and two official British delegations to international economic conferences to which the council successfully made nominations from its own membership; and the same appears to be true in the case of two major administrative bodies. In addition, not only was the council consulted about appointments to certain lower level bodies, but some of its members were unofficial TUC representatives on others in the sense that they were appointed by personal

[81] *GC Mins.*, 24 July 1929.

invitation. This is not to say that the TUC leaders were satisfied: they indicated they were not when they ordered the com-
pilation of 'a list of recent Government Committees showing in
which cases the General Council had not been asked to
appoint representatives'.[82]

In the case of *ad hoc* consultation, TUC deputations generally
had ready access to National ministers. As we have seen, there
were no more than five refusals and nothing to equal Snowden's
dogged rejections late in the second Labour government's term
of office. During the six years to the end of 1937, the General
Council was officially represented in more than 60 ministerial
deputations of a formal nature, including those shared with the
Labour party: there were only a dozen similar deputations
during the three years of Conservative rule up to mid-1929.
And sometimes, as we have also seen, the initiative for *ad hoc*
consultation came from government leaders themselves during
this time.

The TUC's dealings with National ministers, while important, were only the tip of the iceberg. The General Council and
its staff were in frequent and, apparently, close touch with
government officials, especially those at the Home Office and
the Ministry of Labour. There was less formality at this level.
The TUC's staff was sufficiently diversified to allow the
development of steady 'opposite number' relationships. This
facilitated dealings with civil servants which were not limited
to matters of detail, but often extended to preliminary soundings
on larger issues. Beveridge, chairman of the Unemployment
Insurance Statutory Committee in the mid-1930s, has written
of the value he attached to his relationship with the head of the
TUC's Social Insurance Department.[83] From the TUC side,
Citrine also testified to the efficacy of such relationships in
general when he said, in 1936, that he 'did not know of any
case where the General Council had had trouble in getting
memoranda so as to get a sketch' of forthcoming government
legislation in which it was interested.[84] Later, he recalled that
employers' leaders were envious of the access which the TUC
had at this level.[85]

[82] ibid., 26 February 1936.
[83] See Lord Beveridge, *Power and Influence*, p. 226.
[84] *TUC Report*, 1936, p. 133.
[85] See Citrine, *Men and Work*, p. 251.

In sum, the scale of dealings, especially sub-ministerial, was considerable by earlier standards. And even if National governments did not consult the TUC about high economic policy, they did give it a hearing on foreign and colonial affairs to a far greater extent than their Conservative counterparts of the 1920s. This did not mean that the TUC could claim much success in influencing the character of major public policies. But it could fairly claim to have left its imprint on many smaller matters of concern to the unions at a time when these were mounting in number and significance with the growth of government intervention.

The administrative complexities of depression-induced interventionist policies, as we have seen, were one reason why government should have paid more attention to the trade unions than might otherwise have been the case. The TUC provided an obvious and convenient means of tapping this source of technical information. This was certainly a useful function, and the TUC's spokesmen placed great store on its capacity to furnish such information. But it was only one reason, and almost certainly a minor reason, why National governments went as far as they did in their recognition of the TUC— at a time when it neither held the general strike in its fist nor controlled specific administrative sanctions of any great weight. For government leaders were not primarily concerned with the TUC as a source of technical advice. Thus the Home Secretary displayed little interest in a deputation's offer of 'an immense amount of information' relating to proposed factory legislation: he was plainly much more interested in what he described as 'the authority of the views which from time to time [the TUC] expressed'.[86] His main concern, in other words, was with the TUC as a source of opinion.

It was a matter of priorities. National government leaders believed that the central political problem confronting them was, in Baldwin's phrase, 'to get at the soul of the working people'.[87] The TUC was one obvious channel of communication. In the event, government leaders clearly came to regard it as a most important channel. There appear to be two principal reasons for this.

[86] *TUC Report*, 1936, pp. 132–3.
[87] Quoted in A. W. Baldwin, *My Father: The True Story*, p. 328.

In the first place, there was the pragmatism of the TUC leaders. They had early demonstrated their abandonment of the more doctrinaire posturing of the pre-1926 period by their involvement in the Mond-Turner talks; and the talks had been followed by the development of quite close informal relations between officials of the TUC and the two main employers' bodies.[88] In relation to government itself, they displayed their pragmatism by being prepared to negotiate at one level while fiercely opposing at another. For example, they reported to the Congress of 1937 that 'the fight against the Unemployment Assistance Regulations has been vigorously maintained in conjunction with the Labour Party',[89] as indeed it had. But, simultaneously, they had continued to discuss the detailed terms and administration of those regulations with government—and claimed, as a result, to have secured 'a number of beneficial adjustments'.[90] Their more flexible stance induced Baldwin, in 1935, to make his initial approach on the rearmament issue to Citrine instead of the Labour party leadership. It would have been 'useless', the Prime Minister explained, 'to speak to George Lansbury, a sincere and avowed pacifist . . . Attlee was different . . . but he was . . . bound to follow Lansbury'; and so, 'there was no hope along that line of consultation'.[91] He believed, in other words, that there was a greater chance of swinging the General Council to the government's side on the issue.[92]

In the second place, there was the TUC's authority among the unions, as government leaders conceived it. They clearly believed it was worth making some effort to try and influence the TUC, a belief that implicitly attributed to the TUC a substantial internal authority. Given that belief, government leaders could expect that dealing with the TUC would provide at least reliable information about general union reactions on specific issues and, in particular, about the nature and intensity of union opposition. They could expect to be in a better position to sweeten policy pills for working-class consumption, especially in relation to specific administrative difficulties and grievances.

[88] See Citrine, *Men and Work*, pp. 250–1.
[89] *TUC Report*, 1937, p. 110.
[90] ibid.
[91] Citrine, *Men and Work*, p. 353.
[92] See ibid., p. 353; and Young, op. cit., p. 204.

There was, too, the incidental advantage of demonstrating to the electorate at large the reasonableness of a government prepared to consult with an organization so closely identified with the Labour party.

But it was the combination of pragmatism and internal authority which, potentially, offered an advantage of greater value to ministers. For it offered the prospect of shifting the perimeters of union opposition to particular government policies.

Whatever the precise motivation of National ministers, however, the fact remains that the TUC was accorded a standing in government circles which was quite unprecedented in the case of non-Labour governments. By the end of 1937, moreover, there were other comparable indications of the TUC's enhanced standing outside the labour movement. It shared a joint committee with the British Medical Association, and was on the point of doing the same with the British Association for the Advancement of Science. A number of eminent outsiders served on its Colonial Advisory Committee, including a former permanent head of the Colonial Office; and the National Association of Local Government Officers, while remaining unaffiliated, had overcome its earlier diffidence and joined the TUC committee concerned with local government matters. One other indication of the TUC's standing is the stature of the two men with whom it was most closely identified in the public eye, bearing in mind that neither was a parliamentarian or even held an official position in the Labour party. One illustration is Baldwin's comment, during a private discussion in 1934 about a 'reconstructed Government', that it ought to contain 'a strong Labour leader like Bevin'.[93] His confidant on that occasion, Tom Jones, extended the tribute four years later, a few days after the invasion of Austria: 'Many would like a reconstruction of the Government on more national lines for this emergency, bringing in Bevin and Citrine'.[94]

Political Authority: the Ground Prepared

The General Council celebrated the TUC's sixtieth anniversary in 1928 with the observation that 'it has emerged today with a

[93] Quoted in Thomas Jones, *A Diary with Letters*, p. 123.
[94] ibid., p. 397.

prestige greater than at any time in its history'.[95] There was more than a little whistling in the dark about this remark. It was made at a time when the disaster of the general strike hung green and heavy in union memory. It was also a time when the future role of the TUC was uncertain. Even after the advent of the second Labour government, a mood of uncertainty seems to have persisted. This is evident in the introductory statement of the TUC's submissions to the Macmillan Committee on Finance and Industry. The TUC, it was pointed out with exquisite care,

is the central organization accepted by Governments, and by the Central Employers' Organizations, as representative of the Trade Union Movement as a whole. In this capacity its representatives act as delegates and advisers to the International Labour Conferences, as members of Government Commissions and Committees and as members of such [administrative] bodies as the Railway Rates Tribunal, Railway National Wages Board, etc. Its General Council also participates in the scheme of joint consultation and cooperation that has been arranged with the National Confederation of Employers' Organizations and the Federation of British Industries.[96]

Such laboured self-advertisement before a committee of knowledgeable public men, including a member of the General Council itself, smacks of a somewhat shaky sense of 'prestige'. But this was soon to change as a result of the development of the TUC's political authority. And in that development the Labour government's demise and the Macmillan committee's existence together comprise something of a watershed. The circumstances in which the Labour party lost office loosened constraints which, almost since the party's foundation, had qualified the scope and character of the TUC's role as the unions' political spokesman. Bevin's appointment to the Macmillan committee constituted a signal acknowledgement (if from a Labour government) of the TUC's right to consultation on great issues of domestic policy. But more important, in terms of the near future, was the impression he created by his performance in the committee's deliberations; for he finally laid the ghost, fading as it had been since the Mond-Turner talks, that the TUC leaders were prisoners of the class-war preconceptions which many had read into their use of the general strike.

[95] *TUC Report*, 1928, p. 81.
[96] ibid., 1931, p. 265.

Citrine, of course, was claiming too much with his retrospective assessment of the significance of Bevin's appointment: 'Our right to be heard on intricate financial questions was fully admitted'.[97] Non-Labour governments had still to concede that point in 1937. Bevin, too, was exaggerating when he told the Congress of that year that the TUC 'has now virtually become an integral part of the State and its views and voice upon every subject, international and domestic, heard and heeded'.[98] Nevertheless, both were right in so far as they were implying that the TUC's standing, as an intermediary between unions and government, was greatly enhanced after 1931. And this time, unlike the comparable peaks of 1906–10 and the mid-1920s, there was to be no anti-climactic sequel. By the end of 1937, the most critical steps in the process had still to be taken. But they would almost certainly have been more hesitant, and may well have had different consequences, in the absence of the heightened political authority which the TUC had acquired by this time.

[97] Citrine, *Men and Work*, p. 240.
[98] *TUC Report*, 1937, p. 70.

9

Into War's Forcing-House
1938–1940

HITLER's Austrian invasion of March 1938 brought home the threat of war even to a government which, in the Prime Minister's reverberating phrase of barely a fortnight before, was committed to a 'general scheme of appeasement' for a further twelve months.[1] Trade union attitudes became a major concern of government leaders. They became a critical concern when the war began for Britain in September 1939. The TUC provided a focus for this concern. By May 1940, when Neville Chamberlain resigned, both unions and government had accorded the TUC an enlarged political authority that was to prove the pattern of the future.

GOVERNMENT

On 22 March 1938 Walter Citrine had a private conversation with the Prime Minister. Chamberlain had asked for the meeting because 'he wanted to explain the need for accelerating the rearmament programme to the TUC General Council' before making a parliamentary statement about the German annexation of Austria.[2] He suggested that the full council should meet him at 5.00 p.m. on the following day. This was the first invitation of its kind, from a non-Labour Prime Minister, since 1926.

The timing of Chamberlain's initiative, a few days after the *Anschluss*, has been described as 'pure accident'.[3] This seems improbable. Months earlier the parliamentary Labour party, the TUC's annual Congress and the Labour party conference had all formally abandoned their opposition to rearmament without evoking any such overt response from government leaders. It was only when Hitler's Austrian ambitions were

[1] Quoted in Mowat, op. cit., p. 590.
[2] *GC Mins.*, 23 March 1939.
[3] A. J. P. Taylor, *English History, 1914–1945*, p. 413.

244

exposed that Chamberlain wrote, two days afterwards: 'it is perfectly evident . . . now that force is the only argument Germany understands'.[4] A day later he announced a review of the rearmament programme. The decision to accelerate defence production followed. This was the beginning of 'the period of crisis' characterized by the way the Prime Minister thereafter 'kept the Opposition leaders informed of his actions'.[5] It was also the point at which he sought out Citrine and the General Council.

Ministerial moves to secure the unions' cooperation in the government's war preparations date from this time, though there was a half-hearted air about these efforts until war actually came. Chamberlain appealed for 'the goodwill of the Trade Unions' at his meeting with the General Council on 23 March.[6] The Minister for the Coordination of Defence seems to have had little more to add in follow-up discussions with the engineering unions: as one unionist complained, he 'appeared to be treating us as a lot of children, waving a little flag and asking us to support the Government'.[7] A second meeting with the Prime Minister, held on 26 May at the TUC leaders' request, was no more fruitful. Chamberlain explained to them that he was looking to voluntary arrangements between engineering unions and employers to cope with labour problems in military production. But in the negotiations, begun after his March initiative, the employers refused to talk about anything except suspending traditional union practices and diluting skilled labour, and the unions declined to give a blank cheque merely for the asking. In the event, the Prime Minister preferred to allow the negotiations to lapse rather than intervene as the unions wanted.

It took another international crisis to stir the government into action again. On 22 March 1939, a week after the Germans occupied Prague, three TUC representatives saw the Secretary to the Ministry of Labour, at his request. He told them that the government wished to discuss a number of issues, including labour supply in wartime and the regulation of wages and industrial disputes. The full General Council, by invitation,

[4] Quoted in Keith Feiling, *The Life of Neville Chamberlain*, p. 341.
[5] Ivor Jennings, *Cabinet Government*, p. 501.
[6] *TUC Report*, 1938, p. 227.   [7] ibid., p. 301.

later met the Minister of Labour to hear his proposals. But again, after inconclusive talks with the TUC and employers, negotiations were allowed to lapse.

The lack of determination evident on the side of government was partly a matter of caution, a disinclination to risk the consequences of pushing the unions too hard. The Ministry of Labour's 'reluctance to promote legislation without the prior consent of the TUC' was plain, and was sharply criticized by the Committee of Imperial Defence.[8] On the other hand, there was also a tendency in some government quarters to overlook the unions. It is true that, apart from the occasions already mentioned, union leaders were invited to discuss the schedule of reserved occupations and to help with the voluntary military recruitment scheme, before the introduction of conscription. As well, they were brought into dealings on non-war matters, such as factory regulations and holidays legislation. Yet, in mid-1938, the TUC had to ask the Home Secretary for representation at a meeting on air raid precautions in industry to which he had initially invited only employers' organizations. A similar request in 1939 was twice rejected, if subsequently conceded, by the President of the Board of Trade in relation to an advisory Food Council concerned with the price and supply of food. Again, only when bearded by a TUC deputation did the Home Secretary belatedly explain that it had been 'the intention of the Government from the first' to appoint unionists to advisory bodies associated with the new Ministry of Information.[9]

But the overriding factor, surprising as it may seem with the benefit of hindsight, appears to have been the absence of a ministerial sense of urgency. This was largely, if not wholly, remedied when Britain declared war.

A reconstructed Chamberlain government functioned as a war administration from 3 September 1939 to 10 May 1940. The scale of union-government consultation expanded strikingly during these months. However, the change was not as immediate, nor as wholesale, nor as completely a product of government initiative as implied by the comment that 'the Government drew union leaders into consultation as soon as the

[8] H. M. D. Parker, *Manpower*, p. 59.
[9] *GC Mins.*, 31 August 1939.

Second World War began'.[10] The point is illustrated in an episode which occurred on the heels of the declaration of war. Union leaders learnt of the government's intention to proceed immediately with a Control of Employment Bill, which 'we had never seen'.[11] The TUC protested, and the government then consulted it about the terms of the bill.

Although this sequence was to be repeated, in one form or another, the episode clearly convinced at least some government leaders that the time had come for serious concessions on the score of consultation. In early October the Minister of Labour announced the creation of a National Joint Advisory Council representing unions and employers. The next day the Prime Minister saw a TUC deputation which complained about 'the differing practices of Government Departments on this question of cooperation'.[12] A few days later he read out to the TUC chairman and secretary his instruction that ministers were to consult the unions 'on all matters with which they were concerned'; and talked about possible arrangements with specific departments in terms indicating that he had already taken the issue up in detail with the relevant ministers.[13] Within 48 hours, the TUC leaders had invitations to discuss consultation from the previously aloof ministers of supply, food, education and economic warfare. The pace of their dealings with other ministries quickened. There was also a surge in the formation of formal bodies incorporating trade unionists.

All told, during the eight months of Chamberlain's war administration, at least ten ministries and departments either created consultative bodies with union representation or admitted the unions to existing bodies. The decision, in most cases, appears to have been an outcome of the Prime Minister's October directive. Usually, too, the initiative on the issue of formal representation came from trade union leaders who either first proposed the formation of particular bodies, or had to ask for inclusion in existing or projected ones. There were some notable exceptions to this rule, such as the Export Council, the War Agricultural Advisory Committee, and the National Joint Advisory Council which was suggested, in one

[10] Allen, *Trade Unions and the Government*, p. 33.
[11] W. M. Citrine, *The TUC in Wartime*, December 1939, p. 5.
[12] TUC interview with Prime Minister, *Minutes*, 5 October 1939.
[13] *TUC Report*, 1940, p. 166; *GC Mins.*, 18 October 1939.

form, by the Minister of Labour as early as March 1939. But most ministers, while agreeable enough to *ad hoc* consultation, were plainly less interested than union leaders in a formalized relationship. Presumably, they preferred the situation depicted in the General Council's comment that it 'did not want consultation with the Ministry of Information only when Sir John Reith desired it'.[14] Moreover, the ministerial response to the Prime Minister's directive was by no means uniform. This is illustrated by the varying reactions of the ministers of food, supply and mines, each of whom had previously shown scant sympathy for the TUC's consultative pretensions.

The Minister of Food went all the way. He reversed his earlier refusal to appoint the unions' nominees to some 1,500 local food control committees, concerned with prices and rationing; and agreed to their representation on technical advisory committees dealing with pricing, distribution and storage. He also suggested the formation of a Ministry of Food Advisory Committee, consisting wholly of TUC members, and subsequently consulted it conscientiously.

The Minister of Supply played a cannier game. He quickly agreed to include unionists in existing trade panels and advisory committees for raw materials; to set up area advisory committees on munitions production, with union and employer representation; and to form a National Advisory Committee consisting wholly of TUC nominees. Four months later only two area advisory committees had held their inaugural meeting, and a further two months elapsed before the minister could announce that all of them had been constituted. He held his first meeting with the National Advisory Committee in November: four months later he off-handedly informed parliament that there would be a second meeting 'when there was anything important to consult about'.[15]

The Secretary of Mines gave no ground whatever. Following the Prime Minister's directive, the TUC 'invited' him to appoint unionists to local fuel advisory committees set up earlier to deal with price and distribution problems. 'This communication was not immediately acknowledged . . . but repeated inquiries . . . eventually produced a reply', nearly four months later,

14 ibid., 24 January 1940.
15 John Price, *Labour in the War*, p. 148.

which amounted to a flat rejection.[16] And that was the end of that until the government fell.

The disparity of these responses indicates the varying readiness of Chamberlain's ministers to accept the consultative claims of union leaders. Some were eager to do so. R. H. Dorman-Smith, as Minister of Agriculture, was exceptionally willing; Winston Churchill, as First Lord of the Admiralty, went out of his way to consult Bevin—and, in doing so, forged a personal relationship of immense importance for the future. But 'most were less forthcoming and, on the outbreak of war, displayed much more eagerness to consult businessmen and draw them into administrative positions.

Trade union leaders, on the other hand, did not run as poor a second in this respect as they had during the early stages of the first world war. Moreover, in sharp contrast to 1914, they were consulted, however tentatively, on wartime issues long before war came. In large measure, these differences were doubtless a product of the memories and experience that the ministers of 1939 could draw on. Chamberlain, for example (who first attracted national notice with the speech of welcome he gave as Lord Mayor of Birmingham at the TUC's annual Congress of 1916), had worked quite closely with union leaders during an unrewarding spell as Director-General of National Service in the first world war. And he was adjudged by the experienced Citrine as 'the frankest of all th e Prime Ministers I have met, with the exception of Winston Churchill'.[17] But the direct experience of most of his ministers 'was more limited.

In any case, first world war precedents provided an uncertain guide. Just as, at a more general level, they 'could not reveal the actual weight and proportions and particularity of the war economy' that was to come,[18] neither did they reflect the ambitions of union leaders whose horizon extended well beyond that of their counterparts of a generation earlier. Thus the minister who presumed to stifle claims to direct union representation on local food control committees, by pointing out that there had been no such representation on similar bodies during

[16] *TUC Report*, 1940, p. 194.
[17] Citrine, *Men and Work*, p. 367; and see pp. 361–71 *passim*.
[18] W. K. Hancock and M. M. Gowing, *British War Economy*, p. 53.

the first world war, was quickly disillusioned by union officials determined to have no truck with precedents of this kind.

But perhaps the attitude of those ministers and civil servants who, according to Bevin, 'treated Labour with absolute contempt',[19] is basically explained by the almost complacent air which seems to have pervaded the upper reaches of the government until a few days before it fell. The uneventful early months of the war reinforced the widespread belief that the German economy could not withstand a British blockade. On 4 April 1940 Chamberlain was claiming triumphantly that Hitler had 'missed the bus' because of his failure to attack Britain and France.[20]

Five days later, the German invasion of Denmark and Norway began. British troops evacuated Namsos and Andalsnes three weeks afterwards. The great debate in the House of Commons followed. On 8 May the Labour party's leaders made their fateful decision to divide the house. The government, its majority drastically reduced, won a hollow vote of confidence. The Labour party executive delivered the *coup de grace* by declining to enter a coalition under Chamberlain. Having effectively deposed one Prime Minister in this way, the party's leaders raised another on 10 May when they agreed to serve under Churchill.

Had the Chamberlain government survived to enter on the desperate period that began the same day with the German invasion of the Low Countries, it might well have been converted to the more whole-hearted acceptance of the need to work with the unions which characterized its successor. Nevertheless, the consultative concessions it had made to the unions, particularly during the first eight months of the war, were far from negligible. Despite all their deficiencies, they amounted to a transformation in at least the formal relationship between unions and government. Citrine implied as much in a faintly coy comment on Chamberlain's October directive, recognizing a general union right to consultation: 'it is rather an important acknowledgement of the prestige of the Trade Union Movement when the Head of the State [sic] unreservedly accepts that principle'.[21] Fuller recognition of the unions' right to be consulted, in substance as well as form, came later. But when another TUC leader, W. Holmes, spoke of the way 'old antagonisms' had been overcome in developing 'new relationships with the Government', he was clearly not referring only to the months since May 1940.[22]

TRADE UNIONS

There was no question about official trade union support for the war effort. There was, however, a question of whether union leaders could bring themselves to cooperate actively (and, if so, on what terms) with a government associated with foreign and domestic policies that were not merely opposed but detested by many unionists. An added complication was their deep distrust of its motives, particularly in foreign affairs. And their hostility centred on Chamberlain himself. In these circumstances, it was one thing for union leaders to deal with him when they were seeking concessions. It was quite another matter when he wanted concessions from them—especially given the risk that any agreement on their part might be taken to imply a measure of support for the general policies of his government.

Thus Chamberlain's invitation of March 1938, to discuss rearmament problems, was approached with great caution by the General Council. The invitation was accepted (almost unanimously) only after the council had decided that it would do no more than listen to what he had to say. It was a little more forthcoming in the course of its second meeting with him, in May. On that occasion he was told of the unions' 'grave concern' about certain government policies, and of 'suspicions which existed' about the motives behind the rearmament policy in particular.[23]

But the essential point had been established: trade union leaders were prepared to talk about war preparations, even with a Chamberlain government. It was formally confirmed when the next Congress rejected a proposal to ban such dealings, after Citrine had put the General Council's case.

[21] *TUC Report*, 1940, p. 230.
[22] ibid., p. 74.
[23] ibid., 1938, pp. 228–30.

It is a very old contention whenever a government measure of any kind is passed. . . [and] the trade unions are expected to play a part in its being carried out . . . We had it when it came to the administration of the Un-employment Assistance Board. It was said we should take no part in it . . . We decided against that policy, and we have always decided against that policy, the general reasoning being that it is far better to exert our in-fluence to control these things . . . than to stand outside and have to take the consequences.[24]

A tougher test of Citrine's proposition came a few months later. The Prime Minister again invited the General Council to see him. The TUC leaders were aware that his purpose was to inform them of the government's intention to introduce military conscription. This, they believed, violated an earlier under-taking that he had given them. Nevertheless, the council accepted his invitation by seventeen votes to seven. And a TUC-convened conference of union executives, while opposing conscription, later soundly rebuffed another attempt to con-demn all collaboration with the government.

The readiness of most trade union leaders to cooperate in this way did not mean that they were prepared to play down their differences with Chamberlain and his government. Within hours of Britain's declaration of war, Citrine expressed their intention of 'keeping our Movement quite clear and independent of any governmental action, and retaining our right of criticism during war time'.[25] He also went on to make the equally critical point that 'the precedents of 1914–18, valuable as they may be as a guide, may not be absolutely applicable to our situation today'.[26] This remark was directed to the government. Underlying it was the fact that the union leaders of 1939, unlike their counterparts of 25 years earlier, had a clear conception of the consultative status they wanted from a wartime government seeking their cooperation. There were four requirements.

The first was that they should be put on the same footing as employers. Following the abortive rearmament dealings of 1938, Citrine publicly complained of the 'privileged position' given employers in the discussions, and claimed for the unions the same 'access to information . . . as the employers'.[27] Union protests on this score continued. They sharpened after the

24 ibid., p. 311.   25 ibid., 1939, p. 291.
26 ibid.   27 ibid., 1938, p. 300.

outbreak of war when the TUC accused an uncooperative Minister of Supply of having 'combed the Directory of Directors and . . . Debrett' for the personnel of the Supply Council; while Bevin alleged a prevailing government 'assumption that the only brains in the country are in the heads of the Federation of British Industries, and Big Business'.[28]

The second requirement was that their access to government should be institutionalized, so far as possible, by way of formal consultative bodies. In the summer of 1939, for example, the TUC responded to more modest proposals from the Minister of Labour by suggesting, in detail, an elaborate system of joint standing bodies to deal with wartime industrial regulation. It also pressed for similar arrangements with other ministries. Its persistence eventually produced the October meeting with the Prime Minister, his directive to ministers and the subsequent proliferation of formal consultative bodies with union representation.

The third requirement was that the scope of consultation should not be restricted by an unduly narrow conception of trade union concerns. Citrine, addressing the Minister of Labour and employers' representatives, made the point abundantly clear.

They [union leaders] suspected . . . that the Government was trying to limit the scope of such consultations . . . to what the Government might consider to be 'Labour questions' . . . Trade Union representatives . . . were not going to be told that [other matters of interest to them] were something that lay within the field of the employers and the advice of the Trade Unionist was not wanted upon them.[29]

Finally, the unions wanted direct access to all government agencies handling matters of concern to them. Thus they 'were not prepared to regard the Ministry of Labour as providing adequate contact with other Departments': that was Citrine's response to a suggestion from the Minister of Labour that all 'things of common interest to employers and work people' should be dealt with through his department.[30] And Citrine reiterated the point, with specific reference to the

[28] Quoted in Price, op. cit., pp. 92–3.
[29] Meeting between the TUC General Council and the British Confederation of Employers' Organizations, under the Minister of Labour's chairmanship, *Minutes*, 4 October 1939.
[30] ibid.

Ministry of Supply, when he urged the Prime Minister 'not to be guided into the opinion that contact with the Supply Council through the Ministry of Labour would afford adequate opportunity of expression to the Trades Union Congress'.[31]

During the first eight months of the war there was substantial, though not complete, government acknowledgement of these claims to equality with employers, formalized consultative arrangements, a broad interpretation of union concerns and direct access to responsible authorities. Trade union initiative and pressure were the key to this development. And the union leaders of 1939–40 were distinguished from their counterparts of 1914–15 not only by their much more precise conception of the recognition they wanted from government, but also by the confidence with which they threw their ambitions on to the bargaining table.

TRADES UNION CONGRESS

In May 1938, precisely six weeks after the TUC's first rearmament meeting with Chamberlain, Walter Citrine finished building a family air raid shelter in the backyard of his London home. There is no doubt that, during these weeks, his methodical mind had been turned as well to the larger issue of the TUC's role in the coming war. His foresight, in this case, could not provide as simple a solution as an air raid shelter; but he had ample reason to assume that the TUC was favourably placed to grasp the opportunities offered by the emergencies of war. For one thing, it was administratively better equipped than ever before to handle dealings on complex issues of public policy. But above all, it already had a standing in the eyes of both trade union and government leaders which was well in advance of anything it had achieved before, in the absence of a general strike threat.

Its political authority, however, was by no means complete. To describe the outcome of the March 1938 meeting with Chamberlain as the 'equivalent of Lloyd George's treasury agreement', in the mistaken belief that the General Council agreed then 'to relax craft restrictions in the engineering industry',[32] is not only to err in fact but to exaggerate the

---

[31] TUC interview with the Prime Minister, *Minutes*, 5 October 1939.
[32] Taylor, op. cit., p. 413.

powers assumed by the council. Nevertheless, as we shall see, this meeting was symptomatic of a quite considerable authority. It also indicated the extent to which the TUC had shaken free of the Labour party.

The Party Plays Second Fiddle

Chamberlain had approached the TUC without any reference to the Labour party. When the General Council was informed of his invitation, there was a move to postpone consideration of it in order to allow Citrine to 'explain our relationship with the Labour Party to the Prime Minister'.[33] But the motion was eventually withdrawn; and the implication of that withdrawal was spelt out, after the meeting with Chamberlain, in a resolution which the council adopted unanimously a few minutes before seeing the Labour party leaders.

That the General Council places on record its conviction that in dealing with the Government on behalf of the Trade Union Movement, its conduct must be determined by industrial and not political considerations. Further, that in regard to the appeal of the Prime Minister on the acceleration of the rearmament programme we regard this as exclusively a matter for the Trade Union Movement.[34]

There were later affirmations of this position on other issues. For example, in the case of the local committees associated with the government's voluntary national service scheme, the TUC told the party that the selection of labour representatives was 'a matter for the industrial side'.[35] Again, in the case of an all-party advisory committee attached to the Ministry of Information, it insisted that 'the TUC and the Labour Party should have independent representation, so there would be direct representation from the TUC as a body'.[36]

In some matters, on the other hand, the TUC continued to work closely with the party. The National Council of Labour met frequently during 1938 and the pre-war months of 1939. Thereafter its regular meetings were fortnightly instead of monthly, and it was convened in special session on a number of occasions. In addition, there were frequent meetings of the full executives of the TUC, the Labour party and the parliamentary party. But these joint activities tended to be concerned

[33] *GC Mins.*, 23 March 1938.
[35] ibid., 21 December 1938.

[34] ibid., 25 March 1938.
[36] ibid., 31 August 1939.

less with domestic than with international issues, which also were the subject of several joint deputations to the Prime Minister and the Foreign Secretary during the last months of peace. Even on these issues, however, the TUC leaders seem to have preferred independent action when the opportunity offered. Thus they declined to join an NCL deputation on Spain, choosing instead to raise the topic with Chamberlain at the second rearmament meeting.

Once the war began, there was the hint of a change in the TUC-party relationship with Bevin's complaint about 'the need for more adequate reports to be given to the Movement by the Parliamentary leaders'—who, he claimed, had not informed the NCL of matters which the government 'must have . . . discussed with Opposition leaders'.[37] But the relationship does not seem to have changed at all radically until after the party had filled the role of king-maker in May 1940. And even at that point, the TUC had a hand in the king-making. For when Attlee sought endorsement of his agreement to enter Churchill's government, he asked for it not only from the party executive but also from the General Council.

Internal Authority: First Stage

The General Council asserted its authority in relation to the trade unions merely by meeting with the Prime Minister in March 1938. The issue at stake, acceleration of armament production, touched on the vital industrial interests of major unions. The sensitivity of the issue is reflected in the pains taken by the TUC leaders both to inform Chamberlain of their limited jurisdiction and to reassure the unions that they had not exceeded it.

The Prime Minister was told that the TUC 'could enter into no commitments'; that its powers of intervention did not 'normally' extend to 'matters such as this, which lie more strictly within the province of its affiliated unions'; and that the unions affected should be consulted about 'any specific proposals . . . to accelerate the rearmament programme'.[38] He was also told that the 'suspicions . . . generated' by their meeting 'would have to be dissipated'.[39] Citrine moved quickly to

[37] ibid., 27 September 1939.   [38] *TUC Report*, 1938, pp. 228, 297.
[39] ibid., p. 297.

do so. He saw engineering union leaders the next day, just before they met the Minister for the Coordination of Defence, in order to 'explain the reasons why the General Council had met the Prime Minister'.[40] Affiliated unions in general were then informed by way of a circular.

Citrine underlined the point at the following Congress. He spoke of the General Council's consistent 'cautiousness . . . in avoiding any infringement of the autonomy of the unions'; he emphasized that no promises had been made to Chamberlain, if only because the council had 'no powers to commit any union to anything'—but then added a highly significant qualification.

On the other hand, the General Council have some responsibility for general policy . . . [The] first function of a central body, *even if it has not got those powers*, is surely to do something . . . to try to coordinate the action of its unions . . . The Council have tried to discharge their obligations of leadership, always remembering very prominently the limitations of their authority.[41]

Congress overwhelmingly accepted Citrine's explanation. In doing so, it effectively endorsed not only his qualification but also an earlier expression of it in the circular issued to TUC affiliates after the first meeting with Chamberlain. This asked unions to inform the TUC 'immediately' of any specific proposals they received from government on the arms production issue, a request that was justified on the ground that 'from such proposals general principles may emerge which will affect the whole Movement, and . . . the General Council desire to be placed in the position where it can tender such advice as may be found necessary to avoid . . . any Union being prejudiced by the inadvertent action of another'.[42]

One other notable feature of this episode is the fact that the TUC's leaders accepted Chamberlain's March invitation entirely on their own initiative. They made no formal move to obtain prior authorization from the affiliated unions. Given both the intense distrust of the Prime Minister among the unions and the absence of an actual wartime situation, they left themselves wide open to inevitable charges of duplicity, at worst, and political stupidity, at best. It says a great deal about

[40] *GC Mins.*, 25 March 1938.
[41] *TUC Report*, 1938, p. 299. Italics added.
[42] ibid., p. 228.

their confidence in the General Council's standing that they were prepared to place themselves in this position.

The talks with Chamberlain were a landmark in the development of the TUC's internal authority. They were, however, confined to an exploration, in very general terms, of the possibility of union-government cooperation. The all-important details were left to the engineering unions and employers. What had still to be settled was the TUC's competence to handle war-related matters that were both sensitive and specific.

There was a slight movement in this direction some three months after the 1938 Congress. The General Council had before it an invitation, from the Lord Privy Seal and the Minister of Labour, to discuss a schedule of reserved occupations for use in connection with national service. The council decided against calling a meeting of union executives, and accepted the ministers' invitation despite doubts as to 'whether the Unions would give [it] authority to consult the Government on their behalf in this matter'; but it took the precaution of formally declaring that its purpose was 'simply . . . to elicit information'.[43] The real test was to come.

Internal Authority: Second Stage

On 22 March 1939 the permanent secretary of the Ministry of Labour, at his request, saw Bevin, J. Hallsworth, and H. V. Tewson, the TUC's assistant secretary (Citrine being in the West Indies with a royal commission). He told them that the ministry was considering a plan of industrial regulation in the event of war, and mentioned that the specific items to be covered by the plan included, among other things, wage regulation, control of industrial disputes and the efficient use of skilled labour. The plan, in other words, went to the heart of the trade unions' concerns.

Afterwards, the General Council agreed 'that the discussion should now be placed on a formal basis', although at least one member was unhappy with this and asked the council 'not to go any further without consulting the skilled Unions'.[44] There was more support for his position a week later, when the council

[43] *GC Mins.*, 7 December 1938.
[44] ibid., 23 March 1939.

had before it an invitation to see the Minister of Labour. But the majority accepted the chairman's suggestion that they meet the minister, 'get all the information they could and then decide afterwards what they would do with it'.[45]

When they met the minister they were given a 'secret document', as he emphasized, which set out a number of tentative but precise proposals relating to the items his permanent secretary had mentioned previously. After some discussion, he and his officials withdrew. C. Dukes promptly 'raised the question of whether the Council had the authority to commit the Movement to any policy on this issue'. G. Hicks considered that 'they must get authority before the Council could act'. So did J. Brown. But he envisaged no difficulty in getting it— unlike J. Kaylor who was positive that the leaders of the Amalgamated Engineering Union, at least, would not tolerate such an encroachment on 'the prerogative of their Executive Council'. W. Lawther, G. Gibson and W. Holmes took a different line. They argued against consulting the unions at that stage: the council 'must give a lead and act as a coordinating body', speaking for the movement on 'general policy' and leaving 'the details' to the unions. This was the point made by the absent Citrine at the 1938 Congress. G. Chester alone sought refuge in the hallowed formula of 'further negotiations and consultations without committing themselves'. But it is Bevin's statement of his doubts which provides the most telling indication of the quandary into which the minister's initiative had thrown the TUC leadership.

As regards authority to act for the Movement it was possible for a voluntary body of their character, if they had goodwill within the Movement, to act within certain limitations centrally, and beyond them act as separate trades. Without such goodwill, he thought it was far better to tell the goverment they could not act for the Movement now. Even if they went through the document . . . and decided that certain matters should be dealt with centrally, and others relegated to the trades, he did not believe that certain Unions would agree to that. If so, he thought there was no alternative except for each trade to deal with the document on its own. When such questions as transference or allocation of labour were concerned he did not believe they would act as a composite body.[46]

The meeting was eventually adjourned without a decision being reached.

[45] ibid., 31 March 1939.   [46] ibid.

It resumed five days later. The intervening time had not been wasted. Bevin, for one, had cleared his mind. He opened the debate on the central issue.

The issue before them was a very simple one: Were they prepared to face regulation at all in war-time? He assumed the answer had to be 'Yes'. The second question was, how were they going to construct the machinery? There seemed to be two key points. Should there be a central committee to do the whole business, or should there be local committees to act as agents of a central body, either regional organizations or on a strictly trade basis? He favoured the latter because he thought that it would be far more effective.

In the first instance, he personally favoured a central committee, representing all unions, dealing with a central committee of the Government and of the employers for general questions. But for all matters of detail it should be the industries themselves, including the local committees. They could make a report to the national body, who could report to the Government.

Mr Bevin thought they would need several sets of committess for the different industries . . . What they wanted were autonomous groups . . . That would get rid of any idea that the General Council were trying to take the power out of the hands of the [union] Executives, and would have the added advantage that technical difficulties would be dealt with by the trade, and not by the general, national body. There were certain general questions which obviously applied to labour as a whole which the national body would deal with.[47]

What Bevin had done was to translate into organizational terms Citrine's point which Lawther, Gibson and Holmes had merely parroted five days earlier. The fundamental question of the precise distinction between 'general questions' and 'matters of detail' was still left unresolved. But, as it turned out, Bevin had solved the immediate political problem, although Kaylor remained unconvinced and E. Edwards was still worried. Bevin, however, was masterfully soothing when he wound up the discussion.

He had possibly more experience of group working than others. He knew that it was possible to have a group method in the general movement where there was a virtual autonomy in the industry, leaving the central body with an advisory capacity in the coordinating and guiding sense—a central body which could assist and help and coordinate information . . .

The question would arise as to what would be the subjects remitted to the trades and to the local committees. He thought that the General Council wanted guidance, because there might be disagreement on the functions

[47] ibid., 5 April 1939.

to be remitted. He did not think those functions needed to be absolutely uniform because the character of the trades differed . . .
He believed his suggestion offered a basis of approach without impinging on the rules of a single Union.[48]

The motion Bevin then proposed was deceptively simple, if curiously worded: 'That a machine be constructed for dealing with the matters raised by the Government.' The General Council adopted this motion on 5 April 1939 without taking a vote. It is probably the most important single decision affecting its authority that the council has ever made.

It was Bevin also who pointed out the need to allay the 'suspicion [that] would be aroused in the Unions if they thought the General Council was going to give any commitments to the Government before consulting them'.[49] The result was a brief circular which, among other things, said that the council would submit certain proposals to the unions. A conference of union executives was held six weeks later. It was, however, prompted by the introduction of conscription, and the long resolution it adopted at the council's behest was mainly concerned with the conscription issue. But buried in the body of this resolution, there was one neglected and significantly out-of-key sentence: the conference 'also sanctions the General Council continuing negotiations with the Ministry of Labour on wartime problems of industry on the basis set out in the General Council's Report'.[50] Brown had been right. The council did manage to 'get authority' without a fight.

As it happened, the negotiations thus sanctioned by the conference petered out in July. What mattered more, however, was that when war came the General Council was free, without further debate or doubt, to take the lead even in negotiations involving the kind of issues which had prompted the Treasury conference in 1915. Its own decision of 5 April and, to a lesser extent, the more casual decision of the May conference of executives had paved the way.

There were, too, other indications of an enlarged internal authority. The Bridlington Agreement, adopted by the 1939 Congress, provided a code of conduct in inter-union disputes which helped to entrench the TUC's adjudicating role in this connection. The General Council played a major part in

[48] ibid.   [49] ibid.   [50] *TUC Report*, 1939, p. 264.

relation to formal consultative links between individual unions and government. For example, it settled, in conjunction with the engineering unions, the constitution of the area advisory committees in the munitions industry which it had squeezed from a reluctant Minister of Supply. In a number of cases, it determined whether the union representatives on government bodies with specific industrial concerns were nominated by itself or by relevant unions—and, if the latter, by which unions. In the case of bodies with wider concerns, it successfully maintained the principle it affirmed when it resisted pressure to nominate 'persons outside the General Council' to a royal commission;[51] and so it was able to confine the representational 'plums' to its own membership at a time when they were beginning to fall thick and fast.

Thus, during the two years preceding the fall of the Chamberlain government, the TUC demonstrated a capacity for initiatives once thought well beyond its reach; it also took a long step towards monopolizing communication between unions and government over a wide field. And there was no serious challenge from its affiliated unions. Moreover, Citrine at least was confident of more to come. Publicly, he might reassure unionists at large that the TUC 'had no power to intervene in, or in any way to influence, wage negotiations'.[52] But, privately, he had already confided to an audience of TUC, employer and government representatives 'that he thought a stage would be reached when this question would have to be looked at, *on behalf of the whole Trade Union Movement*, without prejudice, in view of the difficulty of keeping wages apace with prices'.[53] His confidence was expressive of the great change that had occurred in the TUC's internal authority over the fourteen years since he became secretary.

External Authority

The scale of the TUC's dealings with government mounted strikingly during the period. *Ad hoc* meetings became much more frequent from March 1938. Advisory and administrative bodies with direct TUC representation rose in number from 11

---

[51] *GC Mins.*, 28 September 1938.
[52] Citrine, *The TUC in Wartime*, March 1940, pp. 5–6.
[53] *GC Mins.*, 22 November 1939. Italics added.

in 1937 to about 20 at the outbreak of war, and at least a half-dozen more were added by May 1940. By this time the TUC was also associated, in varying ways, with some seven sets of regional or sectional consultative bodies.

The scale of this development is not its only significant feature. There is the extent to which it involved access to the highest levels of government. For example, by May 1940 seven ministries (labour, supply, trade, food, information, agriculture and education) had set up advisory bodies of ministerial standing on which the TUC was represented.

There is the importance to government of the policy matters in relation to which the TUC was granted consultative rights. They included not only labour regulation but also such things as price and profit control, the allocation of raw materials and questions of war finance, which the Chancellor of the Exchequer was prepared to discuss with the Ministry of Labour's National Joint Advisory Council.

There is the element of bargaining reflected in the fact that most of the TUC's consultative gains were extracted from unenthusiastic ministers. Similarly, the prevalence of formal advisory bodies underlines the effectiveness of TUC pressure on the point—first evident, in a major case, early in 1939 with the formation of the Central National Service Committee after the General Council had complained that the administrative structure of the voluntary national service scheme 'did not seem to provide any place in which the Trades Union Congress could function'.[54] The strength of the TUC's negotiating position is also indicated by government policy concessions, especially the way the Control of Employment Bill was emasculated following the General Council's attack on it.

Above all, there is the fact that virtually all of these consultative concessions were made specifically to the TUC, or in response to pressure from it. Moreover, the General Council was invited to nominate the union members not only of major central consultative bodies but also of some sectional bodies, such as the Ministry of Supply's trade panels; and in other cases, such as local food control committees, it was asked to designate which union organizations should have the right of

[54] ibid., 19 December 1938.

nomination. The significance of this is that it reveals a preference, on the part of government leaders, for dealing with the unions through the TUC. The contrast with the first world war is striking. Then, government dealings with the unions were typified by Lloyd George's Treasury conference of March 1915, at which 35 different trade union organizations were represented, the TUC being one of them. There was no attempt by the Chamberlain government to stage similar mass meetings of union representatives. Instead, Chamberlain saw the TUC leaders alone in March 1938; and that continued to be the dominant pattern in his government's dealings with the unions. The contrast is heightened by the fact that Chamberlain, unlike Asquith, did not leave the initial approach to a colleague.

It was not only that, in comparison with the first world war, the Chamberlain government diminished the consultative role of the unions at large in favour of the TUC. It also diminished the Labour party's role. The party was excluded from TUC-government dealings on industrial issues, despite their often farreaching political implications. On other matters, the TUC was sometimes given equal, or even prior, standing. For example, government leaders dealt mainly with the General Council on the question of voluntary national service; informed it of their intention to introduce military conscription before telling Attlee and Greenwood; and conceded it separate representation, alongside the party, in the Ministry of Information's consultative machinery.

The government's concentration on the TUC is readily established. The reasons for it are less certain. The critical government initiative, Chamberlain's approach to the General Council in March 1938, could have been motivated simply by a belief that protocol required it, as a preliminary to dealing with the unions directly concerned. The TUC incorporated all those unions—unlike the nearest alternative, the Confederation of Engineering and Shipbuilding Unions, which lacked the affiliation of the crucial Amalgamated Engineering Union. True, no such protocol had been observed in the similar circumstances of March 1915; but then, apart from anything else, it was the TUC which lacked the affiliation of the AEU's predecessor, the Amalgamated Society of Engineers. The protocol explanation is given added colour by the certainty that, at least after his initial conversation with Citrine, Chamberlain knew the TUC could not actually negotiate on behalf of the engineering unions. One indication of this is that the later ministerial discussions with the unions were arranged before he met the General Council.

However, it seems unlikely that protocol was Chamberlain's only, or even his main, consideration. For there was an advantage which he could hope to gain from drawing the TUC into the field. The problem confronting him was that the cooperation of the engineering unions was the key to his government's plans for accelerating the rearmament programme, and the leading officials of these unions included men known to be intensely suspicious of the government's motives. The obvious calculation follows: if influential support could be enlisted within the labour movement, it might be possible to reduce the impact of their hostility on the negotiations. The TUC would have appeared the most hopeful source of such support for two reasons. In the first place, there was the relative moderation of the TUC leaders, coupled with the demonstrated strength of their commitment to rearmament. Chamberlain's picture of the Labour party leaders was quite different: then, as later, he was incensed by what he saw as their 'partisanship and personal prejudice'.[55] In the second place, there was the general political stature of the TUC leaders by 1938, which was far in advance of their counterparts' 23 years earlier. Together, these perceived attributes offered Chamberlain the possibility of inducing the TUC to exert effective influence, favourable to the government, on the engineering unions. The exercise might well have been seen as a long shot, but it was plainly worth trying.

Chamberlain's initiative, of course, did not come off on this occasion. Nevertheless, he and his ministers persisted in dealing with the TUC on war-related matters of close concern to the unions. At no stage did they turn to the first world war device of Treasury-type conferences. They edged, instead, into a consultative relationship with the TUC which was unprecedented in its closeness and exclusiveness.

Such a relationship, given the great and increasing importance which government leaders obviously attached to con-

[55] Quoted in Feiling, op. cit., p. 430.

ciliating the unions, is inconceivable in the absence of an assumption on their part that the TUC was capable of acting as the authoritative union spokesman on many, if not all, major issues. They had no reason to confer privileged status on a body whose competence they believed to be confined to side-issues. To do so would have been to court antagonistic responses from the very trade unions whose cooperation they wanted. In other words, for government leaders to act as they did, they *had* to believe that the TUC leadership exerted real influence in the trade union movement.

The TUC leaders themselves were well aware that their consultative ambitions could be realized only if this belief existed in government circles. Dukes said as much during the General Council's crucial debate on the invitation to consider the Minister of Labour's proposals concerning industrial regulation in wartime.

> He really thought that if they did not take part in providing machinery to deal with the various problems, they were inviting the Government to go over their heads . . . He did not believe that they could afford to say to the Government that they were incapable of acting, and he thought it would be a tragedy if they said they had no authority.[56]

Tewson made the same point in another way: accepting the invitation, he said, 'would be an encouragement to the Government to consult [the TUC] again on questions of national importance'.[57]

The General Council did accept the invitation, as we have seen. This decision was as critical for its external authority as for its internal authority. The implicit effect, in the absence of any challenge from the affiliated unions, was to confirm that government leaders were dealing with a body fully capable of representing its constituents on major wartime policy issues. They may even have been led to over-estimate the TUC's internal authority. As Citrine had disarmingly remarked to the 1938 Congress, 'sometimes even Governments make the mistake of assuming that the Trades Union Congress has greater power than in fact it possesses'.[58]

Mistaken or not, some such assumption was plainly made by Chamberlain and his ministers. It was sufficient to ensure government recognition of the TUC in a manner and on a

[56] *GC Mins.*, 5 April 1939.   [57] ibid.   [58] *TUC Report*, 1938, p. 297.

scale that accorded it an unparalleled external authority by May 1940. But the accolade was bestowed with Chamberlain's fall from office, when Churchill told Attlee and Greenwood that 'it was vitally important that organized labour in industry should be directly represented' in his cabinet.[59] There were only two possible candidates. They were Bevin and Citrine, the dominant figures on the General Council.

Established Political Authority

In the early months of the first world war the TUC had been hemmed in by the Labour party, the Joint Board, the General Federation of Trade Unions and the War Emergency Workers' National Committee. In the wartime months of 1939–40 there was only the Labour party to provide anything like a comparable competitive threat, and it had no Arthur Henderson. Effectively, the TUC stood alone on the industrial side of the labour movement.

Its intermediary role between unions and government, already more substantial by 1938 than in 1914–15, was even weightier by May 1940. The Chamberlain government had conceded it access to an extent and on terms that were unprecedented. The affiliated unions had conceded it an independence of action that was equally unprecedented. Nor was this new political authority confined to the level of high policy. It was reinforced and, in a sense, enlarged by an involvement with such things as the negotiation and administration of an above-ration petrol allowance for union officials, and the provision of lists of local officials who could be consulted by government inspectors. These and similar functions, small enough in themselves, added to the TUC's usefulness in the eyes of both unions and government.

But perhaps the most telling measure of the TUC's new political authority lies in one point of contrast between the two great wars. It is possible, as we have seen, to give an adequate description of union-government relations during the whole of the first world war with only the barest of references to the Parliamentary Committee as an independent actor. On the other hand, the General Council's role is central to any

[59] *GC Mins.*, 12 May 1940.

similar account of even the first eight months of the second world war.

Digging deeper into this contrast, there is a further point to be made. That is the extent to which, by May 1940, the TUC's authority as a political intermediary had been entrenched owing to the General Council's success in both monopolizing and formalizing key channels of communication between government and the trade unions. For in doing so, as it turned out, the TUC had secured for itself an intermediary role that was to endure, in its essentials, through the remaining years of war and far beyond.

IO

Confirmation and Consolidation
1940–1976

THE intermediary role that the TUC had acquired by May 1940 was confirmed and strengthened during the succeeding wartime years. Peace brought some modification and many adjustments, but there was no reversion to pre-war patterns. Despite fluctuating relations with both unions and government, during the next 30 years the TUC consolidated a political authority of greater weight than it had possessed at any time before 1940. It also established a towering presence in the world of British pressure groups at large.

THE WARTIME COALITION: 1940–45

Churchill's government took office as the German panzers stormed into France and the Low Countries. Even a Chamberlain administration would probably have been infused with the acute sense of danger and urgency which, as many have remarked, characterized the new regime. On the other hand, Churchill may have not needed this spur to suggest to Attlee and Greenwood that one Labour member of the coalition should be a trade union man. His eye, he made clear to them at the time, was on Bevin.[1]

Bevin's appointment as Minister of Labour was without precise precedent. Both John Hodge and G. H. Roberts, the first two to hold this office following its creation by Lloyd George in 1916, were also trade union officials. Each was an MP and had been a member of the Labour party executive for several years. Hodge had also held a seat on the TUC Parliamentary Committee for a brief time in the 1890s. But neither carried anything like Bevin's weight in the labour movement of their day. He was not only leader of the country's largest union but

---

[1] See Winston Churchill, *The Second World War*, vol. 1, p. 526.

a longstanding and dominating member of the TUC General Council. He himself emphasized these connections by insisting that he would accept ministerial appointment only with 'the full backing of the General Council and the Executive of his own Union'.[2]

The exceptional nature of his appointment is underlined by the fact that he was not a parliamentarian at a time when 'it was generally expected' that the new minister would be drawn from existing Labour MPs.[3] It signified Churchill's recognition that 'labour relations . . . were the critical point of the war economy'.[4]

The Importance of Bevin

The new Minister of Labour was no mere symbol of union-government cooperation. His talents secured him membership of the war cabinet within five months, and he remained a member until the coalition was dissolved. His stature in that select company was such that Lord Beaverbrook could describe him, to Churchill, as 'the most powerful man in your Cabinet'[5] —an opinion confirmed by the comment, from a less partial source, that 'all the ministers except Bevin were in practice Churchill's instruments'.[6] He made of the Ministry of Labour what it had never before been, a major department of state. Impelled by his thrusting ambition, it 'now took with both hands all the specific responsibilities which hitherto it had been trying to fob off upon other departments', and thereafter asserted its hegemony relentlessly.[7] His political weight is illustrated by the 'official view' of the possibility of containing union wage demands, on which the success of the government's economic policy hinged: 'anything beyond what could be achieved by the informal . . . influence of Mr Bevin was not worth attempting'.[8]

Bevin's influence among trade union leaders was the foundation of his strength as a minister. He won their approval by

[2] *GC Mins.*, 12 May 1940.
[3] Parker, op. cit., p. 87.
[4] Taylor, op. cit., p. 512.
[5] Quoted in Williams, op. cit., p. 228.
[6] Taylor, op. cit., p. 482.
[7] Hancock and Gowing, op. cit., p. 150; and see Bullock, op. cit., vol. II, pp. 12, 15–16, 23, 26–7.
[8] R. S. Sayers, *Financial Policy, 1939–1945*, pp. 46, 67.

playing a major part in relation to policies that helped reduce the sources of union discontent, such as the extension of Chamberlain's food subsidies and rationing policy, the introduction of price control, heavier income tax rates and much tighter profit restrictions than in the first world war, the abolition of the 'household' means test for unemployment benefit and for supplementary old age pensions. He also resisted, successfully, continuing pressure for wholesale industrial conscription and statutory wage controls. And he encouraged, in a variety of ways, employer recognition of unions.[9]

At the same time, he played a crucial part in the introduction and application of policies which cut into traditional union values. But he did so with a 'mixture of legislative audacity and administrative circumspection' which sweetened the pill.[10] The audacity is reflected in the sweeping powers he secured for himself, within a few days of entering the government, through the Emergency Powers (Defence) Act; and in the way he acted to outlaw strikes and to impose restrictions on labour mobility in 'essential' industries. The circumspection is reflected in his insistence that legal compulsion was purely a last resort. Thus he agreed to define an industry as 'essential' only when he was satisfied with both its conditions of employment and its employers' negotiating arrangements with relevant unions; and he used the power to penalize strikes with judicious care. Similarly, he sought to secure the benefits of wage control and industrial conscription by way of persuasion and agreement. This involved, of course, a heavy emphasis on consultation with employers and trade unions.

Bevin's dealings with the trade unions set an influential example owing to the ascendancy of himself and his department within the war administration. He emphasized consultation from the start. The programme he submitted to cabinet, shortly after taking office, was informally discussed beforehand with Citrine and at least one leading employer. Two days after cabinet received it, Bevin outlined it to the National Joint Advisory Council; and three days later explained it at a TUC-convened conference of union officials. There followed a

[9] See, e.g., G. S. Bain, *The Growth of White-Collar Unionism*, pp. 161–2, 164.
[10] M. M. Postan, *British War Production*, p. 145.

marked expansion in the number and variety of formal consultative bodies operating under the aegis of the Ministry of Labour. Above all, Bevin appears to have brought to his ministerial role the conviction he had acted on as a union leader, that consultation was an important aspect of the policy-making process.

He neither supposed, his biographer points out, that 'consultation could be a substitute for a policy' nor treated it as 'an exercise in public relations' designed simply to secure approval of his proposals: 'he expected the members of a committee to express their own views and frequently modified proposals to take account of them'.[11] He demonstrated, at the outset of his ministry, the importance he attached to consultation by taking on the chairmanship not only of the established National Joint Advisory Council, but also of three other major bodies of his own creation—the Factory and Welfare Advisory Board, the shorter-lived Labour Supply Board and the Joint Consultative Committee, formed as a smaller edition of the sixty-member NJAC in order to facilitate quick consultation about Bevin's use of his awesome regulation-making powers. But the strongest confirmation of the value he attached to consultation is provided by his treatment of the JCC in particular. This committee played 'a key role' throughout his term as Minister of Labour, and 'all the major decisions on manpower and labour policy were discussed in advance with its members'.[12]

Union–government Relations

The growth in union–government dealings after May 1940 is reflected in two things, as the outline of Bevin's role suggests. One was an elaboration of the consultative structure established under the Chamberlain government. This involved an expansion in the unions' opportunities for representation on standing advisory and administrative bodies in the case of both departments with which they already had such formal links and those with which they did not. The Ministry of Labour, given its greatly widened jurisdiction under Bevin, is the most dramatic example of the former. Soon after his accession, the

[11] Bullock, op. cit., vol. II, p. 96.
[12] ibid., pp. 22, 96.

lone National Joint Advisory Council was joined by something like a dozen central bodies with union representation, as well as scores of industry, regional and local committees of one sort or another. Departments with which the unions had no existing formal connection either created bodies, on which the unions were given representation alongside other interests, or admitted them to bodies formerly restricted to other interests. Before long, union leaders were associated in this way with 18 separate departments, including the ministries of labour, supply, production, shipping, food, health, home security, reconstruction, pensions, education, information, works, fuel and power, agriculture and fisheries, together with the Treasury, the Board of Trade, the Colonial Office and the Lord Chancellor. As this list indicates, there was no longer any question of the unions' consultative access being confined to narrowly industrial issues. The point is underlined by Churchill's discussion of strictly military matters with two TUC officials in 1944, and by his eagerness to back a TUC investigation of the Greek political situation in 1945.[13]

The second, and more subtle, reflection of the growth in union–government dealings is the greater importance which ministers seem to have placed on consulting union leaders. Bevin's zeal in this respect may well have been unique. The concerns of his ministry, in any case, were more closely and completely enmeshed with those of the unions than any other. But there was evident among ministers in general a disposition for dealing with the unions that was decidedly more pronounced than in Chamberlain's day. The extent to which it was a result of Churchill's influence or Bevin's example is impossible to assess. It certainly owed a great deal to the change from phoney war to total war which coincided so precisely with the change of prime ministers.

Inevitably, in such a complex set of relationships, there were frictions. Many were the product of hesitation or misunderstanding, and were eventually put right. Thus the 'initial rebuff' encountered by a TUC committee before it got to see a Conservative Minister of Health, and the 'apparent reluctance' of some regional civil servants to consult their union counterparts.[14] Sometimes, on the trade union side, difficulties were

[13] See Lord Citrine, *Two Careers*, pp. 200–2, 210.
[14] *TUC Report*, 1941, p. 101; 1943, p. 131.

exaggerated. For example, the TUC followed up a Congress resolution expressing 'profound dissatisfaction' with a number of Ministry of Supply committees, only the find that few of the unions directly involved had grievances of any substance.[15] But there were other cases in which union complaints seem to have been more soundly based.

Lord Woolton, when Minister of Reconstruction, seldom initiated meetings of the Reconstruction Joint Advisory Council. To make matters worse, he was apt to cancel meetings prompted by union or employer representatives, doing so 'often at short notice and sometimes for reasons which seemed to imply that [he] did not attach any substantial importance' to the RJAC.[16] Ministerial attitudes to the principal advisory body concerned specifically with production problems were also a continuing source of grievance. In its initial form, as a wholly TUC body attached to the Ministry of Supply, this body was 'rather disappointing' because of the minister's reluctance to introduce discussion items; it was still 'rarely consulted by the Government' after being reconstituted to include employers and linked to the cabinet's Production Executive; and the complaints remained the same following its final transformation into a body attached to the Ministry of Production, which was headed by a Conservative until the end of the war.[17]

Nor was it only Conservatives who were faulted in this respect. Herbert Morrison, as Minister of Home Security, had drawn an early and 'most emphatic protest' (though he later 'expressed regret') for neglecting to consult the TUC before issuing a regulation.[18] In 1943 Citrine accused Labour party ministers in general of 'failing to give the TUC as much information as [it] got from Conservative ministers'; and shortly before the coalition broke up, he told Attlee to his face that 'I couldn't remember a single occasion when he [Attlee] had ever helped us since he had taken office'.[19] Even Bevin did not escape unscathed. Citrine had an early row with him about his treatment of the members of the short-lived Labour Supply

[15] ibid., 1943, p. 106.
[16] ibid., 1945, p. 175.
[17] ibid., 1941, p. 156; 1942, p. 83; 1943, p. 100; 1944, p. 129.
[18] ibid., 1941, pp. 106, 166.
[19] Bullock, op. cit., vol. II, p. 244; Citrine, *Two Careers*, p. 226.

Board, and he was the chairman of the body advising the cabinet's Production Executive which, as we have seen, the TUC claimed was rarely consulted.

But these complaints represent exceptions rather than the rule. The TUC's annual reports convey the clear impression that the unions encountered comparatively few serious difficulties in securing access to government when and how they wanted it. They struck bad patches, and most notably so in early 1942 according to Citrine, whose comment refers to ministers in general: 'There was, at that time, a rather lofty contempt for consultative machinery; it was quite discernible to myself and others'.[20] However, as this remark implies, that situation did not persist. A more accurate characterization of the war period as a whole is provided by another comment from the same pen. Once Churchill, on Citrine's prompting, had reiterated Chamberlain's directive to ministers about consultation, union leaders 'had very little to complain about ... with [government] officials falling over themselves to demonstrate their desire for cooperation'.[21]

This general pattern of close consultative involvement gave colour to Aneurin Bevan's talk about 'the corporate rule' of business and union leaders.[22] But the notice government took of the trade unions is easily exaggerated. It was unquestionably much greater than in the first world war, and the difference shows up not only in consultative arrangements but also in the use of union officials as full-time members of the war administration. At the same time, the contrast is drawn too sharply in the statement that, while the first world war administration consisted of career civil servants, businessmen and 'the intellectuals, mostly university teachers', that of the second world war was 'in the hands of much the same three groups, with the addition this time of trade union officials'.[23] This overlooks the smattering of unionists in the first war administration. More seriously, it implies an equality of treatment between unionists and businessmen in the second which is almost certainly untrue. For, Bevin apart, the highest administrative level to which a trade union official might realistically aspire seems to have been

[20] Citrine, *Two Careers*, p. 139.
[21] ibid., pp. 31–2.
[22] Quoted in Michael Foot, *Aneurin Bevan*, p. 461.
[23] Taylor, op. cit., pp. 507–8.

membership of a top-drawer executive body, like the short-lived Labour Supply Board, or the office of 'confidential adviser' to a minister. Inspectorial posts, industrial relations officers in supply departments and membership of some local administrative bodies: these were the staple full-time appointments for unionists. The opportunities for businessmen were certainly more varied.

There are other indications that businessmen were, if not invariably, given preferential treatment. Towards the end of the war, for example, the TUC leadership was dismayed to discover that 'directors or managing directors of firms' had been appointed to 'the overwhelming majority' of full-time chairmanships available in relation to local committees and appeal boards concerned with demobilization, while union nominees filled less than a quarter of these posts.[24] On an earlier occasion two ministries nominated private industrialists to represent them on an inter-departmental committee dealing with labour efficiency in munitions production: the TUC failed to convince the government that 'if outside employers were to be brought in . . . then the TUC should be asked to supply two nominees'.[25] Even Bevin appointed a leading employer to a committee inquiring into the use of skilled men in the armed forces, and declined to grant the TUC matching representation 'despite vigorous protests'.[26] And there was one episode (having to do with, of all things, the price of fish) which showed that consultation could be heavily lopsided in favour of employers, even on an issue touching the most intimate industrial interests of union members.[27] But a more subtle and, one suspects, more pervasive form of discrimination was indicated by the remark, in 1943, of a prominent official referring to relations in his own industry. Government and the employers had 'fully consulted' his union 'on all questions affecting the interests of our members'—yet, he added, 'it cannot truthfully be said that the Union has been regarded as an equal partner on all matters affecting the industry'.[28]

[24] *TUC Report*, 1945, p. 169.
[25] ibid., 1943, p. 106.
[26] ibid., 1942, p. 95; and see Citrine, *Two Careers*, p. 94.
[27] See R. J. Hammond, *Food*, vol. II, pp. 54–5.
[28] Quoted in Fox, op. cit., p. 556.

The TUC's Role

Citrine's ambition for the TUC was precisely that it should be regarded as 'an equal partner' on virtually all matters affecting the country: 'no matter what the subject might be— apart from purely military questions—I staked our claim to be speedily and thoroughly consulted on all possible occasions'.[29] In line with this aim, he and his colleagues worked to establish close and regular access to government at as many points and as high a level as possible.

They did not altogether ignore even a parliament that had delegated so much of its legislative power to ministers. They moved in 1943 towards a closer relationship with the parliamentary Trade Union Group, by way of monthly briefing sessions; but this, like similar attempts earlier, soon faded. They circulated MPs about the Education Bill a little later, and fed the parliamentary Labour party with amendments to the Pensions Bill of 1944. But the focus of their attention, and in this they were in tune with the growing tendency of the unions to keep their major officials out of parliament,[30] was ministers and their departments.

By mid-1941 the General Council and its staff were 'engaged in almost daily consultation' with government; and the council's report for that year found it 'impossible to give even an indication of the innumerable consultations' of the preceding twelve months.[31] These and later dealings were conducted almost wholly through either consultative bodies or informal discussions. The formal deputation was used only occasionally. The annual round of post-Congress deputations to ministers was discarded altogether.

The TUC was involved at some remove in virtually every major aspect of the trade unions' consultative relations with the Churchill government. Its nominees, usually General Council members, had seats on almost all of those central bodies, with official union representation, which were concerned with matters of interest to the unions at large. And even in the case of the only important exceptions to this rule, the Labour Supply Board and the Factory and Welfare Advisory

[29] Citrine, *Two Careers*, pp. 24–5.
[30] See H. A. Clegg, *General Union in a Changing Society*, pp. 153–6.
[31] *TUC Report*, 1941, pp. 91, 141.

Board whose unionist members were selected by Bevin personally, there are indications that TUC leaders were informally consulted (quite apart from the fact that the FWAB included two General Council members and one TUC staff member). Often, too, the TUC was the effective nominating agent when it came to central bodies with narrower industrial or occupational concerns. Usually it either selected its nominees for such bodies from names sent in by interested unions or simply forwarded the full list of those names. But sometimes it nominated General Council members, as in the case of the various 'controls' concerned with the distribution of raw materials.

The more narrowly sectional a body, in industrial or occupational terms, the less likely the TUC was to be directly involved. This tendency, although still evident, was much more muted in relation to regional and local bodies of a nonsectional type. In these cases, the TUC usually sent on all nominations submitted to it, but quite often made from them either a short list or its own selections.

The General Council 'cautiously', Citrine's word, encouraged the trades councils to act as its local counterparts, handling 'the same sort of problems [locally] that we are dealing with nationally'—but came down on them heavily when they ventured to make representations to government on matters of '*national* policy', and reminded them that 'the function of declaring policy for the Movement generally belongs to ... Congress and the General Council'.[32] On the other hand, the council moved more boldly at the regional level. In 1940 it formed twelve TUC Regional Emergency Committees, one in each of the designated defence regions, to work with the government's Regional Commissioners in order to provide for 'the carrying on of production in the event of invasion'.[33] They were, of course, spared the full enormity of their anticipated task. Instead, they carried out more mundane consultative functions in the TUC's name. Later, when victory rather than invasion loomed, the General Council decided that 'the Trade Union Movement should formally adapt its machinery' to the fact that a number of ministries 'had delegated ... considerable ... authority and autonomy to their Regional Controllers': the committees were renamed Regional Advisory Committees

---

[32] ibid., 1940, p. 231; 1944, p. 52.   [33] ibid., 1941, p. 169.

and empowered to 'act as the agent of the Trades Union Congress' under the council's direction.[34] The significance of this organizational innovation is that it enhanced the TUC leadership's ability to exert a controlling influence on union-government relations below the national level. Its grip on the regional committees is indicated by the fact that while their ordinary members were elected by the full-time union officials of each region, their chairmen and deputy-chairmen were chosen by the General Council—and, in most cases, the chairman selected was a council member.

There were also less obtrusive aspects to the TUC's intermediary role. It was frequently used as a post office by government departments. At their request, it sent out to unions a great deal of informational material, some of which was 'strictly confidential' like certain arrangements concerning future 'military operations' which it circulated not long before the Normandy landing.[35] At their request also, it garnered the reactions of relevant unions to such things as production quotas and changes in the schedule of reserved occupations. Similarly, the affiliated unions funnelled a huge variety of detailed grievances and proposals for administrative action into the TUC. As a result, it took up with government, for example, complaints about specific individuals in the armed forces whose civilian skills were not being utilized, and claims concerning the rationing and billeting problems of particular occupational groups. It also handled, among other things, all applications by union officials for call-up deferments, and obtained the permits officials needed to enter restricted areas and work-places. The value that TUC leaders attributed to this transmitting role is implied in their invitation that 'trade unions who have anything to suggest, or any complaints to make', about the government's proposed air raid and invasion precautions in industry, 'should let the TUC know all about it'.[36] Another indication is the stream of TUC circulars, sometimes several in one week, and the quarterly issues of *The TUC in Wartime* which informed affiliated unions about government decisions of concern to them.

[34] ibid., 1945, p. 161.
[35] ibid., 1944, p. 153.
[36] Citrine, *The TUC in Wartime*, June 1940, p. 8.

The TUC's minimal intermediary function was that of bringing together appropriate union and government officials. This function normally took the form of a response to a government request for a list of all the unions with members in a particular industrial or occupational sector, or with a likely interest in submitting nominations for a particular committee. Sometimes, but not often, it involved convening trade union conferences for government spokesmen to address, such as a number of local and regional conferences on air raid warnings and industry, and the conference of union executives at which Bevin spoke shortly after becoming a minister.

Internal Authority

The massive gathering that Bevin addressed on 25 May 1940 is the second world war's nearest counterpart of Lloyd George's Treasury conference in March 1915. But the differences are vital. First there is the TUC's role. The conference of 1940, unlike that of 1915, was convened by the TUC and chaired by its senior official, and the key resolution was moved by its secretary. Then there is the difference between the decisions of the two conferences. That of 1915 agreed, for the duration of the war, to rely on arbitration rather than the strike and to relax trade practices impeding the dilution of skilled labour. The 1940 conference decided no such substantive policy issue. The resolution it adopted, with only four dissentients, looked both to the past and the future in totally different terms. As to the past, it endorsed 'the action of the General Council in giving its full support to the . . . measures that must be taken to protect our people', the specific issue here being the council's support for the Emergency Powers (Defence) Act of three days earlier. As to the future, it gave the TUC leadership something of a *carte blanche* by expressing 'complete confidence in the General Council and [its] representatives on the Consultative Committee appointed to advise the Ministry of Labour'.[37]

The contrast sharpened a few days afterwards when the council and its members on Bevin's Joint Consultative Committee agreed to the recommendation paving the way for Order No. 1305, which banned strikes and made arbitration compulsory if industrial negotiations failed. Much later, in

[37] ibid., pp. 4, 33.

1944, they also agreed to accept Bevin's controversial defence regulation 1AA, which provided substantial penalties for inciting strikes—a decision evoking a strong, if unsuccessful, challenge that lured Citrine into the breath-taking emptiness of: 'We had to do something, and we did it unanimously'.[38]

Both the readiness and the ability of the General Council to take decisions on such critical issues, without being repudiated by its affiliated unions, denote an internal authority of a high order. This conclusion is reinforced by other indicators. In particular, there are the refusals to act on policy proposals from affiliated unions, not because of any countervailing Congress resolution, but simply on the basis of the council's own judgement of the circumstances. In 1942, for example, the weighty Confederation of Engineering and Shipbuilding Unions asked the TUC to press government for an immediate revision of the official cost-of-living index. It was coolly informed that the council had already decided that to pursue this matter in wartime would be 'inadvisable'.[39] Again, two powerful affiliates, the Amalgamated Engineering Union and the Electrical Trades Union, were rebuffed with equal firmness in 1944. They had separately asked that the government be urged to classify extra wartime travelling expenses as an allowable tax deduction. 'The General Council decided that [such a scheme] would be difficult to administer . . . and that there was not sufficient evidence of hardship . . . to justify . . . approaching the Chancellor on the matter.'[40]

Trade unions also channelled into the TUC an unprecedented flood of sectional issues, some of which were quite closely related to their central industrial interests. Thus the negotiation, 'at arm's length through the TUC', of the Ford motor company's first collective agreement with the unions; and the requirement of a union conference which agreed, as a wartime measure, that the Home Office might make specific exemptions from the legislative prohibition against wage-payments in kind, but 'only after consultation *through the TUC* with the Union or Unions concerned'.[41] Moreover, when it came to transmitting

[38] ibid., June 1944, p. 20.
[39] *TUC Report*, 1943, p. 149.
[40] ibid., 1944, p. 177.
[41] H. A. Turner, G. Clack and G. Roberts, *Labour Relations in the Motor Industry*, p. 194; *TUC Report*, 1942, p. 126. Italics added.

sectional claims to government, the TUC was not always prepared to accept a passive post-office role. This was strikingly evident in the case of union claims for supplementary food rations on behalf of specific categories of workers. The General Council consistently refused to urge such claims on the Ministry of Food unless they satisfied criteria which the council itself had formulated.[42]

There were, of course, limits to the intermediary role the TUC was allowed to play, especially in relation to issues impinging directly on the sectional industrial interests of the unions. Thus it took no part in the negotiations about applying the principle of diluting skilled labour to specific industries. And the General Council's caution in this area is evident in its circular to affiliates 'suggesting that we should be empowered' to press for legislation giving legal force to agreements on the forty-hour working week.[43]

Both the extent and the limits of the TUC's internal authority are illustrated by its activities in matters of particular interest to the engineering unions. During the first world war, as we have seen, these unions dealt quite independently with government. Their industrial position was certainly no weaker in the second world war, but this time they allowed the TUC a considerable voice in their affairs. For example, it not only collected their nominations for representatives on important regional administrative boards of concern to them, but also made the 'final selection of the nominees put forward to government in each case'.[44] Again, after the TUC had persuaded them to form inter-union production committees at the works and district levels, they agreed 'to carry [this] joint working ... to the national level' by setting up a central committee (the National Advisory Committee for the Engineering and Shipbuilding Industries) on which half the seats were held by General Council members.[45] Yet the TUC played no part in the negotiations with employers about setting up works production committees. On another issue, it was the TUC leaders alone who discussed with employers and the Ministry of Labour the question of legislation providing for the postwar restoration of

[42] See *TUC Report*, 1941, p. 163; 1944, p. 143; and Hammond, op. cit., p. 621.
[43] Citrine, *The TUC in Wartime*, June 1944, p. 11.
[44] *TUC Report*, 1940, p. 185.
[45] ibid., 1942, pp. 84–6.

trade union practices abandoned during the war, a matter of special importance to the engineering unions. Yet the General Council twice found it advisable to safeguard its position in these negotiations by convening full-scale conferences of those unions.

The crucial point, however, is that the constraints imposed on the TUC by its affiliated unions still left room for the exercise of an internal authority that is impressive by earlier peacetime standards, and awesome by the standards of the first world war. A key factor in the situation was the ambition and enterprise of the TUC's leaders. They seized every opportunity of extending its activities and increasing the unions' reliance on it. Their ambition shines through the careful phrasing of an offer to act at the level of basic union concerns: 'Whilst the General Council do not intervene in the domestic affairs of affiliated organizations, they are at all times willing to offer advice and assistance on any phase of work with which a Union may be concerned.'[46] Their enterprise was such that they were prepared to initiate action without worrying greatly about their formal competence to do so. By 1944, they were also prepared to admit as much to Congress.

The General Council have not asked for specific powers to undertake all the wide range of functions which they [have come to] perform. The Council have tried to interpret or anticipate the desires of affiliated Unions in the field of activities they pursue and the Unions have through Congress almost invariably approved the constant extension of functions.[47]

Another factor of importance was the absence, as we have seen, of interunion bodies with comparably broad claims. The TUC's relations with the Labour party, the only body capable of posing a direct competitive threat, seem to have been little troubled by the jurisdictional disputes of the past. The two continued to cooperate in the National Council of Labour, which was reconstituted in 1941 to include representatives of the Cooperative Union. The NCL met fortnightly for a time following Chamberlain's departure, and thereafter appears to have held regular monthly meetings during the remaining war years. It mounted ministerial deputations on a number of topics, including coal supplies and purchase tax. Attlee was one

[46] ibid., 1944, p. 372.
[47] ibid., p. 370.

of its members throughout this period. The party also maintained its two representatives on the TUC Economic Committee and on the TUC Workmen's Compensation and
Factories Committee. The TUC appointed two members of
the party's new Policy Sub-committee, and a couple of special
joint committees were formed. The party showed no interest
in challenging the TUC's role as principal union spokesman.

Finally, there is the vital factor of government response—
the extent to which, and the terms on which ministers
were prepared to deal with the unions through the TUC.
This not only reflected the TUC's *external* authority, but was
also a major determinant of its standing among the unions as
a political intermediary.

External Authority

It was certainly true that 'to a greater extent than before the
Government has recognized the title of the Trades Union
Congress to voice the opinions and the claims of its affiliated
organizations'.[48] The extent of that recognition was actually
much greater than this remark might suggest. On the other
hand, as we have seen, it fell short of an acceptance of the TUC
as the authoritative union spokesman for all purposes.

Thus Bevin used Lloyd George's device of the large union
conference, without TUC sponsorship, on at least two occasions
when he wanted to settle special problems involving building
and shipbuilding unions. His ministry appointed the direct
nominees of individual unions to advisory bodies in particular
industries; and it negotiated with them on the specific application of sensitive policies like dilution. This was true also of some
other ministries, especially those directly concerned with
industrial production.

Moreover, the TUC was sometimes bypassed even in the case
of consultative bodies with concerns of a more general nature.
Bevin almost certainly consulted TUC leaders informally when
he selected the union members of the Labour Supply Board
and the Factory and Welfare Advisory Board: at least they did
not protest his action. In contrast, they lodged a strong objection to the action of the Minister of Fuel and Power who,
'completely at variance with . . . normal practice', failed to

[48] ibid., 1941, p. 269.

consult them about a committee of inquiry to which he had appointed a union official by personal invitation.[49] In 1944 they found it necessary to remind affiliated unions of the 1928 Congress decision requiring unionists to consult the TUC before accepting personal invitations to serve on consultative bodies of general interest. 'Isolated cases', they later admitted, 'have occurred where the TUC has not been consulted by the Government on matters with which it is likely to be concerned, particularly in connection with the selection of the personnel of . . . Commissions and Committees dealing with matters in which Congress is directly concerned.'[50]

'Isolated cases', however, is the correct term. The TUC was clearly the primary focus of ministerial attention when issues of concern to the unions at large were involved, and often in the case of sectional issues as well. Bevin rather dramatically signalled this, within weeks of the Normandy landing, by becoming the first minister ever to attend a regular meeting of the General Council: his purpose was to persuade the council to issue a statement condemning a Yorkshire miners' stoppage.[51] But the more important acknowledgement was the exclusive right that his ministry and others usually conferred on the council in relation to the nomination of union representatives on consultative bodies of a general or inter-industry kind. Moreover, this near-monopoly of nomination was translated into a near-monopoly of access to government, on general issues at least, owing to the council's predilection for nominees from its own ranks.

There was, too, the virtually automatic access on an *ad hoc* basis which the TUC leadership appears normally to have had to ministers and civil servants. Citrine, by his own account, had something of a special relationship with both Churchill and Lord Beaverbrook, the Prime Minister's closest ministerial colleague up to 1942; he had numerous private talks with each of them.[52] A leading employer and a senior civil servant thought enough of his connections to ask him to intercede with Churchill on a defence matter outside the TUC's own concerns, which he did, with complete success.[53] He evidently had

[49] ibid., 1945, p. 193. [50] ibid., p. 216.
[51] See Bullock, op. cit., pp. 301–2.
[52] See Citrine, *Two Careers*, pp. 43, 46–7, 64–8, 91, 97, 116, 126–37, 198–202, 210, 228.
[53] See ibid., pp. 57–8.

cordial personal relationships with some other Conservative ministers as well. As always, on the other hand, his relations with Bevin were basically hostile, and once boiled over in a public squabble that Attlee had to compose.

Equally significant, as a pointer to the TUC's external authority, was the way in which it was often used to vet the claims individual unions made on government. The Board of Trade (with the exception of one early case involving coal miners) invariably sought the TUC's opinion on union applications for extra rations of industrial clothing and footwear, and consistently acted on that opinion.[54] The Ministry of Food's practice in relation to union claims for supplementary food rations was much the same. Then there was the revealing confidence with which, in a matter easily put to the test, affiliated unions dissatisfied with government responses to their members' complaints about local civil servants were told that, if they forwarded 'the facts, carefully verified, to the Trades Union Congress, we will see that the matter is taken up with the Minister and is conclusively dealt with'.[55] This promise implies an external authority which, as we have seen from more decisive indicators, was clearly of great weight.

LABOUR IN POWER: 1945–51

In July 1945 Clement Attlee formed the first Labour government able to boast a parliamentary majority. The peace he inherited was to prove even more perilous, in its own way, than the war that had been won. His administration faced awesome problems of economic reconstruction. Moreover, ideology as well as circumstances committed it to social and economic policies which involved substantially continuing, rather than dismantling, the system of wartime controls. The cooperation of the trade unions accordingly remained as vital a factor in the calculations of government leaders as it had been during the war years. Attlee himself, not long after assuming office, told the TUC's annual Congress as much. 'Just as in the war, so in the period of reconstruction: close consultation by the Government with great organizations such as the TUC is

[54] See E. L. Hargreaves and M. M. Gowing, *Civil Industry and Trade*, p. 320.
[55] *TUC Report*, 1941, p. 271.

essential if changes are to be carried through ... with the active goodwill of all'.[56] As noteworthy as his words, or their later reiteration from the same platform by his Minister of Labour, is the fact that they formed part of the first address that Congress had ever had from a reigning Prime Minister; and he repeated the performance the following year. It is unlikely that the symbolism of this was unintended, or that its significance was lost on his audience.

As it happened, the TUC chairman had already answered the question Attlee was implicitly asking. 'On behalf of Congress I offer the Government the fullest cooperation and assistance.'[57] But it was a qualified offer. Citrine had made the essential point precisely five years earlier when Attlee joined Churchill's wartime coalition.

Our fellows are in the Government, but does that mean that the Trades Union Congress automatically accepts everything that is done ...? ... [Of] course not. Our ... approach to the problems [is] occasionally rather different from ... the men in office. So ... we have tried to preserve an attitude of what one might call watchful though cordial collaboration.[58]

The implications of this position were exemplified, shortly after the 1945 Congress, in the relatively minor matter of a government publicity campaign to promote exports. A request for cooperation from the President of the Board of Trade evoked the response that the TUC, while sympathetic, 'ought not to become too closely identified with a Department of Government in an export drive ... [since] indiscriminate support ... might hamper ... the pursuit of such objectives of trade union policy as ... reduced working hours'.[59]

Trade union leaders, in other words, were determined on the same independence in relation to the Labour government that they had maintained in relation to its wartime predecessor. Nor was their resolve weakened by the revelation that this government was to realize some of their fondest policy aims, especially in the case of full employment, social welfare and industry nationalization—not to mention the repeal, which Chamberlain and Churchill had both resisted despite persistent pressure, of the detested Trade Disputes and Trade Union Act of 1927. They insisted, accordingly, on the continuation of the con-

---

[56] ibid., 1945, p. 316.   [57] ibid., p. 8.
[58] ibid., 1940, p. 233.   [59] ibid., 1946, p. 203.

sultative privileges they had won in wartime. For the most part, they insisted successfully.

Patterns of Consultation

The total victory of 1945 was followed by a much slighter run-down in union-government links, both formal and informal, than had occurred after the Armistice of 1918. Thus although some standing consultative arrangements were abolished or simply withered when their wartime justification lapsed, many others were either maintained unchanged or continued in a modified, and sometimes in a more developed, form; and some new ones were created.

Among those maintained unchanged were the Joint Consultative Committee and the Factory and Welfare Advisory Board attached to the Ministry of Labour. Similarly, at a lower level of formality, the TUC's Rationing and Prices Committee continued to be utilized by the Board of Trade and the Ministry of Food, and its Economic Committee continued to enjoy regular meetings 'on matters of general trade policy' with the President of the Board of Trade.[60] A different, if not altogether dissimilar, fate awaited the National Production Advisory Council. Its formal existence ended along with that of the Ministry of Production, but it was promptly reincarnated in the wider-ranging National Production Advisory Council on Industry (chaired initially by the President of the Board of Trade and later by the Chancellor of the Exchequer); and the addition of an Emergency Committee increased its flexibility. The experience of the wartime Regional Boards for Industry, to cite another instance, was similar except that they were stripped of their administrative functions and converted into purely advisory bodies. Modifications of a different kind are exemplified in the resuscitation of the National Joint Advisory Council (which Bevin had put into mothballs when he formed the more select Joint Consultative Committee) and of 375 pre-war local committees associated with employment exchanges. As to new arrangements, there was the 'intimate contact' achieved following the TUC's creation, inspired in each case by the relevant minister, of a Transport Consultative Committee and a Fuel and Power

[60] ibid.

Advisory Committee.[61] In 1950 these two committees were amalgamated, to form the TUC Nationalized Industries Committee, with the euphemistically entitled Standing Deputation on Iron and Steel—which had been involved for some years in frequent discussions with a Minister of Supply who was 'reluctant to form an official TUC Advisory Committee' for the purpose.[62] The appointment of two TUC representatives as advisers to the British delegation attending United Nations meetings in 1946 was a new development of more symbolic significance: Churchill had refused an identical request in relation to the UN's founding conference at San Francisco.

Another indication of the relatively slight change that peace made to union–government relations is the range of ministries, appreciably wider than in pre-war years, which continued their formal involvement in those relations. The point is illustrated by the fact of trade union representation on a Foreign Office committee considering the admission of women to the diplomatic service; on a trade mission despatched to Iraq by the Department of Overseas Trade; on a War Office advisory committee concerned with Territorial and auxiliary forces; and on the Ministry of Health's Dental Estimates Board. Similarly, the Ministry of Education made 'frequent contact' with the TUC after, as during, the war,[63] and the Chancellor of the Exchequer continued the wartime practice of post-Budget discussions with the TUC's Economic Committee.

Nor did the peace, and the existence of a Labour government, produce any noticeable change in the Labour party's consultative role so far as the unions were concerned. The TUC showed no sign of wanting to utilize it as a channel into government. Formal joint meetings between the two executives were rare, were initiated by the party and, in any case, amounted to direct dealings with government owing to the presence of ministers. Thus at one such meeting in 1946, the party representatives who counselled caution on the issue of 40-hour week legislation included the Lord President, the Chancellor of the Exchequer and the Minister of Health.

[61] ibid., p. 215.
[62] ibid., 1947, p. 272.
[63] ibid., 1948, p. 155.

More surprisingly, perhaps, there was no great change either in the quite different matter of TUC complaints about inadequate consultation. Such complaints, as we shall see, were particularly frequent during the Attlee government's first year in office. Moreover, to union leaders, the government was often guilty of gross imbalances in the representation it allowed them on administrative bodies. When the wartime county agricultural committees were put on a permanent footing, union leaders agitated for more than the two representatives (out of a membership of 12) allotted to them; but without success. They had better luck when they pressed for two positions on the pre-nationalization Control Board for the iron and steel industry: they were initially offered only one, as against the two allocated to employers. The boards associated with nationalized industries proved a much tougher nut on the issue of equal representation with employers. The TUC's annual Congress of 1948 called for heavier representation after being told that there were only nine former unionists among the 46 full-time members of Divisional Coal Boards; one among five in the case of the British Transport Commission; and one among seven in the case of the Railway Executive Committee. There were other unionist-members occupying part-time positions on nationalized industry boards, but the TUC made no bones about its objection to such appointments which it opposed on the ground that part-time appointees were effectively confined to acting 'merely as "labour advisers" . . . [unable] fully to participate in the determination of the general policy of the industry'.[64] Union leaders appear to have made little headway on the issue. By 1951 the central and regional boards of all nationalized industries contained 44 members possessing 'some previous connection with the Trade Union Movement'[65]— but that was out of a total of about 350 members, most of whom were former directors and senior executives of the original companies.

Nevertheless, the scale and level of these and some other administrative appointments constitute a distinctive feature of the unions' relations with the first majority Labour government. By late 1948, for example, no fewer than seven men had been plucked from their seats on the TUC General Council and

<hr/>

[64] ibid., p. 236.   [65] ibid., 1951, p. 543.

placed among the full-time members of nationalized industry boards. Citrine was one of them: after a spell on the National Coal Board, he became chairman of the Central Electricity Authority. Many other union officials were given staff positions in the nationalized industries. The Colonial Office was a major source of employment for others. By late 1947, 19 were full-time advisers to embryonic trade union movements in the colonies; and more appointments followed.

Internal Authority

When the war ended the General Council set about 'developing',[66] instead of disbanding, the TUC Regional Advisory Committees which owed their genesis to the threat of a German invasion. From 1947, conferences of their chairmen and secretaries were convened to discuss common problems. They were made responsible for 'sifting specific production complaints' from the shop floor;[67] and they were encouraged to take an active interest in policy issues relating to production, employment, education and social insurance. They continued to have a hand in nominating the union representatives on government boards and committees at the regional level, and often at the district level as well, notably those concerned with some nationalized industries and with matters involving production, employment, transport and education. At the same time, the TUC maintained its organizational links with the trades councils and the trades council federations, which also retained a nominating function, the councils having a particular interest in committees associated with local employment exchanges and the federations in bodies concerned with war pensions and with the health system.

It is plain enough why the TUC leadership sought not only to perpetuate the RACs but to enhance their status. They were more susceptible to central control than the trades councils and the federations—if only because their chairmen were appointed by the General Council and, with occasional exceptions when none resided in a particular region, were drawn from the council's own members. And central control of the trades councils, in particular, was at times uncertain. Even on the limited issue of making nominations to consultative bodies,

[66] ibid., 1946, p. 200.   [67] ibid., 1947, p. 251.

councils sometimes flouted TUC policy by either neglecting to nominate in the case of approved bodies or selecting representatives who never put in an appearance.[68]

The attempt to promote the RACs was not altogether successful. The General Council admitted on more than one occasion that they 'do not all function with the same degree of . . . support from . . . officials in their area': not only was opposition generated by the obvious threat they posed to the trades council system, but there were suspicions that they represented 'a tendency . . . to encroach on the work of individual unions'.[69] As a result, while some RACs were very active, others were not. Nevertheless, they helped give the TUC's presence more substance below the national level than would otherwise have been the case.

However, when it came to the crunch, what counted most was the national level and the TUC's relations with the official leaderships of its affiliated unions. In this connection it suffered some setbacks in the postwar years. But it also enjoyed successes which, on balance, amounted to the substantial maintenance of the internal authority it had acquired during the war.

As to the setbacks, the miners' leaders were prepared to by-pass the TUC on the two major issues of coal nationalization regulations and supplementary food rations for their members (see below). Most important, there was the 1950 Congress's decision 'to abandon any further policy of wage restraint',[70] a decision which it confirmed by rejecting a proposal in the General Council's annual report for a watered-down version of the TUC's previous wage restraint policy. And this was only the formal *coup de grâce* because although a conference of union executives had approved a tougher version in January that year, the supporting majority had been too meagre to give the TUC leaders any real hope of applying the new policy; and they did not attempt to do so.

There is no question that the action of the 1950 Congress represented a most serious setback for the TUC leaders. At the same time, it is arguable that the rebuff of 1950 is less remarkable than the achievement preceding it. For during a period of more than two years, the General Council had substantially

[68] See ibid., 1949, p. 103.   [69] ibid., p. 204.   [70] ibid., 1950, p. 467.

held trade union officials behind a policy of freezing most wage rates for most of the time. It first secured their support for this policy at a conference of union executives in March 1948, and Congress subsequently confirmed that acceptance by an over-whelming majority in both 1948 and 1949. Throughout the war, in contrast, the council had consistently resisted government pressure for a similar initiative. The fact that it acted on such a sensitive issue in 1948, and held the line until 1950, is more surprising and more significant than the fact of its eventual failure. The delicacy of the operation is underlined by the council's careful use of special conferences of union executives, which served as both a check on and a demonstration of union support for its wages policy.

Moreover, because of the issue's exceptional nature, its fate did not vitally impair the internal authority of the TUC's leaders on other matters. Their impressive, if temporary, success in relation to wage restraint added a tip to the iceberg; and that, it appears, was all that was lost by their eventual defeat on the issue. As defeat loomed, the General Council's chairman, in a remark plainly concerned with much more than wages policy, claimed a very considerable authority when he spoke of the trade unions as having 'always cooperated [with government] when and where they could, in line with the policy *formulated for their guidance by the TUC General Council*'.[71] So far as consultation with government was concerned, his claim was effectively untouched by the defeat.

The miners' leadership, as we have seen, flouted the TUC's authority as an intermediary on two major matters in the immediate postwar years. But this was exceptional behaviour. The typical is exemplified in the action of the powerful Amal-gamated Engineering Union and the Confederation of Engi-neering and Shipbuilding Unions which, about the same time, were 'vitally interested' in certain newly-created Ministry of Supply committees: they relied on the TUC not only to protest at their omission from the committees, but also to handle the subsequent nomination of their representatives.[72] This is not to suggest that, the miners apart, affiliated unions invariably channelled sectional claims on government through the TUC, or were totally subservient to it on representational issues.

[71] ibid., p. 73. Italics added.   [72] ibid., 1946, p. 206; 1947, p. 252.

The General Council itself, on more than one occasion, proclaimed the unions' right to take up directly with ministries what it called their 'individual problems'.[73] Some had their own formal links with government. The engineering unions, for example, evidently carried the burden on the union side in relation to the creation and membership of the National Engineering Advisory Committee to the Ministry of Supply. In any case, the council normally invited nominations from relevant unions when industry representatives were required on advisory bodies with which it was concerned. The same was true of administrative bodies—although an official of the National Union of Bank Employees 'categorically' assured the 1949 Congress that there had been no consultation with his union prior to the appointment of a General Council member to the Court of the Bank of England.[74] Whatever the truth of this, the TUC leaders made no secret of their view that, especially in relation to nationalized industry boards, their choice of nominees was not limited to the members of unions directly involved. And this view was formally endorsed by the 1949 Congress when the NUBE challenged it. But the most striking indication of the TUC's predominance, as the unions' consultative channel to government, is provided by the fact that negotiations on the wage-restraint issue were entrusted entirely to the General Council. There was no challenge whatever to its role in this respect.

External Authority

In 1946 the TUC, in a submission to an investigating body, claimed that governments, employers' associations and 'other national and international organizations' recognized it 'as the only body competent to speak' for trade unionists at large.[75] The British Legion of ex-servicemen, following the pre-war example of the British Medical Association, reinforced the point by forming a standing joint committee with the TUC. Further reinforcement came from major civil service unions which promptly affiliated with the TUC once the prohibition on their doing so was lifted with the repeal of the Trade Disputes and Trade Union Act of 1927. During the same year, however, there were other events which indicated that, even with a

---

[73] ibid. 1947, p. 230.   [74] ibid., 1949, 413.   [75] ibid., 1946, p. 221.

Labour government in power, vigilance was necessary to sustain this claim.

In January the Labour cabinet, acting through the Minister of Labour, made clear that it wanted to deal with trade union leaderships directly, rather than through the TUC, on problems involved in the transition from war to peace. It asked the General Council to convene a conference of union executives for this purpose. The council agreed and, at its insistence, the Prime Minister and the Foreign Secretary attended the conference along with the Minister of Labour. But the TUC leaders were sensitive to the implications of this procedure for their intermediary role. Their acceptance of the government's 'invitation', they carefully pointed out to affiliates, did not mean they agreed that such conferences 'should replace the regular and more detailed consultations which take place through the committees and deputations of the TUC and . . . through the chain of advisory committees . . . with which the TUC are intimately associated': the conference in question was merely 'a useful adjunct' to these procedures.[76]

In May the General Council had cause for more explicit complaint. It rebuked the Minister of Supply for departing from 'the general [ministerial] policy of consultation' when he appointed unionists to two technical committees by personal invitation; and although he then promised consultation 'in appropriate cases', he continued to exclude technical committees from this category until the council enlisted the Prime Minister's support.[77] The Civil Aviation Bill and the Coal Industry Nationalization Bill provided another source of grievance that month. Each included a clause requiring discussion with relevant unions about industrial bargaining machinery. Neither the TUC nor its affiliates had been consulted during the drafting of these clauses. Moreover, that in the Civil Aviation Bill gave consultative rights to two unfriendly non-affiliates. The ministers concerned were apologetic, when reproached, but declined to amend the offending clause on the ground of political difficulties. The Prime Minister later echoed them, but also undertook that the TUC and relevant unions would be consulted about 'any clause affecting industrial relationships' contained in future nationalization measures.[78]

[76] ibid., p. 196.   [77] ibid., p. 206.   [78] ibid., p. 219.

In July, despite persistent pressure from the TUC leaders, the Minister of Fuel and Power refused to consult them about draft regulations on workers' compensation in the coal industry. He preferred to deal with the National Union of Mineworkers alone, on the ground that only 'discussions on detail' were involved.[79] Three months later the Minister of Food was more compliant, on one issue, when he promised to avoid a repetition of his failure to appoint a unionist to a committee of inquiry. However, on another issue at about the same time, this minister sparked a crisis in TUC-government dealings. He granted a supplementary meat ration to underground mineworkers (without consulting the TUC's Rationing and Prices Committee), a decision that flew in the face of the policy steadfastly maintained by the committee since the start of rationing. The incident prompted a meeting in November between TUC leaders and the Prime Minister, together with five members of his cabinet. There was 'a general discussion of the question of consultation with the Trade Union Movement', during which Attlee agreed to 'follow the example of his two immediate predecessors and circulate a note about consultation to all Departments'.[80] The resultant circular urged ministers not merely to consult the TUC on appropriate issues, but also to keep it informed of any dealings with individual trade unions.

Although the circular appears to have improved matters, the TUC continued to find occasional grounds for complaint right up to the time of Attlee's resignation in 1951. In 1947 the Minister of Agriculture rejected its claim that he should have appointed a unionist to a committee of inquiry; and the Prime Minister supported him, with the soothing qualification that this 'exception . . . was without prejudice to the general principle of consultation with the TUC in such cases'.[81] In 1948 the TUC leaders publicly expressed 'concern . . . at the lack of consultation . . . in the case of certain [unionist] appointments to the boards of nationalized industries'.[82] They accepted this situation in relation to the Court of the Bank of England, after discussions with the Chancellor of the Exchequer. Earlier, they had accepted that they were going to get no more than verbal assurances from ministers about consultation in relation

[79] ibid., p. 210.   [80] ibid., 1947, p. 299.
[81] ibid., 1947, p. 275.   [82] ibid., 1948, p. 236.

to unionist appointments to industry boards, despite the stipula-
tion of the 1944 Congress that nationalization measures should
expressly require such consultation with the TUC. In 1949 the
Lord Chancellor refused the TUC representation on area and
local committees concerned with the legal aid scheme, although
he admitted it to the associated national advisory body. In
1951 the Minister of National Insurance did not consult it
about changes in certain welfare benefits, later explaining that
their necessary inclusion in the Budget statement had ruled this
out. More seriously, the General Council was not consulted
beforehand specifically about either of the two momentous
White Papers, *Economic Survey of 1947* and the *Statement on
Personal Incomes, Costs and Prices* of early 1948; and it made no
secret of its discontent on that score.

On the other hand, the central issue these White Papers
raised (wage restraint) was the subject of very close TUC-
government consultation both before and after their publication. Just how close is illustrated by a decision of the TUC's
Special Committee on the Economic Situation in 1949. The
committee's members had been reconsidering the TUC's wages
policy in the light of the devaluation of sterling. They resolved,
'in accordance with their usual practice, [that] the Government
should be informed of the nature of the recommendations
which they were to make to the General Council'.[83] The meeting arranged for this purpose was attended by the Chancellor
of the Exchequer, the Foreign Secretary and the Minister of
Health. It is noteworthy, too, that the TUC's relations with
Treasury, which had been relatively slight before the war, were
particularly close throughout the wage restraint period of
1948–50.

So far as it can be said that the TUC had a special consultative relationship with the Attlee government, that relationship centred on the wage restraint issue. But the critical point
is that the special nature of the relationship did *not* stem
primarily from the 'great deference toward the TUC' displayed
by government leaders, especially during the early negotiations
on the issue.[84] It stemmed, instead, from a most singular concession on the part of the TUC leadership. For in backing wage

[83] ibid., 1950, p. 263.
[84] Gerald A. Dorfman, *Wage Politics in Britain, 1945–1967*, p. 70.

restraint during 1948–50, the General Council accepted in peacetime a policy which it had flatly rejected at a time when Britain was thought to be on the brink of military invasion. And this echoed an earlier concession that is almost as distinctive, because it had no peacetime precedent: the council's acceptance, until 1951, of wartime restrictions on strike action. In other words, the 'special' relationship depended more on the TUC's recognition of the needs of the Labour government than it did on government recognition of the TUC and its claims.

Moreover, for all the intimacy of TUC-government relations on the wage restraint issue, and for all the reshuffling of consultative arrangements, there was no real development in the terms or the forms of consultation under the Labour government. Viewed in this perspective, the TUC's external authority was certainly no less than it had been during the wartime coalition's term of office; but neither was it substantially greater.

THE LONG HAUL: 1951–76

The 1940s foreshadowed the basic pattern of the TUC's experience during the quarter-century following Labour's loss of office in October 1951. The central element remained the same: a national economy under siege. So did the subsidiary elements of government sensitivity to wage movements, to industrial unrest and to the electoral importance of maintaining employment. There was, too, general official union acknowledgement of the TUC's leadership in times of crisis. Its involvement in a wide range of policy issues was accepted by both unions and government.

There were, however, striking variations in the tone and temper of TUC–government dealings during the period. Relations with Conservative ministers, notably amicable under the last Churchill government, cooled considerably thereafter, aided by both a less conciliatory ministerial stance and a leftward shift in the political inclination of key union representatives on the General Council. Symptomatic of that coolness was the government's decision, despite the TUC's opposition, to wind up the Industrial Disputes Tribunal at the close of the 1950s. By the same token, the Conservatives' creation of the high-status and innovative National Economic Development

Council, and the TUC's acceptance in 1962 of representation on it, registered an upturn in relations. And Labour's return to power in 1964 saw a further improvement, for a time, until the shortcomings of a purely TUC-enforced wage restraint policy were revealed by the growing authority of shop-floor organization and the trend to plant-level wage settlements. In 1966 there was no consultation with the TUC before the introduction of an incomes policy backed, for the first time, by legislative sanctions. Thereafter, relations with the Labour government went from bad to worse, plumbing the depths three years later in the dispute over its abortive plan to penalize unofficial strikers. New depths were reached when the succeeding Conservative government pressed ahead with its Industrial Relations Act of 1971. But then, from early 1974, under the last Wilson administration, the TUC enjoyed the most intimate relationship it has ever shared with a government.

One indication of that special relationship was a body whose membership, range of concern and frequency of meeting make it unique in the history of British pressure groups. Known simply as the Liaison Committee, it provided a standing consultative link between the TUC and government leaderships. Also notable, and in some respects unprecedented, were four other political devices which the TUC employed during the 1970s. Three were prompted by the Heath government's industrial legislation: they included a massive campaign of meetings and demonstrations, an administrative boycott of the Industrial Relations Act, and the official threat of a one-day general strike. The fourth, an old-fashioned but unusually crowded lobby of MPs, was used during the last Wilson government's term of office.

Conservative Governments: from Churchill to Heath

Faced with another Churchill administration in October 1951, the TUC leaders voiced their expectation 'of this Government that they will maintain to the full [the] practice of consultation' as developed since the 1930s.[85] Their own desire for consultation was soon put to the test. The government denationalized the steel industry and created an Iron and Steel Board to administer the new policy. The unions were offered representation on the

[85] *TUC Report*, 1952, p. 300.

board. There was strong opposition to accepting the offer. But it was accepted when the 1953 Congress firmly endorsed the General Council's view that acceptance was in line with 'the longstanding and settled policy of the TUC'.[86] The same Congress also rejected objections to TUC representation on two major committees of inquiry, one into London transport and the other into the economics of the National Health Service.

Initially, as it happened, TUC leaders had little ground for complaint on the issue of consultation. Churchill and his Minister of Labour, Walter Monckton, pursued a determinedly conciliatory policy in dealing with the unions. The government moved to consult the TUC as freely and as frequently as had the Labour government. For their part, the TUC leaders might postpone acceptance of government invitations to discuss controversial issues (as in the case of the denationalization of road haulage and the iron and steel industry) until they were informed of the legislative detail involved; but they were prepared to consult in the end.

In 1955 Arthur Deakin died and both Churchill and Monckton resigned. Deakin, Bevin's successor at the head of the Transport and General Workers' Union, had exercised a powerful moderating influence in the TUC General Council. His death not only removed the last man to establish something like the kind of personal ascendancy in its affairs that Bevin and Citrine had enjoyed; it also paved the way for the emergence of the more radical Frank Cousins. And this pattern was to be repeated, its effect being to weaken the council's commitment to collaboration with Conservative governments. Similarly, Churchill and Monckton were succeeded by men of a less conciliatory cast of mind, and their attitudes hardened with the turn for the worse in Britain's economic position from 1955. The consequence of these events was some change in both the scope and tone of relations between the TUC and government from the mid-1950s.

It was, on the other hand, a limited change in that it appears to have been confined to the broader reaches of domestic economic policy. In this respect there was a distinct decline in dealings after the failure of the Eden government's attempt to

[86] ibid., 1953, p. 257.

negotiate a wage restraint policy with the TUC in 1956. The break was neither open nor official. It was a matter of a tacit understanding on both sides that the possibility of agreement on the issues involved was too remote for either to put much effort into negotiating them. One symptom of the break was the change in the character of the TUC's pre-Budget submissions to Conservative Chancellors of the Exchequer. In the early 1950s, as previously, these submissions invariably included a number of proposals (usually about seven or eight) for specific alterations in budgetary policy. In 1956 the General Council decided to abandon this practice on the ground that 'detailed proposals to the Chancellor would . . . have little influence on Government policy'.[87] Its pre-Budget statements thereafter, while occasionally including one or two specific proposals, were typically limited to a general analysis of the economic situation and an outline of the TUC's hopes in broad terms.

There was also one other important area in which, even before the mid-1950s, Conservative ministers were somewhat less forthcoming than their Labour predecessors. This concerned union representation on the boards of nationalized industries. The number and proportion of unionist-members declined sharply after 1951, and the TUC leaders suspected 'a deliberate policy to confine trade union members to part-time service': by 1959 full-time union representation had fallen from 16 to six, and part-time representation from 28 to 20.[88] In addition, the TUC encountered some government opposition to its nominations in relation to agricultural marketing boards. And there was a drop in the number of TUC nominees appointed as 'user' representatives on Regional Hospital Boards and associated bodies (although the scale of such appointments had been the subject of much wrangling under Labour as well).

Otherwise, however, there was little to distinguish the Conservative governments of 1951–64 from the Attlee government, so far as their consultative relationship with the TUC was concerned. *Ad hoc* consultation at all levels of government remained frequent and, for the most part, free of difficulty. Post-Churchill government leaders, for example, had many discussions with TUC representatives on major issues relating to the European Economic Community, the European Free

[87] ibid., 1956, p. 261.   [88] ibid., 1959, pp. 288–9.

Trade Area and the Organization for European Economic Cooperation. Nor does there appear to have been any significant reduction in the range of formal advisory bodies under the Conservatives, as the General Council implicitly conceded in 1961 when it referred to 'the now well-established machinery of consultation with the Government'.[89] Indeed, the following year that machinery was notably extended by the creation of the National Economic Development Council ('Neddy') which included the Chancellor of the Exchequer as chairman and two other ministers as permanent members; associated Economic Development Committees were subsequently formed in relation to particular industries. At least in part, moreover, the NEDC's creation was a response to TUC complaints about the absence of consultation before the government's 'pay pause' policy was announced in 1961. Government leaders excused this lapse by explaining that they 'had not had time to consult the trade unions before acting', and undertook that the NEDC 'would certainly be consulted . . . before policy decisions were taken' in the future.[90]

The TUC accepted the offer of representation on the NEDC, if only after lengthy consideration. It was the most important consultative decision taken by the General Council since April 1939: then, as we have seen, it had agreed to talk to the Minister of Labour about proposals for regulating labour in the event of war. A rejection of the NEDC invitation would have been a striking deviation from the TUC leaders' traditional policy. What that invitation offered them, for the first time since the demise of the second Labour government's Economic Advisory Council at the start of the 1930s, was the opportunity of joining relevant ministers in regular and continuing discussions ranging over the whole of the economy. In other words, it offered them a formal and highly select role in the process of indicative economic planning.

Acceptance of NEDC membership did not mean, of course, that the TUC was unprepared to bare its teeth on lesser consultative issues. In 1963, for example, it took a hard line when it advised affiliated unions not to submit evidence to the National Incomes Commission, inquiring into the terms of collective

[89] ibid., 1961, p. 97.
[90] ibid., 1962, pp. 241, 253.

agreements. But that was a pale shadow of its action against the next Conservative government eight years later.

The Heath government of June 1970 differed from its Churchillian predecessor, which had similarly succeeded a Labour administration, by its attempt to honour an election promise to curb the unions. The Industrial Relations Act of August 1971 was the result. The Act sought to regulate key aspects of the unions' industrial activities and internal affairs to an extent unprecedented in British legislative history. It also provided substantial legal rights and immunities for unions —so long as they were registered under it. In this connection, moreover, the government had been guilty in union eyes of a 'wilful denial of the facilities for consultation that had been accorded to the TUC by every Government for the previous thirty years': because when it published the outline of its legislative proposals in October 1970, the Secretary of State for Employment bluntly informed a TUC deputation that the 'eight central pillars' of the foreshadowed Bill were 'non-negotiable'.[91]

The TUC's reactions, while not as totally unprecedented as the government's legislation, added up to a departure that was unique in terms of the previous 30 years and striking in terms of the TUC's career as a whole. Its affiliated unions were 'strongly advised' in March 1971, and 'instructed' in September, not to register under the Act.[92] In contrast with the TUC's long-standing practice of cooperating in (and thus hopefully ameliorating) the administration of unfavourable policies, unions were also advised that no unionist should accept appointment to bodies concerned with administering the Act. The General Council took a further step in the same direction when it decided, in June, against entering into consultations about the Code of Industrial Relations Practice which the government proposed issuing as a corollary to the Act. It took another step, a year later in July 1972, when its spokesmen told the Prime Minister that it would decline to take part in scheduled talks on the economy until five dockers imprisoned under the Act had been freed. Two days later, it took what was close to the ultimate step by calling a 24-hour general strike in support of the 'Pentonville Five'—whose prompt release, involving

[91] ibid., 1971, pp. 96, 346.   [92] ibid., pp. 99, 376, 608.

'resort to unusual devices' by the courts,[93] enabled the cancellation of the strike recommendation.

The Industrial Relations Act, as either promise or presence, was from October 1970 a running sore in the TUC's relations with the Heath government. The government's adoption of a statutory wage restraint policy in November 1972 added a second irritant of dominating proportions. One indication of the TUC leaders' alienation was their uncharacteristic withholding, as we have seen, of administrative and consultative cooperation in connection with the Industrial Relations Act. Another, relating to the government's incomes policy, was their refusal in 1973 either to discuss the Pay and Price Code with the Chancellor of the Exchequer or to nominate representatives to the Pay Board and the Price Commission, or even to provide evidence for the Pay Board's investigation of anomalies arising from the policy. For its part, the government neglected to consult the TUC in March 1971 before introducing the Social Security Bill which reduced the entitlement of strikers' dependents to supplementary benefit. On the other hand, the Prime Minister himself had two meetings with TUC representatives about the Industrial Relations Act, and at least four (two at his invitation) about the economic situation, between early 1971 and July 1972 when feelings on the Act ran highest. Moreover, he subsequently sounded them out about incomes and prices restraint on at least ten occasions before the government's policy was announced—a scrupulousness which has been explained, in part, as a Heathian reaction to the 'disastrous state of Government-union relations following the Industrial Relations Act'.[94] On all other issues of common concern, the pre-established pattern of consultation seems to have been maintained in the case of both ministers and civil servants. Apart from the TUC-ordained resignation of the unionist-members of the Commission on Industrial Relations, the composition of pre-existing advisory and administrative bodies appears to have been unaffected; and they operated, formally, as before. The key case is the National Economic Development Council which continued to meet frequently and, in line with

[93] Roy Lewis, 'The Historical Development of Trade Union Law', *British Journal of Industrial Relations*, vol. 14, no. 1, 1976, p. 13.
[94] Colin Crouch, *Class Conflict and the Industrial Relations Crisis*, p. 130.

the practice instituted by the Wilson government, under the chairmanship of the Prime Minister. It continued, that is to say, to function as a major 'meeting point . . . between the two sides', although for some time after the passage of the Industrial Relations Act its meetings were 'rather tense and not very productive'.[95]

At a less formal level, however, the Act inspired some striking departures in the TUC's political tactics. The administrative boycott of the Act is the most dramatic instance. The only other time that TUC leaders appear to have explicitly threatened a boycott of similar type and proportions was in 1920, in connection with unemployment insurance; and on that occasion the threat had quickly turned out to be quite hollow.[96] Second, there was the one-day general strike that the General Council officially called for 31 July 1972 (but did not have to carry through) in connection with the 'Pentonville five', imprisoned under the Act. The last time the TUC had been involved in a comparable action was, of course, in 1926. Third, there was the massive public campaign which the TUC mounted during the period from November 1970 to March 1971 against the Industrial Relations Bill. Among other things, the campaign included hundreds of local and regional meetings, newspaper advertisements, a petition to parliament, a lobby of MPs and a procession through London which, with an estimated 140,000 people marching, almost certainly justified the claim that it was 'the largest . . . demonstration against Government legislation to take place in Great Britain in the twentieth century'.[97] The TUC itself had last used the device of the public campaign, on anything like the same scale, during the controversy over unemployment relief policy in the mid-1930s.

There was one other particularly notable outcome of the Heath government's legislative bravado. The TUC was driven to join forces with the Labour party's parliamentary leaders. The Industrial Relations Act, in other words, effectively closed the gaping rift that had opened between the two during 1964–70.

[95] Jacques Leruez, *Economic Planning and Politics in Britain*, pp. 243, 252.
[96] See 'A Rising Political Authority', in chap. 7 above.
[97] *TUC Report*, 1971, p. 97.

Labour Governments: the Wilson Era

Shortly before the general election which first made him Prime Minister, Harold Wilson gave an assurance to the TUC's annual Congress. 'We shall consult—and I mean consult, not present you with a diktat.'[98] In the event, the TUC leaders found that the contrast he implied was not quite as great, in this respect, as he would have had them believe.

Initially, the signs were encouraging. On the side of consultative bodies, the Conservative-initiated National Economic Development Council was not only retained, but its status was heightened when the Prime Minister became its chairman late in 1967. More industry and inter-industry development committees were set up. The National Production Advisory Council for Industry, a creation of the Attlee regime, was abolished with the TUC's agreement; and the regional boards attached to it were replaced by Regional Economic Planning Councils with wider powers. The trade unions continued to be represented on the new planning councils, and the TUC leadership was admitted to the regular meetings between them and the Minister for Economic Affairs. A TUC leader was one of the nine full-time members appointed to the National Board for Prices and Incomes, formed in mid-1965.

On the side of *ad hoc* consultation, Labour ministers at first were markedly more eager than their Conservative predecessors to involve the TUC in discussions on the broader reaches of economic policy. The new Chancellor of the Exchequer quickly moved to offer 'regular opportunities for consultation' on budgetary matters[99]—an offer which the TUC promptly accepted, although it continued the post-1956 practice of presenting him with only short and generalized Budget submissions. The Labour government was equally quick to initiate discussions on the issue of wage restraint. These continued up to the time, in early 1965, when the government opted for a policy of voluntary restraint. Its decision later the same year to inject a compulsory element into that policy, by way of the 'early warning' system requiring advance notice of wage claims, was also preceded by close consultation with the TUC.

[98] ibid., 1964, p. 384.
[99] ibid., 1965, p. 285.

But in 1966 the government changed tack. In July the Prime Minister met the TUC leaders to inform them that a wage-freeze was to be imposed, for the first time in British history, by legislative compulsion. There had been no prior consultation. The procedure was precisely the same 12 months later when the decision was made to continue the compulsory restraint policy in a different form. Similarly, after the devaluation of sterling in November 1967, TUC representatives were blandly informed that 'the Government had considered, but rejected, the possibility of stricter legislation on incomes'.[100]

By 1968 the TUC leaders were making no secret of their feelings about the government's attitude to consultation on the issue. In March they accepted an invitation from the Minister for Economic Affairs to see him about the government's review of its incomes policy, but at the same time expressed 'some doubts about the value of such a meeting'.[101] Their doubts were speedily vindicated. The minister told them that the government thought it should widen its legislative powers. They opposed the proposition. The government's plans, publicly announced the next day, remained unchanged. At a meeting with a number of ministers a day later, TUC representatives expressed the view that it would 'serve little useful purpose to discuss detail when the TUC and the Government were so far apart on fundamentals'.[102] The General Council reiterated this view in June when it had before it the terms of the government's bill.

The trend in TUC-government relations on this key issue was echoed in the TUC's public reception of successive Labour Budgets. Those for 1964 and 1965 were given a much warmer and more complimentary welcome than any (with the partial exception of the 1963 Budget) brought down by the Conservatives in the preceding 13 years. In 1967, however, the TUC's response was noticeably cooler. The next year it was decidedly frigid: the government's budgetary policy was described as 'based on a wrong conception of the problem and of the strategy' which should be pursued.[103]

In 1969 frigidity became outright hostility. The General Council's chairman began his address to the September Con-

[100] ibid., 1968, p. 345.
[102] ibid., p. 359.
[101] ibid., p. 358.
[103] ibid., p. 362.

gress with a remark expressive of this. 'The second century of the [TUC] opened this year', he said, 'in circumstances like the sixties of last century, when the campaign against the trade unions reached its peak of aggression.'[104] He was referring to the Labour government's move to introduce legislative penalties for use against unofficial strikers.

In January the government had issued a White Paper, *In Place of Strife*, setting out its legislative proposals on the issues raised by the report of the (Donovan) Royal Commission on Trade Unions and Employers' Associations. There were consultations with the TUC both before and after the White Paper came out. But in April the government departed from its original plan, involving the introduction of a single comprehensive bill towards the end of the year: it decided on a short interim bill to deal quickly with 'the immediate problem [of] . . . unofficial strikes'.[105] The bill was to include penal provisions.

During the next nine weeks the Prime Minister discussed the issue with the full General Council or a council sub-committee on no fewer than 11 occasions, and with the TUC general secretary alone on at least seven occasions. Most of these meetings were held in the space of 10 days in June, following the first special Congress convened by the TUC in almost 50 years. The Congress had, by an overwhelming majority in each case, affirmed its opposition to penal provisions, effectively approved rule changes extending the General Council's formal powers in relation to unofficial strikes, and authorized the council to continue negotiations with the government. The outcome, on 18 June, was an agreement under which the government dropped its penal clause proposals in return for the rule changes and 'a solemn and binding undertaking' from the General Council concerning the way in which it would administer the principal rule involved.[106]

Relations between the government and the TUC, and between the Labour party and union leaders in general, reached an historic nadir with this episode. The cleavage between the two sides of the labour movement was perhaps sharper and deeper than it had been on any comparable occasion since the party's foundation. But within 18 months the initial impulse for a reconciliation had been provided by the Conservatives'

[104] ibid., 1969, p. 72.   [105] ibid., p. 211.   [106] ibid., p. 224.

Industrial Relations Bill. The reality of the reconciliation that followed was signified, after the next Labour government took office, in the monthly meetings of a body modestly entitled the Liaison Committee. This committee, originally formed to combat the Industrial Relations Bill, was representative of the TUC, the Labour party executive and the parliamentary Labour party. Its membership included the Prime Minister, the Foreign Secretary, the Chancellor of the Exchequer and a number of other senior members of the Labour cabinet

The existence of the Liaison Committee, the composition of its membership and the frequency of its meetings, alone suggest a unique consultative connection between the TUC and the last Wilson government. In addition, according to the General Council, there was 'a good working relationship . . . on a wide range of economic, industrial and social issues' stemming from the 'social contract', under which the TUC had agreed to establish guidelines designed to restrain union wage claims; and, on other matters, 'close contact [was] maintained with individual Ministers'.[107] There was one complaint about the 'inadequate discussion' preceding the government's 1975 Budget,[108] but it was not repeated the following year.

Moreover, on the side of policy achievement, as distinct from consultation, the TUC leadership bestowed the accolade by suggesting to the 1975 Congress that the trade unions 'should acknowledge the many steps taken by the Government in accordance with [its] undertakings'.[109] In particular, the government, while still a minority administration, had acted to repeal the Industrial Relations Act. Once it had won a parliamentary majority in October 1974, it remedied Opposition-enforced amendments of the repealing measure, the Trade Union and Labour Relations Act; and pressed ahead with an Employment Protection Bill, extending the legal rights of employees and trade unions, together with other measures of close concern to the TUC.

The harmony of this picture was ostensibly marred by the TUC's campaign to have the Home Secretary exercise clemency in the case of the 'Shrewsbury pickets', two building workers imprisoned following an incident in 1972. Among other actions, the TUC urged trades councils and affiliated unions to

[107] ibid., 1975, p. 350.   [108] ibid., p. 346.   [109] ibid., p. 350.

approach local MPs and, in January 1975, mounted a 'national lobby of Parliament' in which some 7,000 unionists took part.[110] The scale of the lobby, certainly unique in the history of trade union political action, may well be unique in the history of the House of Commons as well. But the minister stood firm; and there is no evidence that TUC-government relations suffered at all seriously.

Relations with the Labour Party

Following the fall of the Attlee government, the TUC leaders declared that it was their 'longstanding practice to seek to work amicably with whatever Government is in power'; and affirmed their intention to 'continue to examine every question solely in the light of its industrial and economic implications'.[111] Their determination to steer clear of a party-political identification in dealings with the Conservative government was underscored by Arthur Deakin when he advised Congress delegates to confine themselves to issues of direct trade union concern. 'Congress', he said, 'is not . . . a political forum; what can and must be said against the Government will be dealt with in another place.'[112]

This insistence on the TUC's independence of the Labour party did not entail the abandonment of consultative links with it. The National Council of Labour remained as one such link, but an unimportant one—as it had been from the time the first Attlee government took office. It normally met only once or twice a year, more often than not at the instance of the Cooperative Union; and there were some years in which it did not meet at all. Its function, for the most part, was limited to issuing manifestos on occasions such as May Day, although it had a brief spell of uncharacteristic activity during 1971–2 when it was used as the vehicle for a campaign in support of higher pensions. Apart from this flash in the pan, neither the TUC nor the Labour party were disposed to make anything more of the NCL. A Cooperative Union complaint evoked from the TUC leadership the comment that, while it was useful to have such a joint body, there was no point in 'regular and frequent meetings'.[113] For serious consultation, the TUC

---

[110] ibid., p. 108.   [111] ibid., 1952, p. 300.
[112] ibid., p. 82.   [113] ibid., 1962, p. 286.

and the party relied on procedures which excluded the Co-operative Union.

Each of them continued to admit observers from the other to certain of their standing committees. Occasionally, as on the issue of fuel and power policy in 1959, *ad hoc* joint committees were formed to thrash out specific problems. More commonly, major issues were dealt with by way of special joint meetings of TUC and party representatives. But that pattern changed in December 1970 when, as mentioned above, the Heath government's determination to proceed with its Industrial Relations Bill prompted the formation, on a hesitantly temporary footing, of the Liaison Committee to coordinate action against the bill on the part of the TUC, the Labour party executive and the parliamentary Labour party. From the start, its membership included Harold Wilson, James Callaghan, Dennis Healey and other senior parliamentarians. It was converted into a permanent body with broader functions in January 1972. It met once or twice every month thereafter, while Labour remained in opposition. One of its specified tasks was to formulate 'the wider economic and industrial policies of the next Labour Government'.[114] In the result, it was not only the source of much of the last Wilson ministry's legislative programme, but laid the foundations of the 'social contract' with the unions. Moreover, it evidently retained a highly important role in the TUC's dealings with the Labour government: not only did it continue to meet monthly but Wilson, along with his most senior colleagues, remained a member of it.

The closeness of the TUC leaders' relationship with the parliamentary Labour party under the Heath regime contrasted with the way in which they had previously tended to keep their distance. They had made little direct use of the party and of parliament during the long period of Conservative rule up to 1964—apart from the issues of steel denationalization in 1953, union representation on the Atomic Energy Authority in 1954 and (after careful negotiation with the Conservative administration to ensure success) a private member's bill on trade union amalgamations in 1964. Not only did the emphasis in this respect change markedly during Heath's premiership, but there was an echo of it under the last Wilson government

[114] ibid., 1972, p. 107.

when the TUC organized the massive parliamentary lobby in support of the 'Shrewsbury pickets', a campaign directed primarily at Labour MPs. Nevertheless, the hallmark of the early 1970s was the unusual intimacy of the working relations between the leaders of the TUC and the Labour party. And for this, as Callaghan cheerfully told Congress, they had Heath to thank. 'It is he more than anyone else who is responsible for the TUC and the Labour Movement working more closely together, thinking more like one body, than they have ever done in my lifetime.'[115]

Internal Authority

There were marked fluctuations in the internal authority of the TUC's leadership during the quarter-century to 1976. But, on balance, these served to confirm rather than deny the basic stability of its standing among the unions.

Deakin's death in 1955, as we have seen, ended the era of the truly dominating personality on the General Council. Partly for this reason, and partly because later changes in the leadership of major unions gave the voice of more radically-inclined unionists an unusual weight on the General Council, the new era was one in which the council's unity of purpose was less certain than it had been for more than a generation. An early symptom was its inability to comply with a 1956 Congress instruction by formulating an agreed economic policy. On the other hand, this was not a continuing problem. In similar vein, there was the lack of assurance reflected in the council's decision of mid-1958 not to seek talks with the government about the economic situation, reportedly because a majority of its members thought that such an approach would compromise it in the eyes of the TUC's affiliates. Four years later, however, the TUC leaders were prepared to accept representation on the Conservative government's National Economic Development Council despite the predictably controversial nature of that decision.

Nevertheless, it is continuity rather than change which is the dominating feature of the TUC's internal authority during the period. Although, in some respects, such changes as occurred suggest an extension of that authority. For example, by the

[115] ibid., 1974, p. 396.

1970s, following the significant affiliation of the National and Local Government Officers' Association in 1965 and the National Union of Teachers in 1970, the TUC's affiliates enclosed a massive 90 per cent of all British trade unionists.

As for continuity, the TUC maintained its role as the unions' principal spokesman in relation to government. The correspondence of ministers and their departments commonly included conference resolutions and other statements of opinion from individual unions or industry federations, and these were not limited to sectional concerns. But when closer dealings were involved, even on sectional matters, it seems that the TUC was usually at least informed; and often it was asked either to act for the unions concerned or to arrange for their deputations to be received. Government officials sometimes made direct approaches to particular unions and found that they wanted the TUC involved, if only in a minimal 'post-office' role—which established its right to subsequent intervention if the unions felt a need for its support. On the other hand, it invariably handled matters of general legislative policy and major administrative issues. The subsequent negotiation of administrative detail was often left to the interested unions, although the TUC normally continued to act as coordinator when more than one union was involved. Similarly, it usually collated the views of concerned unions and made a single submission on their behalf to government investigating bodies. And in the case of consultative bodies, it commonly arranged the nomination of members representing groupings of unions, as distinct from the TUC itself. Moreover, its political role tended to assume more importance in union leaders' eyes once it seemed, from 1955, that strike action was a less efficacious source of industrial gains than it had been during the early 1950s.

In 1955, as it happened, the TUC's constitutional power was strengthened in relation to industrial disputes. It was authorized to intervene, without being invited, if negotiations were *likely* to break down: formerly, such an initiative was possible only after they had. But the TUC leadership continued to tread as warily as before. It made no open use of the new power over the next 14 years. Its pre-strike interventions occurred only in response to an involved union's invitation, which was not always accepted. Occasionally, it intervened in actual strikes without being invited, but otherwise awaited (or arranged) an invitation before doing so.

In 1969, as we have seen, the Labour government's move to legislate against unofficial strikes prompted further extensions in the TUC's formal powers—in particular, affiliated unions were subject to 'more definite obligations' about informing the TUC of impending and actual stoppages including, for the first time specifically, unofficial strikes.[116] The immediate outcome of this change was, on the surface, astonishing. During the preceding 12 months, 40 disputes had been reported to the TUC. During the following year, there were more than 180 reports. All of them, as the General Council elaborately explained to Congress, were followed up by the TUC staff who had thus been enabled to make 'a major contribution . . . towards averting or curtailing' disputes involving, at 'a rough guess', a saving of up to three million work-days and more than £10 million in pay.[117] There is no question that the TUC was unusually active in this connection. The scale of its interventions was unique, and its officials' contacts with the government's industrial conciliation staff, while 'always frequent, became incessant'.[118] But the TUC intervenors confined themselves strictly to their customary mediatory role—a fact which scarcely accords with the General Council's earlier promise to Labour ministers that the rule changes represented the acquisition of an 'unprecedented authority'.[119] Moreover, after 1970 and the Conservatives' return to office, the council suddenly lost interest in recording even the number of disputes reported to it. Its annual reports reverted to the old practice of referring, more or less briefly, to only one or two major disputes with which it had some connection. Similarly, it continued to restrict its support of striking unions to such activities as arranging publicity, interceding with ministers and circularizing union organizations. It is difficult to escape the conclusion that the TUC's intense involvement with industrial disputes during 1969–70 was essentially an energetic bit of window-dressing designed, primarily, to save the face of a Labour

[116] ibid., 1970, p. 246.
[117] ibid., p. 247.
[118] Eric Wigham, *Strikes and the Government*, p. 153.
[119] *TUC Report*, 1969, p. 216.

Prime Minister who subsequently made skilful use of the episode.[120]

There was, however, another and less ephemeral development relating to the TUC's industrial role. Following consideration of the Donovan commission's 1968 report, moves were made to create a chain of committees on the pattern of the Steel Industry Trade Union Consultative Committee, which had been formed in 1967 to negotiate with the government's new British Steel Corporation. The pattern involved formal TUC committees, each consisting of representatives of the General Council and of affiliated unions in a specific industry. By the end of 1972 there were eight such committees (covering the 'industries' of steel, construction, local government, transport, health services, fuel and power, textiles and clothing, hotels and catering); a ninth, covering printing industries, was added in 1975. Their stated purpose was not only to 'give the unions in the industry concerned a way of expressing their collective views to . . . the General Council', but also to provide the council with a channel through which it could 'impress on the unions concerned . . . the ways in which other trade unionists would be affected by their decisions'.[121] The TUC leadership evidently had large ambitions for the committees. As the general secretary explained, it was envisaged that they would 'look at' such matters as 'collective bargaining and wages structures, safety and health and so on'—and, more significantly, if they wanted 'to undertake the actual work of wage negotiations there will be nothing to stop them because it will be for the unions to decide'.[122] The latter hope was presumably reflected in the General Council's decision, early in 1970, to disband its Incomes Policy Committee and form a Collective Bargaining Committee concerned with the issues and machinery of collective bargaining in general. In the event, the steel committee apart, none of the industry committees took a direct hand in wage negotiations with employers up to 1976. But all of them were active in other respects. There was, however, one especially glaring gap in their ranks: a committee covering the engineering industry.

[120] See Harold Wilson, *The Labour Government 1964–1970*, pp. 662–3.
[121] *TUC Report*, 1970, p. 518.
[122] ibid., p. 547.

As well as developing these organizational links with industry groups of unions, the General Council maintained its grip on local and regional inter-union bodies. Trades councils continued to be subject to the constraints imposed by the system of annual registration with the TUC. It was the 1973 Congress, following the government's redrawing of county boundaries, which decided to replace the old federations of trades councils with County Associations. The same Congress discarded the old Regional Advisory Committees in favour of eight Regional Councils in England, and a somewhat differently structured Wales Trade Union Council, to coincide with the government's economic planning regions. Like the RACs, the new councils appear to have been kept on a tight constitutional leash. The TUC's dominance in this area is indicated by its decision, in the light of the new county and regional arrangements, to wind up the London Trades Council despite strong opposition from the council itself. That decision effectively disposed of the once-powerful rival with which the TUC had been confronted a century earlier.

In general, too, the TUC leadership maintained its authority in relation to Congress. It claimed, by implication, large discretionary powers in this connection. Action on Congress resolutions was commonly either delayed or denied. Otherwise, the reception of such resolutions was often all but condescending, as recorded in the General Council's annual report. Take the way it treated five resolutions which the 1974 Congress adopted on collective bargaining and the 'social contract'. Two of them, the council 'decided', should be 'taken into account in the development' of the TUC's policy; the third, it 'decided', should also be taken into account, but only subject to specified qualifications; and the other two it (not Congress) was designated as having 'incorporated' in the 'TUC policy'.[123] Well might Hugh Clegg conclude that 'Congress cannot initiate policy, for if it were to pass a positive resolution contrary to the Council's wishes, the Council could ignore it or make only the smallest gestures towards its fulfilment'.[124]

Not that Congress was totally subservient. Far from it. Congress rebellions took two forms. One, which the General

[123] ibid., 1975, p. 269.
[124] H. A. Clegg, *The System of Industrial Relations in Great Britain*, p. 400.

Council certainly took seriously, involved rejecting ('referring back') a section of the council's annual report. An example is the 1955 Congress's rejection of the council's explanation ('there was no real case which could be substantiated in front of a Minister') for its failure to comply with an instruction of the preceding Congress relating to income tax concessions.[125] But this form of rebellion was rare. The other was somewhat less so. It involved rejecting the council's advice about supporting or opposing a motion before Congress. Invariably, the issue at stake in such cases was large and sensitive. Wage restraint and the Industrial Relations Act of 1971 are the obvious examples. The TUC leaders moved, for the most part, with great caution on both issues, as indicated by their tendency to use special conferences of union officials as a means of legitimating decisions that had to be taken before the annual Congress could do so. However, for all their caution, and despite many successes, they were at times rebuffed by Congress on both issues. Moreover, some of their successes were won with such narrow majorities as to qualify, effectively, as rebuffs.

On the wage restraint issue, the General Council was under no great pressure to put its internal authority to the test during the Conservatives' long reign of the 1950s and early 1960s. But the situation changed radically with the election in 1964 of a Labour government confronting a balance of payments crisis, and anxious to restrain wage rises. The council, by a majority, was sympathetic. It agreed to a policy of voluntary restraint, and called a conference of union executives which backed it by a three-to-one majority in April 1965. In September it won from Congress a still solid five-to-three endorsement of its decision to cooperate with the government's new, and compulsory, 'early warning' policy. A year later, it had to be satisfied with a more marginal five-to-four majority when the 1966 Congress approved its reluctant acceptance of a compulsory wage-freeze. It fared better in March 1967 at a second conference of executives which roundly endorsed a TUC-operated procedure for vetting wage claims once the freeze ended.

The tide turned at the 1967 Congress, which met after the Labour government had decided to continue the statutory

[125] *TUC Report*, 1955, p. 451.

restrictions in a different form. A motion rejecting the government's 'intervention in collective bargaining' was easily adopted despite the General Council's explicit opposition.[126] This result was echoed, if not duplicated, in February 1968 when the council's proposals concerning a voluntary restraint policy were approved by only a bare nine-to-eight majority at a third conference of executives (a result which determined the government to continue its reliance on legislative compulsion). Similarly, the 1968 Congress later adopted, by a tiny majority of 34,000 in a total vote of 8.5 million, a motion endorsing the TUC's voluntary incomes policy; and an almost as unimpressive majority of 758,000 was all that could be mustered behind the relevant passages of the council's annual report. The council responded by revamping the TUC's policy and, at a fourth conference of executives in February 1969, was rewarded with a healthy three-to-one majority. But seven months later, Congress again rejected the council's advice and narrowly carried a resolution demanding the repeal of the Prices and Incomes Act.

Labour's subsequent election defeat eased the pressure on the TUC leaders. They shrugged off the Conservatives' requests for cooperation in restraining wages on a voluntary basis. And they were able to go along with a resolution effectively rejecting wage restraint, which the 1970 Congress carried without a division. Similarly, after the government switched to a compulsory policy, they went along with a special Congress decision, in March 1973, instructing them to organize 'a day of national protest and stoppage against the wage control policy and increases in food prices'.[127] They did so with an 'evident lack of enthusiasm',[128] and prudently chose 1 May, the day customarily marked by working-class demonstrations anyway. On the other hand, at the annual Congress six months later, they successfully opposed a motion that would have prohibited them from even discussing incomes policy with the Conservative government. Labour's return to power re-created the pressures associated with a TUC commitment to wage restraint. A motion condemning that commitment was moved at the 1974

[126] ibid., 1967, p. 507.
[127] ibid., 1973, p. 281.
[128] Leo Panitch *Social Democracy and Industrial Militancy*, p. 226.

Congress, and then withdrawn in the face of the General Council's opposition. The 1975 Congress was confronted with an agreement between the council and the government, negotiated in the shadow of a balance of payments crisis and limiting wage claims to a flat £6 for 12 months. It endorsed the agreement, in effect by a two-to-one majority. An even tougher agreement (with a £4 limit) gained a massive seventeen-to-one supporting vote at a special Congress the following year, a result effectively endorsed by the subsequent annual Congress.

Thus, during the period, Congress formally rejected the General Council's advice on a wage restraint issue on two occasions, in 1967 and 1969. In addition, of the many more votes on such issues which the council won at both Congress and conferences of executives, at least three involved unconvincingly narrow majorities.

It was, however, in connection with the Industrial Relations Act that the TUC leaders suffered their heaviest defeat at the hands of Congress since the days of the Parliamentary Committee. The Council successfully recommended to a special Congress in March 1971 that affiliated unions should be 'strongly advised' not to register under the Act. Six months later it urged the annual Congress to follow suit. It was spurned by a five-to-four majority, Congress deciding instead to 'instruct' unions not to register.[129] Paradoxically, this defeat paved the way for what is perhaps the most impressive demonstration of the TUC's internal authority in the whole of its history.

Never before had the TUC instructed all its affiliates to take a particular course of action on pain (as the Congress debate made crystal clear) of expulsion. And for many unions, compliance with the instruction entailed considerable sacrifices, financial and otherwise.[130] Yet, by September 1972, Congress had to confirm the General Council's suspension of only 32 affiliates. By the time of the 1973 Congress, nine of them had been re-admitted to affiliation after complying with the directive, two had disaffiliated of their own volition and one had disbanded. Congress expelled the remaining 20, which accounted for less than four per cent of the TUC's affiliated

[129] *TUC Report*, 1971, pp. 376, 427.
[130] See B. Weekes, M. Mellish, L. Dickens and J. Lloyd, *Industrial Relations and the Limits of the Law*, pp. 255–60.

membership. Four of them had complied and applied for reaffiliation before the new Labour government took office; others did so afterwards. By the end of 1975, 14 of the 20 were reaffiliated, along with one of the two that had avoided expulsion by resigning.

The significance of this demonstration of the TUC's internal authority can be adequately appreciated only in the light of the General Council's initial sense of insecurity when it came to instructing, as distinct from strongly advising, unions not to register. 'The real issue before us is unity, not the Act', the TUC secretary told the 1971 annual Congress in the course of arguing against an instruction.[131] As it turned out, he and his colleagues, along with a great many observers, underestimated the ability of the TUC to coerce unity on this issue.

The wage restraint issue, of course, was a different and more delicate matter, longer-lived and much less conclusively solvable. There are two points to be made. The first is that the TUC broke new ground on this issue. During 1965–9 and 1974–5, it did more than merely urge affiliates to comply with its official wage policy: it scrutinized and passed judgement on many hundreds of their specific pay claims. The severity of the judgements is open to question; so, too, are the thoroughness of the preceding inquiries and the extent to which affiliates accepted adverse decisions.[132] Nevertheless, as the Donovan commission pointed out in this connection, 'such an intervention in the autonomy of [the TUC's] members . . . is an innovation which would have been barely conceivable even a few years ago'.[133] The second point is that the failures of the TUC's internal authority on the wage restraint issue are easily exaggerated. They were balanced, and perhaps outweighed, by successes—less dramatic for the most part, and certainly less unqualified, than that on the Industrial Relations Act; but successes nonetheless. A case in point is the TUC-government agreement on wage increases in 1975. It was, as the TUC secretary admitted, a 'tough policy' from the union angle. It

[131] *TUC Report*, 1971, p. 424.
[132] See, e.g., Clegg, *The System of Industrial Relations*, p. 429; Lovell and Roberts, *A Short History of the TUC*, pp. 172–3; Panitch, *Social Democracy and Industrial Militancy*, pp. 95–7, 163.
[133] Royal Commission on Trade Unions and Employers' Associations, *Report*, p. 194.

was also, as a delegate accusingly commented, negotiated 'without any mandate from this Congress'.[134] But Congress, as we have seen, convincingly endorsed it. The incident, given the nature of the issue, provides an impressive demonstration of the internal authority which the General Council could command, if not invariably maintain, in its latter years.

External Authority

A Guildhall banquet attended by the Queen; royal garden parties for trade union officials; a government reception in the Westminster banqueting hall; a centenary postage stamp; special television programmes and newspaper supplements— these are some of the ways in which the TUC's centenary was celebrated in 1968. They signified a considerable public standing.

So did less transient indicators of specifically governmental recognition: the array of consultative bodies with TUC representation and the ready access which TUC leaders had to cabinet ministers. These were the bedrock indicators of the TUC's external authority, bedrock in the sense that they remained substantially stable throughout the period. But there were other, less rock-like, indicators that were more sensitive to shifts in ministerial attitudes and consequent fluctuations in TUC-government relations. Perhaps the most sensitive was the attention which ministers paid to the TUC when it came to the issue of wages policy, an issue of enduring concern during the period.

In 1952 the Churchill government tried unsuccessfully to negotiate an agreement, with the TUC, tying wage increases to productivity. Four years later, the Conservatives again tried to negotiate a wage restraint policy with the TUC; and, when they failed, turned to other deflationary devices rather than legislating against wage rises. That was a symptom of the TUC's external authority. But by 1958–9, it has been asserted, 'the influence of Congress reached perhaps its lowest postwar trough ... when the government put an end to the Industrial Disputes Tribunal against its wishes'.[135] Arguably, an even lower trough was reached in 1961 when the Conservative

[134] *TUC Report*, 1975, pp. 380, 457.
[135] Clegg, *The System of Industrial Relations*, p. 399.

government imposed a 'pay pause' in the public sector without any prior consultation whatsoever—although it then sought to conciliate the TUC by offering it representation on a new and high-level consultative body, the National Economic Development Council.

Between 1964 and mid-1966 the Labour government sought and obtained, though not without effort, the TUC's support for an incomes policy relying primarily on voluntary cooperation from the unions. As late as February 1966 the Minister for Economic Affairs was privately claiming that the path to effective wage restraint involved 'shifting the wage negotiating authority from individual trade unions ... to the TUC'.[136] Nevertheless, he and his colleagues made no attempt to secure the TUC's agreement before switching to a compulsory wage freeze five months later. This pattern (government decisions made with little or no reference to the TUC) persisted in the case of wages policy for the rest of the 1960s. But there was, in 1969, one significant departure on a related issue—the spectacular flurry of negotiation which scuttled the government's proposal of statutory penal provisions against unofficial strikes. Ostensibly, as the Prime Minister was bound to insist,[137] he had relented in view of the TUC's 'solemn and binding' undertaking to act against such strikes. There is, however, little doubt that he had been forced to cave in. The TUC's undertaking was the best he could get as a face-saver. On the other hand, the role of the TUC in this episode, while obviously of great importance, was not the only factor. Both cabinet and the parliamentary Labour party at large were gravely divided on the issue.[138] Nevertheless, it was an impressive demonstration of the TUC's authority.

The Conservative government thrown up by the general election of mid-1970 provided the occasion for an even more impressive demonstration. Initially, its leaders followed the predominant pattern established by their Labour predecessors. Thus the TUC had to be satisfied with perfunctory consultation about both the Conservatives' initial wages policy and their Industrial Relations Bill which, unlike its Labour namesake,

---

[136] George Brown (statement in a closed seminar attended by the author), Nuffield College, Oxford, February 1966.
[137] See Wilson, op. cit., pp. 660–2.
[138] See Peter Jenkins, *The Battle of Downing Street*, esp. pp. 150–5.

reached the statute book. But then, once the union campaign against the Act began to bite, a great deal more respect was shown the TUC—and not only by government. The point is illustrated by a journalist's remark at the 1972 Congress: 'Congress has been treated this year in the press as infinitely more important than last year when everyone spoke of . . . the end of the TUC as we have always known it.'[139] His opinion, as a comment on the TUC's external authority, was echoed in the TUC leadership's own judgement that its recent 'advocacy has . . . brought about a perceptible change of emphasis in Government [economic] policy'.[140] And both were confirmed by three events in July, a few weeks before the Congress. One was the freeing of the 'Pentonville five' following the TUC's threat of a one-day general strike (see above). Another, the consequence of an initiative from the Confederation of British Industry, was the formation of a TUC–CBI standing committee to supervise a non-governmental conciliation and arbitration service. The third event was more complicated. The Prime Minister suggested that 'a small group' of ministers and TUC representatives should be set up to discuss economic issues arising from the government's decision to float the pound, but accepted the TUC's counter-suggestion that these issues were properly the province of the National Economic Development Council of which he was chairman and the TUC a member. Subsequently, mainly by way of special NEDC meetings, he met TUC representatives on ten separate occasions in an attempt to secure an agreed incomes and prices policy, before resorting to a compulsory wage-price freeze. His evident eagerness to negotiate contrasted sharply with his government's earlier and much more casual approach to the wages policy issue. In general, moreover, the Heath government maintained in relation to the TUC both the forms of the consultative arrangements it inherited and, apparently, much of the substance as well, once the heat had drained from the Industrial Relations Act.

But it was left to the last Wilson government to create what amounted to a new dimension of the TUC's external authority. Before 1974, as we have seen, both the Heath and earlier Wilson governments had tried to draw the TUC behind an agreed

[139] *TUC Report*, 1972, p. 542.   [140] ibid., p. 249.

incomes policy. Each had set minimum conditions; and when these proved unacceptable to the TUC, had opted for legislative compulsion. The leaders of the last Wilson government, however, altered the priorities when they negotiated the 'social contract' with the TUC.

[They] proceeded on the assumption that an incomes policy could be formulated only with a consent that Congress was free to withhold, and could be made good up and down the country only if Congress were determined to make it good. This meant that the terms of the policy would have to be in the main those proposed by the Congress; and that responsibility for the effects on the economy would largely rest with Congress.[141]

The result was a government incomes policy which diverged only marginally from the TUC's initial proposals.[142]

It would not do to construe this as an unqualified victory for the TUC. After all, its leaders conceded a great deal when they agreed to the social contract. They conceded what they had earlier refused the Heath government: a tight limit on wage increases. On the other hand, the twofold *quid pro quo* given them was, to say the least, impressive. First, there was the government's acceptance of almost all the TUC's terms in the case of its incomes policy proper. Second, there were the striking concessions outside the area of that policy, as summed up by *The Guardian*. 'In the past eighteen months, the Government has deferred to the TUC to an unprecedented degree . . . What are essentially its Bills have taken priority in the legislative programme of the Government.'[143]

These, given the political gravity of the issues involved, were extraordinary policy concessions from the government. The existence of the Liaison Committee, giving TUC leaders assured monthly access to the Prime Minister and his most senior ministers, was an equally extraordinary consultative concession. Such concessions indicate a pressure group of quite distinctive significance in governmental eyes.

---

[141] E. H. Phelps Brown, 'A Social Contract in Australia?', in J. P. Nieuwenhuysen and P. J. Drake (eds.), *Australian Economic Policy*, p. 90.
[142] See Crouch, op. cit., pp. 138–9.
[143] *The Guardian*, 1 September 1975; and see Clegg, *The System of Industrial Relations*, pp. 478–87, for a detailed account of the ways this legislation favoured unions and their members.

I I

The Course of a Political Career

THE principal task of the last eight chapters was to describe the TUC's changing political role between 1868 and 1976, in some detail up to 1940 and in outline thereafter. The main task of the present chapter is to take a bird's-eye view of those 108 years in relation to both describing and explaining the changes that have occurred in the TUC's political role.

This task is dealt with in three of the four sections into which the chapter is divided. The first ('Determinants of Change') briefly delineates the factors that have helped to mould the TUC's political role. The second ('Patterns of Change') connects these factors with specific aspects of the TUC's activities which they appear to have influenced. The third ('The Question of Authority') outlines the TUC's changing role in terms of its internal and external authority. The final section ('Some Implications') sets out a few points, drawn from the TUC study, which seem to have some relevance to pressure group politics at large, at least in Britain.

DETERMINANTS OF CHANGE

Following Eckstein,[1] four categories were nominated in chapter I as enclosing likely determinants of the TUC's political role: structure, policy, attitudes and group attributes. The case study justified the assumption that they are each relevant to an explanation of the way the TUC's role has changed—subject, however, in two cases (structure and group attributes) to extensions in detailed formulation which Eckstein may not quite have foreseen.

Structure

There have been massive changes in the structure of government during the TUC's lifetime. The locus of effective decision-making shifted from the legislative to the executive arm with

[1] See Eckstein, *Pressure Group Politics*, chap. 1.

the strengthening of cabinet authority and party discipline. Within the executive itself the role of civil servants, relative to ministers, expanded with the administrative complexities bred of mounting government concern for social welfare and economic management.

On the side of the trade unions, the growth of their membership was accompanied by a trend towards centralized and bureaucratized forms of organization. An accompanying trend (also of advantage to the TUC), towards the settlement of industrial as well as political issues nationally rather than locally, was partially reversed in the 1960s. Other changes in the structure of the labour movement confronted the TUC, from the turn of the century, with competing claims to speak for the unions at large. By 1940 the sources of the most serious threats had either died (Triple Industrial Alliance), declined in importance (General Federation of Trade Unions), or tacitly accepted a jurisdictional division (Labour party). Competition from outside the labour movement, involving the structure of the pressure group system at large, has been less threatening because it does not place the TUC's *raison d'être* in question. But it has been more persistent. For the TUC has always faced opposing interests of significant political weight in policy areas of importance to its leaders.[2]

Policy

Government concerns have expanded enormously during the TUC's lifetime, which embraces the transition from the so-called *laissez-faire* state to the age of the welfare state and the managed economy. One aspect of this expansion is government's assumed responsibility for full employment and economic growth: this has been of great importance to the TUC because

[2] Unlike such other major British pressure groups as the National Farmers' Union, the British Legion and the British Medical Association: see Self and Storing, *The State and the Farmer*, pp. 193, 232; Wootton, *The Politics of Influence*, p. 255; Eckstein, *Pressure Group Politics*, pp. 106–9. Indeed, it was the emergence and activity of the TUC which in the 1870s prompted employers to organize for political purposes on a national inter-industry basis: see Jefferys, *Labour's Formative Years 1849–1879*, pp. 112–13. But that organization soon collapsed and it was many years before the TUC had something like a counterpart on the employers' side. It had a reasonably precise counterpart, in terms of matching coverage, only with the formation of the Confederation of British Industry in 1965. Not, of course, that employers were ever voiceless politically, or without organization in some form.

of the way it heightened the peacetime political significance of union industrial action. A second relevant aspect is reflected in the fact that by the mid-1970s more than half the TUC's affiliated membership claimed the government as 'ultimate employer'.[3] A third is reflected in the consuming emphasis on administrative detail and technical problem-solving in the relations between government office-holders and major pressure groups.[4]

Attitudes

The belief that organized interest groups possess a right to be consulted by government, on policy matters of concern to them, became a firm tenet of the British political culture during the TUC's lifetime.[5] Initially, however, union leaders faced special problems in winning government recognition of that right. Not only did the trade unions stand for the 'lower orders' of a highly stratified society,[6] but their very existence flew in the face of conventional economic wisdom and, in the eyes of many, they were sources of violence.[7] Union leaders themselves added another handicap in the form of expectations which seem often to have been limited by a sense of personal inferiority —evident as much in the aggressive 'class-consciousness' of the Socialist as in the faintly seedy respectability of the Lib–Lab deferential. But the twentieth-century counterparts of both were to gain confidence.[8]

[3] *TUC Report*, 1974, p. 233.

[4] As George Woodcock, TUC secretary, once pungently put it: 'In all my activities I am now down rooting in the undergrowth': *The Guardian*, 29 April 1966.

[5] See Beer, *Modern British Politics*, p. 329; Richard Rose, *Politics in England Today*, p. 253.

[6] The importance of this consideration is suggested by the fact that a century later, in another and more fluid society, 'low status' could still apparently impose a serious political burden on the venerable American Federation of Labor-Congress of Industrial Organizations. See Abraham Holtzman, *Interest Groups and Lobbying*, p. 25.

[7] A simple contrast illustrates the extent of the subsequent change in the attitude of government office-holders. George Howell, the first full-time secretary of the TUC, did not interview a Prime Minister in that capacity; instead, as we have seen, he spent a great deal of time dancing attendance on backbench MPs. Three generations later his successor, Walter Citrine, had frequent private access to two non-Labour Prime Ministers by way of a little-known corridor between the Treasury and No. 10 Downing Street: see Citrine, *Men and Work*, p. 367.

[8] The change in union leaders' expectations is epitomized in three TUC reactions to the appointment of working-class magistrates. In the 1880s, as we have seen, the appointment of a few was received with rapture. In the 1920s, on the other hand, there was a pained complaint that only 719 magistrates had a working-class background; and by the 1970s, the whole issue was treated as a routine and essentially minor matter: see *TUC Report*, 1924, p. 271; ibid., 1976, p. 90.

Group Attributes

Since the TUC was founded, its politically significant resources have both gained weight and become more diversified. Considerable wealth and enormous numerical size are two attributes it now has, through its affiliated unions, as a result of trade union growth. Neither, it is true, can be directed at will by the TUC leadership: the unions have always guarded their financial sovereignty and unionists have never shown an inclination to allow their parliamentary votes to be 'delivered'. If questionable in these respects, howevei, the TUC's 'organizational cohesiveness'[9] has a demonstrably positive side—exemplified dramatically in the general strike of 1926, the boycott of the Industrial Relations Act of 1971 and, more subtly, in the TUC-government agreements of the second world war and the 'social contract' of 1974. Perceptions of that cohesiveness have certainly influenced the TUC's acceptance in government circles. So, too, have the qualities of its leaders. Four stand out in the formative years to 1940. Broadhurst, Shackleton, Bevin and Citrine, each in their own way, had a profound personal impact on the TUC's role in their time—and, in the case of Bevin and Citrine at least, well beyond it.

There is one further attribute which underlies the transformation from the little-remarked group of the 1870s to the brooding presence of a century later. It is the extent of the TUC's policy concerns. They were initially limited to the law relating to employees and trade unions, and a few issues of legal administration. By the time of the first world war they included the whole social welfare area as well; by the 1920s, foreign policy; and by the 1930s, the upper reaches of economic policy. The TUC's specific interests since the second world war have been more extensive than those of any other major interest group outside the labour movement.[10]

PATTERNS OF CHANGE

Seven aspects of the TUC's political activities were set out in

[9] This (Eckstein's term: *Pressure Group Politics*, p. 34) amounts to much the same thing as the notion of internal authority, used in this book.
[10] In the 1970s they ranged, for example, from government borrowings on the international money market to matrimonial law reform, from old-age pensions to industrial safety, from education in Britain to civil rights in the Soviet Union, and from race relations to hospital administration.

chapter 1: points of access to government, methods of communication, forms of pressure, scope of relations, intensity of concern, quality of relations and, last, effectiveness. The nature and scope of the changes that have occurred in the TUC's role may perhaps be more clearly delineated if surveyed with reference to each of these aspects in turn.

Points of Access

Initially concerned almost wholly with parliament, TUC spokesmen eventually concentrated their attention on cabinet and the departments. The friendly backbench MP, once a treasured point of access, was all but abandoned in favour of the parliamentary Labour party on the increasingly rare occasions when the TUC sought to work through parliament. Ministers and civil servants became the focus for TUC lobbyists.

This shift followed the changing balance of power between legislature and executive which, although strikingly confirmed during the first world war, had been underway long before.[11] Despite the TUC's early recognition of this structural change, there was a distinct time-lag in one aspect of its response: it persisted with its futile annual list of private members' bills right up to the war. A vested interest on the part of MP-members of the TUC's leadership was probably one reason for this lag; the current union suspicions about civil servants may also have helped.[12] In time, however, the TUC was to respond with great alacrity to lower-level changes in government structure,[13] encouraged by the expansion in public policy and the accompanying emphasis on administrative initiative.

---

[11] Henry Slesser, writing in 1921, made the point another way. 'With the decay of the prestige of Parliament, we find to an increasing extent that legislative bargains are being driven directly between the Government, the employers' associations and the trade unions': *Trade Unionism*, p. 114.

[12] A resolution carried at the 1911 Congress (and re-affirmed at each of the next three) attacked 'the extensive powers' of senior civil servants, condemned 'the clandestine movement . . . for appointing only University men' to such positions, and spoke of 'arresting this tendency towards a bureaucratic system of government': *TUC Report*, 1911, pp. 222–3.

[13] Thus the TUC's decision to emulate government's administrative decentralization in 1940 by creating its own Regional Emergency Committees, placed on a peacetime footing as Regional Advisory Committees in 1945. In 1974, as we have also seen, the RACs were replaced with Regional Councils parallel to new 'economic planning regions' set up by government.

Methods of Communication

Two trends are evident. In the first place, methods involving the initial communication of TUC claims to and within parliament have lost their former importance,[14] and those homing in directly on ministers and civil servants have been emphasized. This development, obviously reflecting the shift in preferred points of access, may therefore be regarded as a function of the changing structure of government which produced that shift.

The second trend has been a mounting emphasis on direct methods of communication that require the cooperation of government office-holders (see chapter 1).[15] Thus, for a time from the 1890s, the regular and highly ritualized ministerial deputation became the TUC's principal method. That has since given way to two other methods. One is a more informal form of *ad hoc* consultation which may, like the traditional deputation, involve a large number of TUC representatives, but it can involve only one or two. Above all, however, it entails something like genuine discussion rather than the set-piece speechmaking characteristic of traditional deputations. This method, sporadically in evidence for a quarter-century from the time of the Liberals' electoral landslide in 1906, was of progressively greater importance from the early 1930s. The other method of communication, though first available to a very limited extent towards the end of the last century, began to play a vital part in TUC-government relations only from the late 1930s. It involves TUC representation on formally-constituted consultative bodies, both temporary and standing, advisory and administrative. The trend towards these two methods of communication plainly owes most to changing attitudes on the part of government office-holders.

[14] Since the first decade of this century, for example, the TUC has officially endorsed no parliamentary candidates; its leaders have very rarely lobbied backbench MPs, and only occasionally urged affiliated unions and/or trades councils to do so. Its use of the parliamentary Labour party as a means of communicating claims to government, whether Labour or non-Labour, has also declined since the 1930s.

[15] The main method that does not require such cooperation, correspondence, remains well-used; but it has become very much a supplementary method, rather than the primary method it once was. The demonstration/mass campaign method has always been supplementary in character, so far as its use by the TUC is concerned. In any case, it fell into disuse after the mid-1930s until revived in the early 1970s for a time. In modern conditions, given the TUC's ready access to government, mass campaigns and demonstrations smack more of a form of pressure than a method of communication (see below).

Forms of Pressure

The techniques the TUC has used, threatened to use or appeared capable of using, in support of its claims on government, have become more diverse. Initially, TUC leaders had only reasoned argument and their possible influence among working-class electors. The development of public policy has enlarged the importance of argument. It has also placed within the TUC's reach two other forms of pressure: the strike and the ability to withhold administrative cooperation.

Electoral influence and the strike weapon, for the most part, represent 'atmospheric' rather than precisely controllable forms of pressure available to the TUC. The former was a natural outgrowth of the size and steady expansion of the TUC's affiliated membership, combined with the progressive extension of the franchise to the working class. TUC leaders have never been able to 'deliver' the union vote, but on many issues they might plausibly presume to articulate unionists' views irrespective of party allegiance. It would be surprising if governments had not sometimes sensed a genuine electoral threat, tacit and attenuated though it might be, behind major claims advanced by the TUC.

Something the same is true of strikes. Government interest in them mounted from the 1890s as they increased in scale, seriously affected strategic industries, happened in wartime, and occurred at times of economic difficulty under governments committed to full employment. Neither starting nor stopping strikes is normally in the TUC's gift—although, during the 1920s, it was able to lay claim with considerable conviction to the general strike until 1926; and its reassertion of this claim in 1972, on the issue of the 'Pentonville five' carried evident weight in authoritative circles. But, in general, a belief that the TUC may influence strikes, if not control them, has plainly affected the calculations of politicians during and since the second world war.

Reasoned argument, of course, is an infinitely more easily controlled form of pressure. Its importance in TUC–government relations has increased, especially since 1906, with government incursions into the fields of social and economic policy. These have thrown the emphasis on to administrative details which tend to be more readily negotiable, in terms of knowledge and logic, than are grander policy principles flowing from essentially unnegotiable values. The TUC's ability to furnish carefully argued submissions and a wide range of technical information was vastly improved, from the 1920s, with the recruitment of professional staff.

Withholding administrative cooperation, for the TUC, is more readily controllable than strike action—if less certainly so than reasoned argument. It owes its mounting importance, as a form of pressure, primarily to two factors. One is the changing character of public policy. The other is prevailing expectations (attitudes) that groups affected by government policy proposals ought to be consulted. These factors have combined to produce a situation in which the 'whole framework of public administration presumes that private associations will give freely of their advice and assistance ... [and] would be seriously dislocated if they were withheld'.[16] To be sure, the sanction thus vested in private associations is a two-edged sword for a group geared primarily to political activity— especially when, as with the TUC, the great breadth of its policy concerns intensifies its vulnerability to government reprisals in kind. Nevertheless, the TUC has actually refused or withdrawn cooperation in relation to such momentous issues as government wage restraint proposals and the Industrial Relations Act of 1971; it has declined to make submissions to investigating bodies; occasionally, it has refused to discuss certain matters with government representatives; and once or twice it has withdrawn its representatives from a standing consultative body. On the other hand, unlike at least one other major British pressure group,[17] it has never even threatened a boycott extending across more than a very narrow segment of

[16] Finer, *Anonymous Empire*, p. 26. The dislocation point applies, in a really serious sense, not only at the level of an Industrial Relations Act or a wartime dilution policy, but often also at more mundane levels as illustrated by two unusually clearcut cases of departmental dependence on the TUC during the second world war. One concerned union applications for industrial clothing and footwear above the ration. The Board of Trade believed that 'only the solid and resolute . . . support of the TUC in cutting down exaggerated claims prevented the whole award system from foundering long before the end of the [first] rationing year': Hargreaves and Gowing, *Civil Industry and Trade*, p. 320. In the case of food rationing, the TUC leadership and the Ministry of Food 'stood back to back, the former repelling the unions, the latter its fellow Government Departments', who sought supplementary rations for particular employees on the ground of heavy work: Hammond, *Food*, vol. 2, p. 609.

[17] See Self and Storing, *The State and the Farmer*, p. 65.

the policy concerns it shares with government. It is also note-worthy that serious use of this form of pressure by the TUC has been confined almost entirely to its latest years, at the height of its prestige and assurance.

It is prestige as well which largely accounts for the TUC's virtual abandonment of the public campaign since the 1930s. A commentator fairly remarked some years ago that the TUC stood 'outside the world of campaigns . . . because the government accords [it] such full recognition'—but then wisely added the caveat that it 'still holds the campaign in reserve'.[18] It did indeed, and was later to employ that form of pressure against both the Conservatives' Industrial Relations Bill, in 1970–1, and the Labour government's stand on the issue of the 'Shrewsbury pickets' in 1975.

Scope of Relations

TUC–government dealings once involved only a few matters, most of them related to law reform. In the course of a century, the few became a horde of policy and administrative issues ranging from the industrial and the social to the economic and the international The widening scope of government policy was obviously crucial to this process. But it was not solely a matter of government initiative and TUC response.

The TUC itself has also filled the role of innovator in this respect. In the first place, it has injected into its relations with government (without necessarily originating, in the larger sense) issues which were not already established concerns of public policy. Old-age pensions, economic planning and full employment are examples. In the second place, it has extended its mutual field of interest with government by choosing to intervene in policy areas which it had previously ignored, although government had not. The major case is foreign policy.

Intensity of Concern

The importance attached by union leaders and government officer-holders, respectively, to the TUC's political role has been subject to marked fluctuations, especially before the second world war. Policy, in the form of a sensitive issue, has been a necessary but not sufficient condition of high intensity

[18] J. D. Stewart, *British Pressure Groups*, p. 122.

in both cases. Its impact has depended largely on the TUC's competitive position (structure of the labour movement) and on government office-holders' perception of the TUC's organizational cohesiveness (group attributes).

In the 1870s, and again in the 1970s, severe legal restrictions on the unions' freedom of action were associated with manifest peaks in the intensity of union leaders' concern with the TUC's political activities. But their reaction in the early 1900s, after the Taff Vale judgement had raised exactly the same kind of issue, was much more muted. The reason is that the TUC's competitive position then was totally different, owing to the parallel involvement of the Labour party and the General Federation of Trade Unions in the campaign to remedy the judgement. Its weak competitive position, further sapped by Shackleton's departure, largely explains the almost contemptuously slight reliance which union leaders placed on it in their dealings with government during the first world war. After 1931, of course, Bevin and Citrine turned the tables on the Labour party. The TUC, as a result, entered the second world war as the acknowledged union spokesman on sensitive issues of general concern. It has retained that position to such effect that, as a perceptive observer put it at the start of the 1960s, 'by and large the unions now attach more importance to ... political action [through the TUC] than they do to their direct involvement in politics' through the Labour party.[19]

Until Churchill and Lloyd George cut their dash in the aftermath of the Liberal triumph of 1906, ministerial concern about consulting the TUC seems to have involved at most a mild interest. Since then innovatory social policies, and policies thrust on government by the exigencies of either total war or an economically perilous peace, have helped produce peaks of intensity on the side of government leaders. But other factors have qualified their reactions. The stark contrast between the first world war and the second world war, in the matter of ministerial reliance on the TUC as an intermediary with the unions, is largely explained by the stark contrast between the TUC's competitive position in 1914 and in 1939. Similarly, the importance of ministerial beliefs about the TUC's organizational cohesiveness is underlined by the fact that its spokesmen

[19] Allan Flanders, *Management and Unions*, pp. 31–2.

were first admitted, in any serious sense, to the traditional inner sanctum of foreign policy in the early 1920s when it was widely believed that the TUC leaders held the general strike in their hands.

Since 1940, on the side of both unions and government, intensity of concern has remained at once relatively high and, in broad terms, stable. There have, however, been some fluctuations. Thus the Heath government's Industrial Relations Bill initiated a period of exceptional intensity in the case of the unions. Similarly, on the side of government intensity, a low point connected with incomes policy during 1966–9 was followed by a resurgence for a while in 1972, and a highpoint in 1974 and later.

Quality of Relations

Greater ease and informality (intimate-antagonistic continuum) and a significant element of bargaining (soft-hard continuum): this has been the secular trend in TUC–government dealings. To a degree, both aspects of that trend go hand in hand. Genuine negotiation—even, perhaps, genuine consultation—was scarcely possible in the circumstances of the TUC deputations of the nineteenth century, and later, which often met ministers with the press in attendance. The number present, the public nature of the occasion, the standard procedures observed, all combined to encourage oratory rather than discussion. This suited ministers with an intention to divert rather than negotiate—as, for example, was usually the case with Lloyd George in his dealings with various interests about the National Insurance Bill.[20] But when he knew he had to strike a bargain, as with the Labour party on one occasion, he met Ramsay MacDonald and G. N. Barnes on their own and in private.

TUC deputations became less bulky, and their encounters with ministers somewhat less public, before the first world war.

---

[20] He 'developed a perfectly uncanny art of "receiving deputations" ', according to a closely involved civil servant. 'He almost invariably allowed the speaker introducing the deputation to make his points fully . . . His replies were more or less to the point, as he chose, and were full of fun; everyone was soon smiling; the most unlikely proposals were promised full consideration; the deputation broke up for informal chatty conversation, which everyone enjoyed, and finally went away fully satisfied that it would probably get almost all that it had asked for'. W. J. Braithwaite, *Lloyd George's Ambulance Waggon*, p. 63; see also p. 193.

Nevertheless, privacy and discussion do not seem to have been given much weight in TUC–government dealings until the mid-1920s. Informal, confidential and really small-scale (down to one-to-one) exchanges began to figure at all significantly at the ministerial level, and became frequent at the departmental, only during the 1930s. They emerged as a major feature of the TUC's relations with government from the time of the second world war. From this time, too, those relations embodied an element of serious negotiation much more commonly than ever before.[21]

Informality and confidentiality obviously depended, at least in part, on a dulling of nineteenth-century class attitudes and prejudices. Personalities played a part. Bevin and Citrine, in particular, won obvious respect from prime ministers and others, and powerfully influenced the TUC's reception in government circles as a result. Greater ease in TUC–government dealings could also be expected as an outcome of frequent and low-key contact, produced by public policy developments which proliferated administrative matters that were conducive to dispassionate discussion because they did not raise issues felt to be fundamental.[22]

Policy and structural factors were crucial to the emergence of a significant bargaining element in the TUC's relations with government. The imperatives of military survival and the peace-time problems of a teetering economy were most conducive to the intrusion of public policy into areas which generated the view in government circles that it was desirable to secure some form of cooperation from the trade unions. The structure of the labour movement, and specifically the TUC's competitive position and cohesiveness, is the other factor. Critical weaknesses in its competitive position were resolved during the 1930s. Its cohesiveness, a more delicate issue, was affirmed on key issues shortly before and during the second world war. TUC representatives have since shown themselves capable of entering into a true negotiating relationship on major matters by

[21] It was therefore entirely appropriate for George Woodcock to assert, at the 100th Congress, 'We are the bargainers': *TUC Report*, 1968, p. 551.

[22] The point is confirmed, in part, by Aneurin Bevan's comment relating to the National Health Service Bill of 1946: 'In making the regulations consultation between the TUC and the Government would have to be much more frequent and in more detail than the discussions which have taken place on the general lines of the Bill itself.' *TUC Report*, 1946, p. 85.

trimming demands and accepting compromises on their own initiative. And they have been right more often than they have been wrong about what their affiliated unions will accept.

Effectiveness

The TUC's success as a pressure group, it was argued in chapter I, may be assessed at two levels. One is that of access to government office-holders (primary effectiveness). The other concerns substantive policy and administrative issues (secondary effectiveness).

As to primary effectiveness, it is a relatively simple task to tot up (roughly) the dealings between TUC representatives and government office-holders, at different times. The picture that emerges is one of a literally colossal expansion in the frequency and range of the TUC's access to government, both *ad hoc* and by way of formal consultative bodies. On the other hand, the picture becomes rather less spectacular if the varying claims and expectations of TUC leaders are taken into account. The leaders of the nineteenth century were, arguably, very much more successful than the totting-up procedure implies. By the standards of their modern counterparts, their claims to access were extremely modest and their expectations exceedingly restrained. They did not expect much more than they got. In that sense they might be regarded as highly effective.

But there are yardsticks other than expectations. Two are particularly revealing. The first is embodied in the fact that the nineteenth-century TUC leaders did not have virtually automatic access, on request, to government office-holders from the Prime Minister down. Their modern counterparts do. It is a vital difference. The second yardstick has to do with the access of employers. There is no doubt that during the TUC's first half-century, and more, major employers and the leaders of employers' groups enjoyed substantially easier access to government office-holders. One reflection of this is the striking difference between the roles accorded businessmen and union officials in the administration of the first world war. As late as 1938, Walter Citrine found it appropriate publicly to attack consultative discrimination favouring employers[23]—although he

---

[23] 'We ... have consistently, and will consistently object to the employers having any privileged position ... the trade unions must be treated in the same spirit of full access to information ... as ... the employers': *TUC Report*, 1938, p. 300.

was later to record an episode which implied that the boot, by the 1930s, was actually on the other foot.[24] During the second world war, more certainly, TUC leaders had essentially the same access to government as employers' representatives. They seem substantially to have retained that position for almost 30 postwar years. But in 1974 they became something more than equal. For the continuation of the Liaison Committee, created when Labour was in opposition, gave them alone access to the last Wilson government in a form that appears to be unique.

There can be no doubt about the great and sustained rise in the primary effectiveness of the TUC. That, in itself, probably tells us something about the TUC's secondary (policy) effectiveness, but not much. For there is no necessary correlation between primary and secondary effectiveness. Persuading government office-holders to listen is one thing; persuading them to accept what they hear is obviously a quite different matter.[25] On the other hand, access of the kind and on the scale that government has accorded the TUC is not to be had merely for the asking, but signifies mounting government recognition of the TUC as an organization of unusual political weight. It seems unlikely, in these circumstances, that there is no correlation at all between recognition in this form and recognition in the form of policy concessions.[26] Yet the nature of the correlation remains obscure; and, because of this, the TUC's primary effectiveness is of only suggestive help in

[24] 'Forbes Watson [director of the British Employers' Confederation] usually had a grumble against the Government He felt that they were keeping his organization too much at arm's length. *He envied the ease with which the TUC was received in Whitehall.* I thought to myself: "This is all wrong. Why should the employers not have the same facilities ... ?" What is more I did my best to help this along ... I remember on one occasion when Forbes and I were going to the Ministry of Labour. Just as we entered the building he turned to me and said, "We owe this to you", referring to the fact that we were both received with such facility': Citrine, *Men and Work*, p. 251 (emphasis added). Another comment on the same page of Citrine's memoirs, that government departments were 'scrupulously careful' to offer the TUC and the BEC consultative representation on equal terms, is perhaps closer to the truth.

[25] Arthur Balfour, then Prime Minister, once illustrated this point in the reasons he gave his private secretary for agreeing to meet a TUC deputation. First he could 'see a certain difficulty in refusing': second, the interview 'would give him the opportunity to say things which he intended anyway to say in the King's Speech': cited in K. D. Brown, *Labour and Unemployment*, pp. 42–3.

[26] Although V. L. Allen seems to believe that there is not: see *The Sociology of Industrial Relations*, p. 208. C. Wright Mills, on the other hand, accepts that there may be: see *The Power Elite*, pp. 263–4.

assessing its policy effectiveness. In any case, of course, the assessment faces the added complications (enumerated in chapter 1) which make it such an uncertain business.

At least it is quite clear that the raw number of the TUC's substantive claims which evoke a more or less sympathetic governmental response has tended to be greater in the later than in the earlier years of its history. But that conclusion glosses over both the difficulties outlined in chapter 1 and two fairly obvious points. One is that the raw number of rejected claims has also mounted.[27] The other is that many, and probably most, of the successful claims concern issues that are marginal to the central concerns of trade unions and their members.

The TUC virtually opened its long career with a momentous policy achievement, the Conspiracy and Protection of Property Act of 1875. This measure not only embodied the TUC's dominating objective, at that time, but also went to the heart of the unions' interests. Almost a century later, on an issue equally central to their concerns, the TUC could claim a resounding victory when it crippled the operation of the Industrial Relations Act of 1971. There is not much to distinguish these two achievements until attention is paid to the importance of each measure to the government leaders of the day. The 1875 Act did not engage the central interests of a Conservative government whose Prime Minister, while ready enough to dish the Whigs on this as an other issues, was preoccupied with different and mainly foreign matters. The 1971 Act, on the other hand, touched the most sensitive policy concerns of a Conservative government whose Prime Minister was deeply and publicly committed to the measure. Put in another way, the achievement of the 1870s involved securing the legislative support of a government only mildly interested in the issues at stake. In comparison, the achievement of the 1970s involved the much more formidable task of frustrating the

---

[27] Not all rejections, of course, are final. Often acceptance is merely postponed, though sometimes interminably. The TUC does not give up easily. The annual reports of its executive body are customarily splattered with such phrases as 'continuing to press', 'persistent efforts', 'again protested', 'continuing pressure', and 'reiterated their strong opposition'. Its most abiding major failure concerns the issue of nationalizing all land. A resolution advocating such nationalization was first adopted by the 1882 Congress. The 1973 Congress followed the example of many others, in the preceding ninety years, and reiterated the principle.

intentions of a government whose leaders had determined on new procedures for dealing with problems they regarded as among the most critical confronting them. This contrast alone provides ample purchase for the conclusion that the TUC's secondary effectiveness has increased strikingly over its lifetime —with one critical proviso. There is no steady or consistent pattern of development connecting the 1870s to the 1970s. The secular trend is one of growth, but of growth punctuated by fluctuations which are much wilder and more sporadic than those figuring in the record of the TUC's primary effectiveness.[28]

There is, similarly, no stable pattern when it comes to the myriad administrative and middle-range policy matters in relation to which success and failure are usually entangled and often obscured. It may be that the failure rate has tended to be proportionately higher in the case of claims located outside the industrial-economic-social welfare area; but even that is uncertain. As for major policy issues possessing a special importance for either the TUC or government, or both, there is something to be said for the commonplace conclusion of other pressure group studies: a determined government carries the day in the event of direct conflict on such an issue. The general strike episode of 1926 is, probably, the most dramatic illustration of this point in modern British history.[29] Nevertheless, there are two crucial qualifications in the case of the TUC. First, it was unquestionably the victor in an equally significant encounter, its campaign to disable the Industrial Relations Act of 1971.[30] Second, government has gone out of its way more than once to offer *quid pro quos* in order to ensure

---

[28] This is probably to be expected given that, in comparison with access claims, the potential range and variety of policy claims are infinitely greater, and the resolution of such claims tends to be less conclusive. The danger in trying to discern a steady long-term trend is illustrated by the conclusion one writer reached about the period 1868–1921. It 'is clear that [the TUC] exercised an important and growing influence on Government policy': B. C. Roberts, *The Trades Union Congress, 1868–1921*, p. 360. This is not an unreasonable summation of the years 1868–1910 (at least as far as 'growing influence' is concerned); but as an overview from the standpoint of 1921, it totally ignores the deep slump that occurred in the TUC's influence during the last decade of the period.

[29] More recent illustrations are government resort to compulsory wage restraint in 1966–9 (Labour) and 1972 (Conservative), and the enactment, as distinct from the enforcement, of the Industrial Relations Act of 1971.

[30] Its successful campaign against the Labour government's proposed Industrial Relations Bill in 1969 is another, if less clearcut, case in point.

the TUC's support for major policies whose reception was otherwise doubtful.[31] The TUC, in short, has come to be treated by government as if it were a force to be reckoned with in relation to virtually all matters in which it declares an interest. It has been accorded the status of a very superior veto group.

Changes in the character of public policy and in the structure of the labour movement seem largely responsible for the rise in both the primary and the secondary effectiveness of the TUC. The extensions of public policy have diversified and strengthened the forms of pressure available, or presumptively available, to it. The structural changes have resulted in its emergence as principal union spokesman after a period of intense competition for the role. On the other hand, its competitive position within the structure of the pressure group system at large has contributed heavily to its failures on policy issues, because its claims have almost invariably been opposed by influential organized groups, especially those representing employers.[32] For this reason, above all, the TUC may well tend to be much less effective, in terms of the extent to which it realizes its *policy* goals, than other less obtrusive groups with more specialized aims and no, or weak, opposing interests.

THE QUESTION OF AUTHORITY

A political role of widening scope and increasing, though still fluctuating, weight: this is the pattern traced so far. Underlying it, partly as cause and partly as consequence, is a political authority that is greatly enlarged in relation both to the trade

[31] Examples are the employment exchanges and the unemployment insurance scheme, before the first world war; the labour control and strike-banning policies of the second world war; and the 'social contract' of 1974.

[32] Thus ministers of all political colours have shown a distinct preference for 'agreed' legislation on issues of particular interest to the TUC. Not that they have invariably clung to the principle; but they have often used the absence of agreement to justify inaction on matters pressed by the TUC—though usually in a more oblique fashion than the minister who rejected a TUC proposal on the ground that it 'would range employers and doctors against' the health insurance scheme: *TUC Report*, 1931, p. 154. The influence, and importance, of employer group opposition was, for example, of great moment in the years immediately preceding the second world war. It was apparently the major reason why government leaders failed to follow up preliminary talks with the TUC about the Defence White Paper of 1936, discontinued the war-preparation discussions initiated by the Prime Minister in March 1938, and temporarily abandoned the Minister of Labour's pre-war proposal of a National Joint Advisory Council.

unions (internal authority) and to government office-holders (external authority). A brief survey of the three dimensions of that authority (exclusiveness, control and importance) substantiates this.

Internal Authority

Exclusiveness, as defined in chapter 1, refers to the extent to which the TUC is able to monopolize the communication of union claims to government. The TUC has achieved an effective monopoly in relation to policy issues of concern to the unions at large. It has also come to control the communication of many, perhaps the greater part, of those sectional union issues requiring government action.

Particular unions have at different times questioned, qualified or denied the TUC's intermediary role on issues of sectional concern: the coal and cotton unions in the nineteenth century and the engineering unions during the first world war are weighty examples. Since the early 1930s, however, there has been a massive growth in the volume of such issues which unions have channelled through the TUC. Union leaders, since the early 1920s at least, have displayed even fewer hesitations about placing the carriage of general claims in the TUC's hands.[33] It is, of course, precisely the issues of general union concern which have been the subject of competition from other inter-union bodies. All of these challenges were beaten off—though in the case of the most pressing, from the Labour party, not until the 1930s.[34]

[33] Citrine's comment to the 1940 Congress, if a little arch, illuminates the importance of the distinction between general and sectional claims. 'The Trades Union Congress . . . can only deal with those questions which are common to the Unions as a whole. We cannot deal with questions of domestic policy . . . in a particular industry If we tried to deal with these problems except at the specific request of the Unions concerned we should very soon be told to mind our own business.' *TUC Report*, 1940, pp. 230–1. It is true that there are many general issues on which the TUC has been technically by-passed—but almost invariably, in recent times, by totally inconsequential procedures as a Prime Minister's comment to Congress suggests: 'I frequently receive letters and resolutions from unions affiliated to Congress, asking . . . that Britain's influence . . . be thrown behind some great issue in world affairs'. ibid., 1966, p. 394.

[34] The resulting *modus vivendi* was stated, much later, by a party stalwart who would certainly have wished it otherwise: 'in its relations with the Government of the day the TUC is not obliged to act through Labour Party channels, nor is it bound to accept the judgement of the Labour Party on industrial questions, or even on political matters which have economic implications'. Herbert Morrison, *Government and Parliament*, p. 145. In actuality, the TUC has successfully asserted the right to act as chief trade union spokesman even in 'political matters' lacking obvious 'economic implications'.

Control refers to the TUC leadership's ability to select the claims it submits to government, and to determine the means by which and the form in which they are communicated. Selection is critical. For a long time the TUC leaders simply acted as a pipeline for each and every Congress resolution concerned with government action; and, officially, they had little hand in bringing the issues involved before Congress. This changed from the mid-1920s under the influence of a Bevin, a Citrine and, crucially, a burgeoning full-time staff. The leadership came to play the major part in initiating and formulating major policies adopted by Congress. It also came to discriminate between Congress resolutions, to the extent of deciding that some were not worth pursuing with government. It even came, increasingly, to negotiate highly sensitive issues with government in the absence of prior authorization from Congress.

From about the same time, the mid-1920s, TUC leaders also became more selective about the means of communication they used. Congress resolutions were no longer automatically directed to ministers. Instead, ministerial deputations were reserved for particularly important resolutions, and other major claims. Lesser Congress resolutions were handled by way of correspondence or direct dealings at the departmental level.

Much earlier, there was a similar change in the TUC leadership's ability to determine the form in which major claims were presented to government. This was accomplished once, from the late 1890s, TUC deputations came to consist at least overwhelmingly, and usually wholly, of members of the Parliamentary Committee and then the General Council. The trend was reinforced, from the early 1930s, when TUC affiliates tacitly accepted that representation on major consultative bodies might be confined to General Council members.

Importance refers to the significance trade union leaders attach to the TUC's political activities, as indicated above all by the extent to which those activities touch vital policy concerns of the unions. This dimension of the TUC's internal authority was subject to wild fluctuations during the 70 years before the second world war, including three particularly dramatic peaks in the 1870s, the 1900s and the 1920s, each followed by a notable trough. Comparatively speaking, the troughs

that punctuated the three decades after the peak of the second
world war were quite shallow. The 1970s, moreover, witnessed
new highpoints resulting from the TUC's involvement with,
first, the Heath government's industrial legislation and, then,
the Wilson government's 'social contract'.

External Authority

Exclusiveness, in this case, refers to the extent to which government office-holders have been ready to confine their union-
dealings to the TUC. The issue was in doubt until the 1930s.
Since then, irrespective of political colour, governments have
evinced a pronounced preference for channelling their relations
with the unions through the TUC.[35]

Control here refers particularly to the readiness of government office-holders both to meet TUC spokesmen on request
and to initiate such meetings themselves. From the start,
ministers and parliamentarians in general usually acceded to
TUC requests for interviews, although refusals (and evasions)
were far from uncommon. Ministers, at least, hardly ever
initiated meetings before the turn of the century. Then, for a
time, a new pattern was set by leading Liberals, first in opposition and then in government, when they sought out the TUC
on a number of occasions. It was, however, largely by-passed
by similar ministerial initiatives during the first world war.
Such initiatives, with a partial exception in the events preceding
the 1926 general strike, did not again become an element in its
relations with government until the mid-1930s. In the meantime, there were occasional ministerial refusals (both Labour
and non-Labour) to see TUC spokesmen. Refusals have been
extremely rare since 1940. More significant, the initiation of
dealings by ministers and, above all, by prime ministers has
become progressively less unusual. The growth in the TUC's
control is also indicated by the fact that its claims for the
creation of, and admission to, standing consultative bodies
have been very largely satisfied.

[35] Thus, in the early 1960s 'plans for a white-collar confederation were far
advanced. They were abandoned when the government made it clear that they
would not recognize the proposed body on the same terms as the TUC, or allow
it separate representation on joint union-government consultative and planning
bodies': Clegg, *Trade Unionism under Collective Bargaining*, p. 36.

Importance, the significance government office-holders attach to the TUC connection, is indicated (as specified in chapter 1) by the character of government policy concerns, the range of issues on which face-to-face dealings occur, the status of the office-holders concerned and the extent to which serious bargaining is involved. The changes in these four factors—especially since the first world war and, above all, since the second world war—suggest an enormously enhanced importance. In this time, industrial and economic issues, the focus of the TUC's attention, have become central to the concerns of government as well. Secondly, the TUC effectively determines the range of matters on which it is consulted by government office-holders; their dealings, in other words, exclude only those policy areas that it does not care to take up.[36] Third, the TUC's routine dealings with government have come to include not merely the most senior ministers but also the Prime Minister. Finally, genuine negotiation, if not altogether absent before then, emerged as a recurring, though irregular, element in TUC–government relations from the late 1930s.

Political Authority

Popular estimations of the TUC's political authority tend to exaggerate it. Francis Williams's comment still holds good: 'so influential has the General Council of the TUC become in the public mind that the limits of its authority are often overlooked'.[37] Among more knowledgeable observers, on the other hand, there has been a contrary tendency to *under*-estimate the TUC's political authority, if only in the sense of stressing its weaknesses while ignoring its strengths. An over-concentration on the TUC's performance in connection with pre-1974 incomes policies has been largely responsible for this.

Two misconceptions seem usually to be involved. One concerns the nature of the wages issue. To write (in 1972) of 'the progressive diminution of TUC authority to deal with issues, *like the wages issue*, which are of vital importance to the con-

---

[36] Thus the breathtaking claim of a TUC president, Lord Allen: 'In a highly industrialized and economically vulnerable society, *no decision* can be taken by Government without first heaiing and heeding the voice of the organized trade union Movement'. *TUC Report*, 1974, p. 335. Emphasis added.

[37] Williams, *Magnificent Journey*, p. 405.

stituent unions',[38] is to imply that the wages issue is typical of a whole range of issues. It is not. It is (with the one exception of their legal freedom of action) of pre-eminent importance to the unions, the issue in relation to which they are most jealous of their independence. Accordingly, any move by the TUC to restrain them in this respect puts its internal authority to an exceptionally severe test.[39] Government leaders have been well aware of this.[40]

The second misconception involves the assumption that a lack of authority on the wages issue necessarily undermines the TUC's authority on lesser issues. And so the conclusion that the TUC's difficulties in the wage restraint controversy of the mid-1960s 'have gradually eroded [its] ability . . . to participate effectively in producer group politics'—in short, from the standpoint of 1972, it 'has become less rather than more influential'.[41] But wages policy is a very special case, and there is no evidence that the TUC's falterings in that connection have significantly affected its standing on other issues. On a vast range of lesser matters, that is to say, the unions continued to accept its legitimacy as their spokesman and government leaders continued to treat it with every outward sign of respect.

During 1974–6, in any case, the TUC demonstrated convincingly that on occasions its political authority could extend, formidably, even to the delicate issue of wage restraint.[42] The

[38] Dorfman, *Wage Politics in Britain, 1945–1967*, p. 156. Emphasis added.

[39] The TUC leadership's recognition of this is reflected in the extent to which it has convened conferences of trade union executive bodies when it was disposed to support the wage restraint policies of Labour governments. The singularity of this device is indicated by the fact that the conference of executives held in April 1965, to consider wage restraint proposals negotiated with the Wilson government, was the first convened by the TUC since those held on the same issue during the lifetime of the Attlee government.

[40] As the TUC leadership acknowledged, for example, when it admitted that it aimed to 'reinforce the General Council's bargaining position with the Government by securing the explicit support of affiliated unions, through the conference of executives, for the [economic, including incomes] policies the General Council were advocating': *TUC Report*, 1969, p. 420.

[41] Dorfman, op. cit., pp. 145–6.

[42] There is, of course, an echo in this episode of the TUC's role in relation to the Attlee government's wages policy during 1948–50. But there are important differences. On the side of the unions, the TUC was not able to hold them in line with the policy as tightly in the earlier period as it did in the later. On the side of government, the Attlee government had not negotiated the terms of its policy beforehand with the TUC. Nor was there anything like the accompanying affirmation of a special relationship which the Liaison Committee represented in the case of the Wilson government.

Wilson government's concessions in exchange for the 'social contract', and the TUC's ability to hold the unions substantially behind the contract, all bore witness to that.[43] But it is not necessary to rely on such an extreme example in order to justify the proposition that the TUC's political authority has grown notably during its lifetime.[44] That growth has been the principal thread running through the pages of this book. It is reflected, above all, in the contrast between a nineteenth-century Parliamentary Committee, which functioned as Congress's message-boy and had trouble seeing backbench MPs, and a twentieth-century General Council which formulates TUC policy and has ready access to prime ministers.[45]

---

[43] Government leaders had plainly absorbed the conclusion Hugh Clegg had drawn, and publicized, from the experience of the 1960s—'for an incomes policy to work, its sponsors must win the consent of the Confederation of British Industry and the Trades Union Congress': Clegg, *How to Run an Incomes Policy*, p. 50. As far as the TUC leadership is concerned, the contrast between the late 1960s and the mid-seventies in this respect is brought out, perhaps as clearly as it can be, in the quite different tone of two statements, six years apart, both concerning the General Council's support for wage restraint policies. In 1968 George Woodcock explained with elaborate caution that the TUC wished to be notified by the unions of all wage claims, not because 'when you come to us you will find us in a position to tell you exactly what you must do', but because 'we do want to be in a position . . . to use our weight and our ability, our reasoning, to seek to persuade you . . . to allow you to be subject to our influence and hope that it will have some effect': *TUC Report*, 1968, p. 552. In 1974 Len Murray, explaining a similar request, took a notably stronger and more confident line. 'We cannot instruct, but we can advise, and if necessary our advice will be very pointed': ibid., 1974, p. 423.

[44] V. L. Allen effectively denies the proposition, though subject to two hedging adverbs. 'After 100 years, the power situation of the TUC has basically remained almost unchanged': *The Sociology of Industrial Relations*, p. 206. (The term 'power situation' applies to both internal and external authority, as is evident from a careful reading of the context of this sentence: see also, ibid., p. 208.) Certainly, the TUC 'basically' remains as it began—a confederation, whose freedom of action is limited by the wishes of powerful constituents; and a suppliant to government whose claims must run the gauntlet of influential opposing interests. But to regard change as insignificant, unless it involves altering fundamental features of this kind, is to adopt a conception of noteworthy historical change which is far too blunt for my taste. This book has been written on the assumption that there is interest, and importance, in changes which are less than revolutionary.

[45] The contrast is, of course, brutally sharpened not only by the 'social contract' episode, but also by the TUC's role in the successful boycott of the Industrial Relations Act of 1971—a boycott, moreover, that is conceivable as a TUC-managed action at virtually any time from at least the second world war, given a Conservative government as unusually intent as the Heath government on honouring, *in that particular form*, union-curbing election promises. Another notable, if less remarked, illustration of the contrast is the ease with which the TUC in 1974 tossed the London Trades Council, its formidable adversary of a century earlier, into the ash-can of history with its decision to disband the council.

SOME IMPLICATIONS

The TUC's political career can scarcely be described as typical. For one thing it is the career of a pressure group whose position has been profoundly affected by its constituents' access to a virtually unique sanction, the strike. Secondly, there is the distinctive scope of the TUC's policy concerns: relatively broad from the start, in contemporary terms, they have come to encompass a range so expansive as to resemble more nearly the concerns of a political party than those of a normal pressure group. Finally, in achieving its present eminence, the TUC has probably surmounted greater obstacles than any comparable British pressure group. Its story is in the true rags-to-riches mould. There are the unmistakably humble beginnings: the limited expectations of spokesmen acutely aware that they stood on the rim of society and politics—lacking the respectability of employers' associations, let alone anything like the prestige flowing from, say, the 'services rendered' by ex-servicemen or the 'deep mystery' of the medical profession.[46] There is the long struggle in the face of unionist doubters, patronising middle-class advisers, off-handed government office-holders, opposing interests like employers and fraternal competitors like the Labour party. There are the disheartening lapses in fortune, as in the decade from 1910, and the shattering reverses, as in 1926. But, eventually, there is the triumphant emergence as one of the indisputably weighty components of the British political system, with leaders who dwell at 'a rather Olympian level' in the eyes of union colleagues,[47] are courted by prime ministers, and may aspire to the social cachet of a peerage.[48]

Nevertheless, while lacking typicality in these respects, the TUC's career does have implications which go beyond the particular case. Thus it supports Eckstein's estimation of the importance of structure, policy, social attitudes and group attributes as determinants of pressure-group activity. It is also

[46] Wootton, *The Politics of Influence*, p. 254; Eckstein, *Pressure Group Politics*, p. 70.
[47] Turner, *Trade Union Growth, Structure and Policy*, p. 283.
[48] The president of the 100th annual Congress was Lord Wright, the vice-president Lord Collison. The retiring General Council also included Lord Carron and Lord Cooper. Compare this with the reported social aspirations of late nineteenth-century trade union officials. 'The majority of them are aiming at the dignity of the J.P., or the more solid preferment of the factory inspectorship': Beatrice Webb, *Our Partnership*, p. 24.

suggestive of some other things with a bearing on the nature of pressure group politics in particular, and the character of the British political system in general.

The Importance of Inter-group Cooperation

Walter Citrine once wrote of the 'unceasing conflict of organized groups within society'.[49] This is a conception which has rightly been emphasized by students of pressure group politics. But unlike some of the students, Citrine was manifestly aware that 'unceasing conflict' does not necessarily preclude cooperation. His earlier enthusiasm for the Mond-Turner talks is indicative of this. And later, by his own account, he helped the director of the British Employers' Confederation gain readier access to Whitehall because 'I sensed that there would be many occasions upon which it would be as well if the Government knew there was an identity of view between our organizations, although our representations might be made separately'.[50] The collaboration he foresaw was subsequently evident on a number of issues.[51] Eventually, in 1967, it flowered into a standing joint committee with the Confederation of British Industry.[52] The committee, which operated in a very public way, was an early casualty of TUC–CBI differences over the Conservatives' Industrial Relations Bill three years later. In 1972, however, the connection was revived in the form of more private but fairly regular meetings, basically between the representatives ('the Neddy six') of each body on the National Economic Development Council.

The point here is that opposing groups learn to do business with each other rather than relying entirely on government to sort out their competing claims.[53] In particular, they come to

---

[49] Citrine, 'Labour and the Community', in Percy Redfern (ed.), *Self and Society: The First Twelve Essays*, p. 31.

[50] Citrine, *Men and Work*, p. 251.

[51] Sometimes it was emphasized at the expense of government. For example, in 1964 when the Ministry of Labour suggested a tripartite meeting to consider certain proposals concerning the investigation of unofficial strikes, the British Employers' Confederation said it would prefer a discussion with the TUC alone; the ministry acceded: *TUC Report*, 1964, p. 150.

[52] Similar joint committees, as we have seen, were formed with the British Medical Association in 1937 and the British Legion in 1946.

[53] But it is to be emphasized that the TUC's relations with the CBI, and its predecessors, have never involved (see Grant and Marsh, op. cit., pp. 147–52) the tightly negotiated tripartite agreements with government, on key economic issues, which would seem to be required to fit the notion of 'corporatism'—though the

accept the advantage, where possible, of pressing joint claims on government.[54]

The Importance of Formal Consultative Bodies

TUC leaders, especially since the 1920s, have shown a decided preference for channelling their dealings with government through formal consultative bodies. They have pressed vigorously for the formation of such bodies, or for their admission to operative ones, in most policy areas of interest to them; and almost invariably they have accepted government initiatives along these lines with alacrity.[55]

The advantages involved, while clear enough in the case of bodies with specific administrative powers, are less obvious in the case of purely advisory ones. In principle, there is no reason why *ad hoc* consultation, subject to its being granted on request and as requested, should not be just as useful or useless in

---

literature which has recently restored that term to prominence is somewhat confusing on this point, as on others: see, e.g., Schmitter, 'Still the Century of Corporatism?', *The Review of Politics*, vol. 36, January 1974, pp. 85–131; Panitch, 'The Development of Corporatism in Liberal Democracies', *Comparative Political Studies*, vol. 10, April 1977, pp. 61–90; Lehmbruch, 'Liberal Corporatism and Party Government', *Comparative Political Studies*, vol. 10, April 1977, pp. 91–126; and Cawson, 'Pluralism, Corporatism and the Role of the State', *Government and Opposition*, vol. 13, Spring, 1978, pp. 178–98.

[54] It does not follow from this that Kwavnick is right when he argues that 'the real struggle of group politics' is not between 'groups representing opposing interests', but between 'rival groups attempting to represent the same interest': *Organized Labour and Pressure Politics*, p. 19. It is certainly true that the most serious threats to the TUC's hegemony have come from inside, not outside, the labour movement—and above all from the Labour party. But that is in the past. Moreover, the cooperative relationship between the TUC and the CBI has by no means obviated serious policy differences between them. Kwavnick's proposition may well hold in the Canadian case that is his focus (though he states the proposition in general terms); but the TUC's circumstances are a world apart from those of the Canadian Labour Congress.

[55] Very occasionally, they have hesitated. The Conservatives' proposed National Economic Development Council, which eventuated in 1962, is the major case. It was presented as something in the nature of a *quid pro quo* for the government's 'pay pause' policy in 1961. Union leaders in general were intensely hostile to the policy and suspicious of the government's stated intentions. The TUC leaders, emphasizing that 'we . . . are not interested in any advisory body which is divorced from the centre of power' (*TUC Report*, 1961, p. 376), sought and obtained government undertakings about the nature, procedures and standing of the NEDC. Just the same, they did not agree to join it until after the government announced its abandonment of the 'pay pause'. The importance they attach to the NEDC in particular (despite its proclaimed shortcomings from time to time), and to this kind of formalization in general, is suggested by their insistence in 1972 that discussions sought by the Prime Minister on incomes and prices policy should be conducted within the NEDC rather than, as he wanted, on a more informal basis outside it.

achieving the TUC's policy aims.[56] But, then, policy outcomes are not the only criterion.

Membership of advisory bodies is valued because it signifies, or is taken to signify, 'privileged access' to the government office-holders concerned[57]—especially when it excludes other groups representing the same interest or sections of it, as in the case of the TUC's affiliated unions. Such access buttresses a group's internal authority.[58] Membership of advisory bodies also tends to enhance the wider public prestige of pressure groups.[59] It 'indicates publicly that [they] are regarded as rightful bodies to advise government';[60] and gives a ring of stability and regularity to their relations with government which is less readily conveyed, at least to outsiders, by *ad hoc* dealings.[61]

The consultative ideal for a pressure group involves something more. It involves a situation in which there is assured access to government office-holders whose decision-making competence encloses all the group's principal policy interests, and whose relations with other groups are relatively distant or non-existent. In practice, the achievement of such a special client relationship requires a group which at once lacks a ' "natural" opposition group'[62] and possesses policy aims limited enough in

[56] Certainly, representation on a formal advisory body in itself gives no assurance of policy effectiveness, as suggested by comments on some major ones involving the TUC. The second Labour government's Economic Advisory Council 'quickly degenerated into futility', largely because the Prime Minister 'seldom paid any attention to its advice': Milne-Bailey, *Trade Unions and the State*, p. 351. The wartime Central Joint Advisory Committee to the Production Executive of Cabinet and its replacement, the National Production Advisory Council, both 'failed' because of the 'determination of the responsible officials and ministers to exercise an untrammelled authority': Scott and Hughes, *The Administration of War Production*, p. 470. The National Economic Development Council was condemned by the TUC leadership for 'no longer . . . fulfilling its original function' but, instead, functioning 'more as a sounding board for [Wilson] Government policies': *TUC Report*, 1968, p. 374.

[57] Truman, *The Governmental Process*, p. 459.

[58] Hence the TUC leadership's policy of confining nominations to its own ranks in the case of general bodies, and its obvious interest in exercising the nominating function in relation to representatives of sectional union groupings.

[59] It has been remarked that bodies with 'general advisory functions' are, on the whole, 'unprofitable' because they tend to do little more than rubber-stamp reports: Vernon and Mansergh, *Advisory Bodies*, p. 436. Nevertheless, if the TUC leadership's behaviour is any guide, it is the generalist rather than the specialist advisory body which (especially if it operates at the ministerial level) is regarded as the more impressive status symbol.

[60] Stewart, op. cit., p. 8.

[61] Not that modern TUC leaders, as is perfectly evident from their annual reports, display any disposition to neglect the prestigeous aspects of *ad hoc* meetings with ministers.

[62] Wootton, op. cit., p. 255.

range to be catered for, in the main, by a single ministry.[63] Both requirements are beyond the modern TUC—although the second was not in the TUC's early years when its concerns were much more limited than they have since become, and those of the Home Office were more varied. The change in this respect has been a function not only of the expansion in the TUC's policy interests, but also of the increasing diversity of government's administrative structure.[64]

On the other hand, it is arguable that the TUC was involved in a special client relationship of a most exceptional kind under the last Wilson government—in that it could be regarded as achieving such a relationship, not with a single ministry, but with the government at large. The Liaison Committee provided the main operational link. It also provided the symbol of a highly unusual relationship by reason of its composition, the frequency and regularity of its meetings, the weighty nature of the issues dealt with, and the manner in which they were handled. The Liaison Committee appears to be unique in British politics. It is, at the same time, part of a pattern in that

[63] The British Medical Association and the National Farmers' Union, for example, each have the advantage of a special client relationship: see Eckstein, *Pressure Group Politics*, pp. 38, 52, 110–11.; Self and Storing, op. cit., pp. 78, 232. Trade union leaders are aware of the advantages of such a relationship, as George Howell long ago suggested with his reference to 'the usual timidity of a Government department in dealing with the vast vested interests more or less committed to its care': Howell, *Labour Legislation*, 2nd ed., vol. II, p. 267. One or two individual unions have been able to establish something approaching such a relationship—as illustrated in the way the Mines Department and the Ministry of Agriculture, at the instance of the unions concerned and against the announced policy of the TUC, pressed the Ministry of Food for extra rations for miners and farm workers during the second world war.

[64] By the time of the first world war, as we have seen, so-called 'labour matters' were apportioned among a number of ministries. To Ben Tillett, this 'meant confusion and overlapping', and he preferred to have 'Labour recognized by one direct head of Cabinet rank': *TUC Report*, 1908, p. 154. Lloyd George created the Ministry of Labour eight years later (though the minister was not admitted to cabinet until 1919), but its policy range did not encompass, even then, the TUC's principal interests. The gap in this respect has widened as the TUC's concerns have expanded. Hence the TUC's consistent rejection of ministerial suggestions, especially prevalent after the great expansion in the Ministry of Labour's scope during the second world war, that it channel its dealings with government through that ministry. In any case, a special client relationship with the Ministry of Labour, in the strict sense, has been ruled out by the ministry's broadly equivalent respect for employers' views. Thus there is no parallel with the Canadian experience recorded by David Kwavnick, in which 'the relationship which develops between the minister of labour and the [Canadian Labour] Congress leadership makes him their spokesman in the cabinet and in relations with other ministers. He is "their man" and can be approached on many matters which do not fall within his jurisdiction': Kwavnick, op. cit., p. 140.

it reflects the TUC leadership's longstanding preference for a relationship with government which is institutionalized by way of formal consultative bodies.

The Importance of 'Responsibility'

The TUC's fervent advocacy of formalized consultative procedures gives colour to the first part of Eckstein's proposition that 'the British . . . behave like ideologists in regard to rules and like pragmatists in regard to policies'.[65] Its career also supports the second part of the proposition in so far as pragmatism is akin to what Max Weber once described as the 'ethic of responsibility'.[66] A readiness to negotiate and, above all, to compromise on policy issues is a critical element of that ethic.

Critics to the left have perennially spied danger in consultative links between trade unions and government.[67] As one puts it, 'the modern technique of enmeshing labour in a net of advisory and administrative bodies' is a means of 'taming the labour movement'.[68] These critics have a point; although it is not quite as devastating as they imagine. Of course government leaders would like to 'tame' the TUC and perceive close consultative relations as, among other things, a means of approaching this aim.[69] It would be astonishing if they did not. It would be equally remarkable if a close relationship did not make TUC leaders more understanding of the government's position and, sometimes at least, more receptive than they would otherwise have been to its policies or to compromises which leant towards its position.[70] But there is no reason to

[65] *A Theory of Stable Democracy*, pp. 30–1.
[66] H. H. Gerth and C. Wright Mills, *From Max Weber: Essays in Sociology*, p. 121.
[67] They prefer a more remote relationship in the belief that it better preserves the ideological purity and the political purpose of organizations assumed to be intrinsically opposed to capitalism and, therefore, to governments presiding over mixed economies. The ideal from this viewpoint, so far as a trade union peak organization like the TUC is concerned, appears to be something like a 'radical pressure group' which seeks fundamental changes in the political system, shuns virtually all direct dealings with government, and draws attention to its aims primarily by way of demonstrations, general strikes and, possibly, violence: Willey, 'Pressure Group Politics: The Case of SOHYO', *Western Political Quarterly*, vol. 17, December 1964, p. 723.
[68] E. J. Hobsbawm, *Labouring Men*, p. 338.
[69] An involved civil servant's diary comment on Lloyd George's discussions with labour leaders in 1911 puts this intent in a nutshell. 'Chancellor's business, of course, is to keep them quiet': Braithwaite, op. cit., p. 189.
[70] Thus Walter Citrine, referring to private meetings he had with Chamberlain and with Churchill before and during the war, effectively acknowledged the influence on him of prime ministerial confidences and implied that the TUC's

suppose, *a priori*, that the policy benefits of such a relationship run the government's way only.[71] In the case of the TUC, it is clear that they have not.

In general, a close consultative relationship (given its primary dependence on government perceptions) implies some governmental respect for the group concerned and a willingness at least to contemplate substantive policy concessions to it.[72] Such a relationship is likely to be proffered only to a group with political resources of some substance. It is also more likely to be forthcoming, and its intimacy to be heightened, if the group's leaders seem capable of being swayed in their official opinions, if not converted from them. Thus, in 1935 Baldwin consulted Citrine on the rearmament issue in preference to the leaders of the parliamentary Labour party: he did so, it is clear, because he perceived, in the case of the TUC's leaders but not in the case of the party's, the possibility of modifying their position on the issue. What is involved here is the image of 'responsi-

---

policy stance was, as a result, less remote from the government's than would otherwise have been the case. 'The confidential information I received on such occasions was of the utmost value to me in trying to guide the policy of the Trades Union Congress . . . I always tried, in the light of my knowledge, to look at our problems objectively': Citrine, *Men and Work*, p. 367.

[71] Apart from policy outcomes, of course, a close consultative relationship has a value for TUC leaders on the assumption that it enhances (or they believe that it does) their standing among the unions. Thus Citrine's intention of impressing his audience is evident from the terms in which he told the 1938 Congress about the General Council's pathbreaking meeting with Chamberlain on rearmament. 'The Prime Minister made to us a confidential statement . . . He said to us that . . . because he wished to let the General Council understand exactly how the Government viewed the situation, he wanted to speak to them with a maximum of intimacy . . . The statement that the Prime Minister made to the General Council was very intimate': *TUC Report*, 1938, p. 296. At the lower level of the administration of wartime food rationing, there was no need for the importance of a close relationship to be spelt out to the unions. First, the Ministry of Food's policy on supplementary rations was in line with the views of the TUC, which had vigorously opposed re-introducing the first world war practice of providing supplementary rations on the ground of heavy work alone. Secondly, the ministry normally declined to consider union claims for supplementary rations unless they had been forwarded through the TUC's vetting machinery.

[72] And it facilitates presentation of the group's case. Citrine, plainly not a man prepared to play Boswell to a Prime Minister's Johnson, was thus provided with exceptional opportunities for putting the TUC's views on great issues by virtue of his private conversations with Chamberlain and Churchill (see footnote 70). Whether he ever actually influenced their thinking on a specific issue is unknowable, but he was certainly in an unusually favourable position to do so. The favourable outcome of a close relationship is clearer at the more humdrum level of wartime food rationing, in the administration of which the TUC played an intimate and important role (see preceding footnote). As a result, the Ministry of Food conceded, if sometimes with great reluctance, *any* union claim for supplementary rations which was endorsed by the TUC's representatives: see Hammond, *Food*, vol. 2, pp. 609, 623.

bility' which the TUC leadership projected once the dust of the 1926 general strike had settled.[73] And it gained, in this respect, from the contrast with the more dogmatic, 'principled' position with which the Labour party leadership was associated for most of the 1930s, especially on defence issues.

The TUC leadership has continued, on the whole, to project the image of 'steady, sober, British opinion' which a Congress president once evoked.[74] One element has been acceptance of the existing political system. This is symbolized in the alacrity with which (Ernest Bevin, most notably, apart) royal honours have usually been accepted;[75] and, more importantly, in the explicit rejection (after 1926) of the 'political strike'.[76] Another element was the tendency to disavow a sectional or class-

---

[73] Clive Jenkins has expressed this feature in slightly different terms, but his dating is the same. 'Since the Mond-Turner talks at the end of the 1920s, this current of accommodation has been visible': in Blackburn and Cockburn (eds.), *The Incompatibles*, p. 228. The change involved, especially in comparison with the early 1920s, was described by Citrine in his valedictory address to Congress. 'There was a time when it was essential . . . for denunciation to be the characteristic note of the speeches made . . . to . . . Congress . . . But . . . now the delegates listen rather more carefully to what a delegate says than to how he says it . . . We have passed from the era of propaganda to one of responsibility . . . Our claim to consultation . . . has now been acceded to': *TUC Report*, 1946, pp. 268–9. Citrine's point had been made, if in a more abstract and much more elegant fashion, many years earlier by Robert Michels. 'The commercial traveller in the class struggle is replaced by the strict and prosaic bureaucrat, the fervent idealist by the cold materialist . . . Oratorical activity passes into the background, for administrative aptitudes are now of the first importance. Consequently, in this new period, while the leadership of the movement is less noisy, less brilliant, and less glorious, it is of a far more solid character, established upon a much sounder practical competence': Michels, *Political Parties*, pp. 316–7.

[74] *TUC Report*, 1950, p. 354.

[75] A resolution regretting that 'active leaders of the Trade Union Movement should accept honours' was easily defeated at the Congress held after Citrine accepted a knighthood: *TUC Report*, 1935, p. 426. The absorptive capacity of the political system, in this respect, is further illustrated in the autobiography (*My Life of Revolt*) of David Kirkwood, fiery wartime leader of the Clydeside shop stewards. After a long parliamentary career, this erstwhile revolutionary—a sensitive soul with a remarkable literary talent—died an admirer of the House of Commons, and a baron.

[76] Thus in 1952 the General Council firmly turned its face against 'suggestions that political opposition to the Government and its policy should be reinforced by industrial action': *TUC Report*, 1952, p. 90. Five years later, after the council had rejected two proposals 'to use industrial action to attain a political objective' (ibid., 1957, p. 292)—in relation to the Suez adventure and to legislation decontrolling rents—the point was elaborated in Sir Thomas Williamson's presidential address. 'As a Movement we renounce any challenge to the sovereignty of Parliament. If we dislike a Government . . . we resist the temptation to dislodge it by industrial action. In a democracy, trade unionists, like all other citizens, have political rights. But we cannot and ought not to claim political privileges because we are trade unionists': ibid., 1957, p. 77. This principle, it is to be noted, was not infringed by the TUC's boycott of the Industrial Relations Act of 1971.

oriented motivation.[77] A third was the TUC leadership's expressed readiness to deal with all governments, irrespective of their policies or political colour.[78] Above all, there has been its essentially pragmatic approach, based on limited aims[79] and a belief in the necessity of compromise.[80]

[77] This is a longstanding feature of the TUC's public posture. At one end of the chronology, there is Broadhurst's claim, in relation to the TUC-supported criminal law reforms of the 1880s, that they were 'by no means a solitary example of the way in which the efforts of the Parliamentary Committee were exerted, not merely for the working classes, but on behalf of the community at large': Broadhurst, *Henry Broadhurst, M.P.*, p. 77. At another end, there is the 'one point' that Citrine asked Congress to remember. 'The Trades Union Congress is not merely the custodian of the interests of its unions; it is also . . . a forum of public opinion. It is a body which in the essence of its creation and existence has obligations to the general community as such': *TUC Report*, 1938, p. 301. And, in the same vein, there is the assertion that 'no other body was . . . better qualified to submit nominations of men and women who could represent the point of view of the general public' on regional hospital boards: ibid., 1956, p. 131. A powerful general secretary of the Transport and General Workers' Union, Jack Jones, much later pinpointed the central issue in the most direct terms: 'the union I lead and myself personally have never supported the idea that trade unionism is a licence for any group to look after themselves and to hell with the rest': ibid., 1975, p. 460.

[78] This, as we have seen, is a point that has often been made. One critical occasion, on which it was asserted by a Congress majority of almost two-to-one, involved the issue of whether some members of the General Council should have accepted appointment as members of the board which the last Churchill government set up to regulate the iron and steel industry following its denationalization. Sir Lincoln Evans, one of the members concerned, made the point in one way. 'The essence of the question is this: can the Trade Union Movement . . . accept responsibility and discharge it only when there is a Labour Government in power, and refuse to discharge it when any other Government is in power? . . . The TUC has never qualified the demand for trade union representation on public boards with any reservations at all as to whether it should be a Labour Government or whether it should be any other Government': *TUC Report*, 1953, pp. 416–7. This attitude extended to a feeling, which persisted for most of the 1950s, that it was 'unwise and unnecessary' publicly to attack Conservative governments of the day; and among some members of the General Council there was a distinct sense of 'regret' when this position was abandoned: Len Murray (then head of the TUC's Economic and Research Department), personal interview, 15 May 1959. It is noteworthy, too, that during the long struggle over the Heath government's Industrial Relations Act, the TUC continued to deal with the government on a wide range of other issues.

[79] 'We are not', as one Congress president put it at a time when the point needed underlining, 'concerned with chimerical notions of ushering in a social millennium that is just round the corner, but with organizing the wage-earners, and using the power of our organization to secure for them positive, practical and immediate benefits': *TUC Report*, 1934, p. 74.

[80] Thus the General Council opposed the appointment of 'independent experts' to the National Economic Development Council on the ground that 'they would have no responsibility and would not feel constrained to compromise in order to reach agreement': *TUC Report*, 1962, p. 253. George Woodcock was at pains to make no apology for this emphasis in a later, more general statement. 'Above all in this business we need flexibility. We need—I am not ashamed of the phrase at all—room for those shoddy, shabby, dirty compromises which are the essence of practical people trying to do a job': ibid., 1967, pp. 539–40. And one of his successors as TUC secretary, Len Murray, made a similar point when attacking a

Nevertheless, the TUC's image of responsibility is tinged with devil. The TUC leadership, in other words, has not been so 'responsible' that governments could always take it for granted—and least of all on issues of great moment to them both, as the history of wage restraint policies (contemplated or adopted) shows.[81]

The Importance of Labour Governments

The question of whether the party character of British governments distinctively affects their relations with particular pressure groups is sharply raised in the case of the TUC. Despite periodic declarations of independence, the TUC is firmly identified in the public mind with the Labour party and with Labour governments. In fact, its relations with such governments have been generally different from its relations with other governments, if not usually in quite the way or to quite the extent that is often assumed. (For obvious reasons, Labour governments did not play a really major role in the pre-1940 developmental period of the TUC's career.)

The *points of access* utilized by the TUC have been affected only marginally by Labour governments. Occasionally, the presence (and anticipated actions) of one has encouraged the TUC to devote some attention to backbench Labour MPs in order to reinforce direct representations to government leaders. But that is all.

---

motion ('Composite Motion 9') which advanced, as he put it, 'a shopping list' of economic and industrial claims. 'It is a list we should like to go shopping with. But where does the motion mention the things that the Government can properly ask for across the counter in return? . . . What basis for a deal with the Government does Composite 9 offer?': ibid., 1975, p. 456.

[81] Conservatives, for obvious reasons, have tended to be exceptionally wary on this issue in particular, a point illustrated by Harold Macmillan's diary record, written in 1956 when he was Chancellor of the Exchequer and on the point of making a public plea for wage restraint and price stability. 'I sent a copy [of the speech] to Tewson (Secretary of TUC) who was rather alarmed at such a clear appeal to the Congress (which is just about to meet). I made some alterations to help his point of view. Tewson is a good fellow': Macmillan, *Riding the Storm*, p. 58. Of course, it was not merely that Tewson was a good fellow. Softening the opposition, let alone securing the support, of the TUC for his plea would have been an invaluable gain for Macmillan. Such an outcome, if not likely, was at least possible; and he would have been well aware that in 1952, 1953 and 1954, the TUC's annual Congress had expressly rejected anti-wage restraint resolutions. But perhaps the most revealing aspect of this episode is the fact that the Chancellor sent the TUC secretary a draft copy of his speech for *comment*, and not simply for information.

As to *methods of communication*, it was a Labour government (the second) which was responsible for the most forward-looking innovation, before 1939, in terms of the status and high policy concerns of consultative bodies to which it admitted the TUC. Subsequently, there was not a great deal to distinguish Labour from non-Labour governments in this connection[82]— until 1974, when the highly select Liaison Committee was continued in operation under the last Wilson government, with the same membership and on the same terms as when Labour was in opposition.[83]

The presence of a Labour government has tended to inhibit the use TUC leaders make of the *forms of pressure* available to them. They have been inclined to pull their public punches and, in general, to adopt a more acquiescent posture than when Labour's opponents hold office.[84]

The second Labour government extended the *scope of relations* between the TUC and government by giving the TUC representation on consultative bodies concerned with the upper reaches of economic policy. The National governments of the 1930s did not follow this lead, but they did produce an innovation of their own by going a long way towards conceding the TUC a voice in the area of defence arrangements—just as their counterparts of the early 1920s conceded it a voice in relation to foreign policy. Since 1940, on the other hand, the TUC appears to have had total freedom in determining the

[82] True, it was a Conservative government that created the imposing National Economic Development Council with TUC representation. But it was a Labour government which transferred the NEDC chairmanship from the Chancellor of the Exchequer to the Prime Minister. Honours, roughly, even?

[83] The emergence of the Liaison Committee has been interpreted as 'the kind of development . . . where the Labour Party relates to the trade union movement as an external interest group rather than as an integral element within its own structure'; and this is seen as an 'innovation': May, *Trade Unions and Pressure Group Politics*, pp. 49–50, 52. In formal terms, however, the Liaison Committee was far from being an innovation. It was the last in a long line of virtually identical bodies (the Joint Board, the National Joint Council and the National Council of Labour) stretching back to 1905. What was different about the Liaison Committee was that its constituents, and above all Labour's parliamentary leaders, took it seriously as a negotiating arena when in opposition; and when those leaders were in office, not only did they retain their membership of the committee but it continued to meet as frequently as before.

[84] Of course there have been exceptions, most notably the TUC leadership's decisive role in the fall of the second Labour government in 1931; its determined and successful opposition to the first bill emerging from the *In Place of Strife* White Paper of 1969; and the massive, if unsuccessful, lobby it mounted in 1975 on the issue of the 'Shrewsbury pickets'.

nature of the issues involved in its dealings with governments, irrespective of their political complexion.

As to *intensity of concern*, the importance which unions have attached to the TUC's intermediary function does not seem to have been much affected by the colour of the government of the day.[85] On the side of government, however, Labour ministers have tended, if anything, to take the TUC a little more casually than their non-Labour counterparts—at least before 1974. With the accession of the last Wilson government, the TUC leadership entered a period in which it was treated with unique delicacy by government leaders.

One thing, at least, is crystal-clear concerning the *quality of relations* between the TUC and Labour governments. It is that joint membership of the labour movement provides no assurance of congenial informality in TUC–government dealings (intimate-antagonistic continuum).[86] Walter Citrine has testified that in general, during the 1930s and early forties, he enjoyed more relaxed and intimate relations with Conservative leaders (including Baldwin, Chamberlain and Churchill) than he did with their Labour counterparts.[87] Moreover, the TUC's negotiating position (soft-hard continuum) has tended to be weakened, when Labour is in office, by the political loyalties which TUC leaders have evidently shouldered. The key case is wage restraint. No Conservative government has secured the TUC's consent to such a policy. Labour governments have—and at the cost of much smaller policy concessions than those demanded

---

[85] Although, as the 'much' implies, there is a marginal qualification in that special institutional or personal links with Labour politicians have sometimes enabled unions to by-pass the TUC in relation to Labour governments, in a way that would not otherwise have been open to them.

[86] Personal hostility between colleagues, like civil wars, can generate a singular bitterness, as the notorious feud between Ernest Bevin and Herbert Morrison illustrates. Labour ministers, too, are more prone to raise union hackles by assuming that their background entitles them to instruct rather than consult—although few are likely to have been quite as *gauche* as John Hodge, simultaneously a serving trade union official and the first Minister of Labour, in one recorded address to a gathering of union leaders. 'Instead of promising an inquiry, he spoke from his own experience of steel, and practically intimated that no other system but that which had succeeded in the steel trade was worth anything. . . . The usual objection against appearance of dictation at once came to the front from trades such as carpenters and joiners. . . . They would not admit the contention. What did a man connected with steel know about wood?' Askwith, *Industrial Problems and Disputes*, p. 422.

[87] See Citrine, *Two Careers*, pp. 356–8.

of their Conservative counterparts.[88] They have also got away with consultative omissions in this connection that the TUC leadership would not have tolerated from a Conservative government.[89] But, eventually, the problems this created led to a quite different negotiating relationship from 1974, which reflected a considerable strengthening of the TUC's position.

From 1974, also, there was a matching shift in the TUC's *effectiveness*. On the score of access (primary effectiveness), the TUC leadership of the 1920s and pre-war thirties had rather more trouble seeing Labour than Conservative and National ministers; but it did better from Labour in relation to formal consultative bodies. Since then, up to 1974, both its ease of access to ministers and the formal consultative arrangements available to it have been much the same whatever the government's colour. The key difference, in the case of the last Wilson government, was the already-mentioned Liaison Committee. As for the TUC's policy (secondary) effectiveness, the pre-1974 picture is one of decidedly mixed fortunes. On the credit side, there are broad policy areas—social welfare, education, foreign affairs, for example—in which Labour governments have tended to act more in tune with TUC thinking than have non-Labour (although it is, of course, questionable that this owes much to the TUC as such). Similarly, there are the union-directed legal disabilities which non-Labour governments have refused to remedy (and have sometimes created) but which Labour has speedily redressed when in office.[90] Against this, there is a wide

[88] On the Conservative bids, see especially Dorfman, *Wage Politics In Britain*, p. 85; and Panitch, *Social Democracy and Industrial Militancy*, p. 226.

[89] Thus, the Attlee government made no attempt to consult the TUC before issuing its momentous White Paper of 1948, *Statement on Personal Incomes, Costs and Prices*, which put the case for wage restraint in quite extreme terms. The TUC leadership, while protesting vociferously about the lack of prior consultation, speedily agreed to the government's proposal for a wages standstill. Eighteen years later, the *New Statesmen* could fairly talk of 'the humiliation inflicted by the government on the TUC' in relation to the same issue. 'It now appears to be firmly established . . . that consultations with the TUC on measures which vitally affect trade union interests always follow rather than precede those measures': *New Statesman*, 29 July 1966, p. 157. The reference is to a Labour government's intention to introduce, for the first time in British history, a statutory (i.e., compulsory) wage-freeze. Despite this, the TUC leaders, and Congress, reluctantly accepted the freeze, though there were later changes of mind.

[90] The repeal of the Trade Disputes and Trade Union Act of 1927 by the Attlee government in 1946 is one example; another is the first Wilson government's enactment of the Trade Disputes Act of 1965 which restored an immunity that the unions thought they had before the decision in *Rookes* v. *Barnard* ([1964]AC, p. 1129).

area of industrial policy within which Labour has tended to follow the non-Labour practice of normally requiring the agreement of employers, as well as unions, before taking legislative action.[91] Above all, there are the economic policy issues on which Labour ministers have disregarded TUC wishes and acted, or sought to act, in ways that their non-Labour counterparts either would have adopted themselves[92] or, while favouring, had not previously dared to adopt.[93] The 1974–6 picture of the TUC's policy effectiveness is more straightforward. It includes, above all, the substantial restoration of the trade unions' traditional legal immunities, with the repeal of the Conservatives' Industrial Relations Act; an Employment Protection Act which significantly extended the legal rights of trade unions and individual employees; a voluntary and generously negotiated wage restraint policy, skilfully packaged as a 'social contract'; and signs of an unusual deference, on the part of government leaders, to the TUC's views on economic matters in general.[94]

[91] For example, the TUC in 1964 proposed to the relevant Labour minister certain arrangements relating to the use of compulsory arbitration in industrial disputes. The minister replied that he 'would consult' employers on the matter. Subsequently, he decided to do nothing after discovering that the Confederation of British Industry was 'not in favour of the proposal': *TUC Report*, 1965, p. 147; ibid., 1967, p. 151.

[92] The second Labour government fell on such an issue in 1931.

[93] Thus the Wilson government's Prices and Incomes Act of 1966 which provided criminal sanctions against strikers, in certain circumstances, as a means of enforcing an incomes policy. Corresponding legislation by the same government in 1967–8 and by the Heath government in 1972–3 followed this precedent; and so did the Wilson government's proposed measure, eventually withdrawn, for dealing with unofficial strikes in 1969.

[94] This is not to say that the relationship is fairly described in terms of a government that was 'largely subservient to [the] wishes' of the TUC's leaders: Wigham, *Strikes and the Government 1893–1974*, p. 191. The TUC secretary expressly denied this interpretation early in the piece. 'In the six months [the Wilson government] has been in office its achievements have by any standards been impressive. Not that it has slavishly adopted the TUC's views at all points. We have had arguments and no doubt there are more to come. The Government is not our captive, and we are not in its pocket': *TUC Report*, 1974, p. 422. It was, of course, in the interests of both the TUC and the government to have this disclaimer made, true or not. But the secretary later gave more substance to the point in the course of explaining the nature of the negotiations about the permissible level, under the government's incomes policy, of wage rises for 1975–6. 'They [government leaders] said that they would prefer an agreed policy but that they would have to act themselves if there was no agreement. That was made perfectly clear to us': ibid., 1975, p. 458. And, in any case, there was an unfavourable side to Labour's policy performance: see, e.g., Minkin, 'The Party Connection: Divergence and Convergence in the British Labour Movement', *Government and Opposition*, vol. 13, no. 4, Autumn 1978, pp. 477–8.

It was certainly arguable, in the late 1960s and early seventies, that Labour governments did not make a great deal of difference to the TUC, in the sense of advantaging it, especially in relation to its policy effectiveness.[95] And looking back, in effect, on the TUC–Labour party connection from a 1973 vantage-point, it was not unreasonable to conclude that 'each experience of Labour government has tended to deepen the partners' awareness of the inhibitions their alliance imposes, and weakened their sense of mutual advantage'.[96] But all this was to change with the advent of the last Wilson government. There can be no doubt that the alliance was reinvigorated by the combination of a distinctively conciliatory Labour government and the recent experience of a tough and aggressive Conservative administration.[97] The TUC's relationship with the last Wilson government probably brought popular preconceptions about the responsiveness of Labour governments to union pressure closer to reality than ever before. Up to then, while it could be said that such governments, on the whole, made a difference to the TUC's political activities which was favourable to its aims, the difference tended to be pretty marginal and decidedly uncertain.

The Importance of Being on the Side of History

Underlying the TUC's career are two closely linked secular trends. One is the trend to central (national) political organization. The other is the trend to public policies encompassing social welfare and economic management.

[95] This is a point which is made with particular force by Lovell and Roberts, *A Short History of the TUC*, p. 187; and Dorfman, op. cit., p. 142.

[96] Martin Harrison in Kimber and Richardson (eds.), *Pressure Groups in Britain*, p. 78. This view echoed an earlier prediction from the historians of the TUC: 'All the signs point to a weakening of the Labour alliance and a gradual shift towards a position of [TUC] neutrality in the future': Lovell and Roberts, op. cit., pp. 186–7. That prediction seemed to have been borne out when the TUC secretary commented to the 1970 Congress that 'the TUC does not sing one song when Conservative governments are in power and another when Labour Governments are in power. We deal with Governments strictly on the merits of the issues': *TUC Report*, 1970, p. 631. Of course, his claim rings a little hollow in the light of the TUC's consistently less flexible attitude towards wage restraint, both before and after 1970, when Labour has been out of office.

[97] Jack Jones, leader of the TUC's largest affiliate and one of the architects of the new accord, underlined the point to Congress. 'Ken Gill asks if we have learnt anything from the past. Yes, we have. The lesson we have learnt is that at all costs we have to keep a Labour Government in office': *TUC Report*, 1975, p. 477.

As to the first, the TUC was founded at a time when the administrative apparatus of government was rudimentary by later standards, and when the activities of organized interests were of marginal political significance. Since then, a vast bureaucratic structure has emerged to administer government policies of increasing complexity, a broadening range of interests have been prodded into generating their own central organizations to treat with government, and pressure group activity has moved from the margins to the centre of the British political system. The TUC caught this wave much earlier than most.

As to the second trend, the TUC's career is interlaced with most of the major domestic policy innovations that have transformed the face of British public policy in the last century. In the end, moreover, the TUC has been on the winning side more often than not—despite the opposition of organized interests of a higher social and, presumptively, political status. The fact that innovatory causes espoused by the TUC have so often succeeded, in sòme measure, against opposition of this calibre reflects the progressive democratization of British politics and the consequent drift of public policy. These circumstances virtually guaranteed the broad policy effectiveness of any long-lived organization which was at once pragmatic in temper and backed policy innovations favouring the improvement of working-class conditions of life over a wide area.[98]

The TUC's present eminence as the doyen of British pressure groups probably owes a great deal to these historical congruencies. This, to be sure, is a conclusion that may well seem, as it stands, either loaded or too tame, or both. Loaded, because some will be inclined to misinterpret it as implying that the TUC is on the side of the angels—which is what being on the side of history is often, thoughtlessly, taken to mean as a matter of course. Too tame, because the long historical perspective flattens out current policy concerns, to which popular perceptions of contemporary institutions tend to be anchored, and ignores the fact that the TUC of our own times is enveloped in an incessant swirl of controversy about its position on great

---

[98] The essentially reactive nature of this role has been suggested by George Woodcock. 'All I can do is to try and see the way things are going, and help them along': quoted in Sampson, *The Anatomy of Britain Today* (1965), p. 612.

issues of economic management and income distribution. The controversy is, in part, about the historical appropriateness of the TUC's specific policy stances. But judgements on that issue are beyond the scope of the present work. What is within its scope is the implication of the TUC's career, during its first century, that the long-term effectiveness of pressure groups may depend above all on the extent to which their aims happen to coincide with political groundswells.

Bibliography

THERE are two sources on which I have relied above all others: the published annual reports of the TUC for the period 1869–1976; and the unpublished minutes of the Parliamentary Committee and the General Council for the periods 1872–4 and 1888–1940. The *TUC Reports* (the full title followed the pattern of *Report of Proceedings of the 75th Annual Trades Union Congress* until 1962, when the reference to 'proceedings' was dropped) have been issued in relation to every Congress since the second of 1869. Since the 1870s they have invariably incorporated, as well as a detailed account of Congress proceedings, the relevant annual report of the Parliamentary Committee or General Council. I was unable to locate the Parliamentary Committee's minutes for 1875–88, a period which corresponds almost precisely to Henry Broadhurst's term as secretary. (There is a tantalizing reference to those for 1875–85 in the Webbs' *History of Trade Unionism* at p. 362.) Incorporated in the minutes of both the Parliamentary Committee and the General Council, during the period to 1940, are minutes or accounts of other meetings including those of standing joint bodies, such as the Joint Board and its successors; of temporary joint bodies, such as the Mediation Committee of 1919; and of *ad hoc* meetings with other bodies such as the Labour party executive. When quoting from such minutes I have normally followed the practice of citing the Parliamentary Committee or General Council minutes in which they are incorporated, rather than citing them separately.

A variety of reports, circulars, and brochures issued by the TUC to its affiliated unions from time to time was also consulted, including *The TUC in Wartime* published quarterly during the second world war. The use made of other primary material from non-governmental sources, notably Labour party and trade union reports and the public press, was selective and determined primarily by 'leads' from other sources. No attempt was made to consult the records of government departments (although I had access, by courtesy of Robert Manne, to some relevant Foreign Office papers for the 1920s). That task, especially given the long time-period and large number of departments involved, was beyond the resources of a researcher entirely dependent on his own efforts and able to spend relatively little time in the country of his subject. In any case, the TUC's own accounts of its dealings with government are, for the most part, very full; and it is precisely those aspects of the study that have to do with government structure, policy and attitudes which are best covered in available published works.

SECONDARY SOURCES

The following list includes books (novels excepted) and articles quoted or cited, together with some others of particular value to the study.

HISTORIES: GENERAL

BEST, Geoffrey, *Mid-Victorian Britain, 1851–1875* (London, 1971).

BLAKE, Robert, *The Conservative Party from Peel to Churchill* (London, 1970).

BOGDANOR, Vernon, and SKIDELSKY, Robert (eds.), *The Age of Affluence, 1951–1964* (London, 1970).

BRAITHWAITE, William J., *Lloyd George's Ambulance Waggon* (Bath, 1970).

CALDER, Angus, *The People's War: Britain 1939–45* (London, 1969).

CHURCHILL, Winston S., *The Second World War*, 6 vols. (London, 1948–54).

CLARK, G. S. R. Kitson, *An Expanding Society: Britain 1830–1900* (Melbourne, 1967).

COLE, G. D. H., and POSTGATE, R., *The Common People, 1746–1946* (London, 1961).

COWLING, Maurice, *1867: Disraeli, Gladstone and Revolution* (Cambridge, 1967).

DANGERFIELD, George, *The Strange Death of Liberal England* (London, 1966).

DAVISON, R. C., *British Unemployment Policy* (London, 1938).

FEUCHTWANGER, E. J., *Disraeli, Democracy and the Tory Party* (Oxford, 1968).

GEORGE, David Lloyd, *War Memoirs*, 2 vols. (London, 1938).

GILBERT, Bentley B., *The Evolution of National Insurance in Great Britain* (London, 1966).

GRAINGER, J. H., *Character and Style in English Politics* (Cambridge, 1969).

HALEVY, Elie, *A History of the English People in the Nineteenth Century*, 6 vols. (London, 1951).

HAMMOND, M. B., *British Labor Conditions and Legislation during the War* (New York, 1919).

HANES, David G., *The First British Workmen's Compensation Act, 1897* (New Haven, 1968).

HANHAM, H. J., *Elections and Party Management* (London, 1959).

HOHMAN, Helen F., *The Development of Social Insurance and Minimum Wage Legislation in Great Britain* (Boston, 1933).

HURWITZ, Samuel J., *State Intervention in Great Britain: A Study of Economic Control and Social Response* (New York, 1949).

LOWELL, A. Lawrence, *The Government of England*, 2 vols. (London, 1908).

MACCOBY, S., *English Radicalism, 1853–1886* (London, 1939).

—— *English Radicalism, 1886–1914* (London, 1953).

MARWICK, Arthur, *The Deluge: British Society and the First World War* (Harmondsworth, 1967).

MOWAT, C. L., *Britain Between the Wars 1918–1940* (London, 1955).

McCALLUM, R. B., *The Liberal Party from Earl Grey to Asquith* (London, 1963).

NOWELL-SMITH, S. (ed.), *Edwardian England, 1901–1914* (London, 1964).

PERKIN, Harold, *The Origins of Modern English Society, 1780–1880* (London, 1969).

SAYERS, R. S., *Financial Policy, 1939–1945* (London, 1956).

SMELLIE, K. B., *A Hundred Years of English Government* (London, 1950).

SMITH, F. B., *The Making of the Second Reform Bill* (Melbourne, 1966).

SMITH, Paul, *Disraelian Conservatism and Social Reform* (London, 1967).

TAWNEY, R. H., 'The Abolition of Economic Controls, 1918–1921', *Economic History Review*, vol. 13, 1943.

TAYLOR, A. J. P., *English History, 1914–1945* (London, 1965).

TREVELYAN, G. M., *British History in the Nineteenth Century* (London, 1923).

—— *English Social History* (London, 1944).

VINCENT, John, *The Formation of the Liberal Party, 1857–1868* (London, 1966).

WILSON, Trevor, *The Downfall of the Liberal Party, 1914–1935* (London, 1966).

WOOTTON, Graham, *Pressure Groups in Britain, 1720–1970* (London, 1975).

WRIGLEY, C. J., *David Lloyd George and the British Labour Movement* (Hassocks, 1976).

HISTORIES: TRADE UNION AND LABOUR PARTY

BAGWELL, Philip S., *The Railwaymen* (London, 1963).
BASSETT, R., *1931: Political Crisis* (London, 1958).
BAUMAN, Zygmunt, *Between Class and Elite* (Manchester, 1972).
BEALEY, Frank, and PELLING, Henry, *Labour and Politics 1900–1906* (London, 1958).
BIRCH, Lionel (ed.), *The History of the TUC 1868–1968: A Pictorial Survey of a Social Revolution* (London, 1968).
BRIGGS, Asa, and SAVILLE, John (eds.), *Essays in Labour History, 1886–1923* (London, 1971).
BROWN, Kenneth D., *Labour and Unemployment, 1900–1914* (Newton Abbot, 1971).
CALHOUN, Daniel F., *The United Front: The TUC and the Russians, 1923–1928* (Cambridge, 1976).
CITRINE, W. M., *The Trade Union Movement of Great Britain* (Amsterdam, 1926).
CLEGG, H. A., *Some Consequences of the General Strike* (Manchester Statistical Society, 1954).
CLEGG, H. A , Fox, Alan, and THOMPSON, A. F., *A History of British Trade Unions since 1889*, vol. 1 (Oxford, 1964).
COLE, G. D. H., *Labour in the Coal-mining Industry, 1914–1920* (Oxford, 1923).
—— *Labour in Wartime* (London, 1915).
—— *Self-Government in Industry*, 5th ed. (London, 1920).
—— *A Short History of the British Working Class Movement* (London, 1948).
—— *Trade Unionism and Munitions* (Oxford, 1923).
—— *Workshop Organization* (Oxford, 1923).
—— *The World of Labour* (London, 1913).
COLE, G. D. H., and MELLOR, W., *The Greater Unionism* (Manchester, 1913).
CROOK, W. H., *The General Strike* (Chapel Hill, 1931).
DAHL, Robert A., 'Workers' Control of Industry and the British Labor Party', *American Political Science Review*, vol. 41, no. 5, October 1947.
DAVIS, W. J., *British Trades Union Congress: History and Recollections*, 2 vols. (London, 1910).
Fox, Alan, *The National Union of Boot and Shoe Operatives, 1874–1957* (London, 1958).
FROW, Edmund, and KATANKA, Michael, *1868 Year of the Unions* (London, 1968).
GILLESPIE, F. E., *Labour and Politics in England, 1850–1867* (London, 1966).

GLASS, S. T., *The Responsible Society* (London, 1966).

HARRISON, Royden, *Before the Socialists* (London, 1965).

HOBSBAWM, E. J., *Labouring Men: Studies in the History of Labour* (London, 1964).

HOWELL, George, *The Conflicts of Capital and Labour* (London, 1878).

— — *Labour Legislation, Labour Movements and Labour Leaders*, 2 vols., 2nd ed. (London, 1905).

— — *Trade Unionism New and Old*, 4th ed. (London, 1907).

— — 'Trades Union Congresses and Social Legislation', *Contemporary Review*, September 1889.

INMAN, P., *Labour in the Munitions Industries* (London, 1957).

JEFFERYS, James B., *Labour's Formative Years: 1849–1879* (London, 1948).

Labour Year Book (London, 1916, 1919).

LOVELL, John, and ROBERTS, B. C., *A Short History of the T.U.C.* (London, 1968).

LYMAN, Richard W., *The First Labour Government, 1924* (London, 1957).

MCBRIAR, A. M., *Fabian Socialism and English Politics* (Cambridge, 1966).

MACDONALD, D. F., *The State and the Trade Unions* (London, 1960).

MACDONALD, J. Ramsay, *The Socialist Movement* (London, *c*.1912).

MARTIN, Roderick, *Communism and the British Trade Unions, 1924–1933* (Oxford, 1969).

MILIBAND, Ralph, *Parliamentary Socialism* (London, 1961).

MUSSON, A. E., *The Congress of 1868* (London, 1955).

ORTON, W. A., *Labour in Transition* (London, 1921).

PELLING, Henry, *A History of British Trade Unionism* (London, 1963).

— — *The Origins of the Labour Party, 1880–1900* (London, 1954).

— — *A Short History of the Labour Party* (London, 1962).

PHILLIPS, G. A., *The General Strike: The Politics of Industrial Conflict* (London, 1976).

— — 'The Triple Industrial Alliance in 1914', *Economic History Review*, 2nd series, vol. xxiv, no. 1, 1971.

POIRIER, Philip P., *The Advent of the Labour Party* (London, 1958).

PRIBICEVIC, Branko, *The Shop Stewards' Movement and Workers' Control, 1910–1922* (Oxford, 1959).

PRICE, John, *Labour in the War* (Harmondsworth, 1940).

PRITT, D. N., *The Labour Government, 1945–51* (London, 1963).

RENSHAW, Patrick, *The General Strike* (London, 1975).

ROBERTS, B. C., *The Trades Union Congress, 1868–1921* (London, 1958)

SKIDELSKY, Robert, *Politicians and the Slump: The Labour Government of 1929–31* (London, 1967).

370 *Bibliography*

SLESSER, Henry H., *Trade Unionism*, 2nd ed. (London, 1921).
SYMONS, Julian, *The General Strike* (London, 1957).
THOMAS, J. H., *When Labour Rules* (London, 1920).
THOMPSON, E. P., *The Making of the English Working Class* (Harmondsworth, 1968)
THOMPSON, Paul, *Socialists, Liberals and Labour* (London, 1967).
TRACEY, Herbert (ed.), *The Book of the Labour Party*, 3 vols. (London, 1925).
TURNER, H. A., *Trade Union Growth, Structure and Policy* (Toronto, 1962).
WEBB, S. and B., *The History of Trade Unionism* (London, 1950).
WERNER, Herbert E., *British Labour and Public Ownership* (London, 1960).
WIGHAM, Eric, *Strikes and the Government, 1893–1974* (London, 1976).
WILLIAMS, Francis, *Magnificent Journey: The Rise of the Trade Unions* (London, 1954).

POLITICAL AND ECONOMIC STUDIES

BAGEHOT, Walter, *The English Constitution* (London, 1949).
BEER, Samuel H., *Modern British Politics: A Study of Parties and Pressure Groups* (London, 1965).
BIRCH, A. H., *The British System of Government* (London, 1967).
— — *Representative and Responsible Government* (London, 1964).
BROMHEAD, P. A., *Private Members' Bills in the British Parliament* (London, 1956).
BUTT, Ronald, *The Power of Parliament* (London, 1967).
CASTLES, Francis G., *Pressure Groups and Political Culture* (London, 1967).
CAWSON, Alan, 'Pluralism, Corporatism and the Role of the State', *Government and Opposition*, vol. 13, Spring 1978.
CHURCHILL, Winston S., *Liberalism and the Social Problem* (London, 1909).
CLEGG, H. A., *How to Run an Incomes Policy: and why we made such a mess of the last one* (London, 1971).
COATES, R. D., *Teachers' Unions and Interest Group Politics* (Cambridge, 1972).
CROUCH, Colin, *Class Conflict and the Industrial Relations Crisis* (London, 1977).
DERTHICK, Martha, *The National Guard in Politics* (Cambridge, Mass., 1965).
DICEY, A. V., *Law and Public Opinion in England*, 2nd ed. (London, 1926).

DORFMAN, Gerald A., *Wage Politics in Britain, 1945–1967* (Ames, Iowa, 1973).

ECKSTEIN, Harry, *Pressure Group Politics: The Case of the British Medical Association* (London, 1960).

—— *A Theory of Stable Democracy* (Princeton, 1961).

ECKSTEIN, Harry, and APTER, David E. (eds.), *Comparative Politics: A Reader* (New York, 1963).

EDELMAN, Murray, and FLEMING, R. W., *The Politics of Wage-Price Decisions: A Four-Country Analysis* (Urbana, Illinois, 1965).

FINER, S. E., *Anonymous Empire: A Study of the Lobby in Great Britain*, 2nd ed. (London, 1966).

GERTH, H. H., and MILLS, C. Wright, *From Max Weber: Essays in Sociology* (London, 1961).

GLEASON, Arthur, *What the Workers Want* (New York, 1920).

GRANT, Wyn, and MARSH, David, *The Confederation of British Industry* (London, 1977).

HOLTZMAN, Abraham, *Interest Groups and Lobbying* (New York, 1966).

JACOBS, Paul, and LANDAU, Saul (eds.), *The New Radicals* (Harmondsworth, 1967).

JENNINGS, Ivor, *Cabinet Government*, 3rd ed. (Cambridge, 1961).

KEYNES, J. M., *The Economic Consequences of the Peace* (London, 1919).

KIMBER, Richard, and RICHARDSON, J. J. (eds.), *Pressure Groups in Britain* (London, 1974).

KRISTIANSON, G. L., *The Politics of Patriotism: The Pressure Group Activities of the Returned Servicemen's League* (Canberra, 1966).

KWAVNICK, David, *Organized Labour and Pressure Politics: The Canadian Labour Congress 1956–1968* (Montreal, 1972).

LASKI, Harold J., *Parliamentary Government in England* (London, 1938).

LEHMBRUCH, Gerhard, 'Liberal Corporatism and Party Government', *Comparative Political Studies*, vol. 10, April 1977.

LERUEZ, Jacques, *Economic Planning and Politics in Britain* (London, 1975).

MCKENZIE, R. T., *British Political Parties* (London, 1955)

MCKENZIE, Robert, and SILVER, Allan, *Angels in Marble* (London, 1968).

MACKINTOSH, John P., *The British Cabinet* (London, 1962).

MARSHALL, Alfred, and Marshall, Mary Paley, *The Economics of Industry* (London, 1879).

MICHELS, Robert, *Political Parties: A Sociological Study of the Oligarchical Tendencies of Modern Democracy* (Glencoe, Illinois, 1958).

MILLS, C. Wright, *The Power Elite* (New York, 1959).

MINKIN, Lewis, 'The Party Connection: Divergence and Convergence in the British Labour Movement', *Government and Opposition*, vol. 13, no. 4, Autumn 1978.

MOODIE, Graham C., and STUDDERT-KENNEDY, Gerald, *Opinions, Publics and Pressure Groups* (London, 1970).

MORRISON, Herbert, *Government and Parliament* (London, 1954).

MULLER, William D., *The 'Kept Men'?* (Hassocks, 1977).

NIEUWENHUYSEN, J. P., and DRAKE, P. J. (eds.), *Australian Economic Policy* (Melbourne, 1977).

NORDLINGER, Eric A., *The Working-Class Tories* (London, 1967).

OLSON, Mancur, *The Logic of Collective Action* (Cambridge, Mass., 1971).

OSTROGORSKI, M., *Democracy and the Organization of Political Parties*, vol. 1 (London, 1902).

PANITCH, Leo, *Social Democracy and Industrial Militancy* (Cambridge, 1976).

—— 'The Development of Corporatism in Liberal Democracies,' *Comparative Political Studies*, vol. 10, no. 1, April 1977.

POTTER, Allen, *Organized Groups in British National Politics* (London, 1961).

REDFERN, Percy (ed.), *Self and Society: The First Twelve Essays* (London, 1930).

ROSE, Richard, *Politics in England Today* (London, 1974).

SAMPSON, Anthony, *Anatomy of Britain Today* (London, 1965).

—— *The New Anatomy of Britain* (London, 1971).

SCHMITTER, Phillipe C., 'Still the Century of Corporatism?' *The Review of Politics*, vol. 36, January 1974.

SELF, Peter, and STORING, H. J., *The State and the Farmer* (London, 1962).

SHANKS, Michael, *The Stagnant Society* (Harmondsworth, 1961).

SHONFIELD, Andrew, *British Economic Policy Since the War* (Harmondsworth, 1958).

—— *Modern Capitalism: The Changing Balance of Public and Private Power* (London, 1965).

STEWART, J. D., *British Pressure Groups: Their Role in Relation to the House of Commons* (London, 1958).

TRUMAN, David B., *The Governmental Process: Political Interests and Public Opinion* (New York, 1959).

WALKLAND, S. A., *The Legislative Process in Great Britain* (London, 1968).

WILLEY, Richard J., 'Pressure Group Politics: The Case of SOHYO', *Western Political Quarterly*, vol. 17, no. 4, December 1964.

WILLIAMS, Philip, 'Public Opinion and the Railway Rates Question in 1886', *English Historical Review*, vol. 67, no. 26, January 1952.

WOOTTON, Graham, *Interest-Groups* (New Jersey, 1970).

—— *The Politics of Influence: British Ex-servicemen, Cabinet Decisions and Cultural Change (1917–57)* (London, 1963).

ZEIGLER, Harmon, *Interest Groups in American Society* (New Jersey, 1964).

ADMINISTRATIVE AND LEGAL STUDIES

ALLEN, C. K., *Law and Orders*, 3rd ed. (London, 1965).
BEVERIDGE, William H., *British Food Control* (London, 1928)
CARR, Cecil T., *Delegated Legislation* (London, 1921).
CHESTER, D. N., *The Nationalized Industries* (London, 1951).
CLEGG, H. A., *Industrial Democracy and Nationalization* (Oxford, 1951).
CLEGG, H. A., and CHESTER, T. E., *The Future of Nationalization* (Oxford, 1953).
DEARLE, N. B., *Dictionary of Official War-time Organizations* (London, 1928).
HAMMOND, R. J., *Food: Studies in Administration and Control*, 3 vols. (London, 1951/1956/1962).
HANCOCK, W. K., and GOWING, M. M., *British War Economy* (London, 1949).
HARGREAVES, E. L., and GOWING, M. M., *Civil Industry and Trade* (London, 1952).
HENDERSON, Hubert D., *The Cotton Control Board* (Oxford, 1922).
History of the Ministry of Munitions, 12 vols. (London, 1920–22).
LEWIS, Roy, 'The Historical Development of Trade Union Law', *British Journal of Industrial Relations*, vol. 14, no. 1, March 1976.
PARKER, H. M. D., *Manpower: A Study of War-time Policy and Administration* (London, 1957).
Political and Economic Planning, *Advisory Committees in British Government* (London, 1960).
POSTAN, M. M., *British War Production* (London, 1952).
ROBERTS, David, *Victorian Origins of the British Welfare State* (New Haven, 1960).
SCOTT, J. D., and HUGHES, R., *The Administration of War Production* (London, 1955).
SUTHERLAND, Gillian (ed.), *Studies in the Growth of Nineteenth-Century Government* (London, 1972).
VERNON, R. V., and MANSERGH, N. (eds.), *Advisory Bodies* (London, 1940).
WEEKES, B., MELLISH, M., DICKENS, L., and LLOYD, J., *Industrial Relations and the Limits of the Law* (Oxford, 1975).
WHEARE, K. C., *Government by Committee* (Oxford, 1955).
WOLFE, Humbert, *Labour Supply and Regulation* (Oxford, 1923).

TRADE UNION AND INDUSTRIAL RELATIONS STUDIES

ALLEN, V. L., *Militant Trade Unionism* (London, 1966).

— — *Power in Trade Unions* (London, 1954).

— — 'The Re-organization of the Trades Union Congress, 1918–1927', *British Journal of Sociology*, vol. XI, no. 1, March 1960.

— — *The Sociology of Industrial Relations* (London, 1971).

— — *Trade Union Leadership* (London, 1957).

— — *Trade Unions and the Government* (London, 1960).

ASKWITH, Lord, *Industrial Problems and Disputes* (London, 1920).

BAIN, George Sayers, *The Growth of White-Collar Unionism* (Oxford, 1970).

BIRCH, Alan, *The Structure of the British Trade Union Movement* (Manchester Statistical Society, 1957).

BLACKBURN, Robin, and COCKBURN, Alexander (eds.), *The Incompatibles: Trade Union Militancy and the Consensus* (Harmondsworth, 1967).

CLAY, Henry, *The Problem of Industrial Relations* (London, 1929).

CLEGG, H. A., *General Union in a Changing Society* (Oxford, 1964).

— — *The System of Industrial Relations in Great Britain*, 3rd ed. (Oxford, 1976).

— — *Trade Unionism under Collective Bargaining* (Oxford, 1976).

— — KILLICK, A. J., and ADAMS, Rex, *Trade Union Officers* (Oxford, 1961).

COLE, G. D. H., *British Trade Unionism Today* (London, 1945).

— — *An Introduction to Trade Unionism* (London, 1918).

FEATHER, Victor, *The Essence of Trade Unionism* (London, 1963).

FLANDERS, Allan, *Management and Unions* (London, 1970).

— — *Trade Unions*, 3rd ed. (London, 1960).

GOODMAN, J. F. B., and WHITTINGHAM, T. G., *Shop Stewards in British Industry* (Maidenhead, 1969).

HARRISON, Martin, *Trade Unions and the Labour Party since 1945* (London, 1960).

HUGHES, John, *The TUC: A Plan for the 1970s*, Fabian Tract 397 (London, 1969).

HYMAN, Richard, *Industrial Relations: A Marxist Introduction* (London, 1975).

JENKINS, Peter, *The Battle of Downing Street* (London, 1970).

LASKI, Harold J., *Trade Unions in the New Society* (London, 1950).

LERNER, Shirley W., *Breakaway Unions and the Small Trade Union* (London, 1961).

LIPSKY, David B. (ed.), *Union Power and Public Policy* (Cornell, 1975).

LLOYD, C. M., *Trade Unionism* (London, 1915).

MARTIN, R. M., 'The Authority of Trade Union Centres: The Australian Council of Trade Unions and the British Trades Union Congress', *Journal of Industrial Relations*, vol. 4, no. 1, April

1962; reprinted in J. E. Isaac and G. W. Ford (eds.), *Australian Labour Relations Readings* (Melbourne, 1966).

—— 'Trade Unions and Labour Governments in Australia: The Relation between Party Policy and Supporting Interests', *Journal of Commonwealth Political Studies*, vol. 2, no. 1, November 1963; reprinted in Colin A. Hughes (ed.), *Readings in Australian Government* (Brisbane, 1968).

MAY, Timothy C., *Trade Unions and Pressure Group Politics* (Farnborough, 1975).

MILNE-BAILEY, W., *Trade Union Documents* (London, 1929).

—— *Trade Unions and the State* (London, 1934).

PHELPS BROWN, E. H., *The Growth of British Industrial Relations* (London, 1965).

Political and Economic Planning, *British Trade Unionism* (London, 1955).

ROBERTS, B. C. (ed.), *Industrial Relations: Contemporary Problems and Perspectives* (London, 1962).

—— *Trade Unions in a Free Society* (London, 1959).

ROBERTS, Bryn, *The Price of TUC Leadership* (London, 1961).

Royal Commission on Trade Unions and Employers' Associations 1965–1968, *Report* (London, 1968).

TURNER, H. A., CLACK, G., and ROBERTS, E., *Labour Relations in the Motor Industry* (London, 1967).

WEBB, S. and B., *Industrial Democracy* (London, 1902).

WIGHAM, Eric L., *Trade Unions*, 2nd ed. (Oxford, 1969).

WOODCOCK, George, *The Trade Union Movement and the Government* (Leicester, 1968).

BIOGRAPHIES AND AUTOBIOGRAPHIES

AMERY, L. S., *My Political Life*, 3 vols. (London, 1953/1955).

ARCH, Joseph, *The Autobiography of Joseph Arch* (London, 1966).

ASQUITH, Earl of Oxford, *Fifty Years of Parliament*, 2 vols. (London, 1926).

ATTLEE, C. R., *As It Happened* (London, 1954).

BALDWIN, A. W., *My Father: The True Story* (London, 1955).

BEVAN, Aneurin, *In Place of Fear* (London, 1952).

BEVERIDGE, Lord, *Power and Influence* (London, 1953).

BLAKE, Robert, *Disraeli* (London, 1968).

BROADHURST, Henry, *Henry Broadhurst, M.P.* (London, 1901).

BULLOCK, Alan, *The Life and Times of Ernest Bevin*, 2 vols. (London, 1960/1967).

CHAMBERLAIN, Austen, *Politics from Inside* (London, 1936).

CITRINE, Lord, *Men and Work* (London, 1964).

— — *Two Careers* (London, 1967).
CLYNES, J. R., *Memoirs*, 2 vols. (London, 1937/1938).
COLE, Margaret (ed.), *Beatrice Webb's Diaries, 1912–1924* (London, 1952).
— — *Beatrice Webb's Diaries, 1924–1932* (London, 1956).
— — *The Life of G. D. H. Cole* (London, 1971).
DALTON, Hugh, *Call Back Yesterday* (London, 1953).
— — *The Fateful Years* (London, 1957).
— — *High Tide and After* (London, 1962).
EDEN, Sir Anthony, *Full Circle* (London, 1960).
ESTORICK, Eric, *Stafford Cripps* (London, 1949).
EVANS, Trevor, *Bevin* (London, 1946).
FEILING, Keith, *The Life of Neville Chamberlain* (London, 1946).
FOOT, Michael, *Aneurin Bevan*, vol. 1 (New York, 1963).
GEORGE, William, *My Brother and I* (London, 1958).
HAMILTON, M. A., *Arthur Henderson* (London, 1938).
HODGE, John, *Workman's Cottage to Windsor Castle* (London, n.d.).
HODGES, Frank, *My Adventures as a Labour Leader* (London, c. 1925).
JONES, Thomas, *A Diary with Letters, 1931–1950* (London, 1954).
— — *Whitehall Diary*, 2 vols. (London, 1969).
KIRKWOOD, David, *My Life of Revolt* (London, 1935).
LEVENTHAL, F. M., *Respectable Radical* (London, 1971).
MAGNUS, Philip, *Gladstone: A Biography* (London, 1954).
MIDDLEMAS, K., and BARNES, J., *Baldwin* (London, 1969).
MACMILLAN, Harold, *Riding the Storm, 1956–1959* (London, 1971).
— — *At the End of the Day, 1961–1963* (London, 1973).
NICOLSON, Harold, *King George V* (London, 1952).
OWEN, Frank, *Tempestuous Journey: Lloyd George His Life and Times* (London, 1954).
ROGERS, Frederick, *Labour, Life and Literature* (London, 1913).
SALTER, Lord, *Memoirs of a Public Servant* (London, 1961).
SNELL, Lord, *Men, Movements and Myself* (London, 1936).
SNOWDEN, Viscount, *An Autobiography*, 2 vols. (London, 1934).
THOMAS, J. H., *My Story* (London, 1937).
THORNE, Will, *My Life's Battles* (London, c. 1925).
TURNER, Ben, *About Myself* (London, 1930).
WATSON, Aaron, *A Great Labour Leader: Thomas Burt, M.P.* (London, 1908).
WEBB, Beatrice, *Our Partnership* (London, 1948).
WILLIAMS, Francis, *Ernest Bevin* (London, 1952).
WILSON, Harold, *The Labour Government, 1964–1970: A Personal Record* (London, 1971).
YOUNG, G. M., *Stanley Baldwin* (London, 1952).

Index

377